THE HISTORY OF THE
RUGBY
WORLD CUP

Printed in the UK by MPG Books, Bodmin

Distributed in the US by Publishers Group West

Published by Sanctuary Publishing Limited, Sanctuary House, 45-53 Sinclair Road, London W14 0NS, United Kingdom

www.sanctuarypublishing.com

Cover design: Ash
Front and back cover photographs: © Getty Images

Photographs: © Getty Images, *The Sunday Telegraph* and *The Sun-Herald*
Extract from *The Art Of Coarse Rugby* by Michael Green courtesy of Robson Books

While the publishers have made every reasonable effort to trace the copyright owners for any or all of the photographs in this book, there may be some omissions of credits, for which we apologise.

ISBN: 1-86074-602-0

THE HISTORY OF THE
RUGBY
WORLD CUP

Gerald Davies

Foreword by John Eales

Sanctuary

Acknowledgements

I consider myself the luckiest of rugby men. I have found myself present at every one of the Rugby World Cup tournaments. Equally, I have been blessed on each occasion to be asked to contribute to the rugby pages of *The Times* in London. There I have found good people who have been sympathetic with someone who, it is said, will not allow a simple word in his copy where five can be fitted in. I am grateful to Keith Blackmore and David Chappell, Assistant Editor and Sports Editor, respectively, for their kindness every autumn to keep me as 'part of their furniture'. HTV were also immensely helpful.

I would like to thank the following: Geoff Cooke, John Eales, Sean Fitzpatrick, Chris Harvey, Tim Horan, Kingsley Jones, Jonah Lomu, Iain MacGregor, Rod Macqueen, Marcel Martin, Ian McGeechan, Keith Rowlands, Chris Rea, Sir Nick Shehadie, Chris Thau, Ray Williams and Dudley Wood. Other conversations over many years helped shape the book and to define the period and the events. I played rugby with Rod Smallwood at Grange Road in Cambridge. Thirty years later as top man at Sanctuary he got me to write this book.

One point of clarification: There are eminent rugby administrators who might have expected their names to be more prominently associated with the Rugby World Cup and to have been numbered in these pages. It needs to be emphasised that the book is about the Rugby World Cup and not the International Rugby Board. There is a difference, as I think I have made clear. Also, the book is foremost about the game and the players who have made it the great tournament that it is.

I am very grateful to my daughter Emily for transcribing the taped interviews at home with our son-in-law Paul and, more significantly, to both of them for providing an unforgettable moment while I was on a visit to Sanctuary to discuss the book's progress. After embarking the train in Wales as a mere father, I alighted in Paddington as a grandfather or, in Welsh, *tadcu* to our first grandson, Tom.

Of course, I must also thank Cilla and Ben for tolerating the many absences and silences.

Contents

To the family

Foreword

Although its history is relatively brief, few events in world sport carry the same resounding fascination as the Rugby World Cup. Most of us have lived through its genesis and history, yet somehow its traditions and significance give the sense that it is as old as the game itself.

I vividly remember watching the inaugural World Cup as a gangling 16-year-old and experiencing the first stirrings of its potential; secretly desiring, but never truly believing, that one day I may have the chance to participate. Hosted by the Antipodes, this event awoke in me what a truly international game rugby union is. Of particular interest was Australia's semi-final against the French at the Concord Oval, Sydney. This game was played in front of a meagre 18,000 spectators. Contrast this with the World Cup semi-final in 2003, to be held at Stadium Australia in front of a crowd of 80,000 plus. The game has come a long way over the last 16 years.

Rugby has become such a global team-sport that only soccer stands ahead of it on the world stage. The world now wholly embraces the Rugby World Cup and the colour and excitement it brings. As is the case with events such as the Olympic Games and the Soccer World Cup, people who would not usually follow the sport come together with those who do to enjoy the spectacle and cheer their country to glory.

Rugby has always been a great fraternity that unites people from all walks of life, from all over the world. In Australia, this was vividly demonstrated by the British and Irish Lions supporters in 2001. Their contribution to the series and, indeed, to the Australian economy was unprecedented in this part of the world. A Rugby World Cup does this in an even more extraordinary way as spectators truly become part of the event.

My great fortune was to play in three World Cups and claim the Webb Ellis Cup in two of them. Looking back, each World Cup had its own special moments and atmosphere which, with the common thread of mutual goodwill, has brought them together as the experience of a lifetime.

For me, the World Cup cannot be defined by a single moment but by the camaraderie, the passion and the excitement that the tournament encapsulates. However, there was always something personally special about each of the tournaments in which I was involved.

In '91, it was living the dream: playing with and against some of my heroes. In '95, it was the triumph of a nation. As disappointing as it was not to have won the Cup, it was great to see the Nelson Mandela-inspired Springboks unite the nation behind their team for the first time. And then there was 1999, the culmination of four years of hard work, with some disappointments, but ultimately final satisfaction at the Millennium Stadium in Cardiff.

Not long after the third World Cup, it was thought by some that the onset of the professional era would erode the unique character of rugby and the game would be irreparably damaged. On the contrary, its greatest virtues have remained intact and, indeed, strengthened by the wider expansion and development of the code.

It has been a privilege to read Gerald's absorbing insights into the history of rugby's ultimate prize. From its uncertain beginnings, through the distinctiveness of each tournament, to the success the World Cup enjoys today, Gerald shares with us his consummate knowledge and understanding of the game and its personalities. We find ourselves amid the on-field and off-field action that has made the World Cup what it is today.

I'm sure all who read Gerald's book will look back, as I did, and remember the great moments; the highs and the lows; the agony and the ecstasy. Now, as Australia looks forward to hosting the fifth World Cup, rugby followers around the world unite once again to witness the earthly summit of the game they play in heaven.

John Eales
Australia Captain, 1996–2001

Chapter 1

'To Make An End Is To Make A Beginning'

Events at the Millennium Stadium in Cardiff on the evening of 4 November 1999 would come to illustrate the truth of what had up until that moment been a mixture of surmise and guess work about rugby union, a combination of imaginative concepts and a choice of proposals. Rugby union had been, and to a certain extent still was, in a state of agitation, tossing and turning in a post-amateur ferment of anxiety. Which way was the game to turn? What did the future hold? The game at the Millennium Stadium was played between New Zealand's All Blacks and South Africa's Springboks. The fourth Rugby World Cup was drawing to a close but it was not there yet.

The Rugby World Cup had come into existence in 1987. From that moment events had moved rapidly. By the late summer of 1995 rugby union, after over 100 years as an amateur game, had declared itself an 'open' sport. The mood of rugby union was a mixture of old-world ethos – once admirable, but now seen as fuddy-duddy – and of a new order which was refreshingly bold and adventurous, but which could also be brash in its audacity. Tartly, those subscribing to the new order viewed the sport as if it were inhabited by galumphing blazer-wearers. This opinion was given a public voice by Will Carling during a 1995 television interview in which he referred to the RFU committee as '57 old farts'. The old farts had been doing their utmost to preserve what they saw as the best their game had to offer. Time was running out. The exclusive enclosure of rugby union patricians was being gate-crashed by impudent and, perhaps, unprincipled *arrivistes*.

There were some who wished to hold on to those parts of a code which epitomised gentlemanly good will and of a competition based on the simple ideal of playing a game for its own sake, for the intoxicating thrill of doing so in freedom and for the honour of the jersey. Others understood that the game, as it had been known, was up.

There was the constant threat that the old order was breaking up. And if that was the case, what form should the new order take? On the horizon was a judgement of an order of merit and of world rankings. England had felt they had outgrown the Five Nations Championship as it then was. There were noises elsewhere that the Tri Nations Championship should be enlarged to include England and France. There should be, perhaps, an annual competition between the champions of the Southern Hemisphere and the champions of the Northern Hemisphere. The broadcasters waited with baited breath on the sidelines. There were playing considerations and commercial imperatives. In the autumn of 1999, there was a good deal that hung, nervously, in the air; speculation was rife.

The World Cup was reaching its climax. What did the future hold for rugby union? In what manner had rugby union changed? There were still many doubts and misgivings. There were those who still disapproved that amateurism had been, in their eyes, so summarily discarded. Perhaps there were still alternative ways for the game, which had existed officially since the formation of the first rugby union in 1871, to progress into the 21st century without jettisoning all of the habits and traditions that it had accrued over that time.

Entering its fifth season since the International Rugby Football Union declaration that allowed the game to become professional, rugby union had begun acquiring the trappings of a professional sport. The die, of course, had been cast but, while it was one thing for a club or a union to declare itself professional, it was quite another to acquire the resources to fund the game. If the Southern Hemisphere had moved swiftly to manage its affairs, there was no such equanimity in the Northern Hemisphere. The transformation had been uneasy.

This was the first Rugby World Cup tournament to be held since the game had declared itself an 'open' sport.

New Zealand and South Africa were meeting again in the World Cup. This was the second time. They had played each other first of all in the 1995 final in Johannesburg in the year of South Africa's introduction into the tournament following their period in sporting isolation.

This, however, was not the moment that validated the World Cup as the theatre of true champions. Rather, it was the moment when rugby's two most formidable nations failed to do so and when they played instead for the third and fourth places. This confirmed the 1999 World Cup final as the pinnacle of rugby ambition; it proved that the World Cup was the inspiration and driving force of rugby union. The World Cup alone gave legitimacy to a nation's boast to be world champions. No other claims could be made. Each of these great rugby nations in its time had claimed the world crown for its own without ever truly being able to justify their claim with authoritative and unanimous approval.

Suddenly the rugby world had moved on. Players were now paid to pursue what they once purported to do for the sheer, simple pleasure. Rugby union had once allowed them to furnish their talent and to fulfil their competitive urges in an exhilarating team sport for fun, while those who played at international level were stimulated by the honour of representing their nation. So it had always been. However, this sense of joy and honour might no longer be the essential imperative which moved men and, increasingly, women to choose rugby union as their preferred sport. Henceforth, fun might be gained from a bonus cheque, talent measured by the number of agents' calling cards and loyalty governed solely by a legal contract.

There remained a sense of uncertainty about the future, an apprehension at the way rugby union had already irrevocably changed and a concern that the mutation process, gradual and inexorable, was not yet at an end. For the optimists, there was the excitement of the infinite possibilities that might unfold – of better, more skilful play and of a faster, more mobile game. However, those of an earlier generation harboured a strong sense of sentimental regret for a rugby world that had now passed and were wary of a new one that was not theirs properly to comprehend. After all, we are creatures of our own past and accustomed to the habits and views nurtured over a lifetime. At international level, to play the game for the game's sake had been abandoned for good.

The 1999 World Cup was the first of the tournaments participated in by players who performed for money and by men who believed this to be a new-found emancipation. Theirs was a talent for sale. The Rugby World Cup was the theatre for heroes and now, also, paid entertainers.

The final week of the fourth in a series of World Cups that began in 1987 was coming to an end. Another great tradition was about to be devitalised and stripped of its time-honoured mystique and awesome muscularity. Two nations whose indestructible pride was woven into the fabric of their rugby teams were to meet: New Zealand were playing South Africa, the All Blacks against the Springboks. However you put it, the contest identified the titans of rugby union.

In 1995 they battled themselves into extra time and to a standstill in the final at Ellis Park, Johannesburg. This was the pinnacle of rugby union. The two teams which had for most of the century been competing for the title of the best rugby nation on the planet, without really being able to justify the claim, were for the first time doing precisely that. They were truly the best in the world.

By November 1999, the crown had tilted. The throne was not theirs any longer to occupy. Instead, they were the poor relations of Australia and France who, in an extraordinary manner in two pulsating semi-finals, had leapt ahead to make their way to the final. The All Blacks and the Springboks were humbled by having to contend for the consolation prizes. They were bereft in having nothing left to do other than compete for the third and fourth places. The All Blacks and the Springboks were challenging for the bronze medal.

Honour might be thought to be at stake. After all, it was what had been fought for throughout the generations. The motivation had been inspired by pride: pride in the jersey, the pride of a nation, the pride of performance. Ellis Park in Johannesburg or Eden Park in Auckland had invariably provided the amphitheatre for these immense gladiators; the rugby game provided the means by which each nation held a mirror to its dignity and reputation. In these arenas they laid claim to world supremacy.

The Rugby World Cup changed all that and the match in Cardiff in 1999 portrayed it. Past contests were perceived to be the makings of the champions of the world. The perception was enough. They proclaimed themselves as champions of the world. There were few around to dispute that the All Blacks and the Springboks commanded the great heights.

Statistics, however, suggest that no one team at any one time in any one 12-month period, say, could ever have claimed to be the champions of the world.

Since 1921, when the international series began between the two countries, New Zealand and South Africa had contested for the title of world champions. Others might argue from time to time about the legitimacy of such a claim. After all, nations did not play each other sequentially: only at frequent, but irregular, intervals. There was no proper measure at any given moment.

The All Blacks and the Springboks can make an authentic claim to be champions of world rugby. By 1995, neither Ireland or Scotland had ever beaten New Zealand; Ireland had won once against South Africa; Scotland, three times. Wales had won three times against the All Blacks but had not succeeded against the Springboks; England had won four times against the All Blacks and also the Springboks; and France had won seven times against New Zealand and five times against South Africa. Throughout all these fixtures there was no synchronisation and therefore no judgement as to who should be made overall champion.

By way of example, if England defeated South Africa in 1972 and New Zealand in 1973, and in beating both of them on their own acres in a 12-month period could lay claim to be the top of the world, the statistics will disabuse them. These show that they lost to both Wales and to Ireland in the same period. In 1964 France won a Test in New Zealand and defeated England in Paris, but South Africa beat them in Stade Colombes. Similarly, France won a test series in South Africa in 1993 and New Zealand in 1994, but England beat them in both years. And so it goes on.

However, in 1960 and 1961 the Springboks could fairly claim to be world champions. In that period they played all the seven member countries of the International Rugby Football Board and France (who were not admitted to the IRFB until 1978). Between 30 April 1960 when they defeated Scotland in Port Elizabeth, and 12 August 1961 when they beat Australia, they had successfully accomplished a four-match series – two matches to one with one drawn – against New Zealand between June and August 1960. They defeated the four home unions between December 1960 and January 1961, and between May and August 1961 they beat Ireland in Cape Town and succeeded twice against Australia. The draw against France in Paris in February 1961 stopped them from achieving a full house. Their captains during this period were Roy Dryburgh (full-back), Avril Malan (lock) and Johan Claassen (lock)

New Zealand achieved as much in the mid-'60s, but over a longer period which encompassed 1963 and 1965. Between December 1963 and February 1964 of the Northern Hemisphere season, a draw against Scotland had denied them a clean sweep of the four home unions, and they defeated France. In August 1964, the All Blacks had won a series (2–1) against Australia. But they were not to beat South Africa in a four-match series (3–1) until July and September 1965. Wilson Whineray (prop) was the captain for most of this period but John Graham (flanker) took over for the Australian matches. However, this period of success went beyond the one continuous season restriction.

In the 1980s the full-scale tour of Europe by the All Blacks and the Springboks, which took in the Five Nations, was gradually scaled down and finally done away with, as indeed reciprocal tours between New Zealand and South Africa were in the '90s. If South Africa had won a three-match test series in New Zealand in 1937, the All Blacks did not achieve as much until 1996. The All Blacks succeeded in winning a one-off fixture there in 1992. New Zealand had won 18 fixtures, and South Africa 21, by the time they came to meet for the first time in the Rugby World Cup in 1995.

The Lions cannot be considered in this context. A rota system existed whereby a period of three or four years lapsed between the visits to New

Zealand, South Africa and more recently to Australia. A case no doubt can be made in the period between 1971 and 1974 when the Lions of those years toured New Zealand and South Africa respectively and won. Despite the vast and genuine interest there is in the Lions and the attachment there is to them, how authentic is their claim to be the best in the world, when the best players from four nations combine to play together for but a brief period? The Lions are uniquely different.

In passing, it might be worth noting that of 32 fixtures in New Zealand, the Lions had only won 6 compared to the All Blacks' 24; while of 43 fixtures in South Africa, the Lions had won 16 to the Springboks' 21.

By this time, Australia had emerged as a major force, a change that dramatically came about in the middle of the 1980s when they first accomplished the grand slam of victories in Britain and Ireland. This heralded a time of unprecedented success for a country for which rugby union had held only marginal interest hitherto, with Australian rules and rugby league able to draw on a far wider audience and participation.

Bob Templeton was the inspiration behind rugby union's emergence from a minimalist reference in the stop press column into the mainstream and headline news in Australia. Templeton's amiable, generous spirit and extraordinary enthusiasm was inherited by the wonderful national coaches that followed in his footsteps. This rise in popularity and Australia's success has coincided almost identically with the initiative to inaugurate the World Cup.

Australia's one and only grand slam of Britain and Ireland was in 1984, the World Cup began three years later and since then they have won the trophy twice.

The fixtures between the All Blacks and the Springboks have to be taken in the context of the great historical sweep and tradition of the contest. Their once dominant position must also be placed against the growing power of Australia, who has surpassed both countries in their influence on the World Cup.

It is with this long inheritance in mind that what happened in Cardiff in 1999 might almost be interpreted as a rejection of what had gone before. That New Zealand and South Africa were not able to compete for the gold and silver was an affront to their own sense of esteem in Cardiff and an outrage to the expectations at home. That the bronze was all they could hope for was, in their eyes, for the first time, a humiliating recognition of their own vulnerability and one which the World Cup had exposed.

Thus, if it had been a matter of mere conjecture in the past, the World Cup every four years had introduced a distinctive and unquestioned world order.

The disparities of the past had now gone. If Louis Luyt, President of the South African Rugby Football Union, said in 1995 that South Africa at the first time of competing was at the top where they belonged and that they would have won the previous two tournaments had they not been ostracised, he must have recognised the hollowness of his blinkered view four years later. The rugby world had changed with the potential for a new world order. This in no small measure was due to the Rugby World Cup.

The All Blacks and the Springboks, who had appeared to rule the rugby world for so long that their superiority had only occasionally been disputed and had always assumed that the race for supremacy was theirs to share, found that they really had no stomach to do battle for third place in 1999. Joost van der Westhuizen, the great Springbok scrum-half, tried to persuade himself and everyone else before the game in Cardiff that no self-respecting South African could diminish the importance of any contest between the two rugby nations. It was not to be, however. The quality of the game disproved the notion.

Tradition and honour are meant to play their part. They still do, of course, but others had set a quantifiable target – the attaining of which could alone satisfy a team's and the player's desire. To win the World Cup was the key. To fall short of that higher ambition was not enough for tradition or honour, neither for the Springboks nor the All Blacks. Wales were to return from Rotorua in New Zealand having succeeded in winning third place in 1987. Wales rejoiced. Neither New Zealand nor South Africa was ever likely to echo such celebrations in 1999.

Thus, their world changed for ever. The match was timid and lacking its customary primitive intensity. The brutal power was emasculated. That the All Blacks should play the Springboks was no longer enough. There had to be a higher vision. Once upon a time they played for nothing other than the honour of representing their country, to uphold a reputation and for the sake, as the poet wrote, full of sentiment and nostalgia for lost innocence, of a ribboned coat. There never had been for these two stalwarts of rugby union any such thing as playing up, playing up and playing the game. The game itself, by itself, between the All Blacks and the Springboks, was not the place to maintain a reputation any more.

Fame was achieved by laying hands on the Rugby World Cup trophy. The most graphic illustration therefore was to witness in Cardiff a contest between the game's ruthless giants that was careless and inert, lacking the unrestrained vigour of yore and without the galvanising vibrancy which made them irresistibly gladiatorial. The punishing muscularity had vanished.

Once and for all, the Rugby World Cup had altered the perspectives of rugby union. All else would simply be an illusion of supremacy.

Chapter 2

Genesis Of The Rugby World Cup

The rugby world changed in March 1985 when the International Rugby Football Board held their annual meeting at the Headquarters of French Railways, Paris. André Bosc was one of the top executives of French Railways and, with Albert Ferrasse, was one of the Fédération Française de Rugby representatives on the IRFB. He arranged a 9am train trip on the TGV (which had just started operating) for the members to travel from the Gare de Lyon to enjoy a lunch on the River Rhône in Lyon. In this informal way, the closing arguments and persuasions were made for the momentous decision they were about to take. When they arrived back in Paris to formally continue their meeting, the members of the IRFB were asked to vote on the proposal to inaugurate a 'world rugby cup' as it was then referred to.

This was a decision that had been a long time in gestation. The IRFB were first approached by two companies in the early 1980s. West Nally, a British company owned by Peter West and Patrick Nally, and Mark McCormack's IMG, a trans-continental company with its base in the USA, had each suggested a world-wide tournament. Both were rejected. There was another proposal in 1983 made by Gideon Lloyd of Lloyd International and by Neil Durden-Smith, who was also involved with sports promotion and public relations in London. Once more the suggestion was turned down.

There was a natural resistance to such a tournament. This came almost exclusively from the so-called four home unions who, despite the superiority of the Southern Hemisphere game, considered themselves (administratively, at any rate) to be the guardians of the sport. This essentially meant the 'spirit' of the game and especially its amateur ethos. Scotland (1886), Ireland (1886), Wales (1886) and England (1890) were the original members of the IRFB.

England were late in joining because of a disagreement with Scotland over a disputed try in 1884 which had given England the victory. In 1886, Scotland agreed to accept the Irish referee's decision provided that England would join the International Board on the same conditions as the other three countries.

England would not do so. The matter was put to arbitration that overwhelmingly came out in England's favour. Because of their superior number of clubs England were allowed six representatives to the two each the other three countries were allowed. England could not be out-voted. In 1911 this was reduced to 4.

Australia, New Zealand and South Africa were not included until 1949, when England's representation was reduced to two. The Dominions, as they were then called, had one seat each until 1958 when they were allocated two. France had to wait until 1978 before being received into membership. By this time all the countries had the equal number of two votes each.

The sense of the four home unions' seniority prevailed. It was still perceived as 'their' game.

The retaining of the amateur ethos, which from the days when the Northern Union split rugby in England over 'broken time' payments and which led to the formation of rugby league, was a matter of faith, of religious devotion, indeed, of fundamentalist belief. It was strictly observed and, with hindsight, grew to appear faintly ridiculous. Any player conducting a conversation with anyone associated with rugby league would be construed as entering negotiations with a view to signing a contract. To be present at a rugby league fixture, a player could consider himself as having desecrated rugby union's sacred rites. He could be and was ostracised. In consequence, no player would be welcome to cross any rugby union club threshold.

David Watkins, the mercurial Wales and Newport fly-half, signed a contract in the late spring of 1968 to play rugby league for Salford. He graced both games, representing the British teams with distinction. On his return to Wales he was interviewed by BBC on the Cardiff RFC pitch. When he was seen by a member of the club committee the BBC were asked to terminate the interview forthwith. No such activity was permitted. As a former rugby league player, Watkins was *persona non grata* and could not be allowed on a rugby union pitch. Serious stuff at the time; nowadays this is hard to imagine.

Yet, for all the injustice, intolerance and evangelical piety with which rugby union pursued its doctrinaire policy in defence of amateurism, there was, to begin with, huge sympathy for its defiant stance. By and large, sport was an amateur's pastime. It was only in the dying days of the 20th century that sport came to be acknowledged as a lucrative means of employment. Few administrators needed to go to the barricades to defend what appeared to be a natural way of pursuing their sport.

Rugby union was in a singular position. It had a competitor for its talent. No one competed for cricket players in similar fashion, nor for footballers. Only in rugby did the dichotomy exist. Rugby league, for the amateur cousins, was a menacing presence. With its ever-present temptation and financial inducements rugby league was, and had been since 1895, a persistent threat to the present and future existence of rugby union. This, too, was serious. With rugby league nowadays perceived to be in retreat in the face of the inexorable expansion and worldwide ambitions of rugby union, it is difficult to understand how beleaguered rugby union was in the face of a force that made it appear to be the bully-boy from the 'north'. For Welshmen, 'going north' was the euphemism for going to play rugby league in either Yorkshire or Lancashire, the two counties which had broken away to form the Northern Union.

Amateurism was under constant threat. As a way of protecting the amateur ethos, the administrators, with a strong bias towards Britain and Ireland, shunned any form of officially recognised competition. To sanction official competitions would 'professionalise' a game that recognised only 'friendly' fixtures.

'You have to remember by culture and tradition in those days – up to the '80s – there was little organisation, no competitions in the British Isles,' says Marcel Martin, currently advisor to the Chairman on all Rugby World Cup matters. 'There were the usual matches and traditional fixtures in the UK. I do remember in the '70s going to Scotland to explain the pros and cons of competition. There was no champion of Scotland. No champion of England. No official champion of Wales at any level. No champion club of Ireland. By the late '70s the public wanted something more than friendly matches.'

Martin was first elected to the IRFB in 1986 and remained until 1997, when his place was taken by Bernard Lapasset, President of the FFR. In 1990 he was elected RWC Director and Chairman of RWC BV, the commercial arm of the tournament. He retired from these positions in 2000 and is now Chairman of Biarritz rugby club. He is a distinguished servant of the game and was the longest-serving representative of the Rugby World Cup. He had been there from the start.

The French had their club championship, South Africa its Currie Cup and New Zealand its Ranfurly Shield. Domestic competitions were soon introduced in the British Isles.

This was true also of the international competitions. The Five Nations Championship as it then was, in the minds of the administrators, existed only as a figment of the fervent minds of newspaper journalists and television commentators. The tournament as such did not exist. It was the French, David Hands maintains in his invaluable *The Five Nations Story*, who dubbed it *Tournoi des Cinq Nations* in the 1920s.

As far as the four home unions were concerned, the ten matches were 'friendlies' and were not an inter-connected series of fixtures from which a table could be drawn up and a champion crowned. The grand slam and the triple crown were merely creations of imaginative reporters in a bid to sell newspapers. It was noticeable, however, that each nation was happy to celebrate when the prizes came their way. The wooden spoon for the nation that came bottom was not as welcomed a part of the journalists' fantasy.

It was in 1993 that the tournament was officially recognised with the presentation of a trophy and rules drawn up to regulate the championship. 'I was a member of the committee at the time and I remember that for years Scotland were adamant they would not accept the Five Nations Championship,' says Martin. 'They did not want to feel obliged to play another nation, which they would be if they signed to play in an officially recognised tournament. I was one of two trustees – the other was Bob Weighill of England – when the tournament was formally created and a Cup was donated.' This was eight years after the decision was taken to start a Rugby World Cup.

The RWC had originally surfaced in the Southern Hemisphere. Separately, both Australia and New Zealand had contemplated the idea, but not too deeply. Bill McLaughlin, President of the Australian Rugby Union, had contemplated the matter in early 1979. Ces Blazey, his counterpart in New Zealand, had thought about it too. McLaughlin had discussed it with businessmen in Sydney but had it gone no further.

They had been considering what should be done to celebrate their country's bicentenary during which the concept of a World Cup had reared its head, as well as a fixture with England. They decided upon the latter and so the other, more grandiose idea, went no further.

However, by late 1979 Sir Nicholas Shehadie had become President of the ARU. In time, he, too, pursued the concept of a World Cup. This was indeed prescient of him but there were other pressures, by now, being brought to bear on the game. This was not only the case in Australia but throughout the rugby-playing world. The rugby union authorities were gradually becoming aware of the insistent external threats that endangered the game's well-being, even its continued existence.

There was a dawning realisation that the game could go out of control, lose its players as well as its traditional fixtures. Ultimately, control could shift out of the hands of the people who had hitherto governed rugby union. There was, and had been for some time in the 1970s, an undercurrent of uncertainty, of growing unease and disaffection which if not addressed could turn into a crisis. Money was at the root of this.

It could be said that sentiment, an undue emphasis on tradition, a lack of awareness of the changing nature of sport in society and the exclusivity that permeated rugby union's upper echelon of administrators all helped to promote an encircling mood that was made to appear impassive and complacent.

There was a kind of Edwardian languor which suggested that the guardians of the game were aloof to the rumblings of discontent and disharmony beyond their committee room doors. There was a sense that a revolution was waiting to happen.

Extra wealth was entering the game, making it richer, but the players felt unfairly excluded from it. Television's tentacles were extending into every aspect of sport, and rugby was no exception.

Rugby union was respected for a while for upholding its strongly amateur values. While some sports appeared to sell their souls for a mess of potage – or so it was made to appear at the time – rugby union held out. The view that the game was played for its own sake was sincerely held to begin with, but Mammon was knocking at the gates and was soon welcomed and embraced. This was done, it was claimed, for the game's sake. The high principles which had been upheld for so long, were placed on an altar and consecrated. But it was the player who was the sacrificial lamb. While more and more – more of his time, more of his talent – was demanded of him, it was someone else, from the player's point of view, who always seemed to reap the benefit. The tension was real.

Innocence, which had never been entirely pure in rugby, began finally to part company with amateurism. Those who maintained its essence soon lost the sympathy of the man on the terrace. Hypocrisy, he perceived, had entered the committee room and the equation no longer balanced. It was an age-old tale. The owners (the unions) made the money; the workers (the players) did not. The centre could not hold.

There were ruffians at one gate wanting to smash and grab the game for their own benefit, a few business mavericks at another, whilst within the game itself there was some underground resistance arising from disgruntled players who felt hard done by. Rugby was an emerging sport which was growing richer but in which the players, financially, were not going to have their share. That was short-lived.

Amateurism was at risk. The administrators defended it to the hilt. It was to be their last stand. After 130 years, its foundation was found to be incapable of withstanding the buffeting of the forces at the end of the 20th century.

The seeds of the World Cup had been sown but it was not until 1982 that Shehadie and Blazey finally got together with some urgency to push the issue forward.

If there were winds of change blowing from a variety of directions, the blow that significantly moved matters to its conclusion was the presence of an Australian entrepreneur called David Lord. He was proposing a 'circus' – the very word immediately intimated the superficiality of the scheme he had in mind. He would sign players from all over the world to play in a series of fixtures in a number of venues around the globe. The itinerant players moved as if by caravan from one capital city to the next from which ultimately a champion country would emerge.

There was no depth and no structure to Lord's scheme. There was no connection with the rugby unions and no development of a future generation of players. Quite what the players would be doing in between the short 'circus' seasons was never properly explained. If Kerry Packer had caused convulsions four years earlier, in 1978, and was to revitalise the complacency in the international cricket world, Lord's ill-thought out scheme was doomed to fail. He visited Europe to promote his campaign but his interrogation on 'live' television in front of an audience in Wales exposed the paucity of his proposal. If there had been serious concerns in Australia particularly, Lord failed to convince anyone in Europe that his way forward would benefit rugby.

The alarm bells were ringing, however. This was especially so in Australia and New Zealand, where with more open minds they were prepared to contemplate a different future.

By 1984, both Australia and New Zealand had separately proposed the concept of the World Cup. The IRFB had been taken somewhat by surprise to have two proposals in this way and turned them both down. The Australians were asked to conduct a feasibility study on holding such a tournament.

'At the time,' Keith Rowlands recalls, 'the Board was not happy about it. It wished to stick with the rota of international fixtures that it believed, in an amateur game, to be sufficient for the amateur players at the highest level to play. Such a limit would be one way also of combating the ever-increasing threat of professionalism. This last was a genuine fear. At the time, the rugby unions were only at the beginning of sponsorship and advertising. There were no commercial agents.' Rowlands had enjoyed the game as a player for the Lions, Wales and Cardiff, followed by a distinguished period as administrator for his club, country and on the international stage as one of Wales's representatives on the IRFB. He was to become the first paid Secretary of the Board and in 1999 was tournament director when Wales was the host nation.

Australia and New Zealand, instead of looking over each other's shoulders to see what the other was up to, as is often their wont, decided wisely this time to pool their resources.

Shehadie and Blazey met in New Zealand and formed a combined committee to formulate a plan. When in New Zealand, Dick Littlejohn chaired the meetings; when in Australia, Shehadie did. Ces Blazey was the Chairman of the New Zealand Rugby Football Union in 1977 and had been on New Zealand's Executive Committee since 1957. At the forefront of their minds was a tournament to be shared between their respective countries. The inaugural year was to be 1987, thereby competing with neither the Olympics, nor the football World Cup, nor the Commonwealth Games.

They made their views known to the IRFB. From this a full submission was expected at the annual meeting in Paris in March 1985.

'I have to say that I was concerned about the IRFB representatives and to what extent they reflected the views of their Committees or councils,' said Shehadie, who had played for Australia for the first time in 1947, touring Europe with the Wallabies in 1947–1948 and who later became a prominent businessman and politician in New South Wales and Mayor of Sydney. 'In other words, I did not completely trust them to convey the right message. In any case, this was far too important a topic to leave to a few individuals. There was, too, a special urgency in the matter. There was no time to stall or to get it wrong. There were people in the wings who would and could take the game over. For the game to move forward it was vital that it was rugby men who did so, not entrepreneurs or business people from the television world. We should control rugby union and if a World Cup should come about we would determine its destiny.'

During the Five Nations Championship, Dick Littlejohn and Nick Shehadie – the 'Nick and Dick Show' as it came to be known – canvassed opinion and made their presentations in the Northern Hemisphere. France, who had only been admitted to the IRFB in 1978, were in favour of the concept provided it included countries from outside the eight members of the IRFB. France, excluded for so long from the IRFB, had courted other countries like Italy, Romania, the Soviet Union and others under the auspices of Fédération Internationale de Rugby Amateur (FIRA). Given time, this grouping might have come to be seen as a competing governing body. Whether politically or altruistically, Albert Ferrasse, who was President of the French Rugby Federation and Chairman of FIRA, wanted the developing nations involved.

The outcome of the battle for the hearts and minds of the other four countries was far from sure. Indeed, there was an expectation of firm opposition.

'We had a difficult time,' said Shehadie. 'We had a bad press. The whole matter was treated as something of a joke. There were times when we were treated patronisingly and were left with the feeling that this was "their" game, not ours, and that we in the Southern Hemisphere were doing it for our own purpose. We offered the TV rights to the BBC, for instance, for US$6 million. They did not take it at all seriously and we were told that that the idea would simply not work.'

When they visited Wales, they found that the WRU were lukewarm towards their proposals but were swayed by the persuasive tones of the late Ken Harris, the Union treasurer (1952–1987), who advocated support. England were also in favour. Ireland and especially Scotland were against.

Each of the countries had two representatives making 16 in all. Even though South Africa knew that they would not be invited to play in the tournament – because neither Australia nor New Zealand would allow them entry into their countries – they voted in favour of it. The decision, with Dr Roger Vanderfield of Australia in the Chair, was revealed as six nations in favour and two against (Ireland and Scotland). There was no commitment, however, beyond 1987.

An International Board Tournament Committee was formed. This was made up of Ronnie Dawson (Ireland), Keith Rowlands (Wales), Ross Turnbull (Australia), Bob Stuart (New Zealand), John Kendall-Carpenter (England), with Bob Weighill as its Secretary.

A world rugby tournament was out of the blocks.

Chapter 3

Down To Business...

The IRFB were soon to find out that the decision to hold a World Cup tournament was straightforward in contrast to the dilemmas that were to confront them afterwards amid the plethora of legal detail and commercial and financial imperatives which needed to be clarified. It soon became apparent that there was no adequate structure in place to cope with the new demands.

The 16 representatives were, in effect, volunteers. The IRFB did not have any fully paid officials or executives of any kind. Until 1986 the IRFB did not even have any money of its own. They had relied on the unions paying the expenses of their representatives.

'In 1986,' explained Marcel Martin, 'the Board celebrated its centenary and organised two matches. One fixture was between teams from the Northern and Southern Hemisphere. The other was between a team drawn from the four home unions to play against the rest of the world. One was held in Twickenham, the other in Cardiff.'

The IRFB was an unincorporated company in the UK which suddenly found itself with a surplus of £500,000 on which taxes would have to be paid. Martin was a qualified accountant and a former accounting executive with Mobil for 33 years. Born in Agen in the south west of France, he studied in Paris and later took an MBA at Miami University of Ohio. He was drafted into the Army and served in Algeria during the Algerian war. Although he did not play much, he did referee in France and with the London Society of Referees in England where, he says, he developed 'a fine knowledge and understanding of the London suburbs' and, more importantly, in the '70s did a good deal of lobbying to get France invited to join the IRFB.

He began in rugby administration in an honorary capacity in 1968. This was the year that Albert Ferrasse was elected President of the FFR and, along with Guy Basquet, he ruled French rugby from their card table in Agen. Martin joined the FFR in 1984 and was appointed two years later to be one of the French representatives on the IRFB.

'Until then the accounts of the IRFB were very simple. There was no income and no expense. The system we had was a spread equalisation fund which I put in place and where each representative would put in his real expenses, make a total, divide by eight and charge back to the union. With most of the meetings held in England, in the East India club in St James's Square, it obviously cost more, say, to send a delegate from New Zealand to London than from anywhere else. That was the only accounting in the IRFB. In 1986 we had an income which we didn't know what to do with. This taught everyone a lesson. Tax advice had been given in 1984 but no action had been taken.

'Therefore we needed to put in place a new company. If we start a World Cup and make a profit, we cannot continue as a committee. We must set up companies in tax havens so that we pay minimum tax. We wanted the maximum amount of money go to rugby.

'At the end of 1989 we created companies in a way that is well known in the business world, where you put a parent company in a tax haven. That parent company has a subsidiary. The subsidiary company signs all the commercial contract then gets income. We needed to ensure, as a sporting body, that we paid as little tax as possible. We needed to find the most agreeable terms.'

The IRFB were entering into uncharted territory. They'd always had good intentions, doing things for the good name of rugby. They only met once a year to discuss three topics in the main: the laws of the game, the general outline of future international fixtures and the maintenance of the game's amateur status (with which they were increasingly becoming preoccupied). The IRFB had no experience in other matters, nor indeed up until this moment were they expected to go beyond their limited areas of expertise. The boundaries had suddenly been extended.

By and large, the IRFB was no more than a servant of the eight member unions. In time this relationship, too, would modify and change as a result of the Paris decision to hold a World Cup tournament. The IRFB would gain in influence and control and begin to behave as a world governing body and not merely to serve the whims and fancies of the separate unions.

At each step of the way there were two major concerns. The first, as ever, was for the preservation of the game's amateur status which, with the intrusion of the commercial devices and desires that would inevitably follow the success of the game and its higher profile, would be put under stress.

The other was that the control of rugby union should remain in the hands of genuine rugby men and not be hijacked entirely by outsiders with no feeling for the game other than the financial benefits that might accrue, and the clout and the kudos it might bring them in the sporting world. The IRFB were a group of men with mixed feelings about the step they had just decided to take.

The IRFB is an unincorporated association and, by definition under UK tax law, is treated as a company for taxation. They have made no returns for many years. This was about to change since the Rugby World Cup in due course would generate vast revenue.

Thus, in 1987 the Tournament Committee would be responsible for the structure of the tournament, fixtures, referees and so on, while Rugby World Cup (Property) Ltd was set up to operate the commercial arm of the tournament and was registered in Australia. The Chairman of both entities was John Kendall-Carpenter. Both organisations were the forerunners of what would become respectively Rugby World Cup Limited (RWCL) and Rugby World Cup (Licensing) BV. The former was based in the Isle of Man, with the latter in Rotterdam.

A company incorporated in the UK is regarded as resident there and therefore liable to tax. Ceasing to be a UK resident was not considered as a realistic option for the IRFB but, by locating in the Isle of Man, they were able to take advantage of its tax exemption status. Therefore, an off-shore structure was devised for the receipt of income from the exploitation of commercial rights associated with all tournaments. In 1989 the International Rugby Settlement (The Trust) was created, from which RWCL and RWC (Licensing) BV were instituted.

The Trust, with its single corporate trustee in Barclays International (Isle of Man) Ltd, accumulates and distributes the surplus of the profits from its wholly owned company RWCL. It is not under the legal control of rugby individuals and it can fulfil its functions without falling under the influence of any one political faction among the rugby leaders.

There is an Advisory Committee to the Trust which consists of eight representatives from the Foundation Member Unions to carry out what the Trustee requires in order to comply with the Trust Deed. The Trust distributes the surplus funds, principally, in accordance with the Committee's advice.

RWCL also has the responsibility of organising all the tournaments which include the World Sevens Series, the Women's World Cup and the under-19 and under-21 age-group tournaments.

RWC (Licensing) BV is a wholly owned subsidiary of RWCL and is therefore responsible to that company for its actions. The majority of its income goes to the RWCL with a small portion retained to meet the tax requirements in the Netherlands.

The reason for interposing RWC (Licensing) BV between the owner of the rights, RWCL, and the end licensees is that, otherwise, royalties paid direct by the latter to the RWCL would be subject to high withholding taxes in the countries from which they are being paid. Royalties paid to a Dutch company are, however, subject to low or no withholding taxes. Therefore RWC (Licensing) BV, unlike RWCL, exists purely for tax purposes, but it must not itself trade. If it did, its trading profits would be taxable in the Netherlands at 35 per cent.

There is one more piece to the jigsaw: IRFB Ltd Services. This has a dual function, part commercial, part tax avoidance. Formed initially to acquire the lease of the Bristol premises for the IRFB in the 1990s before later settling in Dublin, it serves as the on-shore office of RWCL. Its role is administrative. It is also a means of passing funds from RWCL to IRFB. For this purpose it cannot be a beneficiary of the Trust. Services make a profit on its activities and pass this profit to the IRFB by way of dividends. So long as Services as a company, continues to provide administrative assistance only, the offshore companies are not compromised. Services pays UK tax in the normal way.

After the 1987 tournament, there was a period of quick consolidation so that by 1989 the main structures were in place. The fine-tuning occurred after 1991 when there was a huge expansion in the commercial potential of the Rugby World Cup.

None of these companies and trusts were in existence in 1985 when the decision was made to hold the World Cup. They were embarking on a learning curve. Since they had no expertise in the matter, they understood the need for an agent to manage the commercial aspect of the tournament. They appointed West Nally, a company with whom they had already been acquainted. West Nally had put forward a guarantee of US$5 million which IMG, the other applicant, had not, while still wanting a share of the profits. These were the decisive factors.

This sum of money provided the surplus that, ultimately, constituted the profit for the RWC tournament in 1987. It had proved difficult to raise money for the initial tournament. That John Kendall-Carpenter had signed the contract three months before it began actually saved the 1987 tournament. It had made a deficit but this was offset by the guarantee. West Nally and other contractors lost money on the event.

In 1987, the gate money remained with the organising unions (in this case Australia and New Zealand) and the same applied with the five nations that hosted the fixtures throughout the 1991 event. The organising unions also received 40 per cent of the commercial income which was divided in a way that gave New Zealand 24 per cent (they had more fixtures) and Australia 16 per cent.

The rest of the profit from the commercial income was distributed in a way that allowed the eight founding members of the IRFB, because they had promised to underwrite the tournament, to receive four per cent each (including Australia and New Zealand), while the other nine countries had two per cent each. Although South Africa did not participate in the tournament, they did help underwrite it and thus participated in sharing the income. Therefore, it was split 17 ways rather than 16. The remaining 10 per cent was given to the IRFB. This was after all expenses of travelling in economy, accommodation and subsistence had been accounted for. Certain countries were given an allocation for their kit, too.

In 1991, unlike four years previously, there was a commercial income. Of that income, 50 per cent remained with the IRFB to fund its increasing activities, while the remaining 50 per cent was distributed among the five nations who formed the organising committee.

After 1987, the need to have specialists to deal with sponsorship, hospitality, publishing, product licensing, travel loyalty, ticket sales and so on became urgent, and the IRFB started making contacts with a company called Keith Prowse & Co Ltd. Allan Callan was part of this company but, seeing the opportunity the Rugby World Cup offered, resolved to set up his own business: Callan, (Jed) Palmer Associated (CPA). Later Cliff Morgan was invited to join, thus the new entity became CPMA. Callan proposed to become the broker and contract manager. From nothing, commercially speaking, this company created the World Cup. At the end of the 1991 World Cup the commercial turnover (excluding gate money) was $20.5 million, with a profit equivalent to half of this.

Yet there had been problems leading up to within a few months of the tournament beginning. They had signed with Keith Prowse's organisation, who were already selling ticket and hospitality packages. Six months beforehand the company was going bankrupt. They had made a down payment against the fee they had already collected from their customers. Before they filed for bankruptcy they made a last payment to Rugby World Cup. The RWC however had a few hundred customers who had bought hospitality packages but were faced with a prospect of no match ticket and no kind of hospitality. With the help of Wembley Plc the critical situation was salvaged at the last moment. RWC did not lose any money.

With the 1995 World Cup going to South Africa, the IRB wanted an organisation with offices worldwide to act as broker and contract manager. CPMA did not have this capacity and, although an agreement had been signed with CPMA that took them beyond the 1995 World Cup, they were ultimately bought out of that contract by IMG.

For 1995, the aspiration was to make a profit equal to the income of 1991. The target was reached.

Chapter 4

1987 Rugby World Cup

Like a misplaced apostrophe, New Zealand drifts between the land mass that is Australia on the one side and the many thousands of almost anonymous islands which festoon the South Pacific Ocean on the other. Lying in the shadow of a nation which can either be seen as bold or aggressive, restlessly forceful or dynamically enterprising, a braveheart or a braggart, New Zealand, consisting of two islands separated by the Cook Strait, arises discretely, almost apologetically, out of the sea. On the map of the world the sheer bulk of Australia not so much protects New Zealand from the rest of the world, but seems to deny its neighbour any access to it, like a bouncer at the door entrance of a particularly desirable party. They live together as most neighbours do. They need to get along diplomatically but are cautious at all times in case one takes undue advantage of the other, especially when one is bigger and appears to be richer than the other. Welshmen know the feeling living next door to England, as Canada do to the United States of America. Each casts a wary eye on the other. As John Kendall-Carpenter, representing the RFU in England, was once rumoured to have said of Wales, after some spat or other: 'We co-exist on mutual trust and understanding. They don't trust us and we don't understand them.' Perhaps this is just the way it is when a small nation exists in the shadow of a larger neighbour. The tension between New Zealand and Australia could be said to have been given most acute expression at another moment in Rugby World Cup history 15 years later when a bit of a rumpus arose over the host and co-host agreement for the 2003 World Cup.

What is certain is that both countries have embraced sport with an abiding interest, even to the extent of it becoming an expression of a national character and identity. Each has an obsessive passion for a particular sport: Australia has taken cricket to its bosom; New Zealand was from the beginning drawn to rugby union.

With a new world freshness, both countries had canvassed unashamedly for a World Cup tournament and it was correct that the reward for the first tournament of its kind should go to the Antipodes; a shared experience of neighbourly hands stretching across the sea. There was also the sense that both Australia and New Zealand had the confidence and belief that the Rugby World Cup was much needed and that they could accomplish what was necessary. For the cynic, there might also have been the sense that were the tournament to come to grievous defeat, a stillborn competition, then it was better for the Europeans who had expressed mixed feelings about it that the fruitless labours should happen far away rather than on the doorstep of the home unions. Most remained hugely sceptical of where all this might lead and believed that if it should lead anywhere, it was bound to be unappetising and unwholesome for the rugby union game as a whole. The four home unions were less than wholehearted in their support.

At any rate, the show was on the road and that road in 1987 led to New Zealand, who were to be the host nation, and to Australia, who would be the sub-host. Three of the four pools (each consisting of four teams) were accommodated in New Zealand. Australia, England, Japan and the USA played all their matches in the Concord Oval in Sydney and Ballymore Oval in Brisbane. Throughout the North and South Islands in New Zealand there were nine venues for the other 12 teams to play.

Not counted among the 16 was South Africa. Although a member of the International Rugby Football Board and one who voted crucially for the tournament, they did so in the knowledge that they would not be participating in the inaugural contest for the William Webb Ellis Rugby Cup. Danie Craven, Chairman of the South Africa Rugby Board, renounced (although reluctantly and in a somewhat bitter and bellicose mood) the chance of an invitation knowing that a team from his country would not be acceptable to the governments of either New Zealand or Australia. The Springboks would begin their World Cup journey in 1995 when their country would host the tournament. This was not known at the time. Indeed, there were no plans as yet for a second tournament. It was still a matter of conjecture and seeing how gently it went.

There was inevitable regret at South Africa's absence in 1987, and later in 1991, but in a climate which had persisted for several years it was well understood that the Springboks could not play anywhere other than in their own country. For all the sporting and political reasoning of 'bridge-building' and 'keeping lines of communications open', to which philosophy the rugby unions for the most part had strictly adhered, South Africa were pariahs of the sporting world. They could not come out to play nor, in the end, could they welcome anyone in. Even the back door was locked. To some minds this would ultimately prove unsatisfactory. No nation who won the tournament could truly believe itself to be world champion without the possibility of encountering South Africa, one of the two most consistently powerful rugby nations on the planet. Hitherto, the Springboks and the All Blacks were the game's major forces, the very recent world-beating exploits of Australia notwithstanding. Over the decades, the title of world champion belonged to one of the two, if it could be said to be attached to anyone at all.

But South Africa, with the constant challenge of the other nations being beyond them because of their politics, were no longer the force they once were. They did not play often enough. The rugby world was moving on. The Springboks were left behind as the standards were being set elsewhere. They themselves had come to realise this because as soon as the despicable and immoral devices of apartheid were dismantled and the way was once more open to them in 1992, the Springboks embarked on a full schedule of international matches.

Their hallowed name resonated of a formidable past and, sadly but inevitably, their standard of play was stuck there too. They were not so finely tuned, much like the heavy-weight boxer who has listened for too long to the tales of his former glories and, yearning to hear the bell ring once more, decides mistakenly and disastrously to come out of an early retirement. In that softer life after the ring his limbs have stiffened, his muscles softened and the responses have become slack and slower. Away from the rigours of the constant challenge he is not quite the fighter he thinks he is nor the fighter his coterie of versatile acquaintances tell him he is. For the present, the Springbok reputation had to be resurrected and restored.

It is doubtful whether the Springboks would have lasted the course in 1987. Admittedly they had faced England in 1984 and won, but England were under strength and, for one reason or another, 18 of their players had declined to travel. For what it was worth, and it was not worth very much, the New Zealand rebel tour under the guise of the Cavaliers also lost in 1986. Other than the South Africans with the in-built laager mentality of those insular years in the rugby wilderness, no one took any measurement from these spurious contests. They were false. It had simply been an attempt on the one hand to keep South Africa within the rugby community – any contact was better than none, however surreptitious and clandestine – and the even less laudable aim on the other of the 'amateur' players grasping the opportunity to pocket some very generous expenses.

At any rate, in a purely sporting sense they were missed. Argentina were invited to take South Africa's place alongside the other seven members of the IRFB. Invitations were sent to eight other countries to take part. Along with Italy, Romania, Canada, Japan, USA (who took Argentina's place among the invitees), Fiji and Tonga, an invitation was said to have been extended to the USSR. But the qualification of having played against one or other of the eight member countries meant that, in the end, an invitation was sent to Zimbabwe.

However, the 1987 Rugby World Cup was not free of all political intrusion. A few days before the tournament began a military coup took place in Fiji. This was led by Colonel Rambuko, a former Fijian player who had toured Britain and Ireland in 1970. In the growing concern, Russ Thomas, Chairman of the New Zealand Rugby Football Union, insisted that Fiji would still send a team but they would arrive later than planned. At any rate Western Samoa had been advised to stand by and if anything might be said to guarantee Fiji's arrival this was it; such is the South Pacific rivalry. Rugby is Fiji's principal sport. The Fiji Rugby Union, founded in 1913, have 600 clubs and 12,000 playing members. At this time they had already won the Hong Kong Sevens three times. They had beaten the Barbarians in 1970 and the Lions in 1977, as well as having taken the scalps of Australia and Italy.

They did eventually arrive and were to make an exotic and memorably flamboyant contribution late in the competition in a way that has become a hallmark of their way of playing. Their quick and spontaneously inventive rugby had mesmerised the whole of Wales when they were the first to invite them on tour in 1964.

In tune with rugby's traditional sense of camaraderie and, in a sport pursued largely for recreation, extending a hand of friendship to your opponents, there was an official banquet in Auckland for all participating teams before battles commenced. There was some regret later that not all the teams congregated together in the one place. Logistically, this was possible but for what was a speculative venture with 'first steps' and uncertainty hanging over its success and consequent revenues, it was too expensive to fly over the four teams from Australia, improbable as this now sounds as we have grown accustomed to each tournament flourishing and prospering from the last.

This diffidence was reflected on the streets of Auckland where the first and the final matches were to be played. There was a steady-as-she-goes, wait-and-see ambivalence abroad on Auckland's Queen Street. There was bunting of the most modest kind, a flag here and there. What manifested itself more clearly than anything managed by the World Cup organisers, across Auckland's main street was the local amateur dramatics production of Gilbert and Sullivan's *Mikado*.

Ian McGeechan, who, with Derrick Grant, was Scotland's coach, felt that the mood was that of a sports jamboree. 'We were all excited by it,' he said, 'but it was not over-serious. No one was quite sure what to make of it all. In Scotland, before we left, there was reluctance about the tournament. It was probably overdue but there remained a feeling that rugby was being railroaded into something that was not entirely fully supported.' For one of the most astute, articulate and gracious of coaches, this was to be the first of the four tournaments that he would attend. He would miss 1995 because of his commitments as Director of Coaching at Northampton.

As ever, the litmus test of mood and substance and of affairs of every and any kind is that fount of all knowledge: the taxi driver. The eternal purveyor of unalloyed opinion who cannot claim any ambiguity, the man who drives the taxi 'gives it straight'. Of course, he knew that there was a rugby competition on but he was far more interested in the FA Cup final from London's Wembley to which, come Sunday morning, with the time difference, he would be listening to the commentary of the Tottenham Hotspur and Coventry match. The Rugby World Cup held little attraction for him.

A similar lack of immediacy had also infected other more pertinent parts of New Zealand's most populated and cosmopolitan city. Lew Prime, the Executive Director of Auckland RFU, was allocated the task, less than a month beforehand, of masterminding the Opening Ceremony at Eden Park where the first match would be held. 'The World Cup,' he concluded, 'is in people's minds but it is not on the streets.' He was, therefore, unlikely to repeat the lavish ostentation of three years previously when the Olympic Games had arrived in Los Angeles, the 'entertainment capital of the world', as Warner Brothers once claimed at the beginning of each of their television programmes. The inevitable modesty at the birth of a new feature would preclude an epic panorama in Cinemascope with no expense spared, and would resemble more a second feature B movie cobbled together on a low budget on the backlot of the studio. This was Rugby World Cup's humble beginnings.

This was the way it had to be. There were no financial guarantees. No sponsors came knocking on the Rugby World Cup Ltd door until very late in the day. KDD, the Japanese International Communications, became the main tournament sponsor. Rank Xerox, Steinlager and Mazda were also official sponsors.

The Rugby World Cup enterprise began on Friday 22 May 1987 in Eden Park in Auckland, the City of Sails, as it is called, standing on the isthmus that divides the Waitemata Harbour from the Manukau Harbour.

A thin rain fell as a watery sun made its best efforts to shine when the dramatic first notes of Strauss's *Also Sprach Zarathustra* struck. Go-go dancers twirled, gymnasts pirouetted, Highland pipes flourished, brass bands marched. Finally, through the gentle rain and the shy sun, the legendary Maori flanker, Waka Nathan, emerged to run a lap of honour and to deliver the match ball to John Kendall-Carpenter who, as Chairman of the IRFB Tournament Committee, opened the tournament of the first William Webb Ellis Rugby Cup.

'This is an historic occasion for rugby union,' he wrote, 'with 16 nations being brought together for the first time to play in a truly international rugby tournament... It is important for future World Cups and for rugby itself that it presents a positive and attractive face to the rest of the sporting world...equally, it is important that this be a happy occasion which embodies one of the greatest qualities of what we consider to be one of the greatest team games – the camaraderie and the goodwill that is created in the club rooms after the match.' Thus began the tournament which, within a decade, was to have major repercussions for the game as a whole.

New Zealand played Italy in the first game. There had been strong reservations about the obvious imbalance between the contestants and about the time – a Friday afternoon, a working day – when no matches had previously been played in New Zealand. In the event, Eden Park, which could then hold 46,000, was only half full.

But, the rugby authorities argued, by playing on a Friday and therefore providing maximum focus for the opening event – without interruption or diversion – a full programme of games could be followed through on both Saturday and Sunday.

As for the unequal nature of the contest and the mismatch between the two combatants, there was a method behind the fixture born out of principle and an aspiration: what the Rugby World Cup might represent and what it might in time fulfil. The new might converge with the old, the past emerging into a new vision of rugby's future.

On the one hand there stood New Zealand's phalanx, founded in 1892, a longstanding member of the IRFB, 1,100 clubs, 180,000 playing members with its All Blacks sobriquet established as the most famous rugby trade name in the world; the silver fern its emblem, the 'Haka' its symbolic anthem to battle. This is a great and awe-inspiring rugby nation. The 3 million inhabitants knew everything there was to know about their men in black.

On the other side, standing against them were Italy, founded in 1928 and with 314 clubs and 26,000 players. In the land where football is king, the 52 million-strong population barely knew that rugby union existed, and if they did it was unlikely to make them pause with their cappuccinos between cup and lip. Those who play the game can be as passionate about it as the man from Whakatane. If Italy had no place at rugby's high table, it did represent a new order which Rugby World Cup was meant to encourage. Rugby needed to move out and embrace a wider world. The first match was symbolic of this aspiration.

The match inevitably emphasised the disparity between the two teams. If the score at half-time suggested that the game was fairly evenly contested, New Zealand scored 53 points after the interval to add to the 17 they had earlier accumulated. This was a record international score which overtook the 60 points Ireland had inflicted on Romania in the previous season. Italy, however, was unable to improve on the six points which Oscar Collodo collected with a drop-goal and penalty.

If the game followed what had been anticipated, with the All Blacks ruthlessly pursuing their objectives with the opposition unable to offer any firm resistance, the World Cup's first ever game required some quality which might lift it out of the ordinary or the predictable. John Kirwan, New Zealand's tall and powerful right wing, provided the special ingredient. His second magnificent try came immediately from the kick-off which had resulted from his first, shortly after the interval.

David Kirk, the All Black captain and scrum-half, took the ball and passed to his fly-half, Grant Fox, who in turn handed it on to Kirwan not far from his own try-line. In full flight, he was an intimidating figure. With his high-knee lift action and pumping arms, looking fearsomely aggressive, he appeared threatening, defying anyone to be so bold as even to think of making a challenge. The Italians did think and they did try but, as flies to a wanton boy, he destroyed them. Slipping a tackle here, pushing someone aside there, feinting and dodging with players clawing at his jersey, he ran 70 metres or so with some half a dozen forlorn would-be tacklers in his wake. He had kept on going. One moment he was in a thicket of blue jerseys; the next, he emerged as if by magic and was free in the open field. This in itself made the opening game memorable. The New Zealand machine, whilst not in top gear, was ticking over satisfactorily.

The game was significant in another respect also. If the All Blacks felt that this was a good start to their campaign in a purely playing sense, they had galvanised public interest after a time when they had gone through an awkward period of deep uncertainty and introspection, of having faced the wrath of a public which believed a noble game had been betrayed and their heroes tarnished. The blight of South Africa had hung over New Zealand rugby since April 1986.

In that month, a rebel team, the Cavaliers, against government censure and bitter public revulsion at their dishonest behaviour, had cut and run like a scheming thief in the night and flown to racist South Africa. This dishonourable action splintered the whole of New Zealand society. It had been in an unforgiving mood ever since.

This animosity filtered through to the All Blacks when they next performed legitimately in their colours. In August and September of 1986, captained by David Kirk, they had lost a three-match Bledisloe Cup series at home to Australia. Later that year, on their tour of France under the captaincy of Jock Hobbs, they lost the second of a two-match series, having won the first. This was the infamous and brutal game in Nantes. Such was the legacy of their visit to South Africa that the scars remained.

This was an event that divided New Zealand. Without exaggeration, family was set against family, father against son, brother against brother. Tight and close communities were split.

'There was a lot of disharmony,' recalls Sean Fitzpatrick, who had insinuated himself into the team as hooker while Dalton was injured and who was to carve a remarkable career for himself over the next decade. 'After the Cavaliers tour, the country was divided against apartheid. Rugby needed a good kick. There had been a general clean-out after losing to France and a lot of new faces came into the team. New Zealand did not know what to expect, nor did the players.'

With this victory, however, old loyalties began to stir afresh. After all, here was a tournament in their own country to determine who the world champion was to be. The match on 22 May, however modest the opposition, gave a reality to all the talk. There were tougher times ahead, honours to be won. This was no time to be divided. John Kirwan's magnificent try was a reminder of rugby's potential for drama as well as beauty.

The ignominious rift was yesterday; now is now. The time had arrived for another chapter to be written.

There was another factor which helped to adjust the New Zealand psyche from the terrors of the past. This came in the form of their captain, David Kirk.

He was not of the common mould of New Zealand rugby players nor their idea of what their leader should be or appear to be. Relatively speaking, his physical attributes were less than robust in appearance. He was a slight figure, almost frail when silhouetted against the thick-set brawn of the Whetton brothers, of Wayne 'Buck' Shelford, of Richard Loe and Steve McDowell. If New Zealand players are often referred to as the unsmiling giants, then here too Kirk was cut from a different cloth. He had a twinkle in his eye which melted the hardest of hearts and had a captivating smile that convinced the most misanthropic parent that there might be something worthwhile in chasing and battling over a mis-shaped leather ball of a morning.

David Kirk was not the first-choice captain. Andy Dalton, the hooker, was. Unfortunately, Dalton had suffered a hamstring injury in training before the World Cup began. Cruel though the fates were to prove for Dalton – he never managed to recover, despite the many declarations that he might – they proved to be benevolent spirits for New Zealand. Kirk was inadvertently thrust into the spotlight and in so doing became the chivalrous face of All Blacks rugby. With his beaming smile, it was easy to forget the dark days of disgrace.

Without any extravagance, New Zealand had, in the first game, begun with care and discipline. They had set a benchmark of efficiency.

The next three days would encompass the rich variety of the World Cup, mixing the old and the new. Saturday and Monday belonged to age-old rivalries: Australia would play England (Sydney), France would play Scotland (Christchurch) on Saturday while Ireland and Wales (Wellington) played on Monday. If Romania and Zimbabwe (Auckland) played each other on Saturday, it was Sunday that introduced us to several other fresh flavours: the USA against Japan (Brisbane), Fiji against Argentina (Hamilton) and Canada against Tonga (Napier).

So it was that, across on the other side of the Tasman Sea, the team that was expected, according to all the soothsayers, not only to meet New Zealand in the final but to beat them, would embark on their quest by playing England at the Concord Oval in Sydney. Because of longstanding sponsorship and advertising arrangements, that meant, therefore, that they could not provide a 'clean' stadium – the Sydney Cricket Ground, where all rugby internationals had hitherto been played, was out of commission. A new, purpose-built stadium had been constructed in the Sydney suburbs.

The issue of a 'clean' stadium and how this is defined would return to haunt the Rugby World Cup 15 years later in finalising the agreements for the 2003 tournament. This would adversely affect the New Zealand team, and not understanding their obligations in this respect would cost them dearly.

'The "clean" stadium issue had been a very important tenet in the organisation of the Rugby World Cup,' says Keith Rowlands. 'As well as advertising at the ground being an issue, so had the matter of ticket sales. In Sydney there was a debenture scheme in place, which meant that the Rugby World Cup organisation could not sell tickets on the market. There was no freedom to sell tickets in the way we wished because of the scheme at the Sydney Cricket Ground.' Rowlands, who became Secretary of the IRFB in 1988, formulated the 'clean' stadia criteria for the benefit of the Rugby World Cup and future tournaments.

Despite being installed as tournament favourites, Australia as a country found little enthusiasm for the World Cup. Set quite a distance behind rugby league, Australian rules, horseracing and cricket in the national sporting interest, rugby union finds it difficult to draw the nation's attention. Potential glory is not enough. Sporting success is what matters, not wishful thinking, not 'potential' anything. Success has to be delivered to arouse the national consciousness and to promote a national identity and sense of well-being. It is hard to imagine any other country which seeks so unequivocally for international recognition and which identifies so starkly and unapologetically with sporting kudos.

It was quiet in Sydney. It was as if the Rugby World Cup did not exist. Yet in Alan Jones, their loquacious coach, Australia had a man who could engage and interest the most inveterate 'couch potato' in the intricacies and contortions of rugby football. No straightforward explanation would do when a well-honed metaphor might conjure up a more colourful image. In this way, he lightened and enlightened many a press conference.

In a world where sentences are often uttered in tedious repetition or in bland order, Jones coined rich phrases. In the press conference there is a palpable wariness on the coach's side of the table, while on the other side, among the media core, there is the desperate need to seek answers to questions which might supply what is thought of as 'good copy'. There is an air of mild hostility or of scepticism. The coach suffers the ordeal of an inquisition. The media have a job to fulfil, to respond to the public's need to know. There is tension.

Alan Jones seemed to thrive on the exposure. And the company of the media would know that, pens in hand, microphones at the ready, a finely tuned phrase would be launched on an expectant world. Wasn't it he who, on a successful tour of Britain and Ireland, referred to a coach's destiny as being one day a cockerel, the next a feather duster?

In 1987 Jones described his hopes for the team as being akin to the 'Gucci Factor'. Explaining, he said that 'long after you've paid the price, the style remains.' He had great ambitions for his team. And why not? After all, he had inspired his team to win the grand slam of victories in Britain and Ireland in 1984. In 1986, Australia had won the Bledisloe Cup series in New Zealand. In the same year, his team had beaten France. These were remarkable achievements by any standards. Out of 20 matches under his guidance, he had won 16. The four defeats were by New Zealand.

His flamboyant personality and his gift of the gab found expression on his own radio programme in Sydney. His commitment to this, so some of his players believed, compromised his role as coach to the national team. If this hardly mattered to begin with, there grew a sense of grievance among some of his prominent players, who began to believe that Jones's mind was not entirely focused on his national team.

Nevertheless, Jones was in exuberant mood at the start of the tournament. Australia were firm favourites to beat England in their opening match. They did so, but not without reservation. Against what was thought to be Australia's biggest scrum and tallest line-out ever, England not only managed to match them but also, for the most part, played the more convincing game. They began with a flourish but Marcus Rose at full-back was concussed early on and replaced by Jonathan Webb. Only last-ditch efforts kept the England wingers Mike Harrison and Rory Underwood from crossing the Australian line in the first 20 minutes. Peter Winterbottom, the flanker, had his chance, and so did Kevin Simms in the centre.

Their frequent transgressions, however, were penalised by Keith Lawrence, the New Zealand referee. By the end of the game, the penalty count went against them by 18–6. This is a huge discrepancy. If they were at the receiving end of his critical eye, they suffered, too, from his momentary blind spot. Lawrence committed a crucial error which turned the game in Australia's favour at a critical time.

This occurred 11 minutes into the second half and came immediately after Harrison, England's captain on the wing, had scored a wonderful try. With Webb's conversion from the touch-line, England's score matched Michael Lynagh's two first-half penalties. If Harrison was enjoying a fine match, so too was Underwood. Australia had no one to match the RAF fighter pilot's pace on the left wing. If Underwood inspired the move by daringly running from near his own line, Harrison fulfilled the ambition after Simms, Webb and Jamie Salmon had each played a part in a magnificent score.

They could play with panache but too often preferred – as they would frustratingly often in the years to follow – to return to the safety of their tried-and-tested forward plan, where Dean Richards and the rest of the pack had a powerful afternoon. This was against a pack of forwards, including Bill Campbell and Steve Cutler (both in the second row), Troy Coker (at number 8, but more familiar as a lock) and Steve Tuynman (wing forward), who were all 6'5" or more.

In the 51st minute, misfortune struck England. With confidence blossoming after more than a week either at Crest International Hotel in Brisbane or at the Rushcutters Travelodge in Sydney, when they had been cast in the Australian press as hapless no-hopers, England were continuing to expand their style on the field. They exhibited some fine running while at the same time succeeding in stifling at source any threat from Australia. Once more, England began running from close to their own line, but Salmon's pass to Simms went astray. David Campese on the right wing kicked on the loose ball. Attempting to pick up the ball while Peter Williams, England's fly-half, put in a tremendous tackle near the try-line, Campese – manifestly to most observers but clearly not for Lawrence – knocked on the ball. Campese knew it and, on getting up, looked hopelessly crestfallen as he realised a chance had gone begging. The referee thought otherwise and awarded the try.

This was the equivalent of a short, sharp and crippling thwack to the solar plexus. It did not knock England out, but it knocked the wind out of them so that Simon Poidevin scored Australia's second try, in addition to Lynagh's third penalty, to win 19–6. Furthermore, England were to lose Rose and John Hall, who had suffered a knee injury. They left immediately for home.

Even if England lost, there was a sense of consolation in that they had managed to play so well. This is not to interpret the defeat in the sense that in Britain we can somehow, with a shrug of the shoulders, turn a failure into a kind of victory. Extolling the virtues of courage and bravery and of a gentlemanly demeanour mitigates the defeat.

England had cast aside those feelings of inferiority which the Northern Hemisphere teams had constructed for themselves ahead of the World Cup tournament and had accepted almost universally the assumption that the battle for the title was to be an exclusively Southern Hemisphere affair. England had proved that they were more than a match for one of those nations that was expected to be there at the final round, whose players had a collective reputation in the imaginations of Europeans so that they had acquired a fearsome but ultimately self-defeating quality of hyperbole. In other words, the opposition dressing room was perceived to be where leviathans dwelled. England, for the moment, had managed to cut one of them down to size.

Elsewhere, too, Europeans had much to be proud of when contemplating what had been an heroic contest in Christchurch. With a River Avon, the city is described as the 'most English of cities outside England' and is situated on the edge of the Canterbury Plains on New Zealand's South Island. Lancaster Park is where France and Scotland opened their campaign. The contest was a powerful affair.

There were refereeing decisions here too which aroused an exclamation or two. Patrice Lagisquet, the Bayonne Arrow (not the 'Express' as others said), had what he thought a perfectly good try disallowed. On the other hand, Serge Blanco, the full-back, had his try allowed to stand by the referee, Fred Howard of England, when the general view was that it should not have been. In this way, France held the lead for the first time. Such questions merely helped add to a match of high excitement.

These were isolated incidents that might or might not have affected the overall result. A single occurrence naturally sets in motion a series of events that, if different, alters the subsequent action and so changes the course of the match. It is erroneous to assume, for instance, that a kicker missing three chances at goal denies a team nine points. Kicking one of these alters the balance of the game: the contest has to restart on the halfway line and the course of the game follows a different pattern. Had Lagisquet's try been allowed, the contest would have restarted at the halfway line, not on Scotland's 22m line, and so who knows what might have happened thereafter?

But what unquestionably did alter Scotland's chances was the injury so early to John Rutherford, Scotland's brilliant fly-half. No sooner had Derek White put his team in the lead after two minutes than Rutherford was taken off on a stretcher. With a damaged knee cartilage and ligaments, the influential fly-half, one of the canniest and most inventive of his generation, would play no further part in the 1987 World Cup.

Ideally built for the position and hugely gifted, Rutherford had a fine nose for a gap and the speed off the mark to exploit it. A genial man, he was a tough competitor and a hard-nosed tactician. Scotland are not well blessed, as Wales are thought to be, with a production line in gifted half-backs, but when they do come along they have special genius for the game. John Rutherford was such a player. Sadly, the tournament ended far too prematurely for him. Indeed, he was not to play for Scotland again.

Doug Wyllie took over the position while Alan Tait came on in the centre. Scotland held the lead from the second minute and were at one stage 16–6 ahead. Philippe Sella and Pierre Berbizier scored a try each to bring France to 16–14. There followed the Lagisquet incident and, with a minute of proper time to go, Blanco's try and conversion in the 79th minute.

Doubt was cast on the correctness of this last score because Matt Duncan, the Scottish right wing, had had a fine run but was injured in the tackle and required treatment, as did Berbizier. Colin Deans, Scotland's captain, expected a stoppage, which the referee did not oblige. Moreover, Howard awarded a penalty to France. While the Scottish team hesitated and turned away, Blanco, ever the opportunist, took a quick penalty and ran clear for half the length of the pitch for the score and conversion.

Scotland were not done yet and took advantage of the generous four minutes of time added on for stoppages. In a final frenzy of attack, Matt Duncan powered his way over for a try in the corner. Gavin Hastings's attempted conversion missed by a hair's breadth and the final score stood squarely at 20 points each. Justice would appear to have been served. Under the circumstances, the blemishes could more easily be forgotten and, perhaps, even forgiven. For all this, no one argued with the magnificence of the contest.

In contrast to this, the third fixture to include the full members of the International Rugby Football Board proved to be the least inspiring. Ireland were to play Wales at Athletic Park in Wellington, the capital of New Zealand and the seat of government. Embracing a natural harbour and surrounded by green undulating hills, there is a natural beauty about the city. There are many beautiful sights to be seen from many vantage points. One natural phenomenon, however, can hardly be said to enchant the visiting rugby player. Wellington is a windy city. The blast is as permanent as Mount Victoria, which overlooks the urban landscape and the beaches beyond. The strong breeze blowing down the pitch is an eternal dilemma at Athletic Park.

Ireland had another desperate dilemma to deal with before a coin had been tossed or a ball kicked. Mick Doyle, the former Irish and Lions flanker and now Ireland's coach, had been rushed to hospital in Auckland after a suspected heart attack. It was a tense time for the ebullient character. Tests soon cleared him.

The wind in Wellington, however, did not clear or cease its influence. Monday brought with it not just a stiff breeze but a howling gale. As ever in such conditions, the contest is unbalanced so that the game turns out to be a game of two conflicting halves: the haves and the have-nots, as it were; to have the wind or not to have it. Donal Lenihan, the Irish lock and captain, won the toss and chose to play with it in the first half. Richard Moriarty, Wales's captain, was pleased, since that was the way he would have preferred it, reasoning that, after a six-week lay-off at the end of the Five Nations Championship, it might take his team time to adjust to playing once more. Mick Doyle was to agree when the match was over.

Losing Phil Matthews, their flanker, weakened the Irish cause and, with only two Michael Kiernan penalties to show for their efforts in the first 40 minutes, there was little to defend in the second period. In a rough and tumble of a game, what ultimately separated the two teams was the contrasting performances of the respective fly-halves. Paul Dean of Ireland never quite came to terms with the influence of the wind and how to manipulate it to his team's advantage, while Jonathan Davies on the other side tacked and turned, rode the storm and steered Wales to a laboured victory, to which he contributed two drop-goals to add to Paul Thorburn's solitary penalty. Mark Ring scored the only try for Wales. The 13–6 scoreline avenged his team's defeat in Cardiff in April.

There was a further significance to this victory. The chances were that the winner of this fixture would end up at the top of Pool 2, which meant they faced the runner-up of Pool 1 in the quarter-finals. This was likely to be England. This was considered to be less daunting than playing Australia, which Ireland, as runner-up of Pool 2, would have to face. Syd Millar, a great prop for Ireland and the Lions and one of the game's most astute and long-serving administrators and guiding lights, was Ireland's manager. He reminded everyone that, however tough the task appeared, Ireland had in fact beaten Australia on the previous three occasions they had met in Australia: in 1967 and twice in 1979.

If attention concentrated on those matches involving the members of the International Rugby Football Board, elsewhere the minnows of the tournament, as it were, were relishing the opportunity of participating with the world leaders. The emerging countries – some of whom, like the USA and Japan (21–18), had not played each other before – were given the chance now. Canada, who had lost 40–14 to Tonga in 1974, were this time able to reverse the score (37–4).

Surprisingly, Fiji, with flair and enterprise, had disposed of Argentina (28–9). The South Sea islanders, however, came up against the All Blacks in their next game on the following Wednesday and were dismantled 74–13. Along the grapevine, rumour had it that Fiji had not bothered to pull out all the stops for this game, preferring instead to hold back in readiness for the Italian match. Winning this game would ensure a passage to the quarter-finals, it was believed.

The strategy did not work. Fiji were to lose to Italy 18–15 in a pool which ultimately would require a try count to determine which country would join New Zealand in the next round. The top two countries in each pool would go forward to the quarter-finals.

These were nervous times, for none more so than Ireland. Since they had lost their first game, they needed to win the next one against Canada, who, with 19-year-old Gareth Rees at fly-half, had looked to be very competent against a Tongan team which had complained that the fixture was played on a Sunday, the day of rest.

If Tonga had one of the youngest player in the tournament (Taliauli Liavaa, their 17-year-old fly-half), Canada unquestionably had the oldest in 37-year-old Spence McTavish. Overall, though, it was the USA who had the oldest team – 12 of them were over 30. Longevity was not the reason they failed to progress further, though. They kept company in the same pool as Australia and England so that, having beaten Japan, they were to lose to both of them by 47–12 and 34–6 respectively. Such a pattern was repeated elsewhere. When the powerful rugby nations came up against the smaller ones, high scores inevitably followed. England scored 60 points against Japan, while Scotland did the same against Zimbabwe. On another windy day in Wellington, France scored 55 points against Romania. This was a score Scotland repeated against Romania and, to confirm that the old order was not about to give way to the new, France registered 70 against Zimbabwe.

With such a discrepancy between teams, record scores were created. No record could have lasted for so short a time as the one established on 2 June. The Romania and Scotland fixture kicked off in Dunedin at 1pm and during it Gavin Hastings scored 27 points, the highest number of points scored by a player in an international fixture. This surpassed Alan Hewson of New Zealand, who had scored 26 points in Australia in 1982. At 3pm, France played Zimbabwe in Auckland. By the end of this match, Didier Camberabero, the French full-back, had scored 30 points.

There was a price to pay for Scotland. Scott Hastings damaged a hamstring and would take no further part in the tournament. France and Scotland went through to the quarter-finals.

If Ireland eventually accumulated 49 points against Canada, they had to work hard for them. For an hour they played wonderfully well under the astute guidance of Rees, who performed with a maturity beyond his years. He was to play in all four World Cups up to 1999 and could be said to be the main influence in promoting and elevating the competitiveness of Canadian rugby over the next decade or so. His running and, especially, his clever kicking ensured that his team were twice in the lead in the first hour against Ireland. However, they could not maintain their impetus and tailed away with Ireland scoring four tries in the final ten minutes.

In the same pool, Wales defeated Tonga in a game full of errors but one in which Wales suffered with a lengthening injury list. Two of their players, winger Glen Webbe and prop Stuart Evans, had played their last game in the 1987 Rugby World Cup.

In an uninspiring contest, Wales beat Canada 40–9, with Rees typically scoring all the points for Canada with his boot. Indeed, Wales scored all the tries, with Ieuan Evans on the wing nailing four of them. He shares the accolade of scoring as many in one game with three others: W Llewellyn (1899), RA Gibbs (1908) and M Richards (1969). As expected, Wales and Ireland went through.

There had been no surprises as yet. In Pool 3, though, there was a dogfight for second place. Argentina, Fiji and Italy were to win a game each. Argentina, who had lost to Fiji, went on to beat Italy, who in turn went on to beat Fiji. It was Fiji who advanced to the quarter-finals. The pivotal score was the 46 points the All Blacks were to register against Argentina's 15, which gave the South Americans a try-differential deficit which put them in third place. Argentina either needed to win the match against the All Blacks or to score three tries against them. They managed only one try. This was disappointing to Argentina, as they had been predicted beforehand, with gifted Hugo Porta at fly-half, to progress further. Italy had beaten Fiji, but the Fijian overall try differential pulled them ahead.

On the other side of the Tasman Sea, Australia and England unsurprisingly advanced, but not without a few eyebrows being raised when the favourites, Australia, played Japan. Toshyuki Hayashi, the Japan captain and lock, and Seiji Hirao, their outstanding fly-half, had given heroic performances to disconcert their opposition. With a quickness allied to commitment and invention, Japan destabilised Australia. They might even have taken the lead at half-time but for a disputed try which favoured Australia. Peter Grigg tackled a player without the ball and Matt Burke latched onto the loose ball to claim the try which gave his team the 16–13 interval lead. In scoring his 24th try for his country, David Campese equalled the world record set by Ian Smith of Scotland.

As expected, the first World Cup quarter-finals contained all the seven International Board teams and Fiji. Furthermore, on the evidence of the 24 matches played in the first 13 days of the tournament, from 22 May to 3 June, it became obvious that New Zealand was the predominant team. From the opening day, they had made a firm and consistent statement of their purpose – first against Italy in Auckland, then against Fiji in Christchurch and Argentina in Wellington. They had scored 190 points in all, conceding 34 with only two tries scored against them. Their 46 points against Argentina was their lowest figure. The reason for this, ostensibly, was that they had made eight changes in the team. After the first two games, once they were certain of qualification into the knock-out stage, they believed they could afford to give others in their squad an opportunity to play.

This was in contrast to the Australians, who had not settled their team. Whether this was because of uncertainty or a matter of choice or policy was never made clear. Certainly injuries to key players – Nick Farr-Jones (scrum-half), Brett Papworth (centre) and Roger Gould (full-back) – was a factor. But by the end of the first round, they had given a taste of the play and of the flavour of the World Cup to all their players in the squad. Furthermore, Tony Coker, Matthew Burke, David Campese and Steve Tuynman had also been chosen in more than one position.

Alan Jones had argued that the World Cup provided a different set of demands. It was having to play three international fixtures in eight days, for instance, to which players were not accustomed. As the teams moved away from the round-robin of the first stage, which had offered a second chance if a team stumbled and lost, and on to the quarter-final step, which was a knock-out stage with no recovery, Jones, as ever, was not short of a graphic metaphor. 'So far it's been bows and arrows,' he said. 'This is hand-grenades time.' For all his bravura approach, however, his Wallabies had not been impressive thus far, whereas the All Blacks had been.

Even in their press conferences, the New Zealand management showed an impressive objectivity and clarity. While other teams expressed doubts about this or that – the dilemmas inherent in a new competition, the injuries they suffered, the wariness they felt about the opposition, the uncertain qualities of the new teams and so on – New Zealand were simply coldly calculating with no sense of tension or nervous agitation. New Zealand were clearly in charge. They were influencing events but not being influenced by events. It hardly mattered who they were playing; the All Blacks 'did the business' in their fashion.

If other teams found it difficult to raise the game against what might appear to be inferior teams, this was not the case with the All Blacks. In each game they registered the points that emphatically reflected the difference between the two teams. No one who had seen them perform was left in any doubt of their superiority. They were fitter than any other team in the tournament, more powerful and with a blinkered clear vision of their purpose. Their skills were such that no unforced error was countenanced, no aimless gestures allowed. In every respect, the All Blacks were setting new and very high standards.

Typically, the All Blacks admitted they were not fully prepared for the knock-out stage, not because of the 'guillotine' factor of instant 'death', but rather because they felt they had not been battle-hardened enough in the first round. The games had been insufficiently competitive to give them a perspective of their true standard and where they stood in relation to other teams in the IRFB.

England, Scotland and Ireland had suffered a defeat each, while Fiji had lost twice and reached this stage by the skin of their teeth. Wales had won all their matches but without engendering any confidence in their play. There was no authority to France's play, either, and they were a long way from demonstrating any sense of their traditional panache; nor indeed did they look like the team that arrived in New Zealand as grand-slam winners and European champions. In other words, every team seemed to be taking their steps cautiously, while the All Blacks had hit the road running.

Yet not everything was immaculately in order for them either. If, unlike all the other teams, they had not had to endure many injuries among their players, their nominated captain, Andy Dalton, had not recovered from his pre-tournament injury. He had yet to play. Nonetheless, he became the centre of attention in another respect.

This brought into focus the question of amateurism, the principle upon which rugby was played and defended as an article of faith for over 100 hundred years of existence. It had been threatened, as we have seen, in rugby's very early years and more recently by the so-called 'boot money', which players were allegedly paid by sports footwear companies to wear certain boots. Amateurism had always been under siege.

These issues had come and gone, but in recent years the amateur ethos seemed to be undermined and increasingly discredited. In the changing circumstances of the sporting world, it was becoming irrelevant. Books were commissioned and written, players were paid to make radio and television appearances, and the opening of supermarkets and similar commercial premises had become a lucrative sideline. The potential for players to be paid for activities of this kind encroached on the amateur ethos. There was a growing sense of hypocrisy in that the unions who governed the game found it acceptable to acquire large sponsorship deals while the players were forbidden to accept any money not only for playing rugby but also for any other off-the-field activity. This was felt to be unjust. A provocative tension was growing.

In Dalton's case, he appeared in a television commercial endorsing a Japanese tractor. Dalton was a farmer. The fact that he was the All Black hooker was not mentioned, although Eden Park, Auckland's rugby stadium, was referred to.

The Scottish Rugby Union complained. The minutiae of the relevant clauses of the amateur regulations were scrutinised. A case could have been made in Dalton's favour. However, it was thought wiser not to pursue the issue any further. Instead, the offending advertisement was taken off the air to quash speculation that it represented the first steps toward professionalism. This, however, was precisely what it had been.

Amateurism was already not only a deeply wounded animal that had survived many an attack throughout the history of rugby union, going back to the time when the schism occurred between the Northern Union in England and the controlling body of the Rugby Football Union, but could now be seriously considered an endangered species. This admirable but ultimately flawed ethos, depending as it did on gentlemanly conduct to agree not to accept money for playing and of the kindnesses of men with time on their hands to enjoy the game for its essential good fun and occasional high jinks, was entering its final stages. The persuasive whiff of money was strongly and persistently in the air.

The clandestine manoeuvres in the dark were embarrassing and, in not being able to ignore its seductive advances, the strict regulations began increasingly to look outdated and petty. Unwittingly, they encouraged dishonesty in the face of which the probity and integrity of the game was constantly questioned. Whatever purity was still attached to rugby union began openly to be seen as corrupted. The commercial worm had wheedled its way into the apple and was not going to go away.

Already, therefore, with the first World Cup not having gone beyond its initial stages, the threat which so many of the game's administrators had always feared was rearing its demon head. Amateur rugby was haunted by the spectre on the horizon. Commercialism had already entered beyond the walls of amateur rugby union in the form of sponsorship and advertising; incipient professionalism was now sabre-rattling at the gate.

If the administrators were attempting to defend pure 'amateurism', others were only too keen to exploit the opportunities which the World Cup presented. The boundaries were being breached. If this could not be achieved officially, there were those who would do so opportunistically and furtively. Were not the pranks so familiar to the school yard, they might have appeared as unscrupulous dirty tricks.

A postscript comment by the Auckland Rugby Union to the NZRFU report in July 1987 reads as follows: 'Despite the circular from the NZRFU regarding the appearance of sand buckets carrying Steinlager signs, it is interesting to note that, two hours before the final commenced, all gold buckets with sand which had been prepared for the occasion disappeared and in its [sic] place lay black buckets with "Steinlager" written on the side. This was the final straw that suggested that any privileges awarded to this company and the present management should be very clearly defined in the future in all respects.'

What other wheezes, one wonders, did the jackanapeses have up their sleeves in the boardroom of New Zealand Breweries?

Andy Dalton's example provided a clear and unmistakable signpost. This represented a double whammy for him. If he had to withdraw from a lucrative commercial deal off the field, he finally had to come to terms with the even more bitter truth that he was going to have to withdraw from playing any part on the field also. This was a painful conclusion.

David Kirk had, in the early matches, proved himself a magnificent general of the team, and the absence of Dalton allowed a new man to emerge and mature in the middle of the front row of the scrum. As the quarter-finals beckoned, Sean Fitzpatrick was about to embark on one of the greatest and most distinguished careers in the All Black jersey.

'I was delighted to be selected to the squad of 26 in the first place. It was very special,' said Fitzpatrick. 'Can you imagine what it was like as a 22-year-old to be part of the All Blacks? Andy had been injured in training, pulling a hamstring. That was the last time he ran on to the field. He'd come out of retirement to play in the World Cup. He was prepared to play against Scotland, but after I'd played in the first three games the management decided that I would continue. I have to say that Andy was tremendous off the field. He did everything to help me. I believe he was the unsung hero, keeping the team together and taking a lot of the pressure off David Kirk.'

At this moment, it was the next match that Fitzpatrick had in mind.

1987 QUARTER-FINALS

These were the killing fields. The arrangement of fixtures in the four-nation pool meant that not only the teams occupying the first and second positions went through – thereby giving a two-to-one chance of progressing – but, on reaching that stage, a team would be given a second and, depending on the misfortune of others, even a third opportunity of marching on, as Fiji had the good fortune to encounter. There was always a comfort zone to be found at the pool stage, but this now came to an end. 'When the death-or-glory time arrives, you don't mess around,' said Brian Lochore, the All Black coach and most genial of men, who received a Knighthood in the Queen's Birthday Honours in 1999.

The quarter-finals were to be played over a three-day period, two in New Zealand and two in Australia. The first, in Lancaster Park, Christchurch, was between New Zealand and Scotland on Saturday 6 June. France would play Fiji on Sunday at Eden Park, Auckland, while Australia and Ireland would face each other on the same day in the Concord Oval, Sydney. On the Monday, Wales would play England at the Ballymore Oval in Brisbane.

New Zealand were true to Lochore's words. It is not in an All Black's character to mess around. Unlike Europeans, for whom there remains, at whatever level, a sense of fun in games, a release from care and the stress of the world rather than an excuse for further ordeal and obsession, for Antipodeans sport is to be pursued as an unsmiling and solemn business. This, to a large extent, explains their excellence, as opposed to the inexactness of the Northern Hemisphere rugby nations, prone as they are to being distracted by sport's conviviality; they can be brilliant one moment, ordinary the next.

The All Blacks put Scotland to the sword. Admittedly, Scotland were shorn of their best players, such as John Rutherford and Scott Hastings, but they were unlikely to have made a difference significant enough to withstand the juggernaut they faced. If the All Blacks had shown glimpses of adventure earlier in the tournament, they were to revert to their roots against traditional opponents with whom they had a long history. They were to find inspiration in the physical presence, raw power and the speed of their forwards for the quarter-final. Buck Shelford, Alan Whetton and Michael Jones personified these qualities. Possession was what they wanted. Possession they found and possession they kept. Scotland were smothered and were finally suffocated into submission, 30–3.

In retrospect, Scotland found the only means of consolation in their defence, which for most of the afternoon held true. They tackled and tackled and then got up again to tackle some more. This was to such good effect that their line was only crossed three times for a score, including one by John Kirwan which was disallowed for obstruction. Scotland conceded only two tries, the first of which came early in the second half from Whetton, who had scored in every game so far. The second was by John Gallagher. Grant Fox, their metronomic kicker at fly-half, converted both of them in addition to his six penalties. Gavin Hastings kicked his team's solitary penalty.

The All Blacks' purpose was efficient without the frills of entertainment; their rhythm was coldly disciplined, like a squadron on parade, and their tactics trimmed of all extraneous detail. The game was utterly in tune with their ambitions. It was monotone and played to a repetitive and predictable rhythm: Ravel's 'Bolero' without the dramatic climax. They were supremely efficient.

In contrast, for those with a taste for rugby's rock 'n' roll, Fiji, the game's spontaneous entertainers, were happy the following day in Auckland to abandon all sense of formal or classical structure. They simply let their hair down in a way only they can. They were playing France, who themselves are not averse to free-flowing rugby, and ignored the strict tenets which others seemed to abide by to almost academic fidelity. Deviation is good and healthy. Fiji supplied it, while their opponents, for the most part, were more circumspect – that is, until they began to realise that they were on the receiving end of the kind of running brilliance of which they were usually the masters. France responded in parts.

With a quiet revolution still going on at home, Fiji looked as if they might just as well have a bit of fun while they were so far away. They could be returning home to an uncertain future. They played with the same joyous sense of abandon that had mesmerised Wales when, in 1964, they had been invited for the first time by a member of the International Rugby Football Board to come on tour. They had provided a vision of another style of rugby, refreshing in its unorthodoxy and spontaneity. This was rugby with a smile on its face, the sun on its back and young at heart.

It was with this invigorating spirit that Fiji approached the quarter-final. If they were not always successful, who at Eden Park would have wished it otherwise? Kaiava Salusalu and Tomasi Cama tore through the midfield. Manasa

Qoro scored a try of sheer extravagance after Tom Mitchell had made a superb break on the wing and had taken them into an early lead.

The sun shone. They could have scored some more but their high-risk game relied on chance, and chance in their case allowed for too many errors. Their fly-half, Severo Koroduadua, was, for instance, a player of star quality. He made a break of pace and panache, but he had a penchant for holding the ball in one hand like a juggler while aiming it this way and that, only to pull it back and go the other way, and on this occasion he saw the ball squirt embarrassingly out of his grasp in the open field. But Fiji were nonetheless leading France in a merry dance.

France's response to the agile gymnastics of the Pacific islanders was atypically pragmatic. In contrast, they rolled and pushed their way forward at close quarters to score two tries from scrummages and one from a line-out. Laurent Rodriguez scored two and played a vital role in setting up Alain Lorieux. Patrice Lagisquet, the Bayonne Arrow, scored the fourth.

Daniel Dubroca, France's captain, insisted that they dared not attempt to match the Fijians. The way to victory was to exercise control. For once they were tasting the kind of medicine they enjoyed dishing out to others. France were forced to resort to the familiar tactics that other teams tended to employ when playing them: tight and controlled, not giving away any space. Not that France gave up entirely; no French team can deny its rich heritage completely, and so they showed a few neat touches themselves. But on Sunday 7 June 1987 they had to be content with second best – in style, at least.

France won the match, but the abiding memory for those who were there is of Fiji scoring the best try of the game. Mocking the instructions that every teacher has given every schoolboy through the ages and dismissive of Koroduadua's blooper, Jone Kobu strode blithely in open space and – here we go again – holding the ball in one hand, gave Jimi Damu a chance to score a try of breathtaking audacity and beauty.

On the day, though, superior French discipline defeated Fijian improvisation with a score of 31–16. Victory was not without its cost, however. Serge Blanco had pulled a leg muscle and it would be touch and go whether he would be fit for the semi-final in six days' time.

The referee in Auckland was Clive Norling of Wales. Universally recognised as one of the world's most accomplished and authoritative referees – in many eyes *the* best referee – Norling was told by the Chairman of the Tournament Referees' Appointments Panel, Dr Roger Vanderfield of Australia, that he would not be required for the remainder of the tournament. This was a puzzling decision. Referees were chosen on their performances during the competition, and some of those still on the referees' panel had committed glaring errors of the kind missing on Norling's report. Admittedly, no assessment of a referee is foolproof and, as with much of rugby union, it is subject to the vagaries of fragile interpretation, despite attempts at codifying this analysis. But Norling's exclusion and the manner in which he was summarily withdrawn from the remainder of the competition was a mystery.

In the third fixture, Ireland were no match for Australia at the Concord Oval in Sydney. Australia lost the services of Nick Farr-Jones with an injury after three minutes, and he was replaced by Brian Smith. Nonetheless, they went on to play a game designed and executed by Michael Lynagh. Purposeful and controlled, his team accumulated 24 points in as many minutes with tries by Andy McIntyre, Matt Burke and Smith. These were converted by Lynagh, who also kicked two penalties. Ireland never recovered from this devastating opening spell. Burke's second try and a third penalty from the fly-half accounted for Australia's full score. Ireland's 15 points came from tries by Hugo MacNeill and Michael Kiernan, who also kicked both conversions and a penalty.

While the three matches so far had gone according to the forecasts, with each providing rugby of a standard worthy of the late stages of a World Cup, the fourth quarter-final played on the Monday proved, by general consent, to be the worst game of the tournament.

This was England against Wales at Ballymore in Brisbane. The fixture brought with it historical and psychological baggage from which neither the English nor the Welsh were quite able to set themselves free or at any stage be allowed to forget. Born of the culture of the victor and the vanquished, of the bigger and superior country making the smaller neighbour feel inferior, and of centuries of monarchical rule and subjection and defeat, this hinterland of discontent originally had nothing to do with rugby, but it was soon incorporated to embrace a social tradition of annual protest. England and Wales battling at rugby has become the primary occasion to express personal and national dissent. This has materialised into an exaggerated and obsessive hang-up which haunts a nation. England, for the world to see, try to play the whole thing down – so much so that they fail ultimately to understand the game's true dimension. Wales, on the other hand, play up the matter for all its worth. Of course, it is way out of all proportion. Neither side gets it right. Usually the sport suffers.

An England v Wales rugby international releases these pent-up and sometimes irrational emotions. If the fixture has a history going back into the mists of time, a more recent event was brought more immediately to bear on this match, too. Four months earlier, the two countries had played a contest of such attrition and intimidation in the Five Nations Championship at Cardiff Arms Park (as it then still was) that an air of deepening melancholy had prevailed.

England, who had been placed favourites beforehand, ended up losing the game. There was no violence, as there had been in the previous encounter in Cardiff, but the quality of the rugby played at Ballymore was dire in the extreme.

The fates had not been friendly companions to England. They were not kindly disposed to them in their opening game against Australia. Their favours were less conspicuous still in Brisbane. Indeed, with the rain, the cloying pitch and the shallowness of their own performance, England found that fortune by this stage had abandoned them completely. Against a Welsh team that simply wished to be stubborn and to adopt spoiling tactics, England were numbingly ineffective. Referee René Hourquet's penalty count went against Wales by a staggering 25–9, a statistic from which England surely should have profited.

Afterwards, both coach Martin Green and captain Mike Harrison could not put their finger on why they should have played so poorly. All the indications in the build-up suggested that England were bringing their game more confidently together and in a more structured fashion than Wales. The only explanation was that the spectre of Wales had been brought to bear once more on England's pre-match mental condition.

This psychological barrier, if such it is, would lead to the next generation of players being given cassette recordings of the Cardiff Arms Park crowd singing 'Hen Wlad Fy Nhadau', Wales's national anthem. This was one way of overcoming their inhibitions about Welsh rugby and its Celtic twilight myths. Considering what was eventually to happen throughout the '90s and beyond, the cunning plan seems to have worked. England's playing record since this time speaks for itself.

For the moment, Wales contrived, largely through English errors, to score three tries by Gareth Roberts, Robert Jones and John Devereux, with Paul Thorburn converting two of them. Jonathan Webb kicked a solitary penalty by way of reply in a final scoreline of 16–3.

Apart from those who gain pleasure in gloating over Wales beating England once more – so that all is well once more in the Universe and God is in his heaven – this was a game of distressingly low standards. While Wales celebrated, this fact was not lost on New Zealand.

Looking not only through the wrong end of the telescope but one which was also pointing in the wrong direction, Welshmen could observe complacently that England had not beaten Wales outside Twickenham since 1963. This was sufficient justification for Welsh pride. The past, though, is a foreign country. They do things differently there. This, for Welsh rugby, was a past which was beginning to recede into the distance and in the 1990s would accelerate away. England would begin their advance to leave Wales struggling to keep pace. English rugby, from this disaster, was set to improve, while Welsh rugby, from this victory, was set to decline.

Yet, had Welsh observers looked on the present with a view to the future, they might have surveyed a world scene that was shifting radically and, more than likely, at a different pace. They should have recognised that the standards to which they should be aspiring were being set elsewhere.

Robert Jones at scrum-half was the only player in this game who showed, by his consistent class, that he had the right to strut his stuff on the world's stage.

If Wales won the battle, it was England who would ultimately win the war. With lessons learnt, embarrassment suffered, England returned home not only to put their house in order but also to start rebuilding it.

Stung by this defeat and aware of the way rugby was to develop in the future, Twickenham's response was to ring the changes that would usher in the era of Geoff Cooke and Will Carling. Within 12 months, Wales was to win the triple crown and championship. They were to win the championship in 1994, too, but these triumphs were brief amid the long, lean years of disappointment and depression that was to engulf Welsh rugby.

This was to come. For the moment, Tony Gray, the coach, and Derek Quinnell, his assistant, had other concerns. The list of injuries included Jonathan Davies (leg), Bob Norster (hamstring) – both of whom were notable and, at this stage, irreplaceable players – Anthony Buchanan (back) and Gareth Roberts (broken nose). This was no time to suffer. The mighty All Blacks lay in wait in six days' time. The semi-finals beckoned.

1987 SEMI-FINALS

Both semi-final matches contained a Northern versus Southern Hemisphere confrontation, but no one, not the most fervent optimist, expected either Wales or France to advance to the final game. This was predicted to be solely the preserve of the Antipodeans. Neither Wales nor France had shown that they could dominate a match or even indicated that, talented players though they had, their individual skills were of a consistent level. They committed too many unforced errors, which made them look inefficient and careless, and too many of those errors would find them on the wrong and more serious side of the referee's whistle. They gave the ball or too many penalties away – quite often both – which meant that the other team controlled the flow of the game.

For France at this stage, there was the fear that fatigue was setting in. Jacques Fouroux, the coach, drew attention to the amount of rugby his team had played over the last two-year period. In that time France had conducted tours to Argentina (1986, series drawn 1–1), Australia (1986, one match) and New Zealand (1986, one match). They had also welcomed the All Blacks to France (1986, drawn series 1–1) and had competed in the Five Nations Championship. 'We are saturated with rugby,' concluded Fouroux. The pack of forwards he chose for the semi-final was to be the same as the one that had played, fought and, against the odds, won the infamous battle (16–3) of Nantes the previous autumn, having lost the first Test 19–7 in Toulouse. Anyone who had been a witness in Nantes would claim the game to be the toughest, the meanest and the most chillingly brutal contest of all. Buck Shelford, legend has it, left the field at the end with his scrotum ripped apart.

Both semi-final fixtures were played in Australia. The authorities were hoping that there would be better support than there had been for the quarter-finals, also based there. The attendance at the Concord Oval for the Australia and Ireland game had been 14,356 and barely 10,000 in Ballymore for the England and Wales match. Both grounds were capable of a 20,000 capacity. This indicated that if the reception for the Rugby World Cup had been cool to begin with in Australia, the tournament as it progressed had failed to generate any momentum within the country.

The game between Australia and France proved to be one of the great games of all time. Some believed it to have been 'the' greatest game of all time. David Hands of *The Times* wondered if there had ever been a game like it. He wrote: 'It was a French colleague en route to the Concord Oval who referred to the "superb ambience" of a Sydney jazz club he had discovered. Five hours later, his countrymen, blowing their own brand of hot music, had created an ambience all of their own as they made their way to the final of the inaugural World Cup.'

For the game, Brett Papworth and Nick Farr-Jones were declared fit to play so that, even though Steve Tuynman was absent, Australia remained strong favourites to win.

The contest was to prove a thriller with the semblance of fiction in that, with so many heroes and villains and the many exits and entrances, we were to be denied knowing the denouement until the dying moments. Indeed, in an exhausting finale of a chase to rescue the treasure that once had seemed lost, and with bodies literally strewn around the arena collapsing from fatigue in their breathless efforts, the guessing game was not resolved in France's favour until the last kick.

There were too many flaws to make the game one of great beauty, but the imperfections, which made for so many sudden twists and turns, acquired the arresting allure of sublime drama. This game had an intoxicating quality, leaving the mind to wonder what other surprising adventure lay around the corner.

Within the game were great players giving wonderful individual performances. David Campese, playing at full-back rather than wing, with his 25th try became the highest try scorer in international rugby. Michael Lynagh, with 16 points to his credit, overtook the Australian test match record held by fellow Queenslander Paul McLean, who had played in 30 tests between 1974 and 1982. Three times Australia were in the lead; three times France recovered.

With their villainous tendency to transgress and to be penalised, France gave away points which Lynagh took with alacrity and which gave his side an immediate nine-point lead. Then Australia lost the services of Papworth at centre and replaced him with Anthony Herbert, and Bill Campbell, the lock, who was replaced by David Codey. Coker, who had moved to lock, won the ball in the line-out only for Lorieux to rip the ball from his grasp and score the try. Didier Camberabero, who had missed a couple of kickable penalty chances, converted from the touch-line.

With Rodriguez in commanding form, he drove his team relentlessly forward to give France the kind of momentum upon which their flowing style thrives. More tries came. Campese and Codey were the scorers for the Wallabies; Philippe Sella and Patrice Lagisquet for France. Lynagh should have given his team a six-point cushion but inexplicably missed a penalty.

Three minutes of proper time were left and the score stood at 21–21. Serge Blanco wanted to run from his own 22-metre line. He erred and knew it. He passed the problem onto Camberabero, normally a fly-half but now on the wing. He was engulfed by Australians. There was a French infringement and Lynagh kicked the penalty.

Camberabero, villain one moment was hero the next. The excitement was pulsating and tangible, and under tremendous pressure Camberabero kicked a penalty to bring the game level once more at 24–24.

If France had miscalculated, it was now their opponent's turn. Lynagh and Campese thought to chance their arm and run. It was a mistake.

There followed a nail-biting passage of play which involved Lagisquet, Lorieux (who had a magnificent game), Denis Charvet and the inevitable Rodriguez. As the action unfolded, there grew, with the momentum, a sense of inevitability in the realisation that a score was probable. The Australian defence, although fine in numbers, was scattered. Without form and preferring discipline, they were at a loss. One pass from a Frenchman found another safe pair of hands and, surprisingly, yet another was in place. They were on song. France were in their natural element of open space with someone always ready to move on.

The ball arrived in Blanco's hands with a 25-metre journey to go. Aware that he was carrying an injury from the previous game, and with all of Australia's gold jerseys converging on the corner flag, his only destination, time seemed to stand still to ask the question: would he make it? In what appeared an eternity, Blanco finally and exultantly did make it. Camberabero converted from the touch-line. It was a closing sequence worthy of a dream.

In the wake of the grand, breath-taking movement, luminous in its sparkle, bodies were left prostrate on the ground; the last gasp, as it were, had been given. When there was no more to give, Brian Anderson of Scotland blew the final whistle.

Without doubt, this game had given the inaugural World Cup its defining moment. Rugby's greatness as a pulsating and compulsive sport, it seemed to say, would not descend into a mediocre conflict simply because so much was at stake, with so much to win or to lose, and with the added pressure upon the victor and the vanquished. Rather rugby, like any sport, given the piquancy of chance and risk, of the fear of being exposed, and of existing in the shadow of the lion's mouth, could rise to more eminent heights of accomplishment *because* of the edge. Mediocrity thrives in a snug and unthreatening cocoon. This game of glamour and adventure at the Concord Oval Sydney gave permanent life to the Rugby World Cup.

'That kind of match,' Serge Blanco would recall, 'where anything and everything might happen, is the sort of game that I hope tomorrow's rugby will give us. After the match we were the happiest men in the whole world. By the time we had changed and showered, the stadium was in complete darkness. We went out on to the pitch, did a lap of honour and we sang. We sang Basque songs for half an hour. It was a way of re-experiencing the emotions through our voices, the instrument of feelings. No one else was there. It was our little secret. It was a moment of sheer magic, so happy, so proud of what we had done...our special time.'

The other semi-final, indicating rugby potential for infinite variety, was of a different kind. New Zealand demonstrated the special requirements of power, discipline and efficiency. There was no imaginative adventure here. Yet in raw strength, disciplined rhythm and sheer simplicity of execution there was a kind of beauty. This was no contest between equally matched teams. There was a vast gulf, a veritable Grand Canyon, which separated them.

The All Blacks laid Wales on a slab and, coldly and dispassionately, dissected its battered and bruised body. Without emotion, and boldly calculating their immense power, they laid waste Wales's inferior effort. This was a match of inequality and imbalance. They had scored two converted tries after ten minutes and had 24 points on the board within half an hour. The contest was effectively over. Wales, as Tony Gray, the Welsh coach said afterwards, were systematically dismantled.

The All Blacks rucked and drove; rucked and drove again. Wales, like Scotland, were left to tackle and to tackle some more. Respite came only because of the intensity of the unremitting physical strain: when a player needed medical attention.

Eight tries were eventually scored, with Grant Fox given the opportunity to accumulate over 100 points for the tournament. Buck Shelford was outstanding. John Kirwan had a flood of possession and scored two tries, and Alan Whetton maintained his record of scoring a try in every match.

The 49 points that the All Blacks scored were the highest number conceded by a team from Britain and Ireland (although Scotland did score eight tries against Wales in 1924). The six points Wales scored included a try by John Devereux (converted by Paul Thorburn) which opened the second half against New Zealand's 27-point lead at that stage.

Wales suffered not only the ignominy of this score but, in the course of the game, Huw Richards, who had taken the lock position after Bob Norster had declared himself unfit, became the first player in the 30 matches of the tournament so far to be sent off the field for foul play. The referee, Kerry Fitzgerald, could have sent off Shelford, too, for the delivery of an outrageous punch on Richards. Fitzgerald was chosen to officiate at the final.

Another player who confirmed his promise was the 23-year-old John Gallagher at full-back. He had made no impression in club rugby in England and had emigrated to New Zealand, joined Wellington and thereafter made his way up the ladder of representative rugby in his adopted country. After playing as utility back in the New Zealand tour to France the previous year, he had won his place at full-back for the World Cup tournament. By the time he toured Britain and Ireland in 1989 he had become an accomplished and immensely influential player. With him, the All Blacks became an outstanding attacking force.

The All Blacks were unquestionably a superior breed in the tournament and would prove the case elsewhere over the next few years under the changed leadership of Buck Shelford. David Kirk was to play one more international after the World Cup against Australia before embarking on further studies at Oxford University, and thereafter following a career first in government administration, and then in business. Between 1987 and 1990 the All Blacks would create under Shelford a record of 12 consecutive victories.

Clive Rowlands, the Welsh team manager, under stress and deep disappointment, passed a comment in the press conference afterwards that he might have regretted in later moments of tranquillity. It was an impulsive response which he will have meant, as is his wont, as a witty riposte, in this instance to hide his sadness. 'The sooner we return home,' he said, 'and to going back to beating England, the better.' A man who believes passionately in his beloved Wales, he was hopelessly disheartened by the margin of defeat. For him, who had given so much to Welsh rugby, and was later to give to British and Irish rugby as manager of the Lions' success in Australia 1989, such humiliation was hardly bearable. Nonetheless, it was a comment that was to reverberate throughout the next decade and more in Wales. This was especially in view of, and in contrast with, England's response to the World Cup and the way they fully embraced it.

Anticipation of the first final of the Rugby World Cup was in itself piquant, but there was the additional ingredient in that the teams represented the two hemispheres that played in two contrasting styles.

1987 THIRD PLACE PLAY-OFF

This is the fixture no one wants to play. Suddenly, the players are out of the mainstream and while they might enjoy staying behind to watch the final and not go home yet, they nonetheless begrudge having to perform once more in a game that is a mere footnote to the narrative of the tournament. The mental strain of previous games fades and is replaced instead by the strain of having to lift the spirit to show a modicum of interest when the chance of glory has gone. No meaning was attached to the game in this first World Cup tournament other than that which the game itself stood for. This is a difficult but a necessary fixture.

Andrew Slack, Australia's captain, made no bones about it and thought the game a waste of time. Wales bemoaned the fixture on other grounds: they had to gather together a pack of forwards from a choice limited and ravaged by injury. They were short of players. They had been fortunate in that they had already been able to call on the assistance of two players who happened to be in the district. Richard Webster from Swansea was on holiday in Australia and was playing for Teacher's North Club in Canberra, as had David Young, also from Swansea. With crippling injuries to the Welsh team, both players, at 20 years of age, had been drafted into the squad and found themselves winning their first caps for their country. Young had already played against England and New Zealand earlier in the tournament. Webster was now chosen to play in the tournament's penultimate game amid the thermal springs of Rotorua.

Wales were the underdogs. The only question, or so it appeared, was: how many points would Australia score?

The doubts that had been expressed about the value of including this fixture were confounded by what eventually transpired at Rotorua. A large crowd was present, a spectacle followed.

After four minutes, Australia were reduced to 14 men. In this short space of time, David Codey had already been warned, but decided to ignore the referee, Fred Howard of England, and to continue taking the law into his own hands. He found the bodies of opponents a convenient place to rest his studs and was sent off.

If this diminished the team's resources, the depletion, as so often can happen, stiffened the team's resolve. Australia's 14 men found the resources to double their efforts. Thorburn and Lynagh began by exchanging penalties and then each failing with attempts at goal. Wales broke the deadlock. If their early adventurous play was prone to error or lacked judgement, they were eventually rewarded. A firm Welsh drive was carried on by the ubiquitous Robert Jones and resulted in Gareth Roberts being pushed over the line by the rest of the forwards.

It proved to be a tight contest. Whatever advantage Wales felt they had because of their extra man, it was the influence of Cutler and Troy Coker which dominated the lines-out. In addition, Wales contributed to their own difficulties by often overplaying their hands. Australia benefited with Matt Burke and Peter Grigg's tries. Paul Moriarty scored the best of the game after a long movement involving Webster, Alan Phillips and Anthony Buchanan. Their three converted tries gave Wales a nicely poised 15–13 lead at the interval.

Nick Farr-Jones came on for the winger Peter Grigg after 47 minutes, resulting in the Australian threequarter line being re-arranged so that Farr-Jones went to scrum-half and Brian Smith, who started at scrum-half, went to the wing.

Two more penalties were exchanged before Lynagh dropped a goal and looked to have settled the issue at 21–16.

The match reached a dramatic climax when Jonathan Davies hoisted a treacherously high ball to the opponent's 22-metre line. Devereux jumped to recover it for Wales. Ieuan Evans took it on, ran into the midfield to join Mark Ring and Thorburn. The full-back sent Adrian Hadley in for the try near the corner flag.

The conversion was still necessary for Wales. This was left to Paul Thorburn. In a long and prolific kicking career he had accomplished many a fine deed, but none was to prove better than this. Under intense pressure and from as close to the touch-line as it was possible, he succeeded. The large crowd, made up mostly of local people who had given Wales their support throughout, gave an ecstatic cheer as the ball sailed through the posts – 22–21 – to leave Australia to ponder how the good fortune they had enjoyed at the start of the tournament had so utterly deserted them at the end.

Between the cup of celebration and the lip of joy, triumph was stolen from them at the last moment. Their two latest defeats had been dramatically contrived in injury time. Thus, Australia, who had been favourites at the outset, were left in fourth position. They were to make amends for this desperate state of affairs in the years to come.

For Jonathan Davies it proved an exciting finish. He was later to conclude that 'winning third place wasn't the be-all and end-all because the biggest prize was on the following Saturday, but it is always nice to finish amongst the medals. We knew we weren't good enough to win the World Cup but we came back with our heads held high. We went on to win the Triple Crown in 1988.'

1987 WORLD CUP FINAL

New Zealand had already made a strong case to be considered the team of the tournament. At no stage throughout their progress had anyone questioned the overall strength of the team, nor had the All Blacks, through their uncompromising attitude and purposeful play, allowed anyone the scope to do so. No chink had appeared in their armour. No team had come anywhere close to being their equal. Theirs had been an imperious march of confidence and application to duty. They had accumulated 269 points in their tournament games and had 43 points scored against them. If they had not played with a freedom of movement, they had, in their inimitable manner, exerted an iron grip on all the games they played. They had scored 40 tries, while only three were scored against them.

They had a formidable pack of forwards against which every other team had to play servant. Everything was subservient to tight control; simple and direct. The principles of their game were incarnate in the dynamic form of Buck Shelford, their overlord at number 8. On the field he marshalled the team.

David Kirk, the captain, was, by and large, a quiet presence. In view of the turmoil that had so recently engulfed New Zealand, he was all the more potent for that and possessed a latent authority that was impressive.

Outside him was Grant Fox, the fly-half (or first five eighths as they are called in New Zealand). It was in response to his extraordinary exploits that the word 'metronome' had first been coined in a rugby connection. He had scored 109 points already. Both half-backs were disciplined and efficient. Outside this pair, and behind Shelford's pack, the threequarters were a supporting act. They played classic All Black rugby which Brian Lochore, their coach, would easily identify with his own playing and leadership days in the mid-'60s.

As always, they had resilience. They did not suffer many injuries and so had no need to change personnel as other teams had had to. What had proved a distraction was the failure of their original captain, Andy Dalton, to recover from his pre-tournament injury. When he did, Sean Fitzpatrick was performing so well at hooker that they had no need to change him. In the event, Dalton did not play at all.

France, on the other hand, had worries aplenty. Neither Blanco nor Lorieux, who had played so magnificently in the semi-final, considered themselves fully fit for the final game. They made the line-up but it had been touch and go.

More than this, it was evident by 20 June at Eden Park that the vivid spark which sustains French rugby had forsaken them. What their coach, Fouroux, had feared and had forewarned finally came to pass. The final of 1987 was a game too far. So much rugby throughout the previous two years had taken its toll and the energy-sapping but glorious semi-final had drained them physically and mentally. France looked a tired team as they entered the arena. Apart from a swift but very occasional riposte, the game was dominated by New Zealand.

There was no colour, but a grim determination to get their hands on the first William Webb Ellis Cup. For the most part, France were engulfed by black jerseys – the most prominent being those of the back row. In a manifestly overpowering trio, the most conspicuous was Michael Jones.

After Fox's attempt at a drop-goal was charged down and Lagisquet failed to gather, Jones latched on to the wayward ball to score the first try. Fox, after converting the score, attempted a second drop-goal and this time succeeded to give a 9–0 first half lead. After the interval, Camberabero reduced the lead with his only opportunity of a penalty all afternoon. France rarely enjoyed any prolonged period of play in the New Zealand half. In the meantime, Fox kicked another four penalties.

Among all the kicks, Michael Jones made his presence felt once more. He made the influential break which led to Kirk's try. Immediately from the restart, Kirk left the French defenders as mere spectators as he sprinted away for 60 metres to give Kirwan his eighth try of the tournament.

The decisive blow had been struck. There was no way back for France. Pierre Berbizier, who had had a wonderful tournament, scored a try in which movement he was involved four times. This was only the fourth try the All Blacks had conceded throughout their six games. They had been single-minded and brilliant executioners in their 29–9 victory.

The lasting image of the first World Cup was of the All Black captain, David Kirk, holding the trophy aloft. A Peter Pan figure with a whole face that smiled and even a twinkle in his eye, physically slight and unintimidating, he seemed an unlikely figure to be leading an All Black team. As he received the William Webb Ellis Cup from Albert Ferrasse, Chairman of the IRFB, the graze around his left eye and the trickle of blood on his cheek were evidence that he had survived a bruising afternoon. He was no softy. He could be as tough, physically and mentally, as men with a more menacing demeanour.

After the South African visit to New Zealand in 1981, followed by the visit of the Cavaliers in 1986, Kirk became the acceptable face of All Black rugby. Alone he represented a public relations campaign on behalf of rehabilitating the name of rugby from what had been a beleaguered state. This was no small consideration. We may not have been charmed by them – that was left to Fiji and France – but we admired and respected their extraordinary achievement. They were far and away the best team in the tournament. They had not seriously been challenged as the scores testify. The Rugby World Cup belonged rightly to them in 1987. They were to prove beyond doubt in the next three years that the whole world was truly their oyster. The true grit of 1987 was to turn into a rugby jewel under Buck Shelford.

MATCHMAKERS

The 1987 Rugby World Cup was dominated by the All Blacks. Therefore, it is not surprising that the tournament's main rugby personalities emerged from their midst. The whole nation had lost faith with rugby and its representatives on the field. After the Cavaliers debacle in South Africa they were perceived to be mercenary and with this moral deficit they could no longer claim any heroic status. Crowned as world champions, they partially restored their reputation. What secured it more firmly was their captain David Kirk.

He appeared like an elf engulfed by the tyrannous power around him, the still, small voice of reason amid the roar and the bluster. Nonetheless, Kirk remained the 'governor' of the side, endowed with a keen intelligence that could effortlessly set aside the merely peripheral to analyse and emphasise the main elements of the day's play. He did so with congeniality that is not customarily associated with the All Blacks. He was far from being an unsmiling giant. Originally from Otago, where he played 27 times for the province, he moved to Auckland in 1985. After playing for the All Blacks on the tour of England and Scotland in 1983, he captained New Zealand against France and Australia in 1986 before relinquishing the captaincy to Jock Hobbs, who took over the leadership in France.

Andy Dalton was the first choice captain for the World Cup tournament but injury eventually meant that he was not to take part. Dalton had been on tour with the Cavaliers and the stigma was still attached to him and the other players. Choosing him as captain was not likely to regain the sympathy of the nation nor re-unite the many divisions which had riven New Zealand society. A farmer who courted further controversy with the tractor television advertisements, the NZRFU may have, through default, been fortunate in the circumstances that allowed Kirk to assume the leadership.

Kirk simply went from strength to strength. He provided New Zealand with an acceptable and genial face of triumph that restored harmony where before there had been dissent. He was a wonderful player, as he showed in the final when he played a crucial part in the two second half tries. He scored the first by finally going past Sella and Dubroca before diving over. Straight after the restart, he defied two tacklers to burst down the narrow side and when held, Shelford was on hand to pass to Kirwan for the score.

Dalton, too, had a further misfortune. He must truly have had a miserable time. Try as he might to get fit, he failed, which must have been an unbearable frustration. What's more, he never played for the All Blacks again. In his stead a young hooker of 22 years of age took his place. Sean Fitzpatrick, who had been selected in 1986 and had been in and out of selectors' favour, was to play in all six of the World Cup fixtures. He was to make the position his own until he retired with 92 caps in 1997, to make him one of the greatest All Blacks players of all time with 63 consecutive tests and the longest spell as captain (51).

'We had a good run throughout,' Fitzpatrick concludes. 'We were miles ahead of all the other countries in terms of fitness and preparation. Our skill levels were greater, too, at that stage. It built a confidence in knowing that no one could get hear you. We grew and grew so that by 1988 and 1989 we were unbeatable really.' The records show it.

He formed part of a formidable and experienced pack of forwards among whom were the Whetton brothers, Gary and Alan, at lock and the flank; Steve McDowell and John Drake at prop; and Murray Pierce at lock. Each played his part. Above them, it has to be said, soared Michael Jones, the flanker, and Buck Shelford at number 8. If Jones was supreme at No 7, all footballing skills and clairvoyance in anticipating where he ought to be, Shelford was the player who led and controlled the black phalanx at forward. If Kirk was Commander-in-Chief, Shelford was Chief of Staff. His authority on the field was unquestionable. His brilliant tournament meant that when Kirk retired and took up his Rhodes scholarship at Oxford University, Shelford took over for an unprecedented period of success.

During Shelford's reign, John Gallagher was to mature into a fine attacking full-back. He had a fine tournament but had only really hinted at the influential player he was to become.

John Kirwan was the player who made his mark during the tournament. From the moment he scored his spectacular try against Italy, he was determined to play an influential role. This was the try that set the whole tournament alight. For all the tension and the apparent concern beforehand that the fear of failure in so prominent a tournament would diminish rather than enhance the game's potential for spectacle and adventure, Kirwan's try gave faith that this would not be so.

He began to wear the silver fern as a 19-year-old against France in 1984 and went on to win 63 caps – 96 if non-internationals are included – before retiring in October 1994; he became top try scorer with 35 to his credit. At 6'3" and 14 stones he personified power and determination and in possession of a hand-off described by Rory Underwood as 'one you did not want to get in the way of'. His gifts were of the direct, no-nonsense kind. His was a job of work, he seemed to suggest, not a matter of entertaining. In this respect he differed from Campese, whose career has run parallel and who dreamt another philosophy.

For a big man, he could certainly side-step – although less adroitly than others in the pantheon. Given half a chance, however, in a crowded patch, shrugging tackles aside he was the deliverer of a powerful finish. He was at his best coming straight on the near shoulder of the ball carrier and, unlike others of his size who might be more cumbersome, he was capable of changing the angle of his run without significant loss of speed. Unless his opponent reached him early enough Kirwan, erect and with a high knee-lift, seemed impossible to stop in his stride. With fair hair and a fine physique the epithet Adonis might well have applied from a distance but, sadly, he rarely smiled and gave the impression, with his abrupt aggression, of a sullen temperament. Perhaps this was merely a reflection of what is perceived to be the brusque manner of an intensely competitive New Zealander.

The tournament was blessed with four other great wingers with different talents: David Campese (Australia), Ieuan Evans (Wales), Patrice Lagisquet (France) and Rory Underwood (England). It was blessed too with the cut and romantic dash of Serge Blanco.

The first World Cup began in modest fashion and ended in glory for New Zealand, only for modesty soon to return. The accomplishments of Saturday can vanish in the cold light of Monday's dawn.

'Another thing that I remember about the events of 1987...' recalls Fitzpatrick. 'We had won but it was not a big night. We went to the pub and had a few beers and Craig Green turned to me and said "We've just won the World Cup, but on Monday morning at 5:45am I'll be standing on the corner of my street with my lunch box waiting to be picked up to go roofing. It will be a normal day". It was bizarre.'

Chapter 5

1991 Rugby World Cup

It is the commonly held belief that 'Swing Low, Sweet Chariot' made its debut as a chorus of celebration at Twickenham in 1988. The song, of course, had been a familiar late-night bar-room ditty along with other such charming sing-a-long favourites as 'Take Them Down You Zulu Warrior', 'Eskimo Nell' or 'Who Killed Cock Robin' and sung in rugby clubhouses up and down England's green and pleasant land, and elsewhere, for decades. It is of a peculiarly English sort, born of the pranks and wheezes of boarding school or College and University students. When rugby spread throughout the colonies and the Dominions, the risqué words or the merely playful insinuations of these sometime indelicate songs of sexual debauchery, formed part of the legacy. Hymns tend to be sung in Wales, or mawkish tunes of sentiment and 'hiraeth' (an inexplicable longing, soulful and ancient, for home). There are rebel songs and folksy love tunes in Ireland, as there are in Scotland, which tend towards romance or to induce a deep-rooted melancholia.

Not so in old-boys' clubs such as the Old Rottinghamians, that fond caricature and jubilant celebration of the English rugby club, at once accurate and exaggerated, authentic yet burlesque, immortalised by Michael Green in his wondrously funny *The Art of Coarse Rugby* – a great description of the variety and disorder that reigns gloriously unchecked beneath the blazered conformity. Among the table-top debris and the late-night incoherence – when the wiser call to go home has been ignored a couple of hours earlier – is the natural home of 'Swing Low, Sweet Chariot'. The song could be performed by actually singing the words or alternatively, at the call for 'actions only', the song could be mimed with bawdy and, quite possibly, carnal declarations.

Suddenly, and without warning, the swelling chorus of 'Swing Low, Sweet Chariot/Coming for to carry me home' rang out when England's winger Chris Oti, of Nigerian descent and Millfield-educated, scored three tries in his team's handsome six-try, 35–3, defeat of Ireland on 19 March. This was originally a song which the Negro slaves sang on the plantations of the South in the USA to lift their spirits when 'the cotton was high' and from which they could somehow glean a modicum of hope.

Once heard at Twickenham it was never to be forgotten. For some obscure reason thereafter, 'Swing Low, Sweet Chariot' has been adopted as an anthem of English rugby as well as on the terraces and in the enclosures of other games when there is cause for national jubilation. This has been a rum and curious development. But, then, so is Tom Jones's 'It's Not Unusual' which is nowadays a favourite in Cardiff where once rang out 'Cwm Rhondda'. It is the patriotic ballads that are sung at Murrayfield and Lansdowne Road – 'Flower Of Scotland' and 'The Fields Of Athenry', respectively.

The emergence of this newly adopted anthem coincided with the resurgence of English rugby and, in its way, signaled the opening of an era of eminence and glory. Their celebratory cup would have been full to overflowing but for England's penchant to falter singularly at critical times when the grandest of prizes were there to be lifted. Between cup and lip England flipped and slipped. Their reputation will be secure in both senses: for their persistent excellence and their frequent little indiscretions.

The 1991 Rugby World Cup was to be a paradigm of the next decade. After the inaugural event in 1987, England recognised, more than any other Northern Hemisphere country, that the old ways of doing things had gone for ever. The west car park at Twickenham may well be inhabited by the cohorts of the Old Rottinghamians and those whose ambitions did not stretch beyond the Extra As team, but to play on the hallowed turf of the old cabbage patch, from which Twickenham had emerged, meant that the mood needed to change. Attitudes required sharpening and the physical prowess of the amateur players, in search of Olympian heights, needed to be closer to the well-honed status of the professional athlete as epitomised by American football. This had not been achieved in 1991 but Geoff Cooke, the national coach, was to set them on the road for others to follow in the hope of arriving at such a destination in the future.

Before the 1991 tournament began, England had only modest aspirations of such a future. Yet with the Rugby World Cup to be played in Europe, with England as joint hosts, and the final to be played at Twickenham, England could be said to benefit from a fair wind behind them. The Rugby World Cup of 1991 was a massive incentive. Yet, the evidence that remained after the initial tournament, with South Africa still in isolation, hinted that the second World Cup would also see the fortunes of the two dominant Southern

Hemisphere countries prevail. Their sheer sense of professionalism fired by competitive imperatives insisted they were ahead of the game as it was played elsewhere. Beyond these, the technical expertise and the tactical awareness and agility of the All Blacks and the Wallabies was demonstrably better than anything witnessed in the Northern Hemisphere.

Europe's hopes rested with England. Wales were in disarray, a condition to which, neglectfully, they were growing accustomed. If at one time they were thought leaders in Europe and had set standards to which others aspired, they were showing incipient signs of decline to which, if once sensitive, they were now growing frighteningly immune. There seemed to be no urgency to correct the downward spiral. The game had aspirations of becoming global in its appeal whereas Wales preferred, seemingly, not to attach itself to this broad expansion and to remain instead as if sealed in their own private village. There was no vision of a world beyond their own backyard; no strategy beyond calling another meeting to resolve the next crisis. They were living a life under siege, but a siege that was of their own creation.

In the preceding two years they had appointed three national coaches in quick succession. In July 1991, Wales had returned from a disastrous tour to Australia. They had lost 63–6 to the Wallabies. There had been failure on the field and a disharmony off it which deteriorated into a distasteful and squabbling disruption. There were examples of boorish behaviour after the last game in Australia.

As a result, Ron Waldron became the latest coach to take part in the Welsh rugby version of the coaches' musical chairs. Others who had immediately preceded Waldron as coach and had departed prematurely were Tony Gray (1985–1988) and John Ryan (1988–1990).

Ron Waldron (1990–1991) left the team due to ill-health with only a few weeks to go before the World Cup began and he was replaced by Alan Davies. No one knew quite what to make of Wales any more. The Welsh Rugby Union was incapable of arresting a decline which now appeared to be inexorable. A once proud institution stood viewing its reputation being dismantled.

As they prepared as best they could in these desperate circumstances, sympathy was the kindest response; ridicule the harshest. The first emotion belonged to those who longed for Wales to regain their former eminence; the latter was what was felt by those glad to see some retribution for the arrogance of the past, especially the period lyrically praised as a 'Golden

Age' in the '70s. For sure, both camps agreed that Wales had fallen from a great height.

It was not expected that Ireland, despite their excitable potency and devil-may-care approach to rugby, could sustain their efforts long enough even during the 80 minutes of a single match, let alone a period of five weeks, to make a lasting impression during the tournament. They were always capable of springing a surprise as they often showed in the Five Nations Championship, but it was always asking too much to repeat the special effort. They played on a whim and a prayer, but so much was left on the hazard that no one, not even the most ardent follower with the most loquacious touch of the blarney, could foresee toasting their own heroes with Guinness at the end. Yet, of all countries, despite the troubles and obsessive divisions within their own land, they inspire the most enduring affection and, indeed, devotion. They are an elevating, effervescent, mirth-loving and mirth-giving people. No amount of optimism, however, could see them survive the demands of the 1991 tournament. They and Wales had ended the international season at the bottom of the Five Nations table.

In not too dissimilar a fashion, Scotland could enjoy the most brilliant success, as they had in winning the grand slam in 1990 under their astute captain, David Sole, but with such shallow roots to rugby in Scotland, the jubilation was periodical and impermanent. Yet they could play the most thrilling rugby with fluid attack and counter-attack of a breathless kind that befits a country whose Border clubs gave the world their own version of exhausting rugby: Seven-a-side. Too often, though, they had a crowd of workaday, jobbing players in their midst outside of whom they had too few performers of genuine greatness. Yet these rare gifted men invariably brought out not only the best in the others around them, but went further, it seems, so as to draw from them performances which they themselves could hardly have thought possible. In addition, with the Thistle on his breast and 'Flower of Scotland' ringing in his ears each player, however modest in earlier achievements, seemed to fill his jersey and to grow taller still at Murrayfield. This was also demonstrated away from home in the summer of 1990 when, in their second test in New Zealand, they only narrowly lost 21–18.

When we consider France we realise how fragile is rugby union in Europe. With the Rugby World Cup arriving in the Northern Hemisphere, there should have been an outpouring of confidence; that kind of conviction that a home fixture gives a club or country. Such a belief was in short supply, other than that which emanated, however cautiously, from England. There was the coruscating, if evanescent, brilliance of France to be taken into account. They could be a source of joy as well as pain.

When the French players spoke the same language of harmony, they built an edifice of beauty. Yet there were times when, for whatever reason, they might begin to argue among themselves so that, as we might imagine with the Tower of Babel when the multitude began to speak in strange and unintelligible languages, the whole edifice of their beautiful game would tumble down. Not that their language would be incomprehensible to one another. When the play was not going their way a series of discordant temperaments would be triggered throughout the team. For the opposition, the sound of their voluble arguments on the field was always the moment to strike for home, as it were; to keep them in a stranglehold in a way England were capable of doing.

In an aesthetic sense they could play rugby as if touched by the gods but, as with the gods, they were not always in a benevolent mood or liberal in conferring their rewards. France could be as brutal as they were in Nantes in 1986, or as sublime as in the Welsh game in 1991 or in 1994 when Jean-Luc Sadourny was to score the 'Try From The End Of The World' against the All Blacks in Eden Park. For sure, they could turn a mean game into a thing of beauty as they were to do – in a way no other team on earth could – against Wales at Wembley in 1998.

If a new resilience and unyielding firmness had appeared to enter the French rugby soul, no one felt able to trust the apparent changes – history being what it is, with a culture nurtured as it had been and national characteristics being what they are. A strait-jacket can withhold the extravagances only for so long before the prodigious capacity to play spontaneously and with panache is made manifest. What mood would France be in?

With England, what you saw was what you got. Theirs was not a multi-layered game with an infinite capacity to surprise. There might have been, but we were never to find out. They kept to the fundamental strength of the team. They stuck to what they knew best, where time and again they had proven the power of their simple game. They had an iron, military discipline and were endowed with the Bulldog spirit. If in the spring of 1988, Dean Richards and John Jeffrey were high-spirited enough to find it worth playing football with the Calcutta Cup on Princes Street in Edinburgh, the current England regime would not tolerate such aberrant behaviour. Geoff Cooke, who began his tenure with England in the previous autumn, was soon to establish a more rigorous attitude. He began on 15 October 1987, the day after a massive storm swept through Britain and Ireland. Cooke was to create his own draught of changes to freshen England's international set up.

The weakness of their playing strategy was that it was so unvarying and, ultimately, predictable. An opposing strategy could be outlined to counter England's well-known areas of power which they had so vigorously and uncompromisingly pursued. They had won the grand slam in March 1991 for the first time since Bill Beaumont's team in 1980 and were to repeat the feat in 1992. Two consecutive grand slams had not been achieved since Wavell Wakefield's team did so in 1923 and 1924. The feat in 1992 meant that this was the third time England were to achieve the double grand slam. They had also done so in the two seasons prior to the declaration of World War I on 4 August 1914.

In Europe their authority had been irresistible and, indeed, absolute. Well, almost. The 1992 grand slam could well have been their third in a row and would have been unparalleled in the history of the game. That they failed to achieve it was an indication of their essential vulnerability. In 1990, they lost to Scotland. Their cardinal flaw – of losing the vital match – became congenital and succeeding generations inherited it. England was imbued with a supreme confidence. Self-belief, however, is one thing; hubris, with its audacious presumption of inevitable success, quite another. Failure to distinguish the one from the other cost them dearly in Murrayfield in 1990 when both the home team and England challenged for the grand slam. Famously, a single moment was believed to crystallise England's sin. Given an opportunity to kick a penalty goal, Will Carling, England's young captain, preferred to ignore the eminently achievable chance to take his side into a three-point lead in the early stages of the game. He decided instead on what he thought to be inevitable. His team, he decided, would score a try and kick the conversion and so double the lead (the value of a goal worth 7 points came into existence in 1992). The prospect was imaginative and sporting but fatally flawed. England spectacularly failed to score the try and went on to lose the match.

The blunder was not only to haunt Carling, but became a sin that would be visited on the generation to follow. The loss and the hubristic decision would hang around like an albatross and the tale would have to be retold.

England nonetheless was a formidable outfit in 1991. They had acquired a resolve to go with their ambition. In addition, there was, as a host nation, a powerful incentive to be present at Twickenham on the final day. There was high expectation, an expanding reputation and a gathering momentum. At the helm was their coach, Geoff Cooke, an astute strategist. He was a shrewd and sympathetic manager of men; a Cumbrian who knew what he wanted and, more often than not, understood the means by which to get it. Unquestionably, Cooke was the architect of England's glory days. Cooke was blunt, practical and unsentimental, although he too could be touched with too much of the brass neck.

Within his winning ways he could be guilty of not respecting the opposition enough. If he and his captain had miscalculated in Murrayfield in 1990, they made themselves appear ungracious, disdainful even, after the Five Nations match in 1991 – England's first victory at Cardiff Arms Park since 1963 – when they failed to turn up at a scheduled post-match press conference.

Yet there was a certainty about England. They had chosen the path they wished to travel and were intent on pursuing it. There was a stark contrast between Wales's response to what happened in the first World Cup and that of England after they had met in the quarter-final in 1987.

England, after losing the game and seeing the future's expanding horizon, went home, did their homework and prepared for a different vision of rugby. They had lost the battle but they were determined to win the war. They began putting into place a system from which they were to reap rich rewards over the next decade.

'This served as a bit of a wake-up call for the RFU,' recalls Dudley Wood, the Union's genial Secretary. 'It was realised that the World Cup was a success and it was here to stay. Suddenly we were in a four-year cycle.'

In contrast, Wales, in beating England and going on to achieve third place in the tournament, became complacent, or rather allowed the malaise already apparent since the beginning of the '80s, to continue. Wales crowed that they were 'third in the world'. Had they the wherewithal and any proper sense of what international competition meant, they should have been dissatisfied and declared that being third was simply not good enough and redoubled their efforts to be better. Instead they carried on as if they had little to learn.

That Wales, in the early part years of the new century, have been unable to recapture their reputation of the 20th century can be said to stem from misinterpreting the episode against England. So happy were they in defeating the old enemy that they miscalculated the importance of being third place when new standards of excellence were being set by New Zealand, whose scores indicated they were far ahead of anyone else. In these circumstances, third place was irrelevant.

In England on the other hand, the World Cup had a profound effect and prompted a major re-shuffle of attitudes which saw Geoff Cooke appointed national coach in the autumn of 1987 and later Will Carling appointed as captain at 22 years of age. Cooke's appointment represented a firm statement of intent and, in time, his vision of the game would transform the whole perception of rugby in England. He would recreate for English rugby the much-longed-for balmy days of its past.

A former Physical Education lecturer, he was at the time head of the Leisure Department at Leeds City Council. He had enjoyed success as coach of the North of England during the time the RFU had superimposed a divisional structure on top of club and county rugby. There had been a reappraisal of the management structure. When Martin Green failed to be re-appointed as coach, Mike Weston, who had a clear idea of what changes were needed but was blocked, resigned. John Burgess, a Lancastrian, former England coach and President of the RFU, wanted change. Danie Serfontein, the Northumberland representative on the RFU committee and President in 1992/93, approached Cooke.

'The key figure behind the scenes was Don Rutherford,' says Wood. 'He had a deep understanding of the game and strong views about how it should be played. Geoff Cooke was a superb organiser and motivator with a keen eye for detail.'

This was the dawning period. England was to hold European rugby in its firm grip throughout the last decade of the 20th century and the beginning of the 21st. Indeed, none of the Southern Hemisphere countries would hold any fears for them either; except, that is, when a contest mattered most. This would hold true to the other four nations in Europe too. As events would unfold dramatically and, for England, perversely and obstinately, this incapacity to secure their reputation by winning the grand slams was a cross they had to bear. In time, the Celtic fringe on Europe's tiny archipelago in the North Sea, as well as France, were to give England a surprise ambush. When the great prizes were in the offing, England faltered. When least expected Wales (1999), Scotland (2000), Ireland (2001) and France (2002) were to scupper their ambitions in turn.

In spite of the colossus they always threatened to be, bestriding their world, they too often exposed themselves as having feet of clay. For the 1991 tournament Cooke also enlisted the assistance of Roger Uttley, the fine and greatly admired former English and Lions forward who was teaching at Harrow

School and John Elliott who, as hooker at Loughborough College, had come close to an England cap but never quite managed it, but had contributed substantially in coaching and selection. The England team was recognisably a team with the same familiar faces forming a considerable and unchanging core of strength. There was a real sense of optimism that England had it within their capacity to break the All Black and Wallaby stranglehold in 1991.

Yet these countries extended their shadow. England's Northern Hemisphere celebrations in 1991 had been short-lived. In their close season they had visited Australia and Fiji and in so doing their progress had been halted. Leaving these shores as grand slam champions they lost three matches in Australia, including the test. For the second time in their history they went down by 40 points (they lost by 42–15 against New Zealand in 1985). If they needed any consolation they had only to turn to the sports pages of the previous week to find that Wales had succumbed to a more humiliating defeat in Brisbane by 63–6. Australia were making their mark.

Australia enjoyed a good preliminary period. They had also played the All Blacks twice to share the rubber. The Australians were thought overall to be the better prepared and were ranked favourites to win the World Cup. Apart from casting England and Wales contemptuously aside, they had defeated New Zealand in Sydney and could have won in Auckland where they narrowly lost 6–3. From being largely also-rans in international terms for almost the whole of the 20th century, the last two decades saw Australia come of age.

Yet, despite living in New Zealand's rugby shadow, they had often played an influential role in the game's development. If they had been prime movers in initiating the Rugby World Cup, they had also been less hidebound and more open-minded than others, helping shape the modern game in the recommendations they made from time to time to change the laws of rugby.

In 1984, after suffering at the hands of the four home unions throughout their history, they completed the grand slam of victories in Britain and Ireland for the first time. Two years later they won the series in New Zealand. They had been favourites to win the inaugural World Cup.

Rugby union had always been a Cinderella sport in Australia, overshadowed by the serious popularity of rugby league, Australian rules, horse racing and, above all, cricket. These sports condemned rugby union to the role of a minority interest, the preserve of an exclusive few and of largely the professional classes. The game did not inspire the mass of a population which, while overtly enthusiastic about sport, are keenest on sports at which they can consider themselves the best. Australia jingoistically likes to follow Australian winners, single-mindedly nationalistic, as exemplified in their discriminatory newspaper coverage. Sporting success is a front page story; failure can very soon be relegated to a back page afterthought.

By the turn of the new century Australian rugby had materialised from being the perennially second-placed to emerge at the forefront of world rugby. To such an extent was the case that they were considered favourites once again to win the 1991 tournament. They had emerged from the shadow that New Zealand had cast over them for so long. They were no longer considered the poor relations.

It was curious that Australia had usurped the throne so long held by its formidable neighbours. In South Africa's continued absence, the race for the title belonged to the two remaining principal nations of the Southern Hemisphere. Western Samoa, who over the years had supplied players to the All Black cause, were represented in their own right for the first time in the tournament. They had replaced Tonga.

If England were to host the final in 1991, the tournament did not belong exclusively to them. The other four countries in Europe, who were members of the IRFB, were also to be involved. The conclusion was drawn after the 1987 competition that it was unsatisfactory to have the competition split between two countries. Logistics, ease of administration, concentration and focus of leadership and management all argued in favour of a single nation in charge. Despite this, the desire of everyone to have a share and not to be left out, determined that, rather than reduce the complement of nations, the tournament should expand so as to encompass the five nations.

The 24 pool fixtures were spread through all the countries: Pool 1 in England, Pool 2 in both Ireland and Scotland, Pool 3 in Wales, and Pool 4 in France. The quarter-finals were to be held in France (in Paris and Lille), Ireland and Scotland. The semi-finals would be in Lansdowne Road and Murrayfield and the third place play-off in Cardiff Arms Park. Twickenham would host the final. In all there would be 19 venues as opposed to 11 in 1987.

There was, perhaps legitimately so, the suspicion that there were selfish financial reasons for this division. Each union wanted not only to share in what was obviously a good thing for rugby and its future development, despite the earlier scepticism, but also to share in the spoils. This was still a fledgling tournament. There remained uncertainties. To what extent could one country manage to administer the tournament? To what extent could one country arrange for all the fixtures to be played? Were the facilities available?

The Rugby World Cup, it was argued, still had a crucial developmental role to play. Extending the scope of the tournament to encompass Gloucester, Otley and Pontypridd, towns that are not associated with international rugby, would help promote the game in those areas. Domestically this was a laudable aim, but it was not one that was universally embraced with any great enthusiasm. Sport Controllers in the television industry, with their sense of theatre and of the dramatic and with an eye on their viewing figures, did not much like it either. They looked at the impact globally.

Indeed, there were those who were sceptical about extending rugby's embrace at all to allow other nations to join in. This sounds strange and hard to realise, but there were people within rugby who believed that it would be far better to keep the sport within the narrow but comfortable field they had always known and controlled; that is, among the members of the IRFB. After all, that was the way it always had been. As an indication of rugby's insularity and the manner in which it only gradually began embracing whole-heartedly a wider community of rugby-playing countries, no international caps were ever awarded to those nations who were not included among the eight members of the International Rugby Football Board.

This was highlighted in 1964. In a bold and imaginative move in that year, the Welsh Rugby Union played Fiji at Cardiff Arms Park. No other country had ever contemplated issuing such an invitation to any country outside the exclusive 'club of eight', let alone a small island in the South Pacific.

In bright sunshine in April, Fiji performed in a manner that had never been seen before in the United Kingdom. Their handling, often one-handed, was singularly innovative and the speed and agility of their forwards and backs was not of the kind that was overly familiar to those in the corrugated shelters and enclosures of Welsh rugby grounds. Such suppleness hardly made Welsh prop forwards feel they were in touch with kindred spirits. Fiji, eschewing the stereotype, played rugby in an openly invigorating style.

If it took quite some time before a new pattern of fixtures was established, this was unquestionably the dawn of a new internationalism in rugby union. No caps, however, were awarded to the players in 1964. This outmoded practice persisted until the inauguration of the Rugby World Cup.

This was a bi-product of the Rugby World Cup in 1987. It was nonsensical and disrespectful of other countries not to present caps against other national teams. Furthermore, who would sit in judgement to adjudicate who were and who were not worthy opponents to deserve the honour. There were many anomalies. How could it be reconciled, for instance, that a player might be awarded a cap for beating Ireland or South Africa, say, but not get a cap when losing to Fiji or Canada?

Such a classification was iniquitous, made more transparent by the presence of 16 teams in the inaugural World Cup. If the old practice was to continue, players would be decorated with a cap only against half of the countries present. Thus, it was dishonourable to determine that eight countries would receive a sign of approval and the remaining eight would be blackballed – the first- and second-class citizens of the rugby world.

The natural instinct for preservation, to keep to what we know and understand and to question or to resist change, was threatened by the instigation of the World Cup. Who knew what the new world would bring? How would the administrative power shift? What would happen to the ideals of an amateur game? The codes of gentlemanly behaviour, upon which so much had hitherto depended and succeeded was open to question. Other forces were entering the game.

To ignore or to attempt to withstand this development was much like Canute on the seashore wishing to prove that there is little sense in opposing an elemental force. There was a compulsion about rugby union moving in this direction which would have been inadvisable to resist.

An early indication that a break with the past was imminent was the awarding of the host broadcasting rights in the United Kingdom not to the public broadcasters, BBC, but to ITV, the commercial television network. For three decades the BBC had been the sole broadcasters of rugby union. If the 1987 contract had been worth £1 million, the contract in 1991 was £3 million with ancillary facilities at £4 million. In France, TFI and Canal Plus had paid £3 million. For the first time the ITV network, in a federal system made up of 15 separate companies, would transmit rugby union live to the nation. Twenty-four of the 32 games would be screened filling 100 hours of television time. This was in contrast to the 28 hours transmitted by the BBC in 1987. The times were changing and inevitably perspectives altered.

Sponsors and suppliers added another £10 million. The six leading sponsors were Heinz, Ricoh, Famous Grouse, Société Générale, Sony and Glass South Africa, who contributed £4.5 million between them. Gate receipts were expected to bring in £16 million. Hospitality suites and match programmes added a further £3.5 million. The gross income was reckoned to be in the region of £39 million. With expenditure between £12 and £15 million, the tournament was expected to make a profit close to £25 million. This contrasted with the £120,000 in 1987 from a gross income of £3 million.

Rugby union was entering uncharted waters without a map or compass. But in the stolid form of Mr John Kendall-Carpenter, they had not only a safe pair of hands, but also a man who believed he had a vision for the future, would pursue it and would not be inhibited by the past, however wonderful that might have been for him and his generation and those that followed. A future had to be shaped. John Kendall-Carpenter was chairman of the Rugby World Cup organising committee and distinguished Headmaster of Wellington School. Three times a Blue at Oxford University (1948–50), he had played as a back row forward for England between 1949 and 1954, winning 23 caps, the last of which was against New Zealand. As representative of the Schools' Union he had been President of the RFU in 1980/81.

A new language had to be mastered. Marketing executives arrived. Advertising agencies were on hand. Highly seductive voices began insinuating themselves into the ears of men who were suspicious, largely, of modern promotional techniques. They would have to understand licensing and merchandising, marketing and commercially exploiting 'an honourable sporting event'. Administrators, hitherto cocooned away from the brasher world of commerce, were told of the 'up-market image' of their game and that along with golf and skiing, rugby was purported to be a sport likely to attract an ABC1 audience. This was a desirable group. Indeed, it was a group constituted of people just like those on the rugby committee – white-collar professionals.

In 1987, the Japanese telecommunications company KDD was the event's main sponsor. It was a sponsor that, at the time, proved hard to come by. If they came late in the day to the party in 1987, sponsors were forming a queue in 1991. The experts were expecting an audience of 2 billion worldwide with pictures beamed into 65 countries. However, only the TV companies in Europe, Japan and New Zealand paid more than a million pounds in fees for the television rights. Australia only contributed £300,000.

The organisers were willing to take low fees or none at all, preferring in such circumstances to be able to spread or introduce the game to a new audience, which would make the sponsors more than happy. Such fees, of course, contrasted with the £200 million that one of the US networks paid for the Olympics.

There was optimism and expectation in some quarters; there was trepidation elsewhere. This kind of expansion was feared. Such blatant commercialisation was interpreted as the worm in the apple. The much-cherished spirit of amateurism and innocent idealism was having to yield to the inexorable temptation of the riches that were on offer. Rugby would soon be on 'easy street' with such riches.

The game itself had begun to accept the need to administer itself more professionally. Keith Rowlands, who had been one of Wales's two representatives on the International Rugby Board in 1987, was now its Secretary, in effect its Chief Executive. He was the first person to be the Board's paid official. A Welsh International in the second row, he toured with Arthur Smith's Lions to South Africa in 1962. Captain of Cardiff RFC, he became a member of the Welsh Rugby Union not long after retiring prematurely from the game in 1967 after breaking a leg. He was subsequently to become an influential and shrewd administrator on the world stage.

If Wales could not keep up with developments on the field, they were surely playing a leading role off it. The Tournament Director for 1991 was Ray Williams. In the last three decades of the 20th century, Williams had made a unique and seminal contribution to rugby, not just in Wales but also throughout the world.

When its reputation was at stake and the values of its rugby mattered, when the national team had been humiliated in South Africa in 1964, the WRU appointed Williams as Coaching Organiser in 1967. The delay in the implementation had been due to an enquiry to look into the requirements of the game in Wales and to see whether such an appointment might transgress the laws governing amateurism. Once the path was clear, Williams became the first person to hold such a position in the rugby world. It is no exaggeration to say that during his tenure in this position, the whole world seemed to beat its path to his door for the seminars and courses he initiated and to hear the ideas he promulgated. He has been a pre-eminent figure of influence on rugby football. Not least of the beneficiaries was Bob Templeton, one of the men to inspire Australia as a world force.

Williams was later, after Wales's Centenary in 1980/81, to become the Secretary of the WRU and, after retiring as an official, to serve on its General Committee and thereafter on the IRFB. He was a man of vast experience and impeccable rugby pedigree.

His task for RWC 1991, to coordinate the event in the Five Nations, was immense. It was a complex format.

One of the endearing and, indeed, enduring memories of the 1987 tournament was the initial gathering of the teams for a banquet before any whistle had blown to begin play. For those teams congregated in New Zealand in 1987 the dinner was held at the Kingsgate Convention Centre in Auckland. There was no similar gathering in Sydney. Before battle commenced a fellowship was established. Taking their first tentative and innocent steps on the world's stage, the organisers hoped to perpetuate those sociable values which have been traditionally associated and inextricably linked with rugby football. Unlike many other sports, particularly those with professional inclinations and responsibilities, rugby union has insistently promoted the idea that no harm can come from sharing a jar or two of beer, breaking bread with your opponents, telling the odd fanciful tale or two. The hail-fellow-well-met camaraderie has been, from time immemorial, an indispensable accessory to the game's nature and style. This needed to be preserved.

On Saturday 29 September, the teams gathered for the welcome dinner in the Royal Lancaster Hotel in London in honour of the 16 teams. Present were the Home Secretary, Mr Kenneth Baker; Peter Brooke, the Secretary of State for Northern Ireland; and David Hunt, the Secretary of State for Wales. If the last two, for political expediency, expressed a degree of partiality, Baker admitted that he dare not declare any bias since he was born in Newport in Wales, had an Irish grandmother and was married to a Scot. Referring to England's second row forward as 'Wayne' Dooley suggested that he was less than well briefed. Present, too, was the Prime Minister's spouse. As a former referee with the London Society Of Referees and therefore not unknown to make the occasional call at Twickenham, Denis Thatcher was unlikely to trip over the name.

In the congenial atmosphere of a Hotel in W2, there remained the solemn thought of the prospects that lay ahead. There was the feeling of intrusion, particularly among those who considered themselves the favourites to win the competition. They felt they had suffered to be there. The emerging nations, however, were delighted to be in such august company, to have the chance of simply being in the same room, and to rub shoulders with their more famous counterparts, as seen on television or read about in newspapers. Hanging in the air was the question of how long such gatherings could continue as a precursor to the physical and psychological challenges ahead.

In the Olympic movement, there are those who look back nostalgically to Tokyo in 1964 as the last of the friendly games before the politics and commerce of the wider world, and the cynicism that can come with both, impinged on the old ethos. The old, for good or ill, will make way for a newer and different world. As rugby moves on and different priorities emerge, will the 1991 Rugby

World Cup be regarded in similar vein? Until a three-line whip was called, there were teams who had rejected the invitation. It cannot have been entirely to France's liking, for instance, that they were summoned from their training camp in Beziers, to arrive in London shortly before the dinner began at 7:30pm, to depart at 10pm to reach their beds in Beziers at 3am. Along with Australia and New Zealand (both at 6–4) and England (6–1), France (7–1) were included in the quartet among whom the spoils were to be challenged. Scotland by virtue of a favourable draw more than anything, were at 10–1. In their pool, they would meet Ireland, their stiffest opposition, at Murrayfield. Their quarter-final draw, provided they came top of their pool, would also be on home turf. As, indeed, they would then be if they qualified for the semi-finals.

In addition, in Ian McGeechan, Jim Telfer, and Derrick Grant, Scotland had a trio of experts whose long experience and coaching talent were second to none. The more it was scrutinised the more favourable the Scottish scenario became. The plot lines were persuasive; the characters strong and appealing.

However, the trail that led to the World Cup was littered with unsettling results. If they defeated the USA 41–12, they went on to lose 24–18 to Canada. If this largely experimental team had mixed results, a fuller complement of their first choice players went to Bucharest and lost 18–12 to Romania. Entering the 1991 tournament, Scotland preferred to dwell on their previous summer tour to New Zealand where they lost both tests but the second by only by 21–18 in Auckland. Scotland had a clutch of talented players whose experience in the hothouse environment of international rugby was invaluable and irreplaceable. Depending on the wins and losses in Pools 1 and 2 and the resultant quarter-final – where they anticipated facing Wales, a strategic point they were soon forced to reassess – Scotland might have the chance to settle old scores with England in the semi-final. The prospect for this would be enhanced depending on the result of the first game of the 1991 tournament. Unlike the opening game in 1987, the match at Twickenham in 1991 was a mouth-watering affair. England, the host nation, were to play New Zealand, the holders of the Webb Ellis Cup.

The game was played on 3 October. This was a Thursday. The opening match in 1987 was on a Friday. With hindsight, the organisers would have preferred the match to have been played on a Saturday. This recommendation was, perversely, ignored. If the attendance at Twickenham was 300 short of capacity on the afternoon, this was not due to the inconvenience of the day of the week. The mishandling of the ticket sales meant that there were 2,000 unsold tickets, which Dudley Wood managed to distribute in the days leading up to the first match.

'Tickets for the World Cup was a nightmare,' recalls Wood. 'There were some acrimonious moments to discuss allocations. Everyone wanted more tickets and as more overseas unions overestimated the number of fans who wanted to travel, there were heavy returns usually late in the day. We were computerised by that time and could deal with most situations at fairly short notice. There was criticism of the size of the allocation to corporate sponsors, or more often their agents. They have a tendency to take over the whole event. The commercial negotiations were in the hands of the IRFB, not the RFU.'

Before the game began there had been a parade of golden oldies holding aloft their national flag in front of children who were there to represent various schools. Finally, a rugby ball, which had begun its journey from the home of the game at Rugby School, arrived at the home of English rugby. Inside was an inscription from the current Headmaster, Michael Mavor, which Prince Edward read to the crowd. The game of rugby, he hoped, would be the winner.

There was much expectation in the air but too much trepidation in the hands of the players when the game began. There were few thrills and far too many spills. These were committed mostly by a tense England. In a cautious game, the All Blacks were awarded 19 scrums to England's 5. The 27 penalties awarded throughout the match confirmed the uneasy flow.

The statistics also indicated that the referee, Jim Fleming of Scotland, heeded the directive issued by the International Rugby Football Board. The game's international governing body had issued strict guidelines to all the referees as to what was expected of them so that divergent interpretations of the laws, whose labyrinthine intricacies is rugby's eternal flaw as a global sport, could be avoided. When such commands are made, the response can be dramatic. The referees know that it is not only the eyes of the world's spectators that are upon them, but also those of the game's assessors and adjudicators, and sometimes the only safe haven is to control the game by stopping it. The sceptic might say that it's better to gain the approval of the assessor who has a form to fill and a report to file, rather than the spectator who is often perceived as wanting uninterrupted action of a frivolous kind.

Thus, the referee is truly the 'man in the middle' who ensures that the two teams play within the laws of rugby and determines who transgresses them. In doing so, he is caught in the crossfire between on the one hand those – the assessors and the law makers – who insist that he operates strictly according to the letter of the laws of the game, where every dotted 'i' and crossed 't' is observed, and on the other, the baying and paying crowd who believe that the referee is nothing but a killjoy intent on stopping rugby's potential to be a free-flowing game of unstoppable running. Interpretation lies precariously and subjectively somewhere in between.

The All Blacks had a huge advantage with the scrummage count going so substantially in their favour. Only a single try was scored, and that by Michael Jones, their tirelessly dynamic flanker. This suggested a nervousness that is not always apparent in their play. They are as tense as any team but do not show it as others manifestly do and as they themselves conspicuously did at Twickenham. In retrospect, these were the early signs that all was not well within their camp. They played well enough but not with their usual knowledge and mastery of the kind which they were to display only sporadically during the 1991 tournament.

Grant Fox kicked the conversion and four penalties. For England, Jonathan Webb responded with three penalties and, as we were to grow to expect, a drop-goal from Rob Andrew that, in fact, raised English hopes by giving them the half-time lead. The gloom descended when the game ended 18–12 against them.

For Alex Wyllie, the former Canterbury and New Zealand back row player and now the national coach, the match was typical of the kind that might start a tour. 'It is not a matter of whether a team plays well,' he concluded, 'but whether, quite starkly, the team wins.' First outings, after the long period of intimidating contemplation of what is to come, are notoriously unpredictable occasions, often stilted and inexact. Long hours of training are only occasions to re-enact and correct the failures of the past and to create the conditions of the future game's possibilities without the hindrance and inconvenience of a challenger in a turbulent cauldron of expectation. Something needs to go bump to make it real.

Australia found this to be the case the following day at Stradey Park, the home of Llanelli Rugby Club. In an unremarkable first half, they nonetheless seemed to be coasting to a victory at 16–7 against Argentina, with tries by Tim Horan and David Campese. Since they rarely come second best to anyone in the scrum, a vital component still to control areas of the game, no one ever gets clean away from the Argentines. Australia understood this challenge since they had lost to Argentina in 1987. The battle was joined between the Pumas and the Wallabies. That they also did well in the line-out was an additional advantage to Argentina so that, obstinately, they nibbled away at the lead to such effect that entering the final quarter of the match they were only four points adrift. The Australians were later to find themselves in similar straits in even more dramatic circumstances in the quarter-final.

In their midst they had a player who could be relied upon, however desperate the circumstances, to leave the opposition rooted to the spot. David Campese scored a marvellous try for himself and then created one for Horan to put the result beyond doubt at 32–19. This double-act of Campese and Horan would surface in an even more dynamic and exhilarating style later in the tournament. This was the great winger's first statement of intent. There would be others. By the end of the Rugby World Cup 1991, David Campese would have created the most enduring image of all.

Such acts of daring individualism: a neat and nimble rugby hustler, a Fast Eddie, flirting outrageously with a twinkle against the massed ranks of the well-preserved and venerable Minnesota Fats. Campese was the twinkle of rugby's youth that made everyone else seem rheumy-eyed and too full with years.

He was not alone. Serge Blanco, of France, was the other player who could match the Australian for flamboyance and charisma. He could not make much of an impression in their muted match in Beziers. France beat Romania by 30–3. If the score was not convincing, neither was their style of play in an error-strewn game. Nonetheless, France were expected to win their group and with England having lost their first fixture, and therefore due to come second in Pool 1, the two countries were expected to meet at the quarter-final stage.

The Fijians, who were thought capable of making strides forward in the world ranking, proved disappointing. They lost 13–3 to Canada, which included three penalties by their prolific points scorer Gareth Rees. Scotland, who had lost to Japan in Tokyo the previous year by 28–24, put Japan to the sword by 47–9. On the same Saturday at Otley, Italy defeated the USA by 30–9, which included a brilliant try by Ivan Francescato and a fine kicking performance by Diego Dominguez. The following day, Ireland scored more than a half century of points against Zimbabwe (55–11).

If there was much that was subdued in all this, the touch paper was lit at approximately 2:30pm on Saturday. At Cardiff Arms Park, Wales had gone down to Western Samoa by 13–16. This was a staggering result at the time. A few of the Welsh players were also left staggering, too; literally so. There were times during the game when the many fierce, chest-high tackles – which were questioned for their legitimacy – left Welsh players strewn all over the pitch and in need of medical attention. Phil May, Tony Clement and Richie Collins had the worst of it and had to be replaced. Such tackling, and its easy acceptance, was a new phenomenon in the Northern Hemisphere.

If this was a bone of contention, even worse for Welsh morale was that their sense of injustice was made more acute in that the try which won the game for the South Pacific Islanders was doubtful. To'o Vaega's disputed try was allowed to stand when the television pictures confirmed that Robert Jones, Wales's scrum-half had first touched the ball. Even so, there could have been little argument that Western Samoa were deserving of their victory.

Under their coach, Bryan Williams, the great New Zealand winger and the first Western Samoan to wear the All Black jersey, they had exploited Wales's weakness and uncertainty. Wales had added to their pressure by declaring beforehand that this was the most important game in their 110-year history. Bringing the burden of history onto a single game is invariably an error of judgement. It attaches a focus and an attention which one game hardly merits, thereby flagrantly accentuating the importance to the point of exaggerated gravity. This has the potential for a fateful come-uppance. In the event of a loss, the game's meaning assumes seismic proportions. The damage to the team spirit is incalculable. The players draw into themselves. Alan Davies, the Welsh coach, claimed afterwards that they spent the next two days analysing what went wrong.

Wales's error was that they had underestimated the Western Samoans. This result was a forewarning to those who were to follow. Other countries would be more aware afterwards of a country and a rugby people of whom they hitherto knew little. The defeat caused a stir. Scrutiny of the Western Samoan squad and the true rugby provenance of their players might have helped draw different conclusions. Although Western Samoa has a population of a quarter of a million people, a further 150,000 people live overseas, especially in New Zealand.

Frank Bunce, who made his mark with Western Samoa, later played with even more distinction as an All Black and was to prove a major influence in that jersey in 1995. Rugby is a game which the Samoans take to in a natural way because of their big-boned and muscular physique, and their easy handling skills.

Asked prior to the 1991 competition to define his country's strengths, Tate Simi, the ever-smiling Western Samoa manager with a mischievous sense of humour replied that, surely, the other rugby countries did not think they had any. If no one else could define their power, then after this match in 1991 the Welsh players most certainly could. Western Samoa had the power and single mindedness of New Zealand, the flair and enterprise of their near neighbours Fiji and the fearsome tackling of Australian rugby league.

The dilemma for them was that their best players would be enticed away from representing their islands to play for others instead. Before 1991 this might have been acceptable since Western Samoa could hardly be said to have made an impression on the world of rugby. The 15,000 people who converged on the rugby stadium in Apia, the capital, to see the game transmitted live on television at 1am believed their moment had arrived. Their technical adviser, Bryan Williams, echoed such feelings when after the match he admitted that perhaps Western Samoa had found their place in the sun.

Things were not so clear and bright elsewhere. The other countries in Pool 3 and beyond were forced to question their assumptions and in the light of the result from Cardiff, to revise their strategy and preparations.

The situation was not without its humour even in Wales. Western Samoa, which had barely merited a second thought hitherto, had suddenly insinuated themselves into a nation's consciousness so that old atlases were dusted down to find out where exactly Western Samoa was on the map. This prompted the wag in the four ale bar to venture to evaluate Wales's plight and to pass judgement that: 'If Western Samoa could give Wales a hiding, imagine what the whole of Samoa might have done.'

Australia and Argentina were the next opponents to wonder what might be in store for them. Even north of the border, in Scotland, there were slight tremors since they, presumably, had set their sights on meeting Wales in the quarter-final. Having lost their first game, Wales could not with any reason expect to beat Australia in their next match, against whom they had fallen in Brisbane in the summer. Two defeats were therefore predicted for Wales and an early exit from the 1991 tournament stared them in the face. They were not going to make the cut. Their destiny lay in the hands of someone else. Western Samoa had to stumble. The flip-charts upon which tactical strategies are born had to be re-written.

In the morning Wales shivered with the cold sweat of realisation that things were not quite as happy as they had been the previous evening, when they could have swaggered confidently with other top seven rugby nations of the world. This victory gave a nudge to shake the old order; to make it at least unsteady. Someone's misfortune is always another's gain. If Wales were the victims in this instance from which Western Samoa immediately benefited, there was an even greater legacy for the World Cup as a whole. A team from outside the International Rugby Football Board had defeated a team from within it. The slow progress of spreading the game beyond the settled and unchanging traditions could be said to have begun. A new nation had made an entrance. How long that journey would prove to be and how much time it would take to accomplish was impossible to predict. All that could be said in October 1991 was that a step had been taken on that uncertain journey.

Wales had been the fall-guys. None of the other emerging countries were able to follow Western Samoa. If the score was 21–12 at half-time, Scotland went on to beat Zimbabwe by 51–12 with Iwan Tukalo scoring a hat-trick of tries. If Japan in their pacy, all-passing, all-running style scored three tries to four to give Ireland a scare, the men in green kept their heads to win by 32–16. England beat Italy 36–6. France, hardly convincing, scored 33 points to Fiji's 9 while New Zealand in their 46–6 win were in similar mode against a plucky USA at Kingsholm in Gloucester.

Since there were no surprises among these scores, the fixtures were of passing interest when compared with the anticipation of events that were about to take place in Pontypool Park, where Western Samoa were due to play Australia. To highlight the difficulties which confronted the South Pacific Islanders, the Wallabies included in their midst Willie Ofahengaue, their marvellous flanker – and a Tongan. For all the geographical closeness of the two countries, the match at Pontypool was the first of its kind between them.

Pontypool Park, with its tree-lined slopes and many a spinney and grove, is a stunning location for rugby matches when the place is ablaze with the ochre and brown colours of autumn. No such aesthetic observation could be enjoyed on 9 October. The mist and rain came with merciless consistency. In the grinding, mauling contest there were no tries, only penalties which successfully went 3–1 in Australia's favour. It was, nonetheless, far from dull. Indeed, it proved a constant tussle of simple sinew and bone, of hard and honest graft and unflinching obstinacy not to give in. This was of the kind they had grown familiar with over the years, in their rugby as well as their jobbing lives in Pontypool, lying in the heart of the industrial valleys of Gwent. The outcome was not settled until the end.

For Australia, there was a heavy price to pay. In the ninth minute of the first half, Nick Farr-Jones, their scrum-half and captain, injured his medial ligament. This, according to the medical prognostications, would keep him in doubt on the sidelines until the quarter-finals at the earliest. It would be touch and go. His country would miss him as both player and inspirational leader.

Farr-Jones cut an unlikely figure as a rugby player. He looked a misfit among the rugged bruisers around him. He appeared much as if Cary Grant, with his New York drawing-room urbanity, had absent-mindedly wandered onto the back lot of a Hollywood film set where Sam Peckinpah was shooting a scene with swarthy, cheroot-chewing desperadoes, who were about to loot and pillage an innocent homestead on the Mexican border. Or you might imagine him with his gold-rimmed spectacles, a swottish charmer in a college tutorial causing the odd don, noticing all the T-shirted and be-denimed deshabillé around him, to lament the erosion of the correctness and refinements of a past which was too distant by now and perhaps, after all, only imagined. He was of that kind mothers wished for their daughters. Like David Kirk of New Zealand in 1987, Farr-Jones possessed an intelligence and an engaging personality which persuaded a response and an attraction beyond the milieu of muddy knees and harsh grunts. He articulated the game's finer points with precision.

The captaincy was handed to Michael Lynagh, a mantle he often took up, and did so with typical composure against Western Samoa. He kicked all his team's points and he, along with his team-mates, gave a big sigh of relief at having survived a very testing and attritional time on the field.

Michael Lynagh, like the great tennis player Björn Borg, had a hardened competitiveness sealed in his close-set and narrow stare. As Shakespeare noted in *Macbeth*: 'There's no art/To find the mind's construction in the face.' Lynagh, for all his soft complexion, possessed an uncompromising look and his short-stepped walk from scrum to line-out and back again had a briskness which told of an unfussy and imperturbable mind. This steadiness of nerve was amply manifest in Pontypool's treacherous conditions and throughout the tournament. He was to have a great World Cup.

Wales, whose nerves were as taut as harp strings, and fearful of the ignominy of an early exit, overcame Argentina by 16–7. This meant that their execution had been delayed. Whereas elsewhere the outcomes had become predictable, there were different permutations in Pool 3. Wales beating Australia would produce one set of conclusions. Argentina winning their last match against Western Samoa produced another. The first of these was unlikely, so the crucial match was the final one to be held in Pontypridd.

Australia had embarrassed Wales in the summer. They were to do so again at Cardiff Arms Park by registering the biggest-ever score in an international at the home of Welsh rugby. The 38–3 scoreline superceded the 34 points which Scotland had attained in 1982 and the same number by New Zealand in 1989.

If this was noteworthy then so were the events at Sardis Road in Pontypridd, but which were less than estimable. In a fractious match tempers were so frayed that the referee sent players off the field for the first time in the tournament. Jim Fleming dismissed Mata'afa Keenan (Western Samoa) and Pedro Sporleder (Argentina) for fighting on the field. Fleming himself was a replacement for Brian Anderson, the original referee, who had retired hurt. Argentina responded angrily to what they interpreted as the dangerous and illegal tackling of their opponents.

After trailing 12–9 at one stage, Western Samoa went on to win comfortably by 35–12. The upshot of this was that it was Western Samoa who progressed with Australia to the quarter-finals. For the first time, one of the eight International Rugby Football Board members failed to go beyond the pool stages of the tournament. In this way it could be said that the Rugby World Cup was achieving one of its aims.

With South Africa still absent, two emerging countries made it to the next stage, since Canada had come second to France in Pool 4. Fiji had done so in the absence of South Africa four years earlier but failed to do so this time. For Romania, who at one time in the 1970s and mid-1980s were expected to make substantial advances in rugby, political upheaval had severe social and cultural repercussions. In rugby, they had become a declining force. Their only success in 1991 was against Fiji (17–15).

Instead it was Canada who were making strides forward. They had not only beaten Fiji (13–3) and Romania (19–11) but in their final game of the pool stage they had only narrowly lost 13–19 to France. Mark Wyatt and Gareth Rees had contributed 33 of the 45 points scored by Canada, thus ensuring that they would meet New Zealand in the quarter-finals.

England, who had beaten the USA 36–6, would play France in a repeat of the previous season's grand slam match in Twickenham in the Five Nations Championship. This game, however, would be in Paris; a prospect to return the compliment, which France relished.

Meanwhile, Scotland had beaten Ireland at Murrayfield in a game in which Gary Armstrong proved to be a vital figure at scrum-half. This meant that Scotland had come top of their pool and consequently would play Western Samoa – a tie which the pre-tournament predictions would have suggested to be a good draw. But by now it was a dubious reward. Peter Fatialofa, the Western Samoa captain, and his hard-tackling colleagues had caused a swift change of mind.

By this stage, with the aid of sudden research and some background knowledge, information had come to hand which boldly outlined the stark New Zealand influence that dominated the team. Along with their captain, Keenan, Pat Lam, Frank Bunce, Timo Tagaloa and Stephen Bachop had all played provincial rugby in New Zealand. They were not the naïve players from a far-flung archipelago in the Pacific, which might have been the first impression when they arrived for the tournament.

Ireland were to face Australia, who had become the tournament favourites to lift the trophy. The All Blacks were not themselves and not striking the high level of play, of discipline and efficiency which had been expected of them after their opening match. They were clearly out of sorts.

They were pedestrian against the USA, and in front of a capacity crowd in Gloucester it was the USA's spirited performance that had drawn attention. For the All Blacks, it was their lack of authority. To everyone's surprise, New Zealand were held for 22 minutes before they eventually took the lead. With six minutes to go, the score stood at 28–6. If a further 18 points were added before the end it did not disguise the fact that New Zealand were not a dominant force.

This was not all the evidence. There was also the performance against Italy to be taken into account. Italy, it is true, had been accused of playing a destructive style as was reflected in the number of penalties awarded against them. There were 37 awarded in the England game which had allowed Jonathan Webb to create a new England record of 24 points in an international. At Welford Road in Leicester the Italians were to accomplish a more polished display. The final score of 31–21 was in the All Blacks' favour but what this fails to indicate is that the Italians outscored their more illustrious opponents by 18–15 in the second half. Furthermore, two Italians were the first to breach the All Blacks defence in the tournament so far. Marcello Cuttitta, who had created such a wonderful impression in 1987, and Massimo Bonomi had scored fine tries. This was in sharp contrast to the two teams who had last met in the World Cup. New Zealand at that time demolished Italy in the opening game by 70 points. This was a satisfying return encounter for Italy while the winners, feeling a little miffed, complained of how Italy were allowed to play on the fringes of the laws. Fortunately for all Europeans, the referee was Kerry Fitzgerald who came from Australia. In such matters as the interpretation of the laws the Antipodeans see more or less eye to eye, which is not to say that they always do with their colleagues from the Northern Hemisphere. New Zealand would face Canada next.

1991 QUARTER-FINALS

Of no small interest at this stage in the progress of the Rugby World Cup was the presence in the quarter-finals of two nations from outside the circle of International Rugby Football Board membership. Fiji had achieved as much in 1987; Canada and Western Samoa had done so this time. Fiji's presence four years earlier in some respects could be said to be by default. Of the eight countries on the Board, South Africa was absent thus leaving a place open at the quarter-final stage. If this was still partly the case in 1991, because with South Africa's continuing absence a place was vacant, Western Samoa had accomplished their right to be present by dismissing Wales from the tournament. There was speculation whether the underdog might achieve the accolade of going even further.

If this were to be the case, the chances were that Western Samoa would be inheritors. There was trepidation north of the border in Scotland in having wrongly anticipated Wales, a known quantity of long-standing even if, in recent years, indifferent quality, as their opponents. Scotland were instead to be confronted not necessarily by a team of alien character, but one of uncertain pedigree. On the evidence so far, the Pacific Islanders were of the kind that had been encountered in New Zealand and therefore relatively familiar. But if the players had been good enough, the argument ran, might they not in the way of these things have qualified for New Zealand and been included among the All Blacks? How good were they? This was their first appearance on the world stage so no one quite knew what to make of them. There had been fluid movement, but the firm memory of their play so far was not so much of this as their undiluted, bone-crunching physicality. Like a wayward juggernaut out of control on the highway, knocking cones to right and to left, so the Western Samoa players left a trail of devastation in their wake. Wales had been unprepared and had been forced to suffer. This was an image which preoccupied Scotland as they contemplated this new and unpredictable phenomenon.

The underdog might have his day elsewhere too. In Lille, New Zealand were preparing to meet Canada. The All Blacks found themselves in the unusual position of not so much concentrating on the forces ranged against them, as attempting to assuage the tormenting demons which were afflicting their own game. They were not playing well. In contrast to four years earlier when, undaunted like a grim destroyer cutting consummately and unscathed through enemy lines, they commanded and won the inaugural tournament, they were no longer creating the clear daylight between them and their challengers that they were so confidently fond of doing. Strangely and uncharacteristically, this was navel-gazing time for the All Blacks. This was a habit which was as much of a stranger to their fearless unconquerable spirit as it would be for them to imagine a dancing, will o'the wisp, finger-tipping passer at second five-eighths. It was out of character.

With untypical introversion entering their game and a caution which inhibited them, every opponent seemed a problem to the All Blacks. Whereas normally – to take liberties with Shakespeare's *King Lear* – 'As flies to wanton boys would Canada be to the All Blacks/They kill them for their sport', this was no longer so, not in 1991 in Lille.

The IRFB member nations occupied the other two matches. For reasons which had been nurtured in the recent history of Europe's Five Nations Championship, the big game belonged to the Parc des Princes in Paris: England versus France. If for a decade in the '70s this hallowed position of Europe's premier fixture belonged to Wales and France, in the two decades that followed, that aura belonged to the historical adversaries whose cultural differences seemed so much at odds across the water from each other. Apart from the occasional intervention from the Celtic fringe, like terriers snapping for attention, the battle royal for European supremacy was joined between England and France. France held sway throughout the '80s, having won six of the nine matches up to 1988, but for the last three years England had triumphed and were to remain unbeaten in the duel until the World Cup match in Pretoria in 1995.

In their last encounter at Twickenham in March, England had won to secure the first grand slam since Bill Beaumont's captaincy in 1980. With France looking to avenge this defeat, the match on 19 October had the makings of a colossal contest. The rivalry was now intense.

The following day in Dublin, Australia would face Ireland. With so much attention focused on Paris, and the perceived discrepancy between the standards and quality of the two teams at Lansdowne Road, this game was relegated as of secondary importance, or at any rate of interest only to the respective teams and their band of supporters. The Australians had dispatched Ireland 33–15 in Sydney in 1987 and the forecast was that it would not be too dissimilar this time. In the event, Lansdowne Road was due for a treat of a game of the kind that myths are made from.

More mundanely to begin with, the underdog upon whose success sport and the generously and interminably romantic often depended, did not have his day. Canada did make New Zealand work hard for their 29–13 victory but

New Zealand, even in automatic mode, had enough will power and nous not to let anything embarrassing slip. The match indicated what had been agreed by most people by now. The All Blacks' machine was far from finely tuned.

If the All Blacks led 21–3 at half-time, Canada, as Italy had done, 'won' the second half 10–8. The All Blacks made it look too much like hard work, which is normally an issue that, even when the opposition give them a hard task, they settle down to solve without ever looking discomposed. Business-like, they merely make the effort look like another day at the office. They work hard to reap their rich rewards.

In 1991 this did not appear to be the case. There was a malaise that had crept into their camp and which had been put down to a disagreement among the management over which style to play. Before departure from New Zealand there was an apparent difference of rugby philosophy between Alex Wyllie, from South Island's Canterbury, and John Hart, from Auckland in the North Island. In the absence of Buck Shelford, the captain who had led them to unprecedented success in the previous three years, there was no charisma or even simply a strong character to restore a sense of clear direction. Shelford had not been selected. He was missed and New Zealand suffered.

At Murrayfield, Western Samoa's colourful adventure came to an end with a 28–6 defeat. Scotland were comfortable winners with Gavin Hastings in magnificent form as he gave a fine display of the full-back 's art. Not only that, but he kicked one prodigious penalty from 10 metres within his own half. He had spearheaded his team's momentum from the start and had stifled his opponent's burgeoning reputation. Here were passages of ebullient play which left an indelible memory.

That Western Samoa felt they had accomplished so much, and presumably beyond what they had originally expected, meant that even in defeat they ran a lap of honour. They also gave one final rendering of 'Manu Samoa', their equivalent of the more familiar All Black 'Haka'. They went home to a rapturous welcome in Apia, where for their televised games 20,000 people gathered in the rugby stadium. Clearly Rugby World Cup was reaching those parts which, hitherto, rugby had not reached.

In Paris and Dublin two magnificent contests were about to unfold, each with its own distinctive flavour.

The first, on the Saturday in Parc des Princes, saw France favourites to win, although neither team, as yet, could take any comfort from their performances to date. For those who could not make up their minds as to the likely outcome, they could always turn to that capricious indicator of form and instrument for judgement: the law of averages. This suggested that with England's recent run of successes then this must be France's turn to win. This rationale was flawed, as it most often is, and was comfort only to the emotional and the nervous.

There were those who believed that England had been bitterly disappointed that they had lost the first game to New Zealand. They had to come to play France in Paris, whereas New Zealand had the easier option of playing Canada. Disappointed they may have been but not 'bitterly' so.

'We had never expected to win,' says Geoff Cooke. 'In fact we could cope with the route that presented itself to us. Psychologically, it didn't matter to us if we lost to the All Blacks. The way it turned out we had France to begin with and we were one of the few nations who had a consistently good record against them. Paris never held any fears for us. And after that we knew exactly what to expect against Scotland in Murrayfield. Each represented familiar territory for us. The other route meant we would have had to face the possibilities of Australia in the semi-final and New Zealand in the final.

'After the first round we and our wives and partners went off for a two-day break in Jersey. It was like taking the cork out of the bottle. Letting off steam in that way meant we might be better prepared for the two big contests that lay ahead. It worked.'

Cooke's strategy was reminiscent of that of Franz Beckenbauer when he managed the German team in the 1990 World Cup in Italy. After the round robin of the first round and before the knockout stage began, he sent all his players home to their wives and families. Having been in each others' company for so long and having spent so much of their time on the training pitch, the players, he argued, needed a break before acquiring the fresh impetus to complete their task. They did so.

England looked to have done so, too. They were trying circumstances.

The match was a full-blooded, frequently tempestuous affair, of unrelenting bone and unyielding muscle. Neither the argument nor, apparently, the physical challenge finished with the final whistle, for as soon as it did blow accusations were levelled by Daniel Dubroca, the French coach, against David Bishop, the New Zealand referee. Dubroca called him 'a cheat'. Not only this, but Dubroca was accused of assaulting the New Zealander. It was, to say the least, a lively encounter. Also, by the time the final whistle blew we had seen the last of Serge Blanco, after his 93rd appearance for France and with a career total of 38 tries making him second only to David Campese in number of international tries scored. For over a decade since beginning in 1980, he had epitomised the unique spirit of French rugby. He was the quintessence of what the French love about rugby football: the free and fluid movement; adventure and the glamour of the cavalier; the delicacy and wit of the consummate entertainer. This is only one side of the affair. It is not all slap and tickle, for all this can unravel and the infatuation end in turbulence and flaming rows. Not even Blanco was immune to the tempestuous undercurrent and, for once in a long career, was involved in the first fracas of the afternoon. He was told later by Bishop that he was within one incident of being sent off the field. Such was the influence of the vigorous preparations and the 'needle' beforehand. There was much hot blood in circulation.

The game ultimately revolved around France's choice to attempt to play England at their own game. Instinctive flair or risk-taking flamboyance had no part to play in the afternoon's battle. This was to be a battle of strength and brute force; animal pride was at stake, pure and simple, the lord of the jungle. France in their machismo vanity (or their blindness) chose to ignore what to others had always been plain to see. If the battleground was to be at the front in the close quarter and the rules of engagement were primarily to be determined by the phalanx of eight men in the scrum, then England might feel at home. This strategy was tailor-made for them. Their success was based on it; they had made the style of game their own. France misguidedly set out to prove that they were better.

With Eric Champ, their flanker, the epitome of in-your-face, won't-take-step-back hawkishness, alongside Marc Cecillon and Laurent Cabannes and the rest, France might well have thought that they were well-equipped to match England. In Mick Skinner, Peter Winterbottom and Mike Teague England had men of the soil, honest and true, and if bodies had to be sacrificed and the soul put to the test, these players could not be doubted. They had proved time and again that they were men to go into the jungle, not only knowing that there would be a goodly chance of survival, but emerging at the other end having had a fine time along the way.

There were no fun and larks to be had in Parc des Princes. England were capable of suffocating a team into submission by sheer pressure. Starvation was part of their campaign, too. This they were able to do with the immense presence of Paul Ackford and Wade Dooley in the line-out, and in Paris they were on commanding form. England were dominant in all the tight phases. For England Rory Underwood and Will Carling, wing and centre respectively, scored the tries and full-back Jonathan Webb kicked three penalties and a conversion. For France, winger Jean-Baptiste Lafond scored a try and Thierry Lacroix, the fly-half, kicked two penalties. But the contest belonged firmly among the forwards. The match may have been the 'death of romanticism' for Jean Trillo, the backs coach for France, but the score of 19–10 was simple joy for Roger Uttley, England's coach.

France failed to retreat with dignity. They departed in acrimony, accusing the referee of cheating. Furthermore, it was alleged that as the teams trooped back to the dressing rooms Dubroca grabbed Bishop by the collar and Pascal Ondarts, the French prop, was said to have aimed a punch at the referee. Dubroca's version was that he 'simply congratulated the referee after the match. I said "Bravo". If I touched him it was a fraternal gesture as I know him so well.' Albert Ferrasse, the President of the French Federation, maintained that Dubroca's English 'was not good enough to abuse the referee seriously'. Russ Thomas, the Chairman of the Rugby World Cup was aware of 'an incident', but since no official complaint was made no further action was necessary. Soon afterwards Daniel Dubroca resigned.

Serge Blanco retired from a game that had graced such a luminous living expression of rugby's capacity for rhapsody and the instinctive gamble. Rugby's dilemma is to reserve a place for such romantic figures to inspire the young in an age so well prescribed for automatons to rule.

Dublin was set for a different mood, a game of unexpected and flourishing drama; a pulsating and feverish affair. The contest reversed all the wiseacres' prophecies into an airy nothing. Once more, when doubts begin to creep in about rugby's capacity for compelling and transfixing suspense, then a game of spectacle and thrilling enterprise makes an entrance in the most unlikely places.

The game in Dublin was supposed to be a forgone conclusion with Australia simply meant to stride into the semi-final without breaking sweat. In the event, a thrilling drama unfolded with nail-biting heroics and cliff-hanging suspense. Admittedly, there was a no-nonsense bare-knuckle bar brawl to open proceedings, but with the hot-headed turmoil out of the way the stage was set for the passion and the glory of rugby.

David Campese was to become the most prominent personality of the 1991 campaign. He set Dublin alight with the first of his two tries when on an angled 30-metre run he crossed over in the 17th minute. Lynagh converted. Two Ralph Keyes penalties brought the game level at half-time.

Lynagh kicked a penalty. Keyes dropped a goal. However, Australia opened a six-point lead when with another Campese touch and Lynagh's conversion the score reached 15–9. Despite Ireland's magnificent performance this looked to have settled the matter, but Keyes's persistent kicks brought the score back so that Ireland were only three points adrift. Pulses were racing. So was Gordon Hamilton, the Ballymena flanker. He chased the ball. He was out on his own but with a long way to go. On he safely went for 40 metres to score a remarkable and, for all the world to believe, a winning try. With Keyes's conversion and barely five minutes to go, feet were for good reason beginning to dance: 18–15.

Only Australia thought and believed otherwise. They still needed a slice of luck. For sure, what luck there was came their way and deserted the Irish. Ireland failed fatally to find the touch-line and so get out of their own half. The ball went short near their own 22-metre line. The line-out led to a scrum, still within reach of the Irish line. Lynagh had taken over the captaincy after Farr-Jones had gone off the field injured. From the scrum, 15 metres out, he called a manoeuvre which they had practised in the days before the game. Campese ran into midfield in the planned move, was held, just, but kept his composure to pass to Lynagh to score the winning try. It was a breathless, comic-strip ending.

It was an heroic contest but one which will return to haunt the Irish, in that having achieved a winning position they found that, with only minutes to go, they were within touching distance of unforgettable greatness and of legend. The score 19–18 will be indelibly imprinted on their memories forever and will be a demon that will, at the call of midnight when sleep will not come, revisit all who played for Ireland that day. Australia moved on.

1991 SEMI-FINALS

The semi-finals held the intriguing prospect of old and familiar foes coming together in combat. A long heritage insinuated itself into both games.

England and Scotland first embarked on their series of duels in a game in Raeburn Place in Edinburgh in 1871, when each side contained 20 players (it was 1877 when teams were reduced to 15). This was the first-ever international match and remained as such for four years, until Ireland entered the fray and later Wales (1881). By the time they met in the 1991 semi-final there had been 108 fixtures in the series which since 1879 had contested for the Calcutta Cup. England accounted for 52 victories to Scotland's 39. Australia and New Zealand, who nowadays compete for the Bledisloe Cup, had played each other 92 times since 1903, but this was the first time for the game to be played on neutral territory. The All Blacks had won 64 of these games against Australia's 24.

If England had beaten Scotland at their last meeting at Twickenham (21–12) to win the 1991 grand slam, on their last visit to Murrayfield the previous season when both teams were contesting for that accolade, England lost (13–7). In their most recent two-match series, Australia had won the first test in Sydney (21–12) and lost the second in Auckland (6–3).

As had happened the previous weekend, we were destined to see contrasting games, with Dublin on the Sunday once more providing the setting for the enthralling entertainment.

The previous day, England, in pitiless mood, broke down whatever resistance Scotland had in the same destructive, power-driving way they had pulverised France in the quarter-final. England were fearful of what might be thought of as 'Fortress Murrayfield' and the manner in which, when pride was being put on the line, Scotland's players would appear to expand in mind and body in proportion to what was demanded of them. In other words, they could rise to the occasion like no one else when faced with England and be inspired to send their historical oppressor's proud army home to the words and the swelling chorus of their cherished 'Flower of Scotland'.

Unquestionably, there was some 'baggage' attached to the confrontation, of which Geoff Cooke, England's manager, was well aware. He and his team were not about to take any risks and would play in the way they knew best, which, to make sense, is as it should be. Roger Uttley, the coach and former great England back row forward who knew when to have manners and when to be unashamedly ruthless, said beforehand: 'It is not a pick-up-the-ball-and-run game. Rugby has always been a game of territory and possession. The England team are playing for themselves. They want to achieve as much as possible, to be remembered for being successful, not for being glorious failures.' They were not to follow these tenets for the entire game, a lapse in focus which they would no doubt come to regret.

Knowing their superior power at forward and exercising it to the full they tormented and frustrated Scotland into submission. With Ackford and Dooley ruling the line-out, Scotland did not win a ball for 20 minutes. Yet for all this, with a flow of possession, domination of territory, with Rob Andrew in such authoritative form at fly-half, and leaving Scotland scratching helplessly around for any scraps from England's brimming table, the contest remained in the balance. Indeed, England might have lost it. Webb at full-back was off-key with his kicks so that the scoreboard did not reflect England's obvious superiority. This kept them on a knife edge. There was no cushion of comfort, which the relentless work of the forwards deserved.

With Finlay Calder, Derek White and John Jeffrey such persuasive and predatory influences in the back row, anything might be possible. When the moment allowed, Hastings could intervene to make a significant contribution in the wink of an eye. No matter how dominant England were and had been, if the score remained close a momentary chance could swing the game in an unexpected direction. Had Hastings been in more conventional mode with his kicking and had he succeeded with a penalty opportunity which, for him, appeared a formality, it would have been his team that would have gone into a 9–6 lead in the last quarter. Throughout the game, England left open, however slight, a window of opportunity. It was to prove to be their Achilles heel, not in this game but in many games to come. This was to be a dangerous and recurring phenomenon and, like the ghost at the feast, would at intervals return to scupper their ambitions.

However, in Rob Andrew, England had in their midst a player who knew, in extreme circumstances, how to win a game and was frequently to do so. Andrew was a disciplined and efficient player, highly motivated and, for all his geniality and smiling presence, he had a substantial block of ice deeply embedded in his temperament. He was unflinching in his understanding of the parameters within which Geoff Cooke's England should play. In determining the purely physical sense of a contest – where, geographically, to play the game, how, tactically, to encourage his own team and frustrate the opposition – Andrew captained the team; his hands were on the tiller.

There were times when you wished he would test the waters and chance his arm a little in the wilder streams of a game; to extend those limits which he seemed always to impose on his own talent. Such men of chance are few. If unable to fulfil other people's expectations of him, Andrew could invariably cast an eye in the direction of the scoreboard, acknowledge what it read and feel vindicated. There are few fly-halves who could do that as often as Andrew did. He was to do so again when playing Scotland as an act of vengeance against the country which had denied him the grand slam the previous year. The score told the very prosaic and pedestrian progress of the narrative. Webb's two penalties had been matched by Hastings's brace.

In the failing light, Rory Underwood had a long run along the touch-line in a desperate attempt to re-ignite the dying embers of England's game. If the wing could not quite do it, then Andrew could. He dropped the goal that put England through and Scotland out of the 1991 Rugby World Cup.

The match, in truth, could have sunk the heart of the less partisan observer. Averting the jaundiced eye away from Murrayfield and looking towards Dublin, the dullness evaporated and a new and clearer vision appeared.

Once more, hope would be restored as once more the Rugby World Cup, with all its intense and often forbidding expectations, provided a spectacle of vibrant and riveting rugby. The difference lay in being able to distinguish between winning the ball to play with it, as opposed to winning the ball so as to deny it to the others; one chooses to attack the opposition's line, the other to defend one's own. With the ball we can score, says one, or, says the other, without the ball the other team can't; positive and negative.

Australia gave New Zealand something close to a run-around at Lansdowne Road, in a manner that hardly seemed possible, considering their opponent's overpowering stature in rugby and the way that those black serried ranks are never less than cohesive and always a cut above the rest. Even if the All Blacks had not been themselves throughout the 1991 tournament, it could hardly have been predicted that they would be dismantled so comprehensively by Bob Dwyer's commanding team. Australia gave such a supremely compulsive performance as to leave their opponents bereft and with nowhere to run. This was a singular experience, unparalleled in its uniqueness. The All Blacks have never before or since been placed in so inferior a position as they were on that memorable day. Australia were superb.

Despite Ian Jones's magnificent efforts in the line-out, the All Blacks were outplayed in the tight as well as in the fast and loose. The trio at the back – Simon Poidevin, Willie Ofahengaue and Troy Coker – were immense where the All Backs are traditionally so strong, while the midfield was tied down by Lynagh, Tim Horan and Jason Little. Farr-Jones marshalled his convoy. Rarely, if at any time in their history, can the All Blacks have been reduced to impotence. If they did find that they had a slice of territorial advantage, they hardly found themselves in a position to threaten the Wallaby line. Indeed, it was not until after the interval that Grant Fox had his first chance to aim at goal. This was the distance that Australia maintained between their line and their Tasman Sea neighbours.

But all this was a sequel to the brilliance of Australia's beginning. After seven minutes, David Campese scored a try of daring magnificence. Entering the line in the fly-half position and running on a long arc and a diagonal sweep from right to left, he aimed for the corner. The All Blacks strangely stood off.

No one committed himself to a tackle. Onwards the charismatic winger ran. Lulled by the thought that he might do something to change his line of running or his pace – to halt, to start, to quicken his speed, to slow down, to pass or throw his familiar 'goose step' – they watched as if mesmerised as he glided past. They were as if transfixed; monuments in a landscape. New Zealand had been hoodwinked and by the time they came to realise it, they were four points down. Lynagh kicked a penalty and the Lynagh/Campese combination conjured another try. Lynagh chipped the ball. Campese gathered behind New Zealand's defence. While he veered in-field, and the cover defence converged, the winger in the same movement flipped the ball over his shoulder, blind to what was behind but where his intuition hinted that Horan might be. The centre received the ball as if by magic and scored. It was 13–0 and New Zealand had hardly been in the contest. They were forced from the start to chase the score and to play, as they say, 'catch-up'.

The crowd were left to admire John Kirwan, who had his fine moments, but left to wonder to what extent the All Blacks missed Michael Jones on the flank, who, because of his religious conviction, refused to play on Sunday. The match confirmed what many had believed all along. New Zealand in 1991 had been well below the standards they had always set for themselves. Fox kicked two penalties and with Lynagh kicking another, the score was 16–6 at the end.

1991 THIRD PLACE PLAY-OFF

A crowd of 40,000 turned up at Cardiff Arms Park to see the penultimate game of the 1991 Rugby World Cup. The compliment was sadly not reciprocated. If there had been reservations about the value of this game in the minds of the players beforehand, the manner of the play, instead of washing away the misgivings as it had done in Rotorua in 1987, simply confirmed them on this occasion. There was little enthusiasm from either New Zealand or Scotland. The spark of intent started and ended with the All Blacks' performance of the 'Haka'. Increasingly over the last decade and more, the All Blacks have turned this Maori battle cry into an intimidating prologue. At Cardiff, Va'aiga Tuigamala broke ranks with his team's alignment and advanced menacingly towards the Scottish players, who stood their ground. When he came face to face with Tony Stanger and John Jeffrey, the New Zealander found that the Scottish flanker merely smiled at him. There was in this instance something intrinsically silly in turning the 'Haka' into an exaggerated threat with pantomime overtones.

The play-off is always a difficult match to play. In this instance, with teams having suffered their defeats in the semi-finals and in New Zealand's case only three days before, it was asking a great deal of the players to overcome their deep disappointment and to give another purposeful and integrated performance. 'I think the third place game is of more commercial value than playing value,' concluded John Hart. 'The tournament comes to an end when a team gets beaten.' It is a problem for the tournament organisers who want to establish a final order of merit and, it has to be said, raise extra revenue. Less of a priority, perhaps, is the need to fill the gap before the final itself is played. In which case, as Hart pointed out, it might have been delayed to a day closer to the final itself.

There was also another salient point to observe. There is constant reference made to the amount of pressure a rugby player has to bear, or any other sportsman or woman for that matter, but it is a fact of sporting life that the ingredient is necessary to make a good contest. Without the 'needle', which brings a sense of earnest and a burden of responsibility, the competitive edge diminishes. With pressure, players are made to care; without it, they become careless. In Cardiff there was too much that was careless. The day was done, the battle over. New Zealand were weary for home now that the spoils belonged to others and not to them. They simply were uninterested in being, in their view, so low in the world's pecking order. Unlike Wales in 1987, the All Blacks were not about to return to their homeland to boast that they were third in the world.

The match had little to commend it other than the try that Walter Little scored. It was the only one in the game and fitting that Little should have scored it. With three minutes remaining, only three points separated the two teams when the All Black centre clinched the victory. It had remained a mystery why the All Black management had persistently ignored the claims of the centre from North Harbour. He had had one full game against Italy, yet he was a lovely player with many delicate touches. He had speed, good hands and a sharp eye for the gap. All these qualities were on display in Cardiff and transparently so, with so much that was inferior around him. His was the one bright light in an otherwise excruciatingly mediocre game, full of errors and rank bad play. Jon Preston, who had missed four of his seven chances at goal, and Gavin Hastings, who had another fine match and twice brought down Terry Wright in full flight and saved certain scores, kicked five penalties between them in New Zealand's 13–6 win.

The game is memorable as the last one played by Finlay Calder of Stewart's-Melville and John Jeffrey of Kelso. They had played 34 and 40 times respectively for Scotland, and from 1986 (Jeffrey had begun in 1984) they were the mainstay of the Scottish back row, their names familiar as a duo with Jeffrey easily recognisable because of his striking blond hair. No longer would we hear the rich Borders brogue of Bill McLaren calling out their names as if forever bracketed together; the one was always present where the other was, like those two inveterate cricket enthusiasts Charters and Caldicott in Alfred Hitchcock's *The Lady Vanishes*. Jeffrey and Calder had played their last. We could only have wished they had a better platform to dignify their end.

1991 WORLD CUP FINAL

The Southern Hemisphere held their grip on the Webb Ellis Cup as Australia, following their neighbours in 1987, won the trophy in front of a capacity 62,500 crowd at Twickenham which included the Queen, the Princess Royal and Prince Edward. If Australia were not dominant in the way they had been in their previous matches they had nonetheless, taking their performances in their entirety, proved themselves worthy world champions. They obstinately refused to knuckle under in the final when England had put them under intense pressure and denied them but a modicum of possession. Their wonderfully varied success and survival instincts on the way to the final were testimony to their deserving of the title 'the best team in the world'. Their reputation rested not on the last game alone.

Australia had shown in their awkward opening game in Llanelli, when Argentina came back within winning distance in the second half, that, like supreme tennis players having dropped their serve, they could respond straight away to recover what was lost. This they were to show more dramatically and graphically when they returned from the brink against Ireland. In that match, with two minutes to go, they were brave in their composure to mount a final winning attack. It was 'the' single moment, if such there can be, which marked them as champions.

Against Western Samoa at Pontypool in the worst conditions of the tournament they showed, despite their rare experience of such persistent rain, that they could adapt their tactics accordingly. They did so, too, without their much respected captain, Nick Farr-Jones. However much the All Blacks had lost their sense of keen direction, the feeling persisted that whichever team lifted the trophy would first have to overcome them. The formidable aura that attaches to them insists that it should be so. When, like an animal in its death throes whose instinct thrashes out in a last bid of defiance, the All Blacks threw themselves into a desperate final lunge, Australia turned to their well-organised defence. This disciplined and unbending defence won the day in the final. Against Wales, whose psyche had been all but destroyed, Australia ran in the points.

It was Australia's remarkably resilient defence that won the day at Twickenham. To undo England, it had to be unbending. Simon Poidevin and Willie Ofahengaue were supreme in covering the ground and turning up at those places where they were most needed. If John Eales had little return from Ackford and Dooley in the line-out, the young Australian lock ensured he made his mark ubiquitously elsewhere. He showed his potential as a fine footballer not just in the engine room. As captain, gifted player and ambassador, he was to become in the next decade one of Australia's greatest sportsmen of all time.

Rob Andrew at fly-half received double the amount of possession as Lynagh, his opposite number, and ran the ball wide and far from the start, but it was Australia who scored the only try of the game. As so often in the match, Australia found themselves deep in defence. To begin with, Will Carling's teasing kick to Underwood was latched on to by Horan, who then managed to break out. From a line-out on England's try-line Ofahengaue won the ball and the pack drove behind him for Tony Daly to be awarded the try. Converting this and kicking a penalty into the blustery wind, Lynagh gave Australia a nine-point lead at the interval, while Webb missed twice for England.

A controversial incident in the second half provided a talking point. With Peter Winterbottom making an extra man in the threequarter line, he saw his pass to Underwood knocked down by Campese. The English winger was in the clear and would undoubtedly have scored. Was it an attempt at an interception or a deliberate knock to concede three points rather than allow the chance for a try ? This score, with the conversion, would have given England a 12–9 lead. This was a point to discuss, but not for too long. Lynagh and Webb exchanged penalties in the second half to give a 12–6 final score. The Wallaby line was not crossed. This was managed only three times in the whole tournament, twice by Argentina in the first game and, of course, by Hamilton after his breathless charge in Dublin.

It was a resounding game full of thrilling rugby but one which posed a vital question about England. To what extent did England, having heard so much adverse comment about their style of play and aware of the advice proffered – from the lofty heights of the media pundits to the sages in the fug of the pub – choose to depart from all their rehearsals and their prepared scripts? At the last and critical moment, when rugby's greatest prize was on offer, England decided to play differently; to play in a style they had not contemplated in the previous rounds. In the final game of the 1991 tournament England committed themselves totally to the running game. To what extent was this misplaced, and by ignoring that area among the forwards where they were most universally feared did they contribute to their own downfall? There had been suggestions that they should play, for instance, such rugby as schoolboys should wish to emulate and that the way they had played hitherto, so the argument ran, was unlikely to achieve that.

This matter of style preoccupies the teams in the Northern Hemisphere in a way that barely matters to those below the equator. It is not a conundrum for them. This was illustrated by David Kirk's rejoinder to a question after his team had won the World Cup in 1987. With New Zealand having been interpreted as efficient, grimly disciplined and somewhat less than free-flowing, Kirk was queried about the manner of their play in tones which suggested: 'Wonderful accomplishment and all that but what about the style...?'

'You Brits,' answered Kirk, 'you make me laugh...' His response simply trailed away as if the question was meaningless and had no need of further amplification. In other words, why worry about such finery as style which so preoccupies the 'Brits'. The objective is to win and to do so in a manner best suited to the talents of the team at that particular time and place.

It was England's dilemma. England's forwards were held with fear, 'if not with respect', as Geoff Cooke acknowledged. This was plain for all to see, as it would also be in 1995. To what extent, though, were England's threequarters held in such esteem?

What of Jeremy Guscott and Will Carling in the centre? What of Rory Underwood and Simon Halliday on the wing? The problem was that no one was in any position to judge since so little had been seen of them in the tournament. It was potential unfulfilled, which Cooke conceded in his pre-match interviews. He had achieved a great deal. He had turned England's lack of good fortune. His team had won 23 of 33 internationals.

Paul Ackford explained that the final sessions of the week were slick with the running game. There was a difference though from the practice on the training field to the execution against Australia. 'When it came to the big day,' he remembers, 'we could not transfer the excellence of the unopposed training sessions to the intensity of the live match. Around half-time, when we started to get on top of the big Aussie forwards, we should have thrown the running rugby option out of the window. We didn't, the rest is history.'

Geoff Cooke explains: 'We decided to change our tactics as a team. The players agreed. Australia went into that game with three players with experience at playing in the full-back position: Roebuck, Egerton and Campese. If we kicked to them they all could position themselves to respond and to do so to our disadvantage. They also had a very powerful pack. They expected us to play in our usual style and they had already beaten us 40–15 in Sydney in July. Rugby is a game of tactics; to out-think the opposition. In the pre-match build-up, the players were comfortable with the change.'

Rugby could inherit a rich legacy from the Australian team of 1991 as the game had from the Cup winners in 1987. New Zealand had set the high standards then and were to do so for the next three years.

Australia, in contrast to England, had allowed the threequarters to flourish. Little and Horan had had their moments. Campese had strutted his stuff. Marty Roebuck, too, had exerted his influence at full-back. Lynagh, appearing for the 53rd time with his partner Farr-Jones at half-back, had been prominent throughout.

Could there ever be a time, for instance, when a wing became such a focal theme in the team's tactics? This might have appeared a small point, but it did indicate Australia's and Bob Dwyer's willingness to shift where the emphasis should lie within any team. The influence of the front five is well understood and the pervasive contribution goes without question. And the line-out? Well, yes. And the half-backs? Well, of course. On such issues there is much to pontificate over through the long winter evenings. How many, however, will put the wing to good use rather than allow him to languish in the hope that something might soon come his way?

The wing is on the periphery of the game; a man who really should be thankful for small mercies. He is an afterthought among the larger issues of the team-talk; a footnote in the coach's manual.

It was always to Dwyer's credit that he accommodated Campese's needs. He was allowed the freedom to run at will. But the essence of his extraordinary talent was recognised within the team and allowances made for it. His gifts were harnessed to the team's strategy and to its ultimate benefit. He was there to attract and to distract attention; he was included or missed. He was never ignored. Few coaches have the wit or the courage to consider the wing in this way as a primary source of interest and around whom schemes might be plotted. No one in the history of the game had implemented the wing's talents and given him his rightful place in a rugby blueprint in quite the way Dwyer insinuated Campese into his tactics.

This, too, would be the legacy of the Rugby World Cup in 1991. The inheritor would be the Rugby World Cup in 1995. While Campese enchanted the world in 1991, a 15-year-old boy in New Zealand might just have been dreaming at that time of how he, too, might one day care to take the rugby world by storm. In four years' time Jonah Lomu would, like a tornado, create havoc on well-constructed defences and turn on their head the preconceptions and prejudices of what a rugby union winger can or cannot accomplish. This isolated position would once more have its time in the sun.

MATCHMAKERS

The outstanding individual player of the 1991 Rugby World Cup was unquestionably David Campese of Australia. If he began with a couple of tries at Stradey Park in Llanelli against Argentina and ended his tournament shadowed by mild controversy at Twickenham when his attempt at an interception was construed as having been a deliberate knock-on and could have resulted in a penalty try, he reached his apotheosis in Dublin. He scored twice against Ireland in the quarter-final and in the semi-final against New Zealand he scored a try himself and created a superlative one for Tim Horan. Coming so close together, the impression remained that he was touched with stardust and that, with sleight of hand and dancing feet, he was capable of conjuring a magical score. Against the All Blacks, the sway of his head or even the wink of his eye seemed enough to mesmerise the defence into suspension. In the mind's eye nothing stirs except the motion of a single man in gold.

It was his good fortune, and ours who watched, that his coach was Bob Dwyer. Australia's coach admitted that much of the team's tactics revolved around their expert wing. It's so often a position that is neglected, making the most gifted of players player feel isolated, but Dwyer knew that with Campese the position could be one of the sources of his team's strengths, so he made the wing a focus of attention. This was not exactly perceptive – Campese's talent was there for all to see – but it might be thought courageous. By and large, rugby coaches are a timid and cautious crowd, preferring to set narrow limits to the core of tactical choices. They are wary of their players, in whom they clearly lack confidence, and wish to curtail their activities. They are of a mind to be negative rather than positive. In their bunker on the touch-line, and incapable of influencing the great events on the field, they are averse to risk. They are neurotically and permanently, according to the body language and facial contortions, on the edge of a nervous breakdown.

To attempt to bring a wing into play is to increase exponentially the margins of error. The more passes are given once the ball is released from the forward's grip and the further it moves away from the steaming pack, so the tension heightens, so the coach's torment increases. No, the wing does not figure large in the coach's personal rugby manual. But with Dwyer, because of Campese, it did. Such prominence to a wing was not be recognised again until four years later in South Africa.

There were great wings around at this time: Ieuan Evans of Wales, Rory Underwood of England, Philippe Saint-Andre of France, John Kirwan of New Zealand, Simon Geoghegan of Ireland. But no team took the position into such prominence as Dwyer did for Australia. If all the others were forced to languish in the margins of the game until it was deigned to be appropriate, Campese was, to Dwyer, deserving of a major chapter. Wingers were always onlookers from the side, rarely partakers of the main event. While each of the other nations could survive without their wingers, since so much of the emphasis was laid elsewhere, Australia would have been dismembered without Campese in 1991.

If the goose-stepping action which he sometimes introduced to disarm a would-be tackler and to deceive him was somewhat unstylish, Campese's manner of play transcended the limits which are so often imposed on his position. He was an original. He was seen at his best during the 1991 Rugby World Cup.

Wherever he went and whichever game he played he carried with him the following poem by Nancye Sims, which is Kiplingesque in its affirming sentiment:

Winners take chances.
Like everyone else, they fear failing but refuse to let fear control them.
Winners don't give up.
When life gets rough, they hang in until the going gets better.
Winners are flexible.
They realise there is more than one way and are willing to try others.
Winners know they are not perfect.
They respect their weaknesses while making the most of their strengths.
Winners fall, but they don't stay down.
They stubbornly refuse to let a fall keep them from climbing...
Winners don't blame fate for their failures nor luck for their success.
Winners accept responsibility for their lives.
Winners are positive thinkers who see good in all things.
From the ordinary, they make the extraordinary.

Winners believe in the path they have chosen even when it's hard,
even when others can't see where they are going.
Winners are patient.
They know a goal is only as worthy as the effort required to achieve it.
Winners are people like you.
They make this place a better place to be.

Another colleague could also claim to have been one of the prominent players in the 1991 RWC. Michael Lynagh had a wonderful tournament. After Nick Farr-Jones's injury in the 11th minute against Western Samoa, the leadership responsibilities rested on the fly-half's shoulders. The scrum-half returned for the quarter-final against Ireland, but once more he retired hurt in the 18th minute of the game. Not only was Lynagh a master fly-half, but he was also a shrewd and assured captain at a time of extreme demand, and no more so than in Australia's first match in Dublin. Both Tim Horan and John Eales confirmed Lynagh's major contribution to the quarter-final victory.

'After Hamilton had scored for Ireland,' says Eales, 'we were left to believe that we were on our plane home. It seemed that our World Cup chance was all over. But Lynagh's captaincy was outstanding. It was as if he had scripted the scenario that was to come. "We're going to kick deep. They're going to kick to touch. Our throw in. We're going to do this, we're going to do that to win the game." That's what he said. And that's how it worked out. It was extraordinary.'

Tim Horan, his colleague on the next two campaigns, recollects the occasion in the same way. 'We were comfortable,' he remembers. 'The match had been wrapped up with five minutes to go. Then the 15–9 lead evaporated. And instead Ireland were ahead 18–15. We need a try to win the game. Our coach, Bob Dwyer, had instilled a confidence in us and that held us together when the pressure was on. We need that against Ireland. Michael [Lynagh] gave us a briefing and said he was going to kick long. He outlined what he would like to happen. And it did...exactly as he said.' He and Eales would return for two more World Cups.

Eales, only 21 at the time, must have learnt from that experience. He would eventually play for his country 86 times and be captain on 55 occasions. 'Lynagh was so composed. His composure and self assurance translated themselves to the team as a whole. He was the reason we didn't have to go home early,' he concluded.

Lynagh had a wonderful tournament as a prolific scorer with his boot, accumulating 66 points in the 6 fixtures, and also as general and a try-maker.

If they had not 'blown it' in the final match at Twickenham, doubtless the whole of the England pack might have been included, collectively, as a personality. Even so, they were immensely powerful and stamped their mark on the tournament. From within their force it would be invidious to choose anyone in particular. They acted solidly as one. From the beginning, England's pack was feared in a way that no other set of forwards were. They seemed to be set apart from the team as a whole. There may have been comments about the All Black team or even individuals within it, and the Australians were respected and came to be looked upon as favourites, but there was a kind of team ethos which applied to them.

For England, it was always the pack of forwards, even though they had immensely charismatic players like Guscott, or Carling, or Underwood and an indefatigable winner in Andrew. It always came back to the forwards in the end. They shaped the team and gave it character. So dominant themselves, they denied the others their chance to an extent that in the end proved to be their Achilles heel. If a team plays what is referred to as an 'expansive' game, they can choose to play differently when they recognise their forward strength; but it rarely, if ever, works the other way around. A team cannot adapt in a day or a week of training from employing a forward-orientated strategy to one that wishes to play with aplomb and to aspire to a 15-man adventure. England were not accustomed to playing that way in a proper contest.

Gavin Hastings had a wonderful tournament. He was the master full-back against Western Samoa. That he managed to kick a penalty goal from ten metres within his own half in that game was a bonus to what was a brilliant and inspiring all-round display.

In Marcello Cuttitta Italy had a wonderful wing who had also played impressively in the World Cup in 1987. He and his colleague Massimo Bonomi scored the first tries against the All Blacks.

Gareth Rees consistently made a difference to Canada. He was a player who singularly kept his team in touch when all could so easily fall apart. No one player exerted such an influence on the progress of his team in implementing their tactics and, along with Mark Wyatt, in kicking goals. Rees was to play in all four World Cups of the 20th century.

The 1991 Rugby World Cup was an outstanding success. The Tournament Director was Ray Williams. He had had a long and distinguished period as administrator first with the Central Council of Physical Recreation (CCPR) and then with the Welsh Rugby Union. While a WRU coaching organiser – the first of its kind anywhere in the world – in the late 1960s and 1970s he had exerted an uniquely eminent influence on the development of the game worldwide. He had made a significant contribution in helping rugby union to change from merely a recreational pursuit to a major competitive sport. This difference is crystallised in the saying: 'People play rugby to be fit and not to be fit to play rugby.' He saw rugby as an athletic pursuit, not merely a leisurely pastime. Williams made his mark on the game not only as an eminent thinker but also as a man of practical ability: he accomplished things, he was a 'doer'.

His conclusion was that 'the 1991 Rugby World Cup was an outstanding success and exceeded all expectations. It took rugby football to a new eminence on the world's sporting stage...'

He tempered his 'critically objective report' by concluding: 'Ideally, the Rugby World Cup should be organised in one country, but using that yard stick there are very few places in the world where it could be held. Scotland, Ireland and Wales would, for various reasons, immediately be excluded and it could only be held in England if soccer stadia were used to stage some of the matches.

'It would appear that for the future at least in this part of the world, the tournament should be confined to the four home unions and that France should be invited to stage the tournament on its own. It has the grounds and the infrastructure...

'One of the greatest shortcomings of the Five Host Unions concept was the failure of the unions to think globally. In the early days of the exercise, the Tournament Director was continually stressing that RWC 1991 was not a series of internationals but that it was a tournament and each host union had an input to make, not for its own sake but as an essential part of the whole... For the most part, host unions acted independently and sometimes even parochially. With the exception of France, they seemed to be over-concerned about finances. "Who pays?" was repeated *ad nauseam* and there seemed to be attempts all along the line to charge as much as possible to the RWC, even when plainly it was a host union responsibility.'

However, if the tournament of 1987 had released the concept of a Rugby World Cup on an uncertain and sceptical world, the 1991 tournament confirmed its place in the universal sporting calendar. If there were any remaining Doubting Thomases, they were left whispering in a gale-force wind.

Chapter 6

1995 Rugby World Cup

'To begin at the beginning', as Dylan Thomas famously began his radio play *Under Milk Wood*, is self-evidently the best place to start a narrative which records the chronology of events: from start to finish, with one event leading to another. The impact of a single fixture upon the next and the consequences of winning or losing are the essence of a tournament which eventually and climactically comes to determine over a period of four weeks who is the best team in the world. There are shades and colours, of course, within a single game, but these are enhanced when placed in the context of all the other matches.

The journey itself is predictable. We know where it starts and where it finishes, but every slight detour in between, the affairs and the course of events, the incidents and the accidents, cannot be foretold. There are many eliminations and additions, exits and entrances, which happily or sadly make up the extraordinary journey. The game is usually the focus; the endeavour to compete and the dream to win; the tragedy that belongs to the vanquished; the ecstasy which embraces the victor and the undefeated. There is the triumph and the disaster, and the secret, as it is so often pointed out, is to treat both impostors the same. Sport is trivial. It is enjoyable and serious: it provokes crying and stimulates laughter; hope and despair; frustration and inspiration. It is also necessary. But necessary in its essential triviality. Hugh McIlvanney, the great sports writer, once said that 'Sport is a nonsense. A very serious nonsense, but still a nonsense.'

The Rugby World Cup of 1995 defies this straightforward convention. The story of the 1995 World Cup in South Africa must begin, not at the beginning, but at the end. On 24 June of that year in Ellis Park, Johannesburg, sport and politics, for once, came together in happy and glorious communion.

There have been controversial instances in the past when politics intruded on sporting occasions. One occurred during the 1936 Olympics in Berlin when, to the scowling resentment of Adolf Hitler, the black athlete Jesse Owens won four gold medals. Race played its part in Mexico in 1968 with John Carlos's upraised salute with the black-gloved fist. Black Africa made their stand in Montreal in 1976, while in 1980 the USA withdrew from the Moscow Olympics. Race had played a direct or indirect role in all of these. The most violent interruption occurred in Munich in 1972 when Palestinian terrorists killed 11 Israeli athletes in the Olympic village.

In 1995, when the President of South Africa, Nelson Mandela, handed the World Cup trophy to François Pienaar, the Springbok captain, there took place one of those instances which may help to define the 20th century. The moment went beyond rugby's narrow boundaries and transcended sport's hopeful horizons to become transformed into iconic historical significance.

This is not to say that the world was suddenly a better place, or that it would necessarily become one, but the moving spirit of the afternoon provided a hint of man's potential for rich and generous deeds born of the nobility of the soul; the need for compassion; to acknowledge strength in choosing forgiveness; and to prefer reconciliation, not recrimination.

A frail black man walked somewhat achingly onto the rugby pitch to present a white man with the World Cup trophy. This was a black man whose very existence was once abhorred because of the colour of his skin, who had to endure the infinite insults of white men and who was incarcerated for over a quarter of a century in a place called Robben Island. In those dark days of soul-searching in his tiny, sparse room when he yearned for the day of his freedom might he not then have had a deep-rooted hunger for revenge against the white supremacists? Was he at that time motivated not by compassion and amnesty, but by retribution and a wish to square the account at long last? He had been dispossessed of his glad confident morning; a life of rich promise abducted. He had reason to be consumed by rage, rancour and bitter regret. Nothing of the kind at any time manifested itself in Nelson Mandela; not a hint of vengeance.

Instead, sporting a baseball cap and wearing the green and gold jersey of South Africa, identical to the team's captain, with the leaping Springbok on his breast, Nelson Mandela epitomised magnanimity and pacification. Not even these motley garments could deny the President his grandeur. Rather they enhanced his lustre. After all, nothing was so representative of the past injustices of apartheid than rugby union. This was the white man's sport; the Springbok jersey was a metaphor for the old regime. Nelson Mandela dignified the Rugby World Cup in 1995 with his noble presence. Without pomp or vainglory, he presented the trophy to François Pienaar, the highly esteemed Springbok captain, in front of a jubilant Ellis Park crowd.

In the declining years of the Millennium, Mandela flourished to become an icon of 20th-century statesmanship. More than that, there was an air about him of the silence and calm of a sage. Other leaders were dwarfed by his genuine stature. No politician could have accomplished what Mandela accomplished on that day without eyebrows being raised and questions asked about the opportunism in being present in the reflected glory of a winning team and the 'photo opportunity' it gave. Nelson Mandela was perceived to be on a pedestal raised so far above pettiness that such cynical manoeuvring normally attributed to politicians was not countenanced.

Pienaar was later to admit that his comment at the time, which encapsulated the mood of their triumph, was spontaneous. Asked to respond to the wonderful support of 63,000 in the ground, he replied: 'We didn't have the support of 63,000 South Africans today. We had the support of 42 million South Africans.' No one was about to argue in the jubilant cheers. Even the All Blacks, in the moment of defeat and intense disappointment, might have found some solace within this unity of the South African nation. They might not as sportsmen, after the heat of the duel and the aftermath of a long campaign, have been able to see anything beyond their immediate sense of despair. Others, regardless of national flag or foreign allegiance, saw that what they had witnessed transcended the winning and the losing of a rugby game. The game was indeed trivial.

The crowd roared their approval of Pienaar's words to end an afternoon which had begun extravagantly when the vast bulk of a Boeing 747, with the message 'Good Luck Bokke' on the wing, flew so low as almost to kiss the high stands and make the earth tremble. The afternoon was replete with extravagant and unforgettable gestures, culminating in the one symbolic ceremony of fellowship and forgiveness, if not entirely of forgetting.

There was a postscript which, in view of the forty years of apartheid policy which had been enshrined within South Africa's constitution and the belief of the white man's superiority, was of a deeply ironic kind. At the official World Cup dinner at the Gallagher Estate, Dr Louis Luyt, the South Africa Rugby Football Union President, delivered a speech which managed to antagonise almost everyone in the room. Whereas the evening should have struck a mood of warm gratitude for the finale of a successful month-long tournament, of good luck to the remaining participants, of congratulation to the winners and of general bonhomie among all the guests, Dr Luyt's closing remarks were misconceived and were received with a mixture of disbelief and mortification. Euphoria had engulfed the whole country in the afternoon and even those with no sense of South African affiliation responded to it with indulgent understanding of the meaning it held for the nation. There had been an unselfish acknowledgement of the moment's appropriateness.

No one was prepared for Luyt's pronounced triumphalism. His miscalculation was almost comic. Perhaps it was meant to be funny but it fell on deaf ears. Standing to speak at the post-match dinner to close the tournament, Luyt announced brazenly that the cup was in the hands of those to whom it rightly belonged. With shameless effrontery he went on to conclude: 'We boasted in 1987 that the real World Cup could not be won in New Zealand because we were not there. It was the same in England in 1991. In 1995 we have proved that if we were there, we would win.'

Furthermore, ignoring Ed Morrison, the English referee who had officiated in the final, Luyt presented a special tournament award of a gold watch to the man he perceived to be the best official: Welsh referee, Derek Bevan. This was not only bad manners to the other officials and particularly insulting to Morrison, but it might have been perceived as something more unsavoury, which did not wholly escape the evening's audience. Bevan was the referee who had been in charge of the semi-final in which South Africa, in less than clear circumstances, overcame France. The presentation was a sensitive moment for Bevan and could have compromised his integrity.

Aghast at Luyt's swagger and rudeness, New Zealand walked out, as did some of the English players. There were others who felt equally aggrieved but stayed, nonplussed by what had motivated the SARFU's President to speak in such an unfeeling manner. The evening deteriorated into puzzlement and acrimony, which François Pienaar recollected in his autobiography by saying that 'on the night when perhaps the greatest parties of all time were being held all over the country, we were stuck in this terrible, sour atmosphere where nobody was smiling.'

Thus, one man's arrogance nearly betrayed a nation, but not quite. The overwhelming impression was of the harmony and grace of a great Rugby World Cup, the best so far, and of a 'rainbow' nation emerging after 40 years of institutionalised bigotry. Rugby World Cup 1995 assumed a dimension above and beyond the trivialities normally attributed to sport. Exaggerated emotions are attached to pastimes which are simply frivolous. In this way a rugby tournament which in normal circumstances would emerge as a mere footnote was transformed into a totemic chapter in the history of the world in the 20th century.

If the 1995 World Cup ended by presenting to the world a permanent image of reconciliation, of dignity and harmony and the emergence of what was known as the 'rainbow' nation, the beginning of the tournament in Newlands in Cape Town had also given a strong sense of South Africa welcoming the world into its warm embrace. For so many years the laager mentality had prevailed in South Africa. They were a country under siege as the worlds of politics, of sport and of trade, turned away from them. On the defensive and deceived by their obstinacy, they had preached to those left to listen that no one could tell them how to run their internal affairs. Rugby authorities, however, kept the door of contact open. As the preferred phrase of the time had it, 'bridges needed to be built'. When South Africa had been expelled from every other sporting organisation, they retained their place on the International Rugby Football Board.

This was in no small part due to Dr Danie Craven, who, as player, coach and administrator, had given over 50 years' service to rugby in the Republic. He was President of the then South Africa Rugby Board (SARB) from 1956 to 1991. A major influence in the game, he died in 1993 and was not to see the World Cup come to his country.

Increasingly isolated, South Africa seemed to welcome visitors only to prove the point that, despite the outside world and its opinions, they could survive. A fiercely proud nation, they reiterated their desire not to pander to or placate overseas opinion.

The embrace was not total. There was cold calculation. A visit from outside gave South Africa and their immoral policy a legitimacy which was hardly accepted elsewhere. This mood was forced to change after 1976, when black athletes boycotted the Montreal Olympics because of New Zealand's rugby tour to South Africa that same year. Scotland decided not to go there in 1978. Australia soon followed, and the four home unions concluded that a Springbok tour to the United Kingdom and Ireland would not be appropriate at the time.

Such was the mood throughout the '80s, which had seen South Africa excluded from the two Rugby World Cup tournaments so far. There were to be a couple of clandestine and renegade operations involving the so-called New Zealand Cavaliers and other players from all over the world, who, with almost cloak and dagger secrecy, entered South Africa to celebrate the centenary of South African rugby in August 1989. There was, in general, pent-up frustration within a nation which enjoys a fanatical support for rugby; a zeal of religious proportions.

On Thursday 25 May Newlands, in the shadow of Table Mountain, formed a crucible of colour and song and of buoyant movement and harmony. The opening ceremony was truly a grand greeting to the world in which South Africa was longing to find its rightful place once more. After the parade of the 16 nations in the colourful and moving opening ceremony, the new national anthem, 'Nkosi Sikelel' i Africa' was sung with such gusto as if everyone in the Republic meant it for the first time. The old theme 'Die Stem' was also sung but not with the same relish as of yore. 'One team, one nation' was the slogan for the period.

The Springboks would play in the World Cup for the first time and for the first time the tournament would be held in one country. It was time to begin.

The first match was between the host nation and the winners of the previous tournament, Australia, who were in Pool A. Australia was a team which had consistently proven its pedigree throughout the vast experience of the component parts of a thoroughbred team. In consequence, they had been installed as the favourites to win the competition for the second successive time. Michael Lynagh, the fly-half, was the world's leading points scorer; David Campese, the winger, was the leading try scorer. There were Tim Horan and Jason Little among the backs, while each of the forwards might lay claim to challenge for a world team position. Bob Dwyer, who had master-minded their win in 1991, remained in charge and, bearing in mind the notoriously short life span of national coaches, had, if anything, enhanced his reputation as the leading light among rugby coaches. He was an astute and modern thinker so that, within their camp, there were key and influential strengths at every level. By consensus there was, man for man, no better team in the 1995 tournament.

To underline their pole position, Australia could look to their statistics since their victory at Twickenham in 1991 to take comfort from the fact that of the 22 international matches played, they had won 18. Their failures were against New Zealand (two losses out of five fixtures), South Africa (one loss from four fixtures) and France (one from two). The only absentee from this list of fixtures against the world's best teams was England, whom they last played in the final in 1991.

If an extra incentive were needed, both teams were conscious that the winner of the first match had the better route to the final, with the losers probably having to face the twin leviathans, England and New Zealand.

After the emotion of the opening ceremony and before the game got underway, there was some conjecture on what effect this outpouring of affection might have on the Springboks. Would they be weighed down by the demands of the afternoon and burdened by their country's expectation? The 'wave of goodwill' was something the South Africa manager, the immense Springbok forward and greatest of captains, Morne du Plessis, had not felt in his country in 25 years of rugby experience. How would his team respond?

South Africa had returned to international rugby in October 1992 when they played, and lost, to their intense rivals, New Zealand. After their re-emergence on the world stage they went on a spree of matches and played 22 in all before they embarked on the World Cup in 1995. Of these they had won ten, lost ten and drawn two. They had lost twice consecutively to England – a feat that had not been accomplished since 1898.

The euphoria worked in their favour. Australia seemed overawed by the atmosphere. If for some they appeared to misjudge the tempo, for others they were patiently building a platform. Their forwards built the foundation and they had a wealth of balls supplied by their line-out which went in their favour by 22 to 5. The misjudgement and unsteadiness was to be found elsewhere. Lynagh erred, Campese hesitated and George Gregan was forced out of his stride by an eager Springbok pack. Even with this fragility the team was in the lead by 13–9 at one stage, but it could not last long.

The Springboks had their own plan which, although limited, was to prove effective throughout their campaign and which can be summarised in two words: pressure and territory. A try by Pieter Hendriks – who had replaced the injured Chester Williams – was started by James Small near the half-way line in a marvellous piece of attack and took them into a 14–13 half-time lead. South Africa closed down their opponents with Joost van der Westhuizen along with Pienaar and Ruben Kruger harrying Gregan. Joel Stransky played an influential role at fly-half, as he was to do throughout the tournament. Crucially, he kicked 22 points in the match, which the Springboks eventually won by 27–18.

This was the start that South Africa needed. They had returned from isolation and were making an impact for the first time. South Africa, the host nation, had defeated the favourites and provided the impact and the momentum from the start. This was especially so, bearing in mind the emotion that had suddenly attached itself to the event. There could easily have been a sense of anti-climax.

Set against this formidable contest, the following day saw Scotland overwhelm the Ivory Coast by 89–0 at Rustenburg (translated as the 'restful village'). Gavin Hastings scored a record 44 points. The 'anoraks' could point out that neither of these high scores created a team nor an individual record. A few months earlier in a World Cup qualifying match, Hong Kong had amassed the seemingly insurmountable score of 164–13 against Singapore with Ashley Billington of that parish having bagged 55 points for himself, which included 10 tries. However, the record books were able to establish that Scotland had created a record for the finals of the World Cup and that Hastings's four tries equalled the number of tries scored by an individual in the finals.

Such was the condition of the World Cup at this stage in its development, with such a wide range of standards and discrepancies in playing strength that new records were frequently being established. Wales, in their opening game against Japan in Pool C in Bloemfontein, were also able to create a record for themselves.

They had arrived in South Africa having lost their previous five international matches and had suffered a whitewash in the Five Nations Championship. In the wake of these defeats, Alec Evans was appointed coach to the team only a few weeks before the tournament began. Prior to this Wales had only scored three tries in their last 9 games. Therefore, the 57 points they scored against Japan were the highest number for Wales and the seven tries were for them the most they had scored in the finals.

Elsewhere, the tournament was taking its predictable course. Canada had defeated Romania by 34–3 in Pool A in Port Elizabeth and Western Samoa were reinforcing the impression they had created four years previously by beating Italy 42–18 in Pool B. To'o Vaega had been inventive in midfield for the South Sea Islanders and Marcello Cuttitta enjoyed the personal distinction of having scored in every World Cup so far.

This was a modest and unremarkable beginning. It was all about to change.

High up on the veldt at 5,750 feet in Ellis Park, Johannesburg, the first stirrings of a rugby tornado were brewing. On 27 May, on the site of what was once a mine dump and brickworks, Jonah Tali Lomu, of Weymouth Rugby Club in Auckland, swept into international view. Weighing almost 18st and standing at 6'5", the All Black with only two previous appearances for New Zealand presented an awesome sight which, while familiar among the heavy-weight players of the forwards, was unknown among the hitherto more delicate occupants of the number 11 jersey on the wing. While there were sceptics on the sidelines who, quite naturally, could well imagine such a big man playing in this position, making his presence felt in attack by physical force alone and providing an obstructive wall of hindrance in defence, no one outside New Zealand was truly prepared for the impact Jonah Lomu was about to make. He was of a kind to confound all the preconceptions about what a man of his immense size was capable of accomplishing. The judgements were all premature; all prejudices were soon to be silenced.

Ireland in Pool C were the first to feel Lomu's elemental power in their opening game. Garryowen winger Richard Wallace was the first to be exposed to the phenomenon. No doubt he will have had his plans to counter the threat, but he could not have imagined how inadequate they would prove to be, as indeed others were also shortly to find out. Any attempts to challenge him would be made to appear clumsy leaving Lomu's opponent, whoever he might be, feeling diminished and helpless in the face of a dramatic force of nature. Such a player had not until now come within anyone's compass, unless John Novak (Harlequins) and Jeremy Janion (Bedford) from the early 1970s, and John Woodward (Wasps) from the 1950s are counted. They were big men, too. At 19 years of age Lomu was a novice and practically unheard of until his arrival in South Africa.

Wallace would have felt stripped and impotent almost from the start. His forlorn attempts at stopping Lomu as the All Black scored their first try gave a warning to cause sleepless nights for those whose task would be to dream up ways and means of halting the rampant wing. Would-be tacklers were cast aside as jetsam and flotsam in his wake as he made his way triumphantly to the line.

In the second half he ran 80 metres, swatting four players out of his path for Josh Kronfeld to score. For those who witnessed it, this was an extraordinary first sighting. His opponents might try to hinder him and obstruct his path but they were no more than hapless victims. It was like plasterboard furniture being cast in the way of a technologically advanced but villainous Robocop or Terminator in a Hollywood movie. Or, to mix the Hollywood allusion, the force was undoubtedly with Jonah Lomu. Playing only his third game for his country, he scored two tries and made two more.

Fine players were made to look inelegant. Rough and tough ones appeared bloodless. Lomu's play, however, was not purely of strength and aggression alone. He was endowed with other more subtle gifts which are normally attributed to those of more modest proportions. Players a fraction of his size can be nimble of foot. Lomu, too, was a fast and balanced runner who could, with a lightness of touch which belied his physical stature, shift and sway, swerve and change direction concisely and economically. He could distract defences and enrage players as they grappled and struggled in an unequal contest. Frustration grew with the embarrassment and, so it came to seem, the unfairness of the duel. Players, you imagined, would be hurled aside muttering hopeless threats of vengeance: 'I'll get you, oh yes. I will do such things. What they are yet I know not, but they shall be the terrors of the earth.' It was a worthy thought, but fruitless.

Yet for all this, Ireland battled bravely and, to begin with, managed to unsettle the All Blacks, having gone into an early lead after Gary Halpin scored a try. Later, Denis McBride also crossed the line after a brilliant run by Simon Geoghegan, a fine winger and match-winner who all too rarely had the ball in his hands. He suffered to languish instead as a spectator on the empty wing. With his blond hair and determined, high-knee stepping style he was a player to inspire drama and to get the crowd on its feet. Ireland did not get to see enough of his talents.

New Zealand had no such qualms. They unleashed Lomu on an unsuspecting and astonished rugby world. He became a sensational figure in the 1995 Rugby World Cup. Indeed, the All Blacks would prove to be a remarkable team.

This evaluation could not have been made prior to their arrival. They had had a poor season entering into the tournament. Both on and off the field there had been a lack of harmony. On the field, they had lost four of their last six internationals. Off the field, Laurie Mains was not secure in his role as national coach. There was acrimony which destabilised the preparation.

In fact, despite losing 43–19 Ireland probably put up the best performance of anyone against New Zealand, apart from South Africa.

England, if the time came, would have every chance to prepare to be the immovable object to meet this irresistible force. They, too, were a formidable team but, despite entering the tournament on the back of a grand slam in the Five Nations Championship, they had not given grounds for optimism in their first match. Will Carling was the same captain as 1991, but England had a new coach in Jack Rowell, who over many years had made Bath the most powerful club in England, perhaps in Europe.

There was a consistency that was inherent in England's performances. Since the last World Cup they had played 18 international fixtures and had won 14, which had included successes against New Zealand, two out of three chances against South Africa and three victories over France. Only Ireland had denied them the grand slam in 1994 which, had England won, would have given them that particular prize on two occasions in three years. The Celtic fringe could always be counted upon to ambush England's best-laid celebrations.

Entering the 1995 tournament they were expected to dent the reputations and expectations of the Southern Hemisphere teams. Expectation and fulfilment are treacherous allies; the one rarely gets to agree with the other and there is usually a falling out. England found what awkward bed-fellows they make when, at Twickenham in 1991, the high hopes and optimism they had elicited beforehand proved ephemeral. They failed to compose themselves to realise their dreams of a victory over the Australians in a World Cup final which they looked set to win. Once more in 1995 they held the hopes of Northern Hemisphere rugby.

France, the other Northern Hemisphere hopeful, were far from pleased with their opening game against Tonga in Pool D, even if they did win with a comfortable 38–10 margin. Pierre Berbizier, who was the scrum-half in 1987 but now the French coach, gave a novel assessment for their ordinary performance. 'There were too many vain egotists,' he said of his players, 'who are too much in love with themselves and the television cameras.'

In the three years leading up to the tournament, France had won a series in Argentina (1992), South Africa (1993) and, most tellingly of all, in New Zealand (1994). The last test in Auckland had produced a try – 'the try from the end of the world' it came to be dubbed – which had seen the ball go through nine pairs of hands before Jean-Luc Sadourny scored. Yet for all this they had been inconsistent in the Five Nations.

They played the Ivory Coast at Rustenburg and won by 54–18, but they failed to please the eye in the way that they usually delight the whole of France and everyone else who believes in searching for whatever aesthetic beauty there is in rugby and drawing the sublime from so rough and tumble a game. However, as they had done in the first World Cup, they would ultimately ensure that their natural flamboyance would emerge to embellish the tournament. France would give good reason why the television cameras should be in love with them; why their own vanity would insist that they would not – could not – let themselves down. They would find it within them to declare to the world their own singular vision of rugby which, while often brutal, can inspire the game's theatre with rhapsody and stardust. If they cannot draw on universal affection, because of the beast in them as well as the beauty, they are nonetheless to the rugby world what Brazil is to football. Their game is full of curves and sweeps and sinuous rhythms, as well as the curses and the vices that rugby is heir to.

They are a feast to the eyes and poetry to the mind, and when on song you wish the game would not come to an end.

But as well as joy there is also tragedy in sport. Amid the drama of a game we can be uplifted one moment with the joy of triumph, only to give way the next to the tears of the vanquished. Yet, for all the memories sport creates – the sweetness of laughter as much as the pangs of momentary despair – sport is ultimately ephemeral.

Joy can frequently come to pass when the blood is stirred to wonder, but tragedy is an emotion which, within the context of a mere match, strains towards exaggeration.

Yet events occur around the actual game which result in tragedy, like Manchester United and the Munich air crash of 1958; the 39 deaths of Juventus supporters at the Heysel Stadium in Brussels in 1985; the 95 who died at Hillsborough in Sheffield; or when Donald Campbell crashed in *Bluebird* on Lake Coniston in 1967. Very rarely indeed can any incident *within* a game be thought of as tragic. There is sadness and disappointment but nothing that can merit the word 'tragedy'. But because of chance and risk and the ever-present whiff of danger, sport has the potential for tragic circumstances inherent within it.

Sadly we are forced most compellingly to consider the frivolity at the heart of sport when tragedy strikes. On the day of the last two fixtures in Pool D, the 1995 Rugby World Cup would embody great glory and profound tragedy. In the sixth minute of the match against Tonga on 3 June at the Olympia Park Stadium in Rustenburg, some 100 miles from Johannesburg, tragedy struck the Ivory Coast winger Max Brito when a tackle left him paralysed.

For all the urgency with which the tournament was being pursued, this heart-rending incident obliged everyone to pause for a time: to ponder the little acts of heroism and to wonder at the thin line and randomness that separates the happy turn of events from ill-fated misfortune and sorrow; to be able to admire the enterprising, inexplicable talent; and to find glory, but never to forget that moment – the non-negotiable second of danger. Max Brito caught the blast of arbitrary and capricious fate.

Without publicity, the RWC have maintained contact with him since the tragic accident. Marcel Martin, who was the RWC representative at the match and who remained with him at the hospital that evening, has visited him almost every year since 1995. Some unions did not have insurance cover for their players. Prior to 1995, the RWC, on its own initiative, set up an 'umbrella' insurance cover so that every union was covered. In the case of permanent disability, a player would receive the sum of £150,000 to help him through the initial period. If some unions have their own insurance scheme, the Ivory Coast had none whatsoever. Without the RWC insurance, Max Brito would have been left without any financial support. Advising his brother, the RWC recommended that a fund should be set up and protected so as to support Brito. This was done. There have been fund-raising activities of all sorts and the RWC, in addition, has continued to make donations to this fund. Brito was invited to the World Cup final in 1999 but could not travel.

This incident highlighted the discrepancies and the imbalance that exists between teams: in fitness levels, in size, and in power and strength. Standards vary considerably so that rugby, with its ambitions to expand and to encompass more nations into its fold, finds that that there are, in fact, gulfs of difference. Since the game was declared 'open' in August 1995, allowing professional sportsmen to be paid for playing rugby union, it is only the future which can determine whether this change, with more for training and preparation, will help close or widen the gap of inequality.

It may well be that, while this change in status may antagonise the traditionalists who adhere fondly to the spirit and ethos of a player not being paid to play rugby union, the change, on the other hand, may well give the game a greater appeal to those new nations where the idea of high-level sport being amateur at international level is anathema.

There was confirmation of this mismatch in power in the game between Ireland and Japan at the Free State Rugby Stadium in Bloemfontein, the most rural of all South African cities and referred to as the 'city of roses'. Japan relied on speed over the ground and quick ingenuity at every phase. Given the chance, Japan would want to run everyone ragged since they were disadvantaged in their size; lack of weight and height limited the manner in which they could play the game. Even if they had imported players from the Pacific islands, this was not enough and Ireland proved as much in the scrummages.

Twice Ireland forced and squeezed the scrum so much that Japan collapsed and in so doing gave away two penalty tries. These were hard lessons. For all of Japan's scintillating running, quickness of thought and unbounded enthusiasm, they could not compete with the palpable solidity of the scrum and line-out. They seemed forever destined to be the 'smiling boys of summer in their ruin', unable to cope with the flint and pitch in the way Ireland could. Ireland won 50–28.

New Zealand, as is their fashion, were unsmilingly ruthless in exposing the underdogs to a more damaging and embarrassing examination. In a business-like manner, they opened up Japan's vulnerability with pitiless execution and re-wrote the record books. Japan were put to the sword and demolished by 145 points, with the All Blacks scoring 21 tries. Underscoring this extraordinary feat was the fact that only six of the All Blacks had played against Ireland in the previous game. This was New Zealand's second string team.

Simon Culhane recorded the most points for an individual player with 45 and kicked the most conversions (20). Furthermore, he broke the record for a player on his international debut, which had previously been set by his colleague Andrew Mehrtens, from whom he had taken over at fly-half. Finally, on the day for the 'anoraks', Marc Ellis, at centre, recorded the most tries in one game (6) so that the only record left for Gavin Hastings to share with Thierry Lacroix was for the most penalty goals (8). Only one penalty was kicked in the match and that was by Keiji Hirose, the Japan fly-half. The biggest cheers of the afternoon in Bloemfontein were reserved, of course, for Hiroyuki Kajihara, the flanker, who scored Japan's two tries.

The All Blacks had overcome Wales five days earlier at Ellis Park. Wales had talked a good game beforehand, as is the only way to prepare against the All Blacks, but they could not reverse a trend of continued failure. Wales had to look back 42 years for their last victory against a foe which, from 1905 to 1953, they could boast of leading three victories to one. Thereafter, until 1997, the All Blacks had won a series of 13 consecutive victories.

If Mehrtens was in fine form with his kicking and Walter Little and Frank Bunce, once of Western Samoa, were superb creators in midfield, the man who caught the eye was the flanker Josh Kronfeld from Otago. He had only played one international for New Zealand prior to the tournament. If his speed and anticipation, for which he was most needed, did not immediately catch the eye, then his skull cap ensured that you did not miss him for long. He scored his team's final try to give them the 34–9 victory. Wales did not cross their opponent's line and, as ever, had to rely on the kicking skills of Neil Jenkins, their fly-half, to kick two penalty goals and a drop-goal.

This meant that, with New Zealand heading the pool and Japan having been knocked out at the pool stage and heading for home, the dog fight for second position and a place in the quarter-finals was between Ireland and Wales. This was not going to be a spectacle that the aesthetes who might yearn for a bit of style and *élan* would relish, nor to the purists of rugby, who might simply want a game well played. Only the pragmatists, knowing the limitations of both teams, would recognise the test of endurance that lay ahead. The score ended with Ireland winning by a hair's breadth at 24–23. The final agonising few minutes made for a tense and dramatic finish but the contest was largely forgettable. Nick Popplewell and Denis McBride had scored tries very early in the first half which disarmed a bemused and unprepared Welsh team. Eddie Halvey, who had replaced McBride, scored Ireland's third. Tries by Hemi Taylor and Jonathan Humphreys brought Wales back into the match, but to no avail. Wales, for the second time, failed to make the cut for the quarter- finals.

This was as poor an advertisement for European rugby as the France/Scotland game was good. On a balmy evening at Loftus Versfeld in Pretoria, where the 'kikuyu' grass was imported from Kenya and first introduced to the playing fields of the Transvaal in 1920, both teams met again in the World Cup to resume a duel in the way which they had so spectacularly begun in Christchurch in 1987. If anything, this meeting was to prove even better.

The match was an immense clash at forward, with both sides also providing sweeping movements in attack. It was from such an expansive counter-attack in the final seconds that France managed to pull a match that seemed to have slipped from their grasp, and to bring it back within their warm embrace. It was tantalising rugby.

Yet, to begin with, it was Scotland's audacity that held sway and took a 13–3 lead into the interval. They needed to keep it, not only to exact sweet revenge for what had happened in 1987, but, ignoring the sentiments of the past, to ensure that, in beating France, they would come top of Pool D. This meant they would avoid playing New Zealand in the quarter-finals. They held the lead. With seven minutes to go they were still seven points ahead at 19–12 with Hastings and Lacroix exchanging penalties. With four minutes to go they lost a little, but were still four in the lead at 19–15. Gavin Hastings had not only scored 14 of his team's points, he had also, in a marvellous game for him, played a critical role in paving the way for Rob Wainwright's try in the first half. For 84 minutes they did hang on to the lead but then, in a grand sweep of a movement, to left and right and to left again, France curved their way to the line which ended with Emile Ntamack scoring in the corner. Thierry Lacroix converted from the touch-line to add to his five successes out of five penalty chances and to secure a 22–19 victory.

The Rugby World Cup in 1995 needed such a match. After the opening fixture in Cape Town, there had been much that was predictable or simply mundane. This match, with its flamboyance and the resilience and the nail-biting drama at the end, gave the tournament a much-needed lift. France's performance cast back the minds of those who had the good fortune to be there to Ballymore, Brisbane, in 1987, when France provided a similar dash and verve to create a rhythm and movement, of a kind which they alone are capable, to give Serge Blanco his last-minute try.

There was no such conviction in England's play in Pool B. Argentina's scrum remained firm and immovable and gave nothing away in an area in which England themselves were justly proud. At King's Park in Durban, England had to rely, as they often had done, on the accurate kicking talents of Rob Andrew. He scored all the points with his boot – six penalties and two drop-goals – in their 24–18 victory. Argentina scored the game's two tries courtesy of Patricio Noriega and Lisandro Arbizu.

At 27–20, there was nothing much between England and Italy either, except that England felt relieved that the Underwood brothers, Rory and Tony, had scored a try each. Andrew again was true with five penalties. For a team that had so dominated the Five Nations Championship, they looked and played without the belief that had hitherto been so clearly theirs. They were uninspiring, strained and unsure. Collectively, their opponents had scored more tries than they had: four to two.

Western Samoa, after being in the international shadow of both Fiji and Tonga for so long, were forging a name for themselves, and were fast becoming a team of which to be wary, if not feared. In the Basil Kenyon stadium in East London, they and Argentina produced the best match in their pool. Inspired by Junior Paramore, their flanker, the scored ended in favour of the Pacific Islanders at 32–26. With ten minutes to go, the Argentines were in the lead by 26–13. Yet, after this wonderful performance, Argentina went on to lose to Italy and finish at the bottom of the pool.

Whether prompted or not by the thrilling game in East London, England produced their best performance against the other unbeaten team in the pool. They scored four tries in their 44–22 victory. In coming top of the pool and Australia coming second in theirs, England would witness a reprise of the 1991 final. There was a history that each team would bring to the showdown at Newlands in Cape Town and which would add a special piquancy to the contest.

The Wallabies had not been too comfortable themselves, as if the defeat in the first game had undermined their belief in their abilities. After beating Romania at the Boet Erasmus stadium in Port Elizabeth 34–3, Canada went on to be difficult opponents to Australia. One unflinching tackle by Winston Stanley on David Campese, and their captain Al Charron's leadership gave notice of the Canadians' intent not to cower before the Australian reputation or anyone else's. They appeared to have taken this resolve a step too far in their next match against South Africa. For the moment, they lost to Australia by 27–11, while Australia had overwhelmed Romania 42–3 at Stellenbosch.

The Canadian underdog, however, was in fighting spirit. There was all to play for in a tournament in which no team so far had looked anything other than nervous and cautious. The All Blacks were the exception. A bit of fire in the belly might upset the balance still further.

South Africa, after their euphoric response at overcoming Australia, were less assured against Romania (21–8). Their final pool game was against Canada in Port Elizabeth. The signs were not encouraging from the start. The game was delayed for 45 minutes because of a power failure in the floodlights. There was to be failure elsewhere too: failure of discipline.

The match provided the most shameful episode of the tournament. Three players were sent off: the Canadians Gareth Rees and Rod Snow, and the Springbok hooker James Dalton. Two others who had been prominent in the brawl – Pieter Hendriks of South Africa and Scott Stewart of Canada – were later cited and banned.

The Springboks went on to win by 20 points without reply. This set them for a quarter-final match with Western Samoa. It also transpired that Chester Williams had recovered from his hamstring injury, which had caused him to withdraw from the tournament before it began. In many ways he had been the focus of much attention. He was the only black player in the squad.

With so much changing politically, socially and culturally in South Africa, Chester Williams was believed to be a wonderful representative of this wind of change. He was the symbol of the new South Africa. His smiling face was on the billboards and on television. 'The waiting is over' read the legend underneath his face. He had suffered his injury in a pre-tournament match against Western Samoa. Pieter Hendriks replaced him in the Springbok squad. Hendricks was given a 60-day suspension by the tournament Disciplinary Committee, and Dalton left the squad and went home. Hendricks's departure allowed Chester Williams to join the squad.

This raised the question as to whether a player suspended because of ill-discipline should be replaced. Should a team in these circumstances not forfeit a player, otherwise the misdeed effectively remains unpunished? The regulations did allow a replacement but on safety grounds and to prevent an imbalance in the squad, such as when a player from the front row, for instance, is suspended. These arguments were pursued at the time.

No one, in the circumstances that prevailed in South Africa in 1995, was so mean-spirited as to dissect the minutiae of these regulations. Certainly no one would wish to do so if the player in question was Chester Williams. He was a much-loved and much-admired person and his withdrawal in the first place had disappointed everyone. He had come to be the living embodiment of what most people wished Mandela's South Africa to be: free of racial inequalities. Chester Williams could wear the Springbok jersey and represent his country on the world's stage not as a token but as a right. The pieces were fitting into place as the quarter-final stage beckoned.

1995 QUARTER-FINALS

For the second time in the four-year cycle of the Rugby World Cup, England had arrived in the tournament as grand slam winners of the Five Nations Championship. For the second time also, they were to play Australia. This time they would meet in the quarter-finals. The two countries had not played each other since their confrontation in the final in 1991. This fixture was the most intriguing contest of the 1995 quarter-final draw. If France, South Africa and New Zealand, according to the runes, were confidently predicted to progress through to the semi-finals, the indications for the match to be played in Cape Town on 11 June were not so easily detected in the clouded crystal ball.

Only one thing was certain: England was the team that the powerful nations of the Southern Hemisphere feared the most. Both Brian Lochore, the New Zealand manager, and Morne du Plessis, South Africa's manager, admitted as much beforehand. Accepting this, there was one other statement that those who had followed England's journey throughout the period immediately after 1987, when their current success began, could declare with equal conviction. They had the fatal propensity to let things slip when their prospects looked the most promising. Like Shakespeare's tragic characters, there was a major flaw which ruined their ambitions. This was not arrogance, but rather than recognising what the past had to teach them and the previous slips and tumbles that had come their way, there was a perception of a repeated presumption of success. Whether this was truly the case within England's camp and within the minds of the players remains uncertain. At any rate, this aura was created and understood to be the case by outsiders. Sometimes the perception alone is enough even if its rightness is not. It is the way their opponents understand matters which stimulates and galvanises them. For sure, England can fail to assess the moment and not properly judge the opposition's reaction. The red rose, it appears, can be such a red rag to so many.

Their match was on Sunday, a day when another north versus south contest would take place. New Zealand were to play Scotland in Pretoria. This would be their third encounter. They had met in each of the tournaments in the World Cup series and for the second time at the quarter-final stage.

South Africa were pitched against Western Samoa in Johannesburg. However, first on the scene would be a purely European confrontation between France and Ireland in Durban.

King's Park stadium was only half full for the two Five Nations teams. As if familiarity bred contempt and they knew each other's habits too well, France and Ireland for an hour played a game of tedious repetition and wariness. On a beautiful day made to inspire fine rugby, both teams played in a restricted, often inept, style. There was no urgency, no will, and what movement there was was limited to the forwards. By half-time Thierry Lacroix and Eric Elwood had kicked four penalties each. In Sella, Ntamack and Saint-Andre for France, and Geoghegan and Brendan Mullin for Ireland, the two countries had players who might have revelled in the conditions. They were capable of unravelling any defence and lighting up any match with their talent. Ireland, captained by Terry Kingston, were obstinate. France, led by Saint-Andre, were wavering and uncertain. Scrum followed line-out and back again.

France's nervousness was epitomised by their fly-half Christophe Deylaud, who normally excels behind the Toulouse pack. His misjudgements disrupted any hope of fluid play. Throughout he attempted four drops at goal, which was added testimony of their edginess. Yet they dominated the line-outs by 18 to 8, enjoyed most of the territorial advantage and in Marc Cecillon, Laurent Cabannes and Abdelatif Benazzi they had the most threatening players.

The Frenchmen began asserting themselves in the final quarter and, after Lacroix kicked four more penalties to give his team a 24–12 lead, they scored two tries by the end. Saint-Andre scored the first and, on a rare visit to French territory and searching for a last-minute try, Mullins's pass was intercepted by Ntamack who ran almost the whole length of the field for France's second try in the fourth minute of injury time. 'We may at some stage be able to drink champagne,' said Pierre Berbizier of his team's lack of sparkle afterwards, 'but for the moment, we are struggling to get the cork out of the bottle.'

There was nothing so drab in Ellis Park. The match between South Africa and Western Samoa was full of incident and movement but not always of the desirable kind. If there were plenty of tries, there were plenty of big hits, too, which incensed the Springboks and the crowd. Mike Umaga's fierce tackle on André Joubert after fifteen minutes was questionable and, after another robust tackle, he was spoken to by the referee. He was fortunate in not having been sent off the field. Joost van der Westhuizen and Mark Andrews were also at the receiving end of what appeared to be recklessly dangerous tackles. Before he went off in the 70th minute, Andrews had scored a try.

After the rumpus in their previous game against Canada, the South Africans had to be more disciplined than they otherwise would have been. South Africa used all four replacements, one of which was costly. Joubert, because of a broken bone in his hand, had to be replaced at full-back by Brendan Venter.

Western Samoa could not touch Chester Williams, though. In his first outing in the World Cup after a hamstring injury, he became the first Springbok to score four tries in an international. For the image of the rainbow nation to achieve reality, the World Cup required an exhibition of brilliance from such a player at such a time. In its way, it was a triumphal moment.

With his first two tries and that of Chris Rossouw, the Springboks went into a 23-point lead. Within ten minutes of the second half, the Springboks had scored two more tries before Western Samoa finished off in a flourish with two brilliant tries by Shem Tatupu and Tu Nu'uali'itia. Tupo Fa'amasino's conversions gave them 14 points against South Africa's 42.

If there were controversial incidents which were obvious to the naked eye, there would appear to have been other furtive actions of a more insidious and nauseous kind. Accusations were levelled against van der Westhuizen who, it was asserted, had made racist comments on the field. 'He said a lot to us and what he said after the game could not be printed,' said Pat Lam, the Western Samoan captain who, it was claimed, had been bitten. Pienaar, the Springbok captain, dismissed the allegations. Bryan Williams, the Western Samoan manager and former great All Black wing, took the matter no further.

The match, on the afternoon of Sunday 11 June at Newlands, gave us the gift of an unforgettable rugby moment. No, it was more than that. Rob Andrew's drop-goal was of such stuff as makes not just rugby but sport the invigorating pastime it is and which compels us passionately to return again and again in the longing to see its likes once more. The match had been a captivating and gruelling trial of strength and endurance with little that was delicate or what one might have imagined to be touches of finesse. Bob Dwyer, the bespectacled and perceptive Australian coach, who has the mien of a youthful professor on the campus of a new university, had commented beforehand that the game was quite likely to be the match of the tournament, and in the same breath added: 'I do not necessarily equate "good" with "open".' He expected a tough contest with high-quality rugby. It was what he got; with spades, as they say.

Australia were the world champions from 1991 and were returning to play against the team they had defeated in a match in which England had been struck dumb and had ever since grieved of the missed opportunity, as others in the Northern Hemisphere had admittedly done.

They were two well-matched teams. After four years, Carling and Guscott would renew their acquaintance with Jason Little and Tim Horan, who had only recently recovered after 13 months with a knee injury. Andrew and Lynagh were true masters of their craft and the epitome of disciplined efficiency, and Campese and Rory Underwood were great wingers but with differing gifts.

Mightiest of all would be the gladiatorial survival of the fittest among the sixteen rivals among the forwards and, within this, the battle royal in the back row of the scrum. Nine Australians and six Englishmen survived from 1991. For pure drama, it proved to be one of the greatest of games. If neither team had played particularly well so far and had failed to impose their personalities on the competition, this took nothing away from the anticipation. There was a history which declared its significance. The significance brought out the best in both.

There were only two tries – one apiece – and in their different fashions, wonderfully executed. England's early control, against the wind, took them to a 13–3 lead. In the 22nd minute Lynagh dropped the ball on England's 22-metre line. Andrew swept up the ball, set Guscott free to pass to his partner, Carling, who in turn sent in Tony Underwood for the try. Converting this and kicking two penalties gave them a comfortable lead against Lynagh's penalty. But either side of the interval, Lynagh's accuracy with the boot and an acute presence of mind brought the game level at 13–13. First he kicked a penalty and then his beautifully judged high kick allowed Damian Smith to reach high, Australian-rules style, to catch and tumble over the try-line.

Andrew traded kicks with Lynagh. The Australian fly-half became the first player to reach 900 points in international rugby. England had to come back twice to level the score at 22–22. There was tantalising emotion. David Bishop of New Zealand awarded a penalty to England. Mike Catt, England's full-back, dispatched the ball into touch on Australia's 22-metre line. From the line-out, in which Eales had been magnificent throughout, it was Martin Bayfield who won the crucial ball for the match's climactic moment.

England drove forward. Three minutes into injury time, Dewi Morris delivered the ball to Andrew. The fly-half, with diamond-crusted nerves, with greatness in mind and triumph at heart, struck for the posts.

It was one of those sporting moments when the earth stops moving and the world holds its breath. And for ever in the mind's eye, those figures, in that particular landscape, do not stir in an eternal unchanging tableau. They wait and they look as the ball, the only thing that moves it seems, sails; upward and onward.

To know the answer it is best to keep eyes fixed on the kicker. Andrew would know sooner than anyone else: of success or of failure. He knows how the strike of the ball felt. He knows the flight and path of the ball. He is in the best position of all to judge. Dejection or jubilation would be writ large on his face.

Andrew was the first to raise his arms in acknowledgement and triumph. He had kicked one of the greatest of drop-goals, coming as it did, when it did and with such a prize in store. After the tumultuous tussle the match had finally turned 25–22 in England's favour. To think that some years ago there was the suggestion that the drop-goal should be removed as a method of scoring or to be reduced in value. Happily, this never came to pass. The drop-goal can be a most dramatic and intriguing intervention as it so abundantly proved in Newlands to help England to some extent exorcise the demons of 1991. Australia went home while England stayed in Cape Town to await the Scots or the All Blacks.

The match at Loftus Versfeld began inauspiciously, even cynically. Derek Bevan of Wales penalised the All Blacks three times early on for intemperate tackles. They were soon to demonstrate, however, that they were not the All Blacks of old. They were playing a high-risk game and were playing to the widths of the pitch where Lomu, in particular, was prowling so dangerously. Within four minutes he was let loose to run 60 metres, twice leaving Craig Joiner and Scott Hastings in his wake to set up the first of Walter Little's two tries during the match.

Lomu then rounded Gavin Hastings to score himself. Hastings kicked three penalties to keep in touch at 17–9 at the interval. The other All Black tries were scored by Andrew Mehrtens, Frank Bunce and, on the day he won his 100th cap for his country, the captain, Sean Fitzpatrick, to give a 48–30 victory in a free-flowing game.

Doddie Weir scored two tries for Scotland and, on his last time in Scotland's jersey, Gavin Hastings got his country's third try. Up to this moment, only Australia in 1978 had managed to score as many points against New Zealand. Australia, though, had won. Scotland had scored 30 points and lost.

1995 SEMI-FINALS

On Saturday 17 June, the heavens opened in a deluge of Biblical proportions on KwaZulu Natal. The rains were of a kind at which Noah himself might once have nodded in recognition. The torrential rain turned King's Park into a lake. The situation was so thoroughly abnormal that the King's Park personnel were ill-equipped to deal with the amount of surface water that was accumulating three hours before the start of the game. The meteorology office advised that the rain would stop at 4pm. The kick-off was meant to be at 3pm.

In the event the game's kick-off was delayed for 90 minutes and at one stage seemed destined not to start at all. Delaying the game by 24 hours would have created such logistical problems, of transport and accommodation in particular. Everyone realised that the conditions were atrocious and that no one was really to blame. Nevertheless, the decision was a difficult one for Derek Bevan, the referee.

There was one inadvertent symbol of the old South Africa, a residue of past injustices. When workers were required to clear the pitch of the surface water, black women came on to mop up and sweep it away. There was not a white person, not even one man to carry out the task. This unrehearsed moment of what unthinkingly went on before 1990 and of supreme political incorrectness in the new South Africa, the rainbow nation, was soon put right. White men joined in.

With both captains keen to play, the match finally began despite conditions which, were it not for the exigencies imposed, would surely have prevented the game from starting. There were some moments that were funny, some absurd and others downright dangerous. The ball would skim over the water one moment, stop dead the next. Players would overrun the ball or slip while in pursuit of it. The scenario was as jerky as a *Keystone Cops* movie, flickering and random; as erratic as the chases in those old Hollywood films. More serious might be the chancy business of being in the mayhem of the ruck, where to be caught at the bottom presented a hazard which put life at risk. There was indeed the risk – hard as this might be to believe with the distance of time – of drowning, as there had been in a match between New Zealand and Scotland in Auckland in 1975. There was a lot of water.

The world's best rugby players might not have had a proper stage on which to parade their talent but they did show courage and an indomitable spirit in what were, by any normal yardstick, unplayable conditions. André Joubert, despite doubts about his damaged hand, was chosen to play and to exert a critical influence on the outcome.

The weather naturally governed the game for which, to begin with, South Africa seemed tactically better equipped. They were more direct whereas, at crucial moments, the French chose to be more expressive only to find they were making little headway. Once again, Deylaud was suspect in his judgement and execution.

Joel Stransky had already kicked South Africa into the lead with a penalty when, with his team at last getting up a head of steam, Deylaud aimed for touch deep into South African territory. He miskicked and failed to reach the target. Joubert gathered the loose ball and ran. The momentum was irresistible and took the Springboks to and over the French line. Ruben Kruger was awarded the try which Stransky converted. The converted try thus broke the sequence of penalty points, which was always likely to be the outcome of the game in such atrocious conditions.

There was another significant factor to keep in mind and which, it could be said, alleviated the referee's dilemma.

Having agreed with captains that the game should be played, Derek Bevan was aware that the onus would be on him, if certain events should prevail, to invoke a sensitive decision. The storm continued to threaten so that the chance had not gone away completely. It was still possible that the game might have to be abandoned. If this occurred before the end of the first half and no tries had been scored, the team to go through to the final would be the team with the best disciplinary record and not the team that happened to be winning at the time. In this case, France would benefit from South Africa's misdemeanours during the fracas against Canada at Boet Erasmus in Port Elizabeth, where James Dalton had been sent off and Pieter Hendriks banned. No one was more relieved than Bevan that this didn't happen since there would no doubt have been a furore if France had been awarded the victory despite the fact that the Springboks were in the lead. Kruger's try invalidated the invoking of this regulation.

Benazzi and Cabannes were on immense form for France and by half-time Lacroix's two penalties left them only four points adrift. Stransky kicked three more penalties and Lacroix four (he missed only one all game). Ignoring the lashing rain, France insisted in indulging themselves with extravagant passes. By the end, with the Springboks having lost the powerful presence of van der Westhuizen early in the second half, France were territorially on top. The score held at 19–15 for the Springboks.

Ntamack crossed the line only to be recalled for a knock forward. Benazzi also looked to have forced his way over but was deemed to have been brought down short of the line. The five-metre scrum that followed had to be re-set four times as the French went for the push-over try. The Springboks line held to ensure an appearance in the final in their first time in the tournament. François Pienaar, their estimable captain, had delivered so far what a nation, patriotic and passionate, expected of its rugby team.

However, New Zealand remained the favourites to lift the trophy. They were playing at a pace and a dimension all of their own. They were manifestly playing a style of rugby, expansive and adventurous, which was different from anyone else. New Zealand, throughout their history, have inspired hyperbole for their awesome power and technical excellence. They did not relinquish their reputation in 1995. Indeed, they enhanced it further and did so by departing surprisingly from their traditional principles of tight and solid control and of predictable and disciplined patterns. They quite simply expanded the boundaries and limitations which coaches and players had imposed on themselves and did so in a manner, full of flourish and immodesty, for which no one was prepared. Such airs and showmanship were out of character with what everyone believed to be New Zealand's solemn and cheerless march.

New Zealand were the last to arrive in South Africa. Not much attention was paid to them in contrast to the salutations paid to Australia, England and France. So low-key had been their arrival that they landed in Johannesburg as if under cover of darkness. With their recent record, which was less than was normally expected by their standards, they were cast in a subordinate role but one with which their captain, Sean Fitzpatrick, was not unhappy. 'We don't mind being cast as underdogs,' he observed on arrival. 'It means we have a point to prove.' This surely must be the first time an All Black captain had uttered the word 'underdog' in relation to themselves.

True, 1994 had been an indifferent season. Philippe Saint-Andre's France had won a two-match series in New Zealand for the first time. The All Blacks had beaten South Africa with two wins and a draw before losing the Bledisloe Cup to Australia. They had also lost to England in 1993. In the time leading up to the Rugby World Cup, Laurie Mains, in fashioning his squad, had been swapping and changing the team with a regularity that worried his countrymen. This had caused a strain and a sullen disharmony between the management and New Zealand's media. This resulted in the appointment of Brian Lochore and Colin Meads, two legends of New Zealand rugby, as part of the management team. If Mains was unhappy with public relations, Lochore and Meads were ideal as front men.

There were sensitivities and uncertainties which were matched by the rumours that the All Blacks' brand of rugby was attempting to break with the past. The eternal verities were no longer so eternal.

After two matches the All Blacks had made their case. Their transformation had been quick and clinical. After seeing them twice I wrote to *The Times* in London from South Africa: 'What has elevated the All Blacks from the rest is the clarity with which they have demonstrated their potency. While others talk of their potential, New Zealand are giving proof of theirs. They have been impressive. There are those who point out that the two teams they have encountered so far have lacked the necessary skills and power to put them to the test. But Ireland and Wales have reputations that are at least recognisable at this level in a way that some countries in the tournament have not. Neither of these two Five Nations Championship teams are as formidable as in times past, but New Zealand are likely to be more wary and respectable of them than they would be of, say, Italy, Romania and Canada against whom England, South Africa and Australia have recently played and been less than convincing.'

There were players in their midst with whom the rugby world at large were familiar. Glen Osborne was an adventurous full-back, Jeff Wilson was swift and a top try scorer. Walter Little was a known talent who had been overlooked in 1991, as was Frank Bunce, who had made his mark with Western Samoa in the same year. Andrew Mehrtens and Graeme Bachop were a wonderful pair at half-back. This much was known.

Jonah Lomu, the 20-year-old on the wing, was an unfamiliar name and since he had been talked about as a back row forward – a number 8 at school – an unknown quantity. No New Zealand pundit had included him in the prospective team to go to South Africa. At the All Blacks squad summer camp in Taupo in February there were those who despaired of Jonah Lomu, who had been capped against France the previous season. He was less than impressive in all the physical and skill tests to which each of the players were subjected. At another camp later in Christchurch it appeared that Lomu was not going to make the final role call of names to go the Rugby World Cup. A month or so later, Lomu's outstanding performances in the Hong Kong Sevens brought him back into the reckoning and he was included in a series of trial matches which Laurie Mains had wanted before finalising his squad for South Africa. He scored two tries in the North-South match in Dunedin and helped create a couple more. The final trial in Whangarei convinced Mains of his worth.

In South Africa, he had taken the World Cup by storm. He was the name on everyone's lips. He appeared unstoppable. Only the late-night talkers or those know-alls in the stand ever had a good game against Lomu. Only they, at a fair distance away, knew how to keep him under control.

In the semi-final the All Blacks would play the team they admitted they feared most. They feared their height, their power and their command at forward. From their experience in Twickenham in 1993 they knew how formidable England could be. Where, asked Brian Lochore, was the weakness? He could not find it among the players. He found the flaw, however, in their tactics. England played to a pattern which, on recent evidence, was inflexible.

Before the game Lochore wondered what England's response would be if they found themselves behind on the score sheet, not by a penalty goal or two but by a converted try which, in the light of England's dearth of tries, would require Andrew to kick three penalties or, knowing England's fly-half's prowess, three drop-goals. To achieve victory in these circumstances England would have to go in search of other methods. Lochore questioned whether they could.

They had found their answer by the time they arrived in Newlands on Sunday 18 June. Dean Richards, Tim Rodber, Martin Johnson and Brian Moore and the rest were mighty men and gave England an impenetrable vanguard. New Zealand for their part were not exceptionally big men, but they were supremely athletic and skilful players. First, though, they had to think of a way to disturb England's pattern.

What they came up with was to provide a first-half performance that was the most extraordinary and extravagant in the history of rugby football. In little more than ten minutes they were to put on a display so comprehensively devastating and of an impact so damaging that they destroyed England, psychologically and physically. In so brief a time the contest for a place in the 1995 Rugby World Cup final was over. There was a very real sense for those who were present, so rapid were the thrusts and the economy with which they were accomplished, of not understanding truly what we were actually seeing. For sure, nothing so compelling, sudden and sublime had been witnessed before to begin a match. No sooner had one magisterial action given us a surprise than another, in swift succession, gave us cause once more to rub our eyes, almost in disbelief at the audacious start. There would only be academic interest in the final score.

The tempo was set from the kick-off. The All Blacks chose to kick away from that side of the field where the English forwards had gathered. Mehrtens kicked to the more open side where Lomu was lurking and where Carling and Tony Underwood collided. The advantage went straight away to the All Blacks. England's forwards could not gather together as a unified phalanx. They were split. This bold first stroke gave the initiative to the All Blacks. England were not allowed the chance to establish their forward-orientated game.

In the second minute the All Blacks scored their first try. Bachop's long pass found Lomu in open space. He dispatched Underwood with a hand-off, beat Carling for pace and, like a large, rampant forest animal, ran through Mike Catt at full-back. From the re-start Bachop threw a long pass which strayed into midfield and was picked up off the floor in one movement from his toes by Little. This began the move that ended 80 metres at the other end of the field with Josh Kronfeld scoring. This devastating start so fazed the normally imperturbable Andrew that he missed a penalty and a drop-goal.

Mehrtens rather prosaically kicked a very earth-bound penalty before we soon returned to the realms of rugby fantasy. Carling attempted a relieving kick out of defence which in more normal circumstances would have given England valued breathing space from this opening onslaught. Instead, the high ball was taken by Zinzan Brooke who promptly dropped for goal. From some 50 metres and at an acute angle, the number 8 succeeded. After the breathless start, this was so cavalier that the crowd looked around open-mouthed in disbelief. With Lomu's second try, New Zealand had scored as many points as the 25 minutes on the clock. Little inspired the winger's third try by half-time and Bachop's try soon after the interval gave them a 35-point lead.

There had scarcely been error in their play; everything had been accomplished with mesmerising speed and agility. Such rugby had not been seen before; they were touched by the gods. Lomu was a significant influence with four tries in all, but to say that he alone made the difference would seriously underestimate the role of the others and the glorious intention behind all that New Zealand did. No other nation had come anywhere near this pedestal of brilliance.

Jack Rowell, England's coach, recognised immediately that New Zealand were aspiring to a different style of rugby. With such high expectations and with every right to have them, Rowell must have been unnerved to find New Zealand occupying those sunny uplands of which coaches and players can only dream. New Zealand had dared to play a game often talked about wistfully and wishfully in the imaginary schoolyard long ago; or proposed in the pub among the many 'what if...' scenarios of rugby's possibilities but, actually, unthinkable to put into practice. In fact, New Zealand had dared and won. By any stretch of the imagination this was an extraordinary display.

If England had not reached the heights of which they were capable in the pool games, apart from the Western Samoa match, they had shown nonetheless in the great contest against Australia that they could generate a style of tenacious and unforgiving pressure, played at their own tempo, which was hard to match. To overcome them needed an unorthodox response. New Zealand did it in the most extraordinary fashion.

England recovered in the second half. Both Rory Underwood and Carling scored two tries each in the second half. Andrew, who had received his MBE in the Queen's Birthday Honours list, converted them all. He also kicked a penalty to give a tinge of respectability which had hardly seemed likely 40 minutes earlier.

No England team had lost by 45 points before and the last player to score four tries against them was Maurice Richards of Wales in Cardiff, 1969.

On 18 June the New Zealand All Blacks were playing rugby of a kind different to any other team on the planet. Indeed, for those who were privileged to witness the performance, it did not seem of this planet at all.

1995 THIRD PLACE PLAY-OFF

The hope was that the match would prove a better spectacle than the mediocre affair in Cardiff four years earlier. In an attempt to add vitality and weight to the occasion, it was decided that the winner would gain automatic qualification to the 1999 tournament. England, it was thought, might seek further motivation in that they had not lost two consecutive matches since 1991. France might likewise be inspired by wishing to avenge their defeat against England in the quarter-final that year as well their loss to England at Twickenham in the recent Five Nations Championship.

Such hopes were to evaporate. The game proved to be the worst of the 1995 competition. There was no glory to be found at Loftus Versfeld.

'It's the hardest game to play,' Gavin Hastings had said in 1991, 'because no one wants to be there.'

Sean Fitzpatrick echoed similar sentiments: 'If you've played in one play-off match you don't want to play in another.'

After this one, Will Carling concluded, 'It was a difficult game to play, but more for mental reasons than anything else. It was a challenge we set ourselves as a squad but we didn't get ourselves up for it and we didn't do it.'

At the end of the first half, Lacroix and Andrew had exchanged penalties. After 10 minutes of the second half the two fly-halves swapped penalties again. For the first time in the history of the tournament the crowd grew restive with boredom and expressed themselves by the occasional slow hand clap. Lacroix nudged his team into the lead with his third penalty.

Then the game came alive. From England's restart after Lacroix's penalty, Ntamack began his run from deep within his own half. He linked up with Laurent Cabannes who had had a wonderful tournament, even in the rains of Durban. His run in midfield was decisive in setting Saint-Andre on his way to the line. The French wing was brought down a few metres short of the try-line. However, from the resultant line-out the French forwards drove and Olivier Roumat emerged with a try.

If Ntamack had instigated the first try, he was to start and finish the next one. Fed by Fabien Galthie, the tall wing began his journey once more in his own half and swaying in and out he sped past Dewi Morris, on his last international for his country, and left Rory Underwood and Mike Catt in his wake. Andrew's last-ditch attempt was too late to deny Ntamack a brilliant score.

The French winger was the one player to light up a dismal evening. The outcome, however it was achieved, proved a pleasure for Saint-Andre, the French captain. This was the first time in six meetings that he had been on the winning side against England and of the team, only Philippe Sella and Franck Mesnel knew what it was like previously to do so.

1995 WORLD CUP FINAL

Saturday 24 June 1995 was the day South Africa felt they were back once more in the forefront of international rugby. After they were embraced back into competing at international level, South Africa had embarked on a swift period of acclimatisation in the three years leading up to the World Cup in their country. Even in the years when they were left out in the cold, the South Africans had continued to believe in their own superiority. 'You are not world champions until you beat the Springboks' had been a mantra of theirs during the previous two World Cups, which hitherto had been taken in good humour accompanied with a sense that for the World Cup to be truly a test of champions, in reality, the tournament needed South Africa's presence. No one disputed it. However, there was a dark side, dare I say, to the claim. They expected everybody to take them at their word: they brooked no argument. They believed themselves to be the world champions and that they would have been in 1987 and 1991.

Yet the fixtures they played throughout the world prior to the 1995 tournament had indicated quite starkly that in their years of isolation they had, clearly and naturally from not having regular contact with the outside rugby world, lost ground. The game elsewhere had moved on tactically, technically and in the requirements of physical fitness and athleticism. If they had grown up to understand their pre-eminence in their talent for the oval ball, they were quickly forced to realise in the brief period since their return to the rugby fold that the world to which they had returned was not quite as it was when they were forced to abandon it.

In 1992, England had beaten them once and in that year and the following one France had beaten them twice in four encounters, with one loss and a draw. Australia had won three of their four matches in the same period and between 1992 and 1994 New Zealand had won three of their four games with the final match drawn. In order to reacquaint themselves to the new standards, South Africa had set out on a hectic and punishing schedule against the world's best rugby nations. It was a road they had chosen to travel with an unerring eye fixed on their distant target of the World Cup.

The journey had not been without its casualties. After New Zealand, their coach, Ian McIntosh, had been jettisoned and replaced by Kitch Christie, whose provincial team was Transvaal. They had twelve months to correct their losing trend. They visited Scotland and Wales, a tour which, by winning both fixtures, helped them redress the balance. By the end of it, however, Jannie Engelbrecht, the manager, was cast aside to be replaced by Morne du Plessis, one of the greatest of Springbok captains who had played throughout the 1970s.

Thus, on 24 June their aspirations were realized. In the footsteps of New Zealand in 1987 and England in 1991, the host nation reached the final. This achievement would always mean more to South Africa. Not only because of their long period of exile from the international sporting arena but, far greater than this, there were the broader dimensions which encompassed the country's release from an oppressive and persecuting regime; the birth of an extraordinary sense of hope, fairness and justice; of a benevolent society honouring the dignity of all men, women and children.

Could a sporting occasion accomplish so much? At that moment, the answer was an unequivocal 'yes'. The grandeur of this vision was manifest on a balmy afternoon on a rugby pitch in a somewhat down-at-heel suburb of Johannesburg. To be there was to be moved to believe in a feeling that went beyond sport and to be given a glimpse of what people in Washington on 28 August 1963 might have witnessed when Martin Luther King Jnr gave one of the most powerful and impassioned expressions of 20th-century oratory: 'I have a dream that my four children will one day live in a nation,' he confided to 300,000 people, 'where they will not be judged by the colour of their skin, but by the content of their character. I have a dream.'

King was assassinated in Memphis in 1968. Four years earlier, Nelson Mandela had been arrested and imprisoned for 26 years, and released in February 1990 at 71 years of age.

The sense of touching that dream had grown during the World Cup. In Ellis Park there was a substance of the dream's truth. The Springboks of June 1995 came to represent reconciliation in a unified South Africa. In the past, the Springboks had stood for white supremacists; a victory for the men wearing the green and gold was a victory for apartheid. The old national anthem of the Afrikaners, 'Die Stem' ('The Voice') and the new one, 'Nkosi Sikelel' i Afrika' ('God Bless Africa') that belonged to the new rainbow nation, had been sung throughout the tournament wherever and whenever the Springboks played.

If South Africa had had the opportunity of choosing their opponents in the final they would have called out but a single name, that of their historical foe in these rugby matters: New Zealand. Other nations have had their glorious afternoons in the sun but for most of the century since battle was joined in 1921 in Dunedin, the All Blacks and the Springboks had fought for supremacy. The sheer will of the two nations had been drawn from a primitive source, inspired by triumph and provoked by the dishonour of failure. They had stood toe to toe, eyeball to eyeball, to carve themselves as champions of the world.

Their confrontation at Ellis Park in 1995 was the first authentic test of this claim. Both the All Blacks and the Springboks kept their teams unchanged from the semi-final matches. Joost van der Westhuizen, the brilliant scrum-half, was declared fit after the fears of the previous game in Durban. He had come off the field after 51 minutes with a trapped nerve in his ribs.

The game, for all its feverish excitement and typically unbending resolve, fell short of the epic encounter that had been anticipated. Nonetheless, it was magnificently emotive and endlessly gripping in its drama that drew ultimately to a terrific climax. There were no tries but the match was no less vivid for that. There were too many mistakes to make it touch the pinnacle.

South Africa had played a cautious game in the main in contrast with New Zealand's hugely expansive style. The latter had to be held in check because if they were given a hint of daylight, Little, Osborne and Wilson, orchestrated by the precocious Mehrtens, would make for the open spaces.

Kruger, Pienaar, giving a leader's performance, and van der Westhuizen, acting as a fourth back row man, closed them down mercilessly. Mulder in midfield was also a tower of strength. The contrast was stark. New Zealand initiated attacks, while the South African strategy was largely defensive and one of containment.

In the line-out, Ian Jones, in the truest sense, had a great game. Impressively and conspicuously he rose high to claim the ball as his own. With total control, as if suspended in the air, he gave Bachop a stream of fine and reliable possession. Try as they might, however, the All Blacks could not find the rhythm that they had so much enjoyed in the other games. Surprisingly, they were in too much of a hurry, too much of a nervous dash. There was the frequency, the desperation, of trying to set Lomu free, and not timing it correctly. For once the All Blacks looked to an individual player to win them the game, while forgetting at the same time their collective strength and discipline. True, Lomu had won them matches but through careful thought and fine judgement.

He was, admittedly, well marked by James Small but the All Blacks had lost their accuracy. When they also lost Mike Brewer, their flanker, at half-time they seemed to lose their way completely. Instead of attempting to regain control by limiting the width of their attack, the All Blacks pursued their tactics to unleash Lomu. They seemed incapable of change.

Meanwhile, the Springboks followed their strategy of a carefully structured, though limited, game. Joel Stransky was the architect at fly-half. Almost third choice before the tournament began, along with Brendan Venter and Hennie le Roux, Stransky very nearly did not take part. However, he had shown from the beginning against Australia that he was the man in charge. He knew the team's strengths at forward and played to them. He knew his team's limitations and sheltered them. He was truly the team's fulcrum, which is as it should be for the fly-half.

Stransky had kicked two penalties and a drop-goal against Mehrtens's two penalties by half-time. The All Black fly-half brought things level with a drop-goal of his own halfway through the second period, but with an easier chance – if there is such a thing in so boiling a cauldron – he failed to hit the mark the second time just before Ed Morrison, the referee, blew for the end of proper time. In 22-year-old Mehrtens's mind, the 9–9 score must be frozen eternally. He had come so close to moving it on in his team's favour but instead, with a chance of victory missed, extra time was to be played. He had enjoyed a brilliant tournament.

With energy dissipating and bodies weakening in the relentless physical struggle, it was more than ever the trial of will. Who, when all else was laid bare, had the last pieces of unyielding iron left in his soul?

Mehrtens kicked a long penalty goal in the first period, and so it was as the minutes died away. Strange and, in many ways, inexplicable feelings strayed into the most hardened of hearts. Was this the way it should be? Was this how it should end ? Was this what the new South Africa deserved? Should the team who had played the most dashing rugby and who had charmed us all along the way take the trophy? Or on such a unique occasion, should there be a more charitable outcome, whose meaning would be interpreted beyond the sphere of mere sport? Should sport and politics only be seen to mix in an adverse sense, one which South Africa knew so well, or should they not also be seen to be a source of good and to be experienced in their benign humanity?

Stransky levelled. For all the endeavour and the creeping tiredness, the defences of both teams remained tight and unyielding as they had been all afternoon. In this prodigious struggle, there was no give, no surrender. Neither line was breached even if Kruger and du Randt thought they had; no try was scored.

With seven minutes left, Stransky, from 30 metres and with Mehrtens close enough to charge down, struck his second drop-goal: 15–12. Thus, the Springboks won the 1995 Rugby World Cup.

Justice was not done to New Zealand, who had performed with exhilarating clarity and vibrancy throughout the tournament, unlike the often-ponderous Springboks. Sport is not about fairness, however much we may wish it, so that on a beautiful Transvaal afternoon and in a transfiguring moment in South Africa's history, the game ended with the fitting result which bespoke of hope and promise. It was a moment of sublime harmony. One team, one nation.

WINDS OF CHANGE

'Anyone who plays rugby very soon finds out there are two sorts,' writes Michael Green in *The Art of Coarse Rugby*. 'The first kind of rugby is called rugger. Rugger is played by fifteen men on each side. These fifteen men are devoted enthusiasts who train like mad. They don't mind at all if someone tackles them at thirty miles an hour and sends them flying into the grandstand; they merely grin and tousle their opponent's hair playfully.

'If they are injured, rugger players are very brave. They pretend it is nothing really and as soon as they are able to stand they hobble back into play and everyone claps them, especially the other side.

'After the game, rugger players all declare what fine fellows their opponents are, and they all cheer and clap each other on the back, and sometimes exchange jerseys. Both teams then wallow in a luxurious bath, eat an enormous tea, and indulge in great bonhomie together in the evening.

'Rugger is controlled by an International Board who issue edicts about open play and the Spirit of the Game. In turn, the board is composed of representatives of the various unions who send round men to speak at club dinners and to exhort everyone to follow the Spirit of the Game. This includes being celibate on Saturday night.

'Games of rugger are controlled by a referee and two touch judges. The referee's decision is final and even if a player disagrees with it, he grins and bears it in the Spirit of the Game.

'Unfortunately, half of the rugby played in this country bears little resemblance to the splendid conception fostered by the Rugby Union. The "other half" consists of the third, fourth, fifth and sixth teams of the less-fashionable clubs or the first and second XVs of the very small clubs. This submerged section of the rugby world play coarse rugby. The rest play rugger.

'The first thing that distinguishes coarse rugby from rugger is that neither side is ever composed of fifteen men. In fact, most extra Bs or Cs wouldn't know what to do with fifteen players. They would have to send three or four off the field before they could begin.

'An old friend – a converted soccer man – who played for the coarsest sides in the country, claimed that he was 28 before he realised there were supposed to be fifteen on each side. When they told him, he thought for a moment and said: "Well, I think that fifteen a side spoils it."

'What a man! His type are the very salt of coarse rugby.'*

---

*Extract taken from *The Art of Coarse Rugby* by Michael Green (Robson Books, 2001)

Rugger was always played in England. Nowadays, visiting Bath, Leicester, Wasps and Newcastle and other points in the English Premiership, I am not certain whether even in England they call rugby 'rugger' any more. Moreover, if they still do at Twickenham, where there is a good deal of role-playing among the hospitality crowd – as there is, I hasten to add, among a similar crowd elsewhere – it serves to emphasise either those of a certain vintage or those who believe that to talk in this way is *de rigueur*. Things have changed. They play and always have played 'rugby' elsewhere.

Furthermore, I wonder to what extent Michael Green's comic vision rings any bells in the hearts and minds of the 21st-century rugby fan. Green's fictional characters, the Penelopes and the Rodneys and the Arthur Symington-Smiths inhabited a once-familiar territory in much the same way that PG Wodehouse's Jeeves, Tuppy Glossop and Augustus Fink-Nottle did. Rugby union's set of intricate laws and richly colourful personalities was never far from caricature. Nonetheless, a good deal has changed.

Green's affectionate and hilarious view of rugby union was familiar to anyone who had ever crossed the threshold of a welcoming clubhouse. Those with a modicum of acquaintance with the game could recognise the fraternal good humour, the tolerance and the tender indulgence, the bountiful frivolity and essential absurdities of an inexact and less than impeccable pastime which was, nonetheless, made compelling by the sheer exuberance of its many possibilities and contradictions. Rugby was tough yet amiable: the fat man could play in the same team as the slim Jim; the slow with the quick; a place could be found for the clumsy as well as the agile; the elegant as well as the graceless; the fit as well as the unfit. At the highest level there was intense drama on the fields of glory where legends played.

For many, what playfulness there was off the field was rather more important than anything that ever was played on it. The atmosphere of the 'third half' – 'le troisième mi-temps' as the French refer to it – was thought by many to be the game's major attraction. The game was amateur. Green managed to exaggerate the triviality of a game whose endless mysteries cannot easily be explained even by the diehard aficionado.

If Green's view found its observance and its apotheosis in England's green-leaved suburbia, the acknowledgement that only a thin line separated a creative and resourceful team game from that which was comical and of interest to the crackpot or deviant, was vividly understood throughout the world. The athlete and the cartoon figure existed side by side. The way Green wrote and the milieu he created may have been a caricature, but it was a spirit of a place that could be recognised and inhabited by a species every rugger-bugger knew. If the incidents themselves as recounted by Green did not actually happen, it did not require too vivid an invention to imagine that they could. The Old Rottinghamians RFC, the rugby club of Green's imagination, lived on the fringes of the game and played in the green belt on the edge of town.

If New Zealand, South Africa and Australia recognised this less than others did, and took sport in a more serious vein, the Southern Hemisphere nations, nonetheless, did accept that there is a funny side to sport. They recognised that there was a social side to the game. It was the 80 minutes on the paddock that was not funny.

Rugby was recreational and a highly sociable activity. It was a game a man – and they were men for the first 100 years – played in his spare time. This was so even at the international level, more or less depending where you lived. For England, Ireland and Scotland, rugby union was a game pursued for its own sake and enjoyment. It was strictly amateur. That was the end of the matter.

Wales had always been ambivalent in their attitude, seeing that the game was not the sole preserve of the middle or professional classes. Strongly of the classes who served the heavy industries of coal and steel, where life was a good deal tougher and more demanding than it was for the largely College and University educated of the other countries, and where originally time-off was not so easily come by, Welsh clubs throughout the decades were quite flexible in their view of amateurism. On the face of it, they complied with the view of the other three unions but behind the scenes at the clubs there was a form of reimbursement. There were what was euphemistically called 'liberal' expenses or 'boot' money, whereby brown envelopes were said to materialise in the boots in the dressing room after the game.

These benefits, it has to be added, were far more modest than the tall stories that have always circulated, would have them. Just as it was once said that, as far as violence on the rugby field goes, an incident was always made to seem more interesting if a Welshman was in the thick of it, so it was with stories where money was concerned. The impression was that there was a mountain of dosh available. The point was that in Wales a blind eye was turned to the strictness of the laws governing amateurism, but more in innocent charity spiced with a bit of club rivalry than ill will or bloody-mindedness. Had the rugby clubs been swilling in money there would have been more movement of players than there was at the time.

Suspicion of the goings-on in France cost them their place for a long time on the International Rugby Football Board. They, like Wales, did not interpret the laws too strictly. Theirs, however, was a view that saw rugby as full of bonhomie and camaraderie, words which have entered the vocabulary wherever the game exists and which are, self-evidently, French in origin.

The player who wears his country's jersey recognises the world that Green created and knows of the colourful and eccentric denizens who inhabit it. However, it was all of a piece. The man who played coarse rugby near to the town allotment, or at the end of Acacia Avenue, or in the shadow of the steelworks did so for the same pleasure as the man who found his crowning glory with a thistle, the fern or the shamrock on his chest, the rose or the three feathers, the wallaby, the springbok or the cockerel.

For over a hundred years they ran and played at will and did so for the sheer unalloyed pleasure of doing so. That was the joy and the honour. To what extent winning the game was important varied from nation to nation; some emphasised it more than others.

In August 1995 the world which rugby union had happily occupied for over a century was changed dramatically. There had never been an untrammelled period when rugby union had not been free of its anxieties about the threat to the amateur spirit, to which the game's administrators had always wished to adhere. It was a matter of faith. However, in the summer of 1995 the International Rugby Football Board turned its back on its long history and declared that the game henceforward would be an 'open' sport. For the second time in ten years the IRFB made a crucial decision in Paris which would alter the whole tenor and attitude of their game.

The game's amateurism had withstood a number of forces from a variety of directions which it could no longer sustain. In the mid-1970s there was the controversy of the payment by manufacturers to players for wearing branded boots. If this centred largely on Wales this was because the Welsh team enjoyed the most prominent profile at the time. Players from all countries were implicated, however. Famously, Andy Ripley, the hugely multi-talented England number 8, ran on to the field at Twickenham wearing an Adidas boot on one foot and a Gola boot on the other. Fond of cocking a snook at orthodoxy and pomposity and anything that might soon become an acceptable conformity, Ripley enjoyed nothing more than questioning that which, through unthinking consent, might border on the absurd. Much as Graham Chapman might interrupt a sketch that had gone on long enough in *Monty Python's Flying*

Circus, so Ripley intervened. 'That's enough,' Chapman would bellow. 'This is now becoming silly.'

This seemed to be Ripley's message as much as it was to highlight in good humour the boot companies' promotional gimmick. Which of the two companies was going to sponsor both of Ripley's feet? The RFU hierarchy were not amused and when Ripley turned out for the following international fixture in Adidas he was pestered for an answer as to why he had made the choice. Sniffing another controversial story, the media clamoured for an answer to which Ripley gladly responded. 'ADIDAS, didn't you know,' he responded, 'is an acronym for All Day I Dream About Sex.'

The controversy over what became known as the 'boot scandal' had grown out of all proportions in Ripley's view and, typically, he saw the funny side of an issue which had grown to be rather ridiculous. Instead of providing a critical examination of the matter, Ripley simply saw the funny side. This was in 1974, twenty-one years before the barricades came down.

Sports sponsorship became manifestly more visible and endorsements more widespread. Television, in particular, along with radio, newspapers and other outlets for promotion extended their coverage of sport. This rendered countless opportunities available for sportsmen to capitalise financially on their fame and their standing among the public, which hitherto had been of only marginal or exclusive interest. Sportsmen were asked to contribute to radio and to appear on television, to participate in programmes that required not necessarily their expertise in their chosen sport but merely that they were recognisably a 'personality'. The cult of 'celebrity', which would reach hysterical proportions in the following century, was in its infancy. Players' expert comments might be required for newspapers and magazines. Autobiographies were contracted. Fees were available.

The rugby union player could not be a part of this. The amateur regulations forbade it. At the same time the administrators found it amenable for their purposes to accept sponsorship for whatever they deemed worthwhile. There were match sponsors, kit sponsors and other deals and contracts which the unions were now ready to acknowledge. The Welsh Rugby Union were the first to have a one-name sponsor for an international fixture. This was Crown Paints, and the game was against New Zealand in 1980.

In the meantime, the number of fixtures at international level was increasing. The demands of time and commitment intensified for the players and the strain on the players themselves began to tell, as well as that between them and their administrators; the exploited and the exploiters. The feeling grew that they were being unfairly abused. Increasingly, there emerged with this heightening tension what was perceived to be the blatant hypocrisy of the game.

Sir Bill Ramsay, uniquely twice President of the RFU in England (first in 1954/55 and again in his union's centenary year in 1970/71) was once quoted as saying at a club's annual dinner that it pleased him very much to see rugby clubs in the 'red'. This meant, he concluded, that a club relied on voluntary effort and therefore ensured that rugby union remained an amateur sport.

In the *Centenary History Of The Rugby Football Union* (UA Titley and Ross McWhirter), he wrote in the foreword, 'Further changes are certain in the future but through all the time one sees the determination to retain our strict amateur belief... Rugby union, as we know it, is not a job of work but a game to be enjoyed in the hours of relaxation, as a relief from the daily toil; if ever it imposes too great demands and interferes with work and home, it exceeds its function.'

The interference had begun. It was to prove unstoppable. The entrepreneurs were waiting on the sidelines. Following in the footsteps of what Packer had forced cricket to achieve, in 1983 David Lord had proposed signing up 200 of the top qualified players to play on a circuit in venues around the world. This had been the route tennis had originally taken before establishing itself as a fully professional sport. In rugby, the entrepreneurs had made suggestions of a World Cup before it ultimately came into being. They were there also to suggest the establishment of a European club tournament in the 1990s.

As Marcel Martin points out, at every stage the ruling body of the game was always reacting to outside forces, instead of themselves promoting new ideas and guiding the game in the right directions. They were always behind the Zeitgeist.

Even among the IRFB, one of their own kind was actively undermining the amateur ethos and promoting the payment of players, albeit clandestinely. South Africa, bitter at the way they were ostracised because of their apartheid policy, had invited the New Zealand Cavaliers to visit the republic in 1986. This caused a furore in New Zealand.

If, when the South Africa Rugby Board were celebrating their Centenary in August 1989, no rugby union accepted an invitation to their party, many players chose or were in some cases advised by unscrupulous committee men, motivated by self-interest, to act independently. Enticed by money (£20,000 was the figure circulating at the time), Welsh players along with other international participants flew out to the Republic. There was a letting of blood in Wales. The President of the Union, Clive Rowlands, and the Secretary, David East, resigned. This might have had significance only as a little local difficulty; other nations also to contend with it, but they chose to deal with the controversy either by ignoring it or by managing it in a more discreet fashion. But the fuss in Wales seemed yet another instance of the Welsh team choosing to wash their dirty linen in public. They failed to keep the controversial issue under control and while the shenanigans were highlighted in Wales it served to divert attention from what everyone else was up to. The focus was on Wales. Others managed to keep their heads below the parapet.

The WRU Committee was divided by acrimony and riven by shame during the conspiratorial South African adventure. The clandestine nature of the trip and the many deceptions that were perpetrated at the time among players and administrators alike, led to the WRU asking for an independent enquiry. The man invited to carry out this review was barrister Vernon Pugh QC. He was little known in rugby circles but of growing repute on the legal circuit. Hitherto he had been associated as a coach with Cardiff High School Old Boys. This was his first step into rugby union affairs at national level and was to lead him with meteoric suddenness and clarity into the firmament of international rugby administration.

The publication of Pugh's report led to the demand for an Extraordinary General Meeting (EGM) of the Welsh Rugby Union. It had found that 'while an individual lack of circumspection or even deceitful behaviour might be explicable, the vitally disturbing feature was that such behaviour seemed so widespread as to be almost endemic to the whole system and its operation.' The EGM was held in April 1993. A vote of no confidence was declared which forced out of office the whole of the General Committee of the Union. The afternoon of long knives in the Civic Centre in Port Talbot in South Wales, momentous as this change seemed to be at the time, soon came to be seen as the kind George Orwell depicted in *Animal Farm*, and would ultimately have more consequences for the rest of world rugby.

The revolutionary zeal with which one set of committee men at the WRU was removed only succeeded, as time passed, in replacing them with a complete set of imitations. Just as the animals in Orwell's fiction began to resemble the previous occupants in form and habit after taking over the farmhouse, so nothing in the end changed at the WRU. Deterioration in Welsh rugby fortunes was set to continue. The root and branch reform of both the playing and administrative structure, which the report recommended was essential and long overdue, is still awaited in 2003.

The Welsh Rugby Union EGM was followed in July 1993 by an AGM. Pugh for the first time stood to be elected as a member of the General Committee and succeeded. Following on from the 103rd AGM of the Union and at the first meeting of the new Committee, as is the procedure, the Chairman of the WRU was chosen. Vernon Pugh emerged as the elected Chairman. The upshot of this parochial argument and internal feuding was, within a few short years, to have a significant influence beyond the limits set by Offa's Dyke.

This was a local spat but one which would reverberate throughout the rugby world and would have repercussions beyond Wales. The true revolution was to take place somewhere else. Port Talbot was significant in the sense that it was in this small town, famous for its steel industry, that the leader of rugby's revolution surfaced into the spotlight. It is worth recounting this particular Welsh saga because it was in this way that Vernon Pugh came to prominence. For what remained of the Millennium and two years into the next one he was to become the driving force of rugby's international administration.

Thus the current of hot air stirring in Wales's backyard would set in motion a whirling turbulence which, accelerating, caused the collapse of the whole edifice upon which rugby had existed for over a century. It was to change the course of the game forever.

Pugh also became one of Wales's two representatives, along with Ray Williams, who had been elected to the WRU general committee, on the International Rugby Football Board. Immediately he acquired another office. With Chairman of the IRFB allocated on a rota basis between the member countries, Pugh found himself, as it was Wales's turn, in the IRFB Chairman's seat. It was a remarkably swift rise. By the end of what remained of the century, he was to emerge as the single most influential and prominent administrator in the history of the International Rugby Football Board. Within two years he was to be instrumental in determining the most radical change in the game's history. There had been other famous controllers of rugby union but no one until Pugh had pushed back the boundaries and extended the game's sphere of influence in the way he did.

A storm was brewing and he was to find himself in the eye of it.

In March 1995, rugby league was developing a Super League which posed a terminal threat to rugby union in Australia and New Zealand. By creating a Super League, television money from Rupert Murdoch's News Corporation threatened to take over Australia's rugby league competition. A new competition was envisaged which would be controlled by television moguls. With vast sums of money at their disposal, a steady recruitment was under way not only to buy rugby league players but also those players in rugby union. This was not just in Australia but also across the Tasman Sea in New Zealand, where new franchises might be created in major cities like Auckland.

With disenchantment setting in among rugby union players who saw their unions entrenched on the matter of amateurism, the threat of major-scale abandonment of rugby union was starkly real. Discussions were well under way. Promises of commitment were made. However, the Rugby World Cup in South Africa loomed. Rugby union players were contented to bide their time until then.

Significantly, on 23 June 1995, the day before the Rugby World Cup final, Louis Luyt, President of South Africa RFU, along with Leo Williams, President of the ARU, and Richie Guy, Chairman of the New Zealand Rugby Council called a press conference. They announced to the world that the alliance of the three countries – known collectively as Sanzar – had signed a contract worth US$555 million with News Corporation for the television rights over a ten-year period. There was no hint that the players would receive any of this money. However, if this might forestall rugby league, there was another competitor in the field to entice rugby union players with the promise of actual money.

For months prior to this, a group led by Ross Turnbull, an Australian businessman and former ARU member on the IRFB had been aggressively promoting a move towards professionalising the game. He had started recruiting players from around the globe. This was a breakaway game. Players would in effect be relinquishing their association with their governing bodies at home. If, to begin with, he was promoting the idea in isolation and unaware of what else was happening, his side finally collided with Sanzar.

There had been many clandestine meetings over many months which are fully recounted in fine detail by Peter Fitzsimons in his book *The Rugby War*. With a driving and dramatic narrative, the book catches the highly secretive, almost espionage stealth, with which the cloak and dagger meetings were arranged. Even after Sanzar had signed the contract with Rupert Murdoch's man at Sky Television, the New Zealander Sam Chisholm, Turnbull, knowing that the unions had not consulted the players, pursued his ambitions. The unions, he argued, could not fulfil their side of the contract without the players' agreement to play. The unions had not consulted them. Turnbull exploited this flaw. For some six months, Turnbull had crossed the globe many times, east to west, north to south. His organisation, World Rugby Corporation (WRC), had kept the players interested in his scheme.

At the heart of the matter was the plain fact that Ross Turnbull's vision of rugby in the 21st century centred almost exclusively on the élite players at the top of the international game. World Rugby Corporation would be in charge of all the contracts and all the subsequent revenue. Such revenue would be spent among the few. WRC would, in effect, control the world game at the high-profile end and would become its ruling body, but a body without responsibility beyond the cartel of major rugby playing nations. What hope would there be in the future for the likes of Uruguay, Georgia, Chile and the USA? They were in the process of developing. Their needs would have been ignored. This was WRC's flaw.

The gap between the view of the administrator and the player's expectations is a delicate one. If this was the case in the amateur days, it was clearly not a matter which the Sanzar consortium, for all their claim to be realistic about a professional future, had fully understood either. They had also ignored 'player power'. When Sanzar had completed their plan and signed the half a billion contract with Rupert Murdoch's television empire the Sanzar consortium had treated the players with similar disdain. They were the last piece in the jigsaw. With Ross Turnbull's determination to keep the players, not to let go and to follow his own dream for a new rugby system, rugby union could so easily have collapsed. They very nearly lost the day when they thought they were bringing rugby into a bright new future.

By the middle of August, the governing bodies of rugby won the day. The rugby men managed ultimately to keep control away from the maverick WRC but it had been touch and go.

For all the flaws that are frequently attributed to the rugby unions and to the IRFB, their responsibilities encompass every aspect of rugby and have to ensure that the game is nurtured and developed from the grass roots upwards and to include the developing countries as well as the established rugby playing nations. All levels of rugby need to be financed and promoted, not just the upper echelon. The battle was for the life and soul of rugby union. Indeed, had the WRC won, the Rugby World Cup would have had its day and the unions throughout the world would have been subservient to the whims of WRC. Rugby union would have had its own Super League played on an annual basis, thus making the Rugby World Cup redundant and putting the IRFB out of existence. There would have been a new world order.

The game was in turmoil. By the time the IRFB convened in Paris in August, the path they had to take had already been paved for them. There was only one route to go. The man who chaired the meeting was the Welshman, Vernon Pugh QC.

He was the man in the right place when the role of the IRFB was changing in any case. With no full-time employees until the beginning of the 1990s, Pugh became its salaried Chairman by the end of the decade. From the small staff in Bristol, the IRFB, with Keith Rowlands as its paid Secretary and with money at last to advance their cause, was in 1996 to establish a full-time administration in Dublin.

In 2002, the Board, which had once been the exclusive preserve of 8 nations, was expanded to include 94 member unions. To accommodate its headquarters, to develop the game worldwide and to finance its various tournaments (the Rugby World Cup, Women's World Cup, the world series sevens and the age-group competitions) and to distribute grants and donations to emerging countries, by the beginning of the new Millennium the IRB (as the IRFB became in 1997) needed to generate its own income. This income is $50 million which is their 50 per cent share of the fee revenue from the four-yearly World Cup.

It is the Rugby World Cup which eventually speeded up the process to bring about the decision to make rugby an 'open' sport and to allow players to make a living out of the game. This had been the original fear of those who made the decision to inaugurate the first World Cup.

Yet in the New Zealand Rugby Football Union's report to the Joint Organising Committee of RWC 1987, presented in August of that year, they concluded with a different prediction: 'The total absence of any discussion, proposals or even media comment regarding professional rugby proved an earlier claim that only regular Rugby World Cup tournaments could successfully diminish aspirations in this area.'

In a world in which sport plays an increasingly dominant role, rugby union would not have been able to survive as a game as nothing more than a casual, recreational interest, a pastime for the amateur enthusiast. Television had encouraged spectator interest which in turn attracted corporate interest and commercial investment. None of this was lost on the rugby authorities who saw, altruistically to begin with, a source of revenue which would benefit the game as a whole. On one side stood a corporate, commercial stream of finances;

on the other were the rugby unions. Between them there was a bit of give and take. In the middle were the players who supplied the 'product' free of charge. It was an untenable position. The centre could not hold. Amateur rugby had to end.

There are still two sorts of rugby but no longer in quite the way that Michael Green had once portrayed it. There were the nations who were equipped to play and to challenge for the World Cup trophy and those who, from a distance, aspired to do so one day and break the monopoly of the mature and the historically powerful nations. There are, in the current jargon, the 'haves' and the 'have nots'. In a tournament which is yet young, the objective must be for the emerging nations to make their significant mark. It has been a remarkable progress for so short a period. From an exclusive band of eight, the membership has accelerated to almost one hundred. It is the World Cup that has allowed so rapid an expansion. It has provided rugby with the vehicle for worldwide exposure and in consequence brought in the requisite level of revenue to finance its many obligations and responsibilities.

Chapter 7

1999 Rugby World Cup

The Rugby World Cup came to Wales in 1999. To say this, as a famous politician said apropos of something totally unrelated to rugby, is to be economical with the *actualité*. High politics may encourage and demand that words be balanced in the scales and used judiciously. Interpretation of the small print of the contract and the nuances of meaning are critical in the negotiations that follow. Rugby union, as indeed every sport understands, is not immune to high or low politics, especially when there are grand schemes afoot and the potential for high revenue. These had not been easy times for rugby union, having established a major worldwide tournament with a vast commercial potential while almost simultaneously coming to terms with the transition from amateurism to professionalism.

There had been some conflict along the way to the 1999 Rugby World Cup as to who should be entitled to do what and where, and how much and how many; who said what and to whom and who had the right to do this or that, and so on.

There had been difficulties. Rugby football had been administered on gentlemanly lines for over a hundred years. Over a handshake and a civilised lunch, agreements were made and fulfilled. The men on whose voluntary shoulders rested the governance of the game in the Northern and Southern Hemisphere conducted their affairs in as amenable and amiable a manner as possible. The game demanded no more. By and large nothing mattered but the good of the game. They were good companions.

Through the Rugby World Cup, rugby union was growing, as was, in consequence, the company of friends. The places at the top table were no longer exclusively for the small band of brothers who had historically come together annually to share their thoughts. Rugby's interests needed to be shared among a wider public and its administration began moving beyond the prerogative of the few. Rugby union was expanding its boundaries to be inclusive of everyone. Inevitably, patterns of behaviour were beginning to change also.

The compacts of the past might not hold. Increasingly, there was a need to know where to draw the line between the genuine desire to be part of what was now believed to be the third great world sporting tournament (after the Olympics and the Football World Cup), and the point where self-interest set in and began to dictate. From hesitancy and misgivings prior to 1987, the subsequent success of the Rugby World Cup made everyone want a piece of it.

Wales were indeed the host nation in that they would welcome the world of rugby to the opening ceremony on 1 October to begin 37 days of intense competition and would, when the time came, say farewell after the champions had been crowned in Cardiff on 6 November. In between those two dates, the Rugby World Cup of 1999, like its predecessor in 1991, would be shared among the four other major rugby-playing countries in the Northern Hemisphere. In actual fact, the Rugby World Cup came to Europe, not just to Wales.

In the bartering that had gone on to secure the Rugby World Cup for Wales and the gentlemanly agreements to share the fixtures so that everyone could benefit, somewhere along the unclear line it had been agreed that the two semi-finals would be at Twickenham. In the way things had been done among amateur administrators from time immemorial, they had made a verbal agreement. There was no record. What's more, John Kendall-Carpenter, who had been such a moving force and guiding influence in the other World Cups, and whom everyone held in high esteem, had died. What had been agreed?

It was this. After 1987, it was decided that the Rugby World Cup was a 'good thing' and should therefore continue with the next tournament to be held in the Northern Hemisphere. The host country would be England with the final to be held at Twickenham. At this point, Keith Rowlands, one of Wales's two representatives on the International Rugby Football Board, had further moved that if that was the case, then the next time the Rugby World Cup returned to Europe Wales should be the host nation. Upon that there was agreement. England, when the time came, disputed the decision.

Since both Australia and New Zealand were the original prime movers for the concept of the World Cup there had been agreement that these two countries should host the inaugural tournament. Since the next one should be in the Northern Hemisphere, England, with its many resources, its locus in Europe and with the assistance of the other four countries, was best equipped to build on the first tournament. They should be the host in 1991. With South Africa returning into the fold they were naturally the inheritors of the third competition.

Rowlands, a most articulate and astute man, became the first IRFB Secretary-cum-Chief Executive in 1998 and retired in 1996.

In 1994 there were two bidders to host the tournament. Australia and Japan put in a joint bid. Wales was the other bidder. Presentations were made in the Swallow Hotel in Bristol, next to the then headquarters of the International Rugby Board before its move to Dublin. This was the first occasion on which the tournament went out to tender, a system which was to be continued in 2002 and which was to produce not a little dissent and acrimony.

I was asked to make the presentation on behalf of the Welsh Rugby Union, a request that was to become contentious. An objection was made on the grounds that I was not a bona fide member of the WRU and therefore ineligible to make the presentation on their behalf. This was not accepted since there was nothing in the rules to say as much.

Wales were awarded the host union status for 1999. This had been awarded partly on the basis that the current Cardiff Arms Park ground would either be enhanced or a new stadium erected. The latter was chosen and was to prove to be a major problem up to the moment of the opening ceremony. Leo Williams, the Australian Chairman of the RWC made several visits to Wales to meet Glanmor Griffiths, the Chairman of the WRU, to check on the progress of the stadium. With the help of the Works Manager, the American general and Vietnam veteran, Dick Larsen, the stadium was ready just in time.

The last event of this stature to come to Wales had been the Empire Games, as the Commonwealth Games were then known, in 1958.

At any rate, the upshot was that of the 41 matches to be played in the tournament spread over 37 days instead of the previous 31 days, only nine matches would in actual fact be played within Wales. The extended period was to accommodate 20 teams, compared to the 16 nations who had participated in the first three tournaments. England would have the same number of fixtures as Wales, having secured the agreement to have the two semi-finals played at Twickenham. Scotland and France would have eight games and Ireland, without a quarter-final play-off or a semi-final fixture, seven.

Legends abound in Wales. A rich heritage of stories belongs there, and tales from the heart of rugby football are found in abundance. Small towns and hamlets have their heroes of steel; Cardiff Arms Park and St Helen's, Swansea, have long been the fields of international praise. Since Wales desperately wanted to find its place in the sun again, the Rugby World Cup would become part of this inherited folklore. It was devoutly wished for.

The '90s, as with most of the '80s, had been a period of brief gestures of hope. There had been but a single triple crown and a shared championship in 1988 and one outright win of the championship in 1994. There was nothing much else to boast about. Each gave a spur to hope for the following season but they were ultimately to prove to be futile glances at a horizon which merely promised a clear dawn. The sun never rose from behind the clouds to bring to pass the longed-for brighter day. A gloom had settled on Welsh rugby.

Thus, Wales were living on remembrances of a once-golden time which, in a Celtic twilight, was so long ago that it also had become part of all the other myths. The feats of the'70s were tales told on grandparents' knees, as were the victories against the All Blacks in 1905, 1935 and 1953 and the triple crowns of 1950 and 1952 after long years in the wilderness.

There are myths in Wales which tell of splendid cities and idyllic hamlets which one treacherous and stormy night the sea swelled to engulf and claim, never to be regained. On a still evening, it is said, bells are heard to ring from beneath the waves to remind the keen and susceptible listener of the glory there once was. So it was that the sense of pride and honour in Welsh rugby had been washed away over the last two decades with only the occasional and temporary reminder for the discerning and patient aficionado of the way things were – a Ieuan Evans, a Jonathan Davies and a Robert Jones. This is indeed a world that has been lost. There was a precious longing for Wales to find its place in the sun once more.

To add to the nation's woes and a periodic reminder of its inadequacy was that, having torn down Cardiff Arms Park and having promised in its tender for the Rugby World Cup to build a new £140 million stadium, there were innumerable delays and procrastinations. The Welsh Rugby Union, from the beginning, were working against the clock to get the stadium erected on time. Contingency plans had to be put in place. When the Springboks came to visit Wales to play in the stadium in June 1999, only 27,000 spectators could enter the ground, sections of which looked like a building site. In fact, that is precisely what it still was in part.

The retractable roof that would make it the only stadium of its kind in Britain and Ireland was not in place. The removable turf was laid down just in the nick of time so that as a trial run Canada and France had fixtures in preparation before the World Cup arrived in town.

Wales were also conscious that in every World Cup so far the host country had reached the final. Wales's own sense of low esteem was exacerbated when, in contemplating recent rugby history, it could be inferred that, for the first time, the pattern would not be followed in 1999. Few could imagine Wales surviving beyond the quarter-final stage.

There were optimists who believed that Wales's fortunes were about to change; indeed, that they already had changed. There was another myth in the making as if bringing to life the folk fantasy of a disfranchised and fettered people everywhere. This took the form of the romantic vision of a braveheart or a knight touched with divine gifts who would come to the rescue of a subdued and oppressed people. In Wales there are myths which whisper of illustrious princes, slumbering in underground caverns, awaiting the day when the trumpet shall sound to call him to arms to restore the lost glory of Wales. It is a gallant vision.

When the clarion call duly came in 1998 to restore Wales's rugby pride, the deliverer or the 'Redeemer', as he was soon to be mischievously dubbed, was not a Welshman at all. He materialised instead from the land of Maori, not Celtic myths. There were those as the Millennium beckoned, with its allegorical mystical and transforming qualities, who were prepared to believe that Graham Henry, from the Land of the Long White Cloud, embodied the fantasy. The long-for Promised Land was, it would appear, within reach.

Henry was a 53-year-old teacher from New Zealand with coaching credentials second to none. He had coached Auckland to 80 wins in 102 matches between 1992 and 1997 and had guided the Auckland Blues to the Super 12 Championship title in 1996, 1997 and runners-up in 1998.

He took over Wales in autumn 1998, soon after they had suffered a 96–13 humiliation against South Africa in Pretoria, and under his guiding hand the Welsh team had won 9 of their last 12 fixtures; the last 8 had been consecutive victories. Among these had been successes against France (twice), England and South Africa. He had also succeeded where other teams from Britain and Ireland had failed: winning a two-match series in Argentina.

If this sounded encouraging for a nation desperate for a hint of success and inspired at least a cheery good will that anything, with the added piquancy of passion, was possible in the topsy-turvy world of rugby, there was a suspicion that the Rugby World Cup administrators might have given Wales a tail wind. Wales were placed in a pool which was awkward rather than difficult. Furthermore, they had broken with the arrangements of 1991 and 1995 which allowed the host nation to play the winners of the previous tournament. In 1999, Wales would begin by playing Argentina. There were those who believed that Wales were playing Argentina and not South Africa as a compromise. Australia would be similarly placed against the South Americans in 2003, but then they were in a privileged position, being both host nation and previous winners.

In mitigation at the time, the RWC authorities explained that the 1999 tournament included 20 teams in five pools of four teams, as opposed to the 16 (four pools of four teams) which had appeared in the previous three tournaments. The top team of each pool would progress through to the quarter-finals while those countries ending up in second place would have a quarter-final play-off in order to go forward. To arrive at the full complement in the last eight, the play-offs would also include the highest scoring third-placed team.

In both England and South Africa the opening matches – England versus the All Blacks in 1991 and South Africa versus Australia in 1995 – set the tone for the tournament. These intense struggles announced to the world that what we were about to witness over the next month or so was a battle of the giants of world rugby. Wales playing Argentina lacked the potency of that image.

The Millennium Stadium, as it had now been christened, was sufficiently ready to accommodate the Rugby World Cup finalists after 65 teams had participated in 133 qualifying matches worldwide. The opening ceremony was unashamedly Welsh in content: Shirley Bassey, Bryn Terfel, Michael Ball, Cerys Matthews and Catatonia, Max Boyce, along with the massed ranks of male voice choirs and dancing schoolchildren. There was a modest budget.

There was no government involvement. What modest contribution there was came from the Welsh Development Agency and the Wales Tourist Board. The Wales Tourist Board had approached William Hague when he was Secretary of State for Wales, before succeeding John Major as Leader of the Conservative Party. This is in contrast to the manner in which the Australian Rugby Union has received support from state and national governments for their tournament in 2003.

This was also in contrast to the £10 million that the government in Westminster had already spent on promoting the campaign to bring the Football World Cup to England 2006; a quest in which they had failed. If they had shown an interest in this, why not give support to a sport which could now rank itself as third in global importance?

As for the opening ceremony there were critics of the overt Welshness of it all. This is a curiosity. Quite what was expected is a mystery. After all, this was Wales welcoming the world into its embrace. By and large the criticism reflected the observers' own prejudices rather than an objective view of the spectacle laid before them. Wales is, in view of the cynics, expected to be parochial so that anything that reflects Wales is seen as insular and narrow-minded. This is part of the stereotype which is frequently reinforced by commentators.

When Manchester opened the Commonwealth Games in July 2002, it was hailed as a celebration of Manchester and the North West. This was interpreted as a warm-hearted Mancunian welcome. It was as if a different set of rules applied. Wales was parochial; Manchester's was an effusive fanfare of welcome from hospitable Lancashire.

If the first World Cup made a profit of £3.5 million, the second in 1991 made £37.7 million and the 1995 tournament, which was the only one hitherto to be held in one country, South Africa, profited by £40 million. There were those who predicted breaking the £80 million mark in 1999. Seventeen countries took television pictures in 1987 with a 300 million audience. Rugby World Cup had five times the audience in 1991 in 103 countries and by 1995, 124 countries with an audience of 2.65 billion put the tournament in ninth position in popular television interest, sixth as a single sporting event.

Wales was ready.

Wales had played and won against Argentina three times in the previous 12 months, once in Llanelli in 1998 and, more remarkably, twice to win the series in Buenos Aires a couple of months before the World Cup began. This latter success was an achievement no other team from Britain and Ireland had ever accomplished.

The game at the Millennium Stadium to start the Rugby World Cup on Friday 1 October 1999 lacked tension and hardly set the tournament alight. Colin Charvis and Mark Taylor were Wales's try scorers while Neil Jenkins kicked both conversions and three penalties. For Argentina, Gonzalo Quesada, their fly-half, kicked six penalties with a control and discipline – but time-consuming precision – which would reap rewards. Consummate as he was as a kicker, Quesada took an unconscionable time in steadying himself and in eyeing the target, and was oblivious to the restless huffing of the crowd. Every time, though, he garnered his reward. After Wales had gone 23–9 in the lead, the Argentine fly-half brought his team back to five points short of the Welsh total.

After much debate and frequent bouts of consternation between the two rugby unions of Australia and Wales, Jason Jones-Hughes from Sydney, who had a father, Gwyn, from Colwyn Bay in North Wales, won his first cap for Wales by replacing Scott Gibbs in the centre. He looked good. With Shane Howarth, who had played for the All Blacks in 1994, and Brett Sinkinson, who also came from New Zealand, Jones-Hughes was another player with dual qualification. As was later found out, Jones-Hughes's credentials and blood line were more valid and sustainable than the other two. The International Board Appeals Committee had declared him eligible to play for Wales 25 days earlier.

Further talking points that arose from the first match in Pool D centred on the Welsh flanker Colin Charvis and the Argentine prop Roberto Grau. They had been involved in brouhaha on the field. Grau had been issued with a yellow card by Paddy O'Brien, the referee, and Charvis had been cited by the match commissioner. Charvis was suspended for the next two matches, Grau for three weeks.

The IRB had declared their intention of cleaning up the image of the game as many of the aggressive and often violent goings-on, to which a blind eye had so often been turned in the past, were unacceptable to the new nations which the IRB wished to encourage to play. What soon became apparent was the inconsistency in the application of the punishments. Two days later, in the match in Wrexham between Japan and Samoa, Brendan Reidy, the prop for Samoa, was cited for punching but he was not suspended. T-shirts emblazoned 'Free Colin Charvis' became a fashionable accessory. When Gareth Thomas, in the game against Japan, lifted his Welsh jersey to expose the T-shirt and the legend underneath it, the authorities were not endeared to Charvis's case.

At any rate, Wales, naïve and uncertain, had survived a dishevelled game to which was attached so much tension by a nervous yet demanding home nation. The embrace of an expectant home crowd in a new stadium, whose intimacy and closeness made it a wonderful venue for team sports, accentuated a fervent and intoxicating sensation. The stadium provided an arresting and dramatic force.

In the evening of the same day in Beziers, Fiji opened their account against Namibia and, with Namibia perceived as the whipping boys of the group, the South Sea Islanders won comfortably enough by 67–18. In the French provinces, Fiji were to endear themselves to the people as much by the exuberance of their personalities as the spontaneity and adventure of their play. Ten-thousand people turned up in the Stade Mediterranée in Beziers to see their first performance and the accumulation of nine tries. Waisale Serevi succeeded with

11 out of 12 shots at the posts. This was a return to form for the Fijians under the coaching guidance of Brad Johnstone, a form which had deserted them in the 15-a-side game ever since the 1987 World Cup. They had failed to qualify in 1991 and had not won a game in South Africa in 1995.

France, however, were expected to come top of the Pool C. Yet France were far from a happy camp. They had won two consecutive grand slams in 1999 and 1998 and with the same management their fortunes had suddenly turned awry for them. A triple grand slam had been expected but the team had contrived to come apart at the seams. Their once-formidable reputation at Parc des Princes had not been transferred to the Stade de France.

In the previous Five Nations Championship they had lost to both Wales and Scotland. Furthermore, in August they had lost for the second time to Wales in Cardiff. In between, they had been to New Zealand and were at the receiving end of a heavy 54–7 defeat in Wellington. In all, they had suffered seven defeats in 11 matches in the previous twelve months. There were rumours of dissension among the players and management under the coach, Jean-Claude Skrela, his assistant, Pierre Villepreux, and Jo Maso, the manager, which would be exacerbated in the days to come.

Canada, belying their status in world rugby, had, in fact, made a contribution which few had contemplated. Gareth Rees, uniquely playing in his fourth World Cup, was a major influence as captain and place kicker and at fly-half. He was a shrewd tactician of a kind impossible to nurture in Canada, but which hinted strongly of the Welsh blood from his parents flowing in his veins. Canada had performed more than adequately in 1995, honourably some would say despite the fracas against the Springboks in Port Elizabeth, in a group which also included Australia. They had reached the quarter-finals in 1991.

On the second day, Canada played France and went into an early lead, a score achieved typically by Rees's boot. If Richard Dourthe kicked a penalty and Stephane Glas scored an unconverted try, Rees's conversion of Morgan Williams's try restored the lead once more. Dourthe soon kicked another penalty. It was a close run thing and at half-time Canada had every right to fair expectations with the score standing at 18–10.

Critically, Rees, Canada's main man, was injured in the movement leading up to France's second try by Oliver Magne. His loss was not apparent immediately as Williams scored another try. With Bobby Ross's conversion, the underdogs were only one point adrift. Canada, however, missed Rees's wherewithal and they finally went down 33–20.

There were three other matches going on during the same day, staggered at various times to satisfy television's insatiable requirements and rugby's need to maximise its audience.

If England had been held to a tight 23–15 in their previous encounter with Italy in Huddersfield 12 months earlier, there was no such closeness in the first game of Pool B at Twickenham on 2 October. With so many Italian infringements and eight England tries, the 20-year-old Jonny Wilkinson enjoyed a glorious collection of 32 points, from 11 kicks out of 13, to set up a scoring record for an England international. This surpassed the 30-point record which Rob Andrew and Paul Grayson shared. Wilkinson also scored his first try for his country. The 67–7 win was a fine beginning for England, with only Diego Dominguez's converted try registering on the score sheet for Italy.

With a 7 o'clock in the evening kick-off, Ireland scored 53 points against the penalty and try scored by Kevin Dalzell, the USA scrum-half. Twenty-year-old Brian O'Driscoll scored his first try for Ireland, while Keith Wood, the hooker with the flair and dazzle of a fire-fly and with the same desire and energy to be conspicuous even in the most shadowy of places, scored four to equal Brian Robinson's tally from number 8 against Zimbabwe in 1991.

More intriguingly, earlier, at Netherdale in Galashiels on the Scottish Borders, Uruguay had beaten Spain by 27 to 15. There were not many there, some 3,761 souls, or so the records tell, and most of those present had their minds elsewhere on the immense contests to come. There will hardly have been a more wondrous, ineffable sense of joy anywhere and at any time throughout the tournament – not even among those who would ultimately hold the trophy aloft at the end – than the cries and the chorus of rejoicing that echoed in the Eildon Hills that night. Other teams had sterner hopes, steeper ladders to climb, reputations to uphold or embarrassments to be avoided, but Spain and Uruguay were free of the inhibitions and fears that harassed others and which harnessed them to the yoke of relentless ambition. Spain and Uruguay were simply glad to be there.

Uruguay's captain, Diego Ormaechea, was a 40-year-old veterinary surgeon and their coach, Daniel Herrera, worked for the Disney Corporation. Pablo Lemoine, the Bristol prop, was the only professional rugby player among them.

Sweet indeed it must have been for Ormaechea, who had played rugby for 20 years and had hitherto worn his country's colours 62 times, when he scored his team's first try in the first half.

There was more that gave poignancy to the presence of Uruguay. Guillermo Storace, the 25-year-old prop, was a member of the Old Christians Club. This was the club that travelled from Montevideo to Santiago in 1972 and whose aircraft crashed in the Andes killing 29 of the 45 passengers. Those who survived in that perilous and inhospitable region did so by eating the flesh of the dead. This gruesome and nightmarish episode was made into a film, *Alive*.

In the crowd at Netherdale was Jorge Zerbino, a 47-year-old farmer who captained Uruguay for 14 years. The club trip to Chile in 1972 was the first he had missed. Only 6 – which included his brother – of his 24 team-mates returned. It fell to Zerbino to keep the club going. There are only 1,200 players from which they could choose their national team. The Rugby World Cup, in its infancy still, embraces, as it must, a complicated spectrum of personalities, of clubs and of nations with a variety of motivations and who are at different stages of evolution. Rugby's story is only gradually unfolding. Uruguay is an essential part of that. They were there, too, to remind everyone of sport's simple pleasures and the joy that moves and the friendship that joins in a common spirit and which all sport, in an increasingly competitive and commercial world, is in danger of losing and of forgetting.

If Spain had gone into a 12–10 lead in the second half, a penalty try and a try each for Alfonso Cardosa, the full-back, and Juan Menchaca, on the right wing in the final quarter, secured Uruguay's victory. Andrei Kovalenko, their Ukrainian-born fly-half, scored all of Spain's five penalties.

In contrast to this, the following day in the same Pool A at Murrayfield, the old guard were confronting each other for the first time: Scotland versus South Africa; the current Five Nations Champions against the World Cup holders. If Scotland lost 46–29 and by six tries to two, they contributed vastly to a game which provided a sparkle that was lacking at the somewhat damp squib of the opening game in Cardiff.

At Murrayfield, it was 16–13 at half-time and the expected destruction of the Scottish pack by a Springbok line-up (including the contest between Os du Randt, the 6'3", 20st prop, and the relatively diminutive George Graham, who had once played at fly-half for his club) was underway. Scotland's scrum stood firm throughout the afternoon. Two Springbok tries in two minutes midway through the second half, however, put paid to Scotland's chances.

Scotland's weakness came from an unexpected area: Gregor Townsend, one of the most gifted players of his generation. His delicate handling was in fine fettle but his kicking out of hand was not as deft as it should have been. Twice Percy Montgomery ran Townsend's less than accurate kicks to set up movements which ended in tries for Robbie Fleck and Ollie le Roux, who had replaced Os du Randt. Towards the end, having cleverly set up Alan Tait for his 17th international try, Townsend passed a high ball in the direction of Scott Murray. Deon Kayser intercepted the pass and ran clear for 45 metres for a try. The other tries were by André Venter (2) and Joost van der Westhuizen, one of only three Springboks in the team who was in the line-up for the final of the 1995 World Cup.

It was disappointing for the Scottish Rugby Union that for this high-profile contest between age-old rivals, the crowd was 10,000 short of the 67,500 capacity at Murrayfield. This was to prove a problem for the SRU during the tournament. The attendance figures were low: 9,400 for Scotland versus Uruguay, 4,700 for South Africa versus Spain and 17,600 for Scotland v Spain.

Crowds were better in Ireland and there was a full house at Ravenhill, Belfast, where Australia began their campaign by romping home with a 57–9 victory playing Romania. In only the second international to be played at Ravenhill since 1954, the Wallabies scored nine tries against three penalties by Petre Mitu, the scrum-half. Toutai Kefu scored three tries for Australia, but the accolade for the fastest try in the tournament was to remain that scored by Tim Horan in 92 seconds, the 29th of his career. This earned him a cheque of £10,000 from Guinness to donate to a charity of his choosing.

A capacity 22,000 spectators turned up at Ashton Gate in Bristol for New Zealand's opening game. This was the first time they would play Tonga in an international fixture. The omens were not good from the moment both teams performed their respective chants simultaneously – the well-known 'Haka' from the All Blacks and 'Ikale Tahi' from Tonga. The tough, sometimes fierce, tackling of the Tongans not only unsettled the All Black play in the first half but drew angry comments from John Hart, New Zealand's coach. Eventually, Siua Taumalolo, Tonga's full-back was cited and banned for 21 days.

Nonetheless, a Tongan did leave his distinguished mark on the game, but he did so playing not in the red jersey of Tonga, but in the black one of New Zealand. Jonah Lomu, born in Tonga, scored two tries, the first in the 7th minute and the next, and the more significant, in the second half, which signalled the end of Tonga's resistance. In a 7-minute spell between the 59th and the 66th minutes, three tries were scored. It had been 16–9 at the break, with Taumalolo scoring all the points for Tonga. Lomu, who was starting the game for the first time in a year after suffering from kidney problems, struck first, with Josh Kronfeld, who had a fine second half, and Norm Maxwell scoring the other two. Despite the good work of Semi Taupeaafe in midfield, Sililo

Martens and Elisi Vunipola at half-back, New Zealand, having survived the early physical onslaught, ran out comfortable winners by 45–9. Byron Kelleher was the other try scorer, while the remaining points came from the accurate boots of Andrew Mehrtens, who collected 20 points in all.

If Taumalolo was cited in this game, there was a strong feeling that Brian Lima of Samoa should have been called to answer for his high tackle on Japan's Patiliai Tuidraki. This had left Japan's replacement full-back in a daze and he later had to be replaced. Brendan Reidy was also not taken to account for his heavyweight style of punching in the same match in Pool D at the Racecourse ground in Wrexham.

There was a growing dissatisfaction that there were discrepancies in the citing procedures. Much of the evidence was provided by the television cameras. Since a citing commissioner could not be present at every ground they depended on notational analysts who were. The system was far from foolproof. When Charvis and Grau were cited after the opening game the citing commissioner was able to call on television executives to provide nine different camera angles of the same incident. The culprits could not avoid detailed scrutiny. The commissioners' work may not so easily be assisted at the smaller grounds or what might be deemed to be less significant fixtures in the tournament where fewer cameras are in use to supply evidence. A lot depends on the role of the television director who makes the decision in choosing the pictures to be transmitted and who might not catch an off-the-ball incident on camera.

Prior to the World Cup in 1995 citing used to be the preserve of the two teams. A citing commissioner had been introduced in South Africa because it took the pressure off the teams who might be persuaded to introduce tit-for-tat tactics – you cite us, we'll cite you. Instead teams could lodge a complaint for the commissioner to investigate.

There were those who believed that the citing procedure could lead to an emasculation of a sport which by its very nature was overtly physical and that the heat of the moment could generate a violent action. Vernon Pugh, the IRB Chairman, believed that punch-ups can arrest the development of the game. In some countries – Germany was given as an example – rugby is perceived to be a brutal sport. With the profile that the World Cup was achieving for rugby, the image that it promoted for the game was important for its future expansion. For the moment there was concern about the lack of consistency.

Graham Henry, Wales's coach, believed that on the evidence that he had seen on television there were nine other incidents that could have been cited but which were not. Inevitably, there was an element of subjectivity. What might be thought a heinous crime for one pair of eyes would be interpreted by another as no more than what is in the nature of a rumbustiously physical sport. This was a dilemma that bedevilled the opening few days of the 1999 tournament.

At any rate, the New Zealand influence in the Japan team was of no avail and they failed to build on the success they had against Samoa in Osaka earlier in the year. Andrew McCormick at centre, flanker Greg Smith, Jamie Joseph at number 8, and Graeme Bachop at scrum-half were all from New Zealand but now worked in Japan. The last two mentioned, from Otago and Canterbury respectively, had played for the All Blacks in the World Cup of 1995.

The All Black influence had a better effect in the Samoa team. Stephen Bachop from Otago, brother of Graeme, and Va'aiga Tuigamala of Auckland, were also All Blacks. In driving rain which added to Japan's woes and hindered their swift running game, Samoa won 43–9. Keiji Hirose's three penalties was their only response to Samoa's five tries. Silao Leaega scored a try in his total of 23 points to add to the two tries each that Brian Lima and Afato So'oalo scored.

The weekend's prospects included England and New Zealand and a chance for the former to avenge the cruel duel and the unceasing agony in the South African sun in 1995. While in Dublin, there was to be the reprise of the 1991 classic quarter-final encounter between Australia and Ireland.

Before these fixtures there was further unease for France with the news that Thomas Castaignede had injured his thigh in training before their match with Namibia and would not participate any further. France were unconvincing once again and although they won by 47–13, Namibia had given them an awkward first half during which the scores were level and which motivated the 34,000 crowd at Stade Lescure in Bordeaux to give them the bird.

There was no chance of such a crowd responding with spontaneous outpourings of disaffection at Murrayfield. In an almost empty stadium the SRU were driven to adopt artificial means and had arranged for pre-recorded chanting and cheering as Scotland registered a score of 43–12 against Uruguay. That they did not score the 70 or 80 pointer that was anticipated was due in large part to a gutsy performance from the South Americans.

'Sometimes winning a game is not only in the score,' concluded Daniel Herrera, the coach, afterwards. 'With a brave heart sometimes you can have a moral victory. For six years we have been working for this. For us to qualify, to win our first game and to do well in the second is like a miracle.' They were able to point to the fact that Argentina, their more powerful rugby neighbour, had only won one match in their previous three World Cup appearances – against Italy in 1987.

Argentina's fortunes were about to change. At Stradey Park, Llanelli, the expected fearsome contest did not materialise. The match was perceived to be a battle between the renowned scrummaging of Argentina and the high body-line tackles of Samoa. In fact, it was a very disciplined affair. Samoa, confirming the reputation they had gained in the World Cups of 1991 and 1995, had a 16–3 lead by half-time.

A transformation took place in the Argentine dressing room during the interval because the trend was reversed in the next 40 minutes. Agustin Pichot, a wonderfully busy and mischievous scrum-half, who sees himself very much as an entertainer guiding the performers as if he were in a circus ring, mastered the events at Stradey Park to his fashion. His partner at fly-half, Gonzalo Quesada turned the scoreboard to his ways. If Alejandro Allub had scored a try, Quesada, taking all the time in the world over his shots at goal, succeeded with a drop-goal and eight penalties altogether. Argentina scored 29 points in the second half without a Samoan reply in the 32–16 victory that suddenly, against the predictions, changed the potential outcome of Pool D.

This was Argentina's first victory in the World Cup tournament since 1987 and placed them in a good position to come second place if they defeated Japan.

This result, too, was a relief for Wales. In anticipating the match against Samoa, Wales were constantly aware and were frequently reminded of the result of their game in 1991. Samoa's loss against Argentina provided Wales with a safety net which meant that, were they to lose against the Samoans again, they could still come out top of their group and so avoid the extra fixture of the quarter-final play-off. Wales had beaten Japan the previous day by 64 points to 15, scoring 38 unanswered points in the second half. Their high score might also be useful were there to be a tie of sorts at the top of the pool.

For all the ease of their win, one of the most memorable highlights was the sight of Daisuke Ohata leaving Wales's defence standing when he ran 40 metres for a brilliant try, indicating that Graham Henry's preference for size before speed exposed his team's weakness.

The other point of interest was Neil Jenkins's accumulation of points during the game, which brought him level with Michael Lynagh's individual record of 911 points. He needed 20 points before the game began and was expected to surpass the Australian's impressive figure but fell a point short. Gareth Thomas had his moment to display his 'Free Colin Charvis' T-shirt, but the authorities remained aloof from the minor demonstration and were, perhaps, even more resolved to stick to their original punishment. This was Wales's 10th successive victory under Henry.

In front of a sparse crowd at Murrayfield, South Africa, with only Jannie de Beer included from the team who played Scotland, beat a plucky Spain by 47–3, while only 3,000 spectators turned up at Lansdowne Road to see the USA relinquish a 17–5 half-time lead to let Romania register their first rugby cup win in eight years. This might have had something to do with Dan Lyle, their captain and stylish ball player, dislocating his shoulder after 30 minutes, not to play any further part in the tournament. He had gained a vast experience playing for Bath in England's Premiership. Kevin Dalzell might have salvaged something of their disappointment had he managed to convert a late try, which would have drawn the match. The score, however, stood 27–25 in Romania's favour.

The crowds still came out for the fixtures in England. For example, 10,000 turned out for the match between Italy and Tonga at Welford Road, Leicester, to see a dramatic ending to the contest. In a close encounter Diego Dominguez thought that he might have managed to draw the game with a penalty kick in the fifth minute of injury time only for the Tonga full-back Sateki Tu'ipulotu to drop a 45-metre goal a minute later. Italy had lost both their matches and were looking at their exit from the competition. The All Blacks were coming their way next.

Canada needed to beat Fiji or else they too would be going no further. Their prospects looked promising when they took a 10–0 lead after fifteen minutes, then 16–5 after 30 minutes. Then Fiji showed why they were popular in the south of France and they cut loose with Viliame Satala scoring two tries to add to the penalty try. In the second half, Nicky Little, who had been preferred to the more famous Waisale Serevi, guided the team tactically and kicked the points. He collected 18 points, but the end came for Canada when Marika Vunibaka scored a superb solo try. Hero one moment, villain the next, he was sent off the field after head-butting the Canadian centre Kyle Nicholls. The Disciplinary Committee declared that the sending off was sufficient punishment and ruled that he could play in the next game.

On the second weekend of the tournament the focus was Twickenham on Saturday and Lansdowne Road on Sunday.

The match between England and New Zealand was, naturally, of enormous significance in a traditional sense. That it should be a World Cup match added to its lustre while the consequences of the result would dramatically change the fortunes of either team, depending on who won and who lost. The loser would have to play an extra game four days before the quarter-final, while the winner would have free time to spend and to gather their energies as they wished before the killing fields of the knock-out stage began.

Added impetus was given to the contest because Clive Woodward, England's manager, had declared that it was the singularly most significant game for England. John Hart responded for New Zealand by retorting that England were putting too much emphasis on one game. 'You can think a match too big,' he continued. 'England have put a huge challenge on themselves. All eyes in the England squad have been on 9 October. The World Cup will not be won or lost then. That will be on 6 November.'

Another factor could not be avoided. Time and time again England were reminded of their humiliation in Cape Town on 18 June four years earlier, when they had been demolished by a team who refused to be drawn into England's suffocating forward clinch. The All Blacks had shown they could out-think and out-pace England and they thrust the elemental force of Jonah Lomu upon them, leaving the England team a bedraggled and motley crew which beforehand had been an unbroken phalanx of white. Never had there been a demolition job quite like it. Where once there had been a fortress, only a ruin remained in Cape Town's dusk. There was much to avenge.

All portents foretold of the mighty clash at forward; the contest would be settled among the bone and muscle of the piano shifters. There should be no expectation of any fine tuning even though one of the finest tuners of his generation, Jeremy Guscott, would be returning to reclaim the centre position and to make his 64th appearance for his country.

However, the more crucial questions were: if all proved to be equal among the forwards, what else did either team have to offer? What did they have in their armoury to break the stalemate? Who would provide the telling difference?

To the All Blacks belonged the combined and ubiquitous gifts of Jeff Wilson, Tana Umaga, Christian Cullen, Alama Ieremia, Andrew Mehrtens and, of course, Lomu. Collectively, they were a more potent force of thrust and pace than Matt Perry, Austin Healey, Phil de Glanville, Dan Luger and Guscott, however dangerous they could sometimes be. Complementing the All Black physical prowess was the All Black mental capacity of abrasive toughness.

Umaga and Ieremia were the first to make inroads. Mehrtens kicked the first penalty before Wilson, winning his 50th cap, scored a try from Umaga and Cullen's fine running. With two further penalties, one either side of half-time from the fly-half, New Zealand were 16–3 in the lead two minutes after the interval. A de Glanville try and a conversion and penalties by Wilkinson, who was having an unsettled afternoon against the outstanding Josh Kronfeld, brought the two teams level.

Twickenham was a bubbling cauldron of excitement and of the echoing 'Swing Low, Sweet Chariot'. Then England's nemesis of four years earlier silenced the sense of jubilation that arrives in the wake of such a striking comeback. Mehrtens passed a long ball to the prowling Lomu, 55 metres out. Guscott, Healey, Luger and Dawson gave a challenge to which Lomu, rampant as always, responded by striking in such a way that he made the resistance seem puny. Lomu makes the contest look unfair. Each player put in his best effort but was merely cast aside as Lomu strode to the line like the rugby colossus he is.

Twickenham was struck dumb by the dark avenger. Whatever there was to win in the line-out, the scrums, the rucks and the mauls, England enjoyed more than their share during the afternoon. But whenever the critical moment came, in winning the 50/50 ball, where Kronfeld was supreme, New Zealand won the day, and any advantage that came their way they made it matter. Byron Kelleher's try made certain that there was no way back a second time for England, as they had managed earlier in the afternoon when they came so close to overhauling the All Black lead.

With the unfearing prospect of Italy to come for New Zealand, England's route now meant an extra fixture to play. In time the All Blacks, with 11 changes from the team which played England, duly dispatched Italy at the McAlpine Stadium in Huddersfield by 101 points to 3. Having done the business, job done as it were, the All Blacks, with 10 days to their next game, transported themselves south, to the French Riviera no less, where they took a holiday in Cannes. So much for nostalgia and the rosy hues of the good old amateur days. Doubtless then they might have had to stay in Huddersfield or travelled north to the chillier streets of Edinburgh where they were due to play Scotland in the quarter-final. Cannes would not have been on the itinerary.

Lomu's two tries against Italy took him to twelve to overtake the record previously held by Rory Underwood as leading try scorer in the World Cup, while Wilson's three took him beyond John Kirwan's record of 35 tries and establishing a new New Zealand record of 37.

South Africa had beaten Uruguay 39–3 and Scotland had accounted for Spain with a 48–0 win.

In the meantime, the much-vaunted meeting between Australia and Ireland failed to meet expectations. Stephen Larkham was back in the team after a year out of action. Damaged knee ligaments and then a broken thumb put him on the sidelines and Rod Kafer had deputised at fly-half during the period, including Australia's 28–7 win against New Zealand in Sydney earlier in the year. Larkham had last played for his country in the 12–11 victory against England in November 1998.

Lansdowne Road was full of colour and song, 'The Fields of Athenry' competing with 'Waltzing Matilda' on the madcap terraces. It was to be hoped that the spirit of 1991 would prevail. Sadly it did not. The game was a poor one in every sense. The unpredictable wind was one reason put forward for the low standard and meant that Larkham and his partner, George Gregan, constantly played the ball back to their forwards.

Australia dominated the flow and the possession with the wind at their backs, yet were only two penalties ahead at the interval, one each by Matt Burke and John Eales. The Australian full-back and his captain together missed another three. Toutai Kefu and David Wilson were simply too fast for the Irish, who at times could not get their hands on the ball. Trevor Brennan and Kefu got their hands on each other in a way that earned the former a ten-day ban while the Australian number 8 had a 14-day suspension. Whatever misdemeanour Brennan committed, he was to find himself at the receiving end of a machine-gun volley of punches from Kefu, but it was Australia who received the penalty.

Typically, it was Tim Horan who made the vital break in midfield and kept on running to score brilliantly under the posts. He was to prove the link also between Joe Roff, who took advantage of Gregan's trademark inside pass to run clear, and Ben Tune, who scored. Burke kicked the conversion to add to his earlier penalty. David Humphreys kicked Ireland's only points in the Wallabies' 23–3 win.

'The match had a bit of baggage because of what had happened in 1991,' commented Rod Macqueen. 'Mentally, though, this was good. It meant everybody was switched on. There were players who had memories of how close it was and what can happen in a match. We wanted to qualify as number one in the pool, as it was the best way for us. We didn't talk about outcomes, only how we were going to play the game. In this case, before the match in

Dublin, players like Jason Little and Tim Horan were able to say what had happened in 1991, how close it was and so on. This helped the team mentally.'

If the All Blacks had come to haunt England, so the vision of Manu Samoa tormented Wales. Nightmarish memories of the 1991 defeat had inflicted damage on the Welsh psyche which still lingered when the physical scars had long healed. What trepidation there was in Cardiff was moderated by the thought that surely it may have happened once but, like lightning, it will not strike twice in the same place. There is no natural law that dictates that this should be so, merely that the chance of such a phenomenon has very long odds. This is much like the law of averages. The nervous sportsman hopes to find some refuge in it, but it is capricious and ephemeral. No one should put their shirt on such a thing happening or not happening. In any event, Samoa were no longer simply making up the numbers. They were very much a part of the tournament, and feared, and were about to make their point once more.

Jenkins was overtaking the record number of caps won by Ieuan Evans, the great Welsh winger. With his 73rd cap to add to his collection, he was expected by the end of the game to be the holder of the world record for individual points scored, ahead of Michael Lynagh. This record was delayed slightly. After Silao Leaega had kicked Samoa into the lead, Jenkins had his chance in the fifth minute but, with the crowd poised to celebrate, the ball hit the post. Finally, after 13 and a half minutes he converted a penalty try to give him the new record.

The Samoan scrum suffered so much that they allowed another penalty try. But, as after Jenkins's missed first attempt at goal, the Samoan response was to run the ball at Wales. They benefited from their own spontaneous but penetrative running and profited from Welsh errors of which there were many. They scored five tries, three of them coming directly from Welsh mistakes. Stephen Bachop with two tries – one of which came by stealing the ball at the back of the Welsh scrum – and Pat Lam – from an interception – were in fine form, as was Leaega at full-back.

Wales were leading 18–10 after 35 minutes and looked to be having an uninterrupted path to the Australians in the quarter-final, without the extra match in between. For the third time in the series between the two countries, Samoa, at 38–31, defeated a demoralised Welsh team which brought to an end Wales's sequence of consecutive victories.

The permutations for the pool were complicated. If Argentina beat Japan, then – with Samoa and Wales – three teams would end up having won two matches with one defeat. If Argentina beat Japan by 69 points they could come top of the pool. If they reached 48 points they would be placed second with Samoa third. If Japan beat Argentina then Samoa would be level with Wales. By virtue of beating Wales, Samoa would go straight through to the quarter-finals.

These varied possibilities occupied the minds of those who turned up for the Saturday evening kick-off in Cardiff. Japan, as ever, ran and played as if their lives depended on it but could not cross the Pumas' line. Hirose kicked four penalties, while Quesada kicked seven to add to the fourteen penalties and a drop-goal he already had. He had contributed 66 of Argentina's 83 pool points and was the leading scorer in the tournament so far. Against Japan there were others who managed to upset his monopoly of the scoreboard. There were tries by Pichot and Diego Albanese to add to the one Allub had scored against Samoa, with one conversion by Felipe Contepomi.

The third best from the five pools, which was Argentina, would go to Lens in France to play Ireland, the runners up from Pool E, while Samoa would play Scotland. Ireland, with nine changes, brought Pool E to a close with a 44–14 win against Romania and in second place after Australia, who had defeated the USA, 55–19, the previous day in Limerick.

Rod Macqueen, a marvellously shrewd, articulate and tough-minded coach, and probably the most accomplished in an era of genuinely talented coaches, had learnt a small lesson in what to say and when to say it. As his team was about to face the USA, Rod Macqueen mistimed his assessment of the tournament. He expressed dissatisfaction with so many 'minnows' allowed entry into the final stage of the Rugby World Cup.

At Thomond Park in their final game of the pool stage, Australia loosened their grip to allow the USA to cross their line for what turned out to be the only try Australia were to concede throughout the tournament. Juan Grobler had achieved the accolade before half-time and with Dalzell converting to add to the drop-goal that David Niu kicked, the score briefly stood at 17–10. Earlier, Alec Parker had missed a try and Dalzell a couple of penalties. By half-time it was 22–10 and 34–19 entering the final quarter. But three tries before the end made a tally of eight tries to one in the final reckoning. The result told its own story. This, at least, had been no less than interesting for the capacity 12,000 crowd.

There were interesting times in France too. Canada, who had been aware that life would be short in the 1999 World Cup after Samoa's defeat of Wales, went out in Stade Municipal, Toulouse, needing a big score against Namibia. This was in case the mathematical equations needed to be worked out for the best third place play-off and that the number of points came into play in determining the final outcome. Canada duly did so (72–11) but to no avail, since they still depended on Japan beating Argentina two days later.

It was a sad end to a team that had held high hopes at the start and which, had they succeeded, would have consolidated their position as an emerging team to challenge rugby's higher echelon. There was also the ignominious early departure of Dan Baugh, who was one of the quartet that was sent off the field in the early rounds. The other three were Marika Vunibaka of Fiji against Canada, the South African Brendan Venter who was sent off at Hampden Park, Glasgow, against Uruguay and Ngalu Taufo'ou of Tonga, who was sent off against England.

Of more concern in Toulouse was the performance of their own country. France had failed to convince in any of their matches hitherto while Fiji, despite Vunibaka's misdemeanour, had enamoured themselves with the public in the south of France. They had been in scintillating running form when the mood struck them of the kind beloved of France themselves.

There was a sense that not all was well in the French camp and such disruption that was hinted at off the field was, it was thought, made manifest in the lack of cohesion on the field. There were those, journalists in particular, who felt that they had not had as full an explanation as they deserved for the injury to Thomas Castaignede. Then Pierre Mignoni, the scrum-half, had to be replaced before the Fiji game by Fabien Galthie, who had played in the 1991 tournament and was now re-introduced to the squad. This was the scrum-half who, having been dropped after the tour to New Zealand, had declared that he would never be part of Jean-Claude Skrela's team again. A special press conference was called to clear the air. In the event it was Stephane Castaignede who began the match against Fiji. From the two undefeated teams so far, one would get a clear run at the quarter-final and, it was presumed, against unfancied Ireland.

France, once again, were only in fitful form; a condition with which Paddy O'Brien, the referee, could identify. There was a higher percentage of random decisions than one would have liked, even in a sport admittedly not short of eccentricity. There was, for example, some curious indecision over whether Christophe Dominici had scored a try or not or whether, before this, Christophe Lamaison had indicated his intention to go for a penalty kick or not. A try, however, was not awarded. Nor was another one for Setareki Tawake, who was adjudged to have knocked on when, in fact, a Frenchman had.

On a beautifully sunny day France had gone into the lead. Richard Dourthe had kicked a couple of penalties and converted Christophe Juillet's try to which Nicky Little could only respond with a penalty. A superb try by Alfred Uluinayau converted by Little, who also contributed three penalties, gave Fiji a 19–13 lead with ten minutes to go. There followed a period of some six minutes when France camped on their opponents' line and at which there followed the drama of a series of eight scrums.

Props were warned, props were yellow-carded until, finally, it was Fiji who were deemed to have transgressed beyond the endurance of the referee's patience and awarded a penalty try. Lamaison's penalty and Dominici's try in injury time secured the victory in a match which, while mostly attritional, had the balance of wonderful movements to provide intense drama. The pool which had originally been thought to belong in France's pocket was, in the end, a chasteningly competitive one for them. Nonetheless, they survived to move on unbeaten to Dublin.

While Australia had appeared in control and confident, yet somewhat diffident and wary, it was New Zealand and England, by the end of the first round of matches, who had looked to be flourishing and fully in charge. The two nations were putting to the sword those nations who deserved to be put to the sword, and against those who were stubborn they took the resistance before calmly overwhelming them. Against each other they had provided an immense struggle for supremacy at Twickenham.

Their opponents had to be weighed in the balance for they were not the same for both of them; the psychology of each game changes, the moods shift and the traditions or the old scores different. England took Italy's resistance and scored 67 points while the All Blacks scored 101 points. The All Blacks had a tough time against Tonga only to score 45 points, while England this time went strolling to score 101 points. This was England's third 100-pointer in 12 months. The USA and Netherlands were the other two.

The score against Tonga had been 38–10 at half-time, but Ngalu Taufo'ou was sent off for punching Richard Hill, to which David Waterson, Tonga's coach, responded by drawing attention to the referee's lack of consistency. Phil Vickery stayed on the field even though he was clearly seen to retaliate against Isi Tapueluelu who had caused the rumpus in the first place by up-ending Matt Perry in mid-air.

After the trauma of the summer's drug allegations against him and the isolation that he must have felt with the stigma that was attached to the affair, Lawrence Dallaglio had been in enormous form throughout in the back row for England.

Thus Australia, France, New Zealand, South Africa and Wales were leading their pools and therefore had a straight passage to the quarter-finals in Wales, Ireland, Scotland and France. Before reaching these destinations, the others had first to make a detour to London (England versus Fiji), Edinburgh (Samoa versus Scotland) and Lens (Argentina versus Ireland) for the three quarter-final play-offs, which were to be played on Wednesday at 1pm, 3.30 pm and 7.30pm, respectively.

1999 QUARTER-FINAL PLAY-OFFS

Teams viewed this round differently. For Fiji, to have reached this stage of the tournament was seen as a natural part of the route of getting to the final. They had not thought otherwise. If they had hoped to get there by an easier route, it was no more than wishful thinking. It was not based on any reasonable analysis. They had only imagined in their dreams that they would come out at the top of their pool. For them to remain in the tournament was reward enough. To be in the play-offs was what they had expected.

England, for their part, did not see it in quite the same terms. For England this match was something of a nuisance; in many ways an unnecessary game, a chore. This was not arrogance. It is as other nations in their position – as tournament favourites – would have perceived it also. Had they beaten New Zealand they could have avoided this extra match, coming as it did and as England would have seen it, four days before the game that really mattered to them. They had every right to believe that they should be present at the quarter-final stage. To play Fiji was another hurdle to overcome.

Brad Johnstone, the Fiji coach, sardonically illustrated the difference in a more pictorial, more colourful way: 'Fifteen guys with fast cars and laptops will be playing against fifteen guys with just rugby balls.' This was Johnstone's way of portraying the haves and the have nots of the rugby world.

If Clive Woodward was wary of the opposition this was not reflected in his selection. Phil Vickery, Matt Dawson and Richard Hill, who had each played in all the fixtures so far, and Danny Grewcock and Phil de Glanville, having played in two, were not on the team sheet. Fiji were a team, however, who had played some ebullient rugby. They were a team, too, that were unpredictable;

anything could happen. Woodward's appeared to be a risky strategy, choosing a team which seemed to be below full strength.

In the match at Twickenham, Fiji showed sufficient exuberance in their attack in the first half to give cause for concern. Had they not been guilty of so many errors the score might have been closer than the 21–3 lead that England held at the interval. Uluinayau always threatened from full-back, ably supported in his attacking endeavours by Vili Satala and Meli Nakauta. Serevi, who had been chosen ahead of Little, was as mischievous in his teasing play as ever. These gave the less than full Twickenham crowd a few nervous moments.

Jonny Wilkinson kicked three penalties in the early periods of each half and went on to collect 23 points in all. There were two tries, in which both Dallaglio and Johnson, his captain, played prominent roles. Both had fine games. Dan Luger was the beneficiary of the first. He ran superbly to fend off the Fijian defence and score his 11th try in 14 matches. The other saw Neil Back leap successfully to recover Wilkinson's high kick to cross the line.

At half-time Woodward had a roll call of injuries. Luger, Healey and Joe Worsley came off. Later, Wilkinson and Matt Perry were to follow them to the dressing room. By the end England had used all seven substitutes. Nick Beal and Phil Greening added two more tries which gave England, despite some threatening attacks from Fiji and tries by Viliame Satala, Imanueli Tikomaimakogai and Meli Nakauta, a 45–24 victory. There was, as England's battered forces indicated, a heavy price to pay.

If Twickenham was less than full, the Scottish Rugby Union were dismayed by the meagre turn out at Murrayfield for the second play-off. Only fifteen and a half thousand paid to be there to see their countrymen take on Samoa. This low turn-out was largely a statement against the high cost of tickets (£35 upwards). The matches elsewhere made up for the sparseness in the Murrayfield stands. If Scotland had yet to exceed six figures, the 30 fixtures played hitherto had attracted more spectators than the 931,000 of 1995 and was expected to top 1.5 million by the close of the tournament.

For the second time in the World Cup, Scotland faced the team that arrived from Cardiff with Wales's scalp safely tucked away. Gary Armstrong was winning his 50th cap. He and Doddie Weir were the only survivors from the 1991 match, as were Vaega, Lima, Lam and Bachop for Samoa. Lam was to retire after the Edinburgh game.

It was the quarter-final then, it was a play-off now. This was a state of affairs which Bryan Williams, Samoa's manager, felt able to criticise by saying that it was expecting too much of players to play three international matches in eight or nine days.

In an extraordinary start, there was a period of 12 scrums in eight minutes after which David McHugh, the Irish referee, awarded a penalty try to Scotland. If Samoa preferred the open spaces for the likes of Tuigamala, Leaega and Lima, they could not master the set pieces long enough to secure regular possession for them. Having noticed how Wales had played naïvely into their opponent's hands, Gregor Townsend chose to pin Samoa back into their own half. The safety tactics and close-quarter drives paid dividends and paved the way for Martin Leslie, the flanker, to score.

For all the pressure Scotland were only 15–6 ahead at half-time. Logan and Leaega had kicked the other points. Three more Logan kicks and a Townsend drop-goal gave Scotland a comfortable cushion of 27–6, but tries by Semo Setiti inspired a come-back for the Pacific Islanders. Lima was to score another try, but by that stage, Scotland, with the help of another Logan penalty and a try by Cameron Murray, were home and dry at 35–20.

If these games had sprung no surprises, the third match did. For the first time, Argentina found their way through to the quarter-finals. Conversely, but also for the first time, Ireland progressed no further. Argentina had won only one game out of eight in the previous World Cups – against Italy in 1987. Having lost their coaches before the 1999 tournament began, they had called upon the services of Alex Wyllie, the former New Zealand flanker of the 1970s and All Black coach in 1991.

It was doubtless at his prompting that Argentina's wonderful scrum-half Agustin Pichot was able to feel outwardly confident before the game in Lens. 'The nations of Great Britain and Ireland,' he said, 'always make such a big point about home advantage that they never, ever feel comfortable about playing away from home. Ireland coming out of Dublin to play will have a problem about playing in France.'

It was 15–9 to Ireland at half-time which was stretched 21–9 midway through the second half. All the points came from David Humphrey's boot (six penalties and a drop-goal). In a monotonous, forward-orientated game Ireland were to squander the lead in the last half an hour when Argentina out-scored them by 19 points to 3. In the 75th minute, after a stalemate of kicks between the Irish fly-half and Gonzalo Quesada (six penalties) the vital score came. Diego Albanese, the left wing, crossed the line and Quesada kicked his first conversion of the tournament, as well as kicking another penalty.

In eight minutes of injury time Ireland laid siege on the Argentine line when every Irishman seemed to enter every line-out and every scrum in a desperate attempt to recover their position. There were a succession of penalties for Ireland but at 28–24 they needed more than a mere three points. The penalty try for which they went in search never came. This was for sure a turn up for the books, not least for France who had based all their preparation on facing Ireland at Lansdowne Road. The Irish public had bought their tickets in expectation of a home team presence and hostelries had made special arrangements of their own with equal certitude.

1999 QUARTER-FINALS

Wales were drawn to play against Australia on Saturday 23 October, while the other three matches would be played the following day. Wales and Australia had come out on top of each others' pools, while in the other fixtures it might be said that France, New Zealand and South Africa, the winners of their pools, had some kind of advantage as they were to play those teams who had had an extra fixture thrust upon them four days prior to the quarter-final round.

Wales could not be said to be confident. Samoa had seen to that. They were in a questioning mood and with their staccato, uneasy play in the other games, they were not in any sense bold, even though they might have been expected to be in front of their home crowd. They were a valiant team working hard against the odds to achieve a goal which always seemed destined to be beyond their grasp. Each match was entered into with all fingers crossed, on a wing and a prayer, in the hope that for all the reservations about their overall competence, they might survive to fight another day. They were a defiant team.

There was always the constant belief, too, that Graham Henry, the coach, would make a difference. Up until their previous game he had, after all, led his team to ten successive victories in the fourteen fixtures over the last twelve months. Had they succeeded against Samoa, Henry's efforts might have gone on to equal, and perhaps even surpass in one season the record of 11 victories achieved in the three seasons between 1907 and 1911.

Wales could draw sustenance from the fact that included in this list of successes were victories against England, France (twice) and South Africa. Less comforting was the realisation that Australia had beaten Wales on their last six encounters, all the victories convincing and unarguable.

Against a team which Henry admitted had no weaknesses and a country he believed to be 'the best sporting nation in the world', Wales were inspired to produce their most competent and refreshingly confident rugby of the tournament. Australia, with a touch of luck and some lenient refereeing which soured the crowd, were nevertheless to prove a stronger and a more skilful team. Gregan, Horan and Burke exerted an abundant and constant influence, whether singly or collectively, of the kind Wales did not so readily possess among the backs; Eales and Wilson were likewise among the forwards. They had the sure-footedness that comes with maturity and familiarity with success. Even the good players like Scott Gibbs, Robert Howley and Scott Quinnell always bring with them to any game the baggage of past failure and this needs to be overcome before any thought of success can attain the patina of probability and authenticity. Psychologically, it was as if there were any number of hurdles in Wales's way, whereas Australia looked down the strait with a clear, unimpeded run.

Their fortunes throughout the game might have gone better had they not had such a poor beginning. Wales, from the kick-off, insisted on playing the game in their own half. They put pressure on themselves. Having got the ball they would not let go and insisted on playing the ball in their hands. A simple kick would have achieved some relief. After six minutes Gregan scored the first try, which Burke converted. Thus, the defiant mood and the mental resolve which everyone had doubtless embraced in the dressing room and the need to take the game firmly to the Wallabies were immediately questioned. So soon into the match, Wales were having to come from behind.

Yet, if the difference between the two teams was manifest on the field, all of Wales as a country remained hopefully buoyant. The game was tightly fought. Whatever superiority Australia showed, however confident they outwardly seemed, it was not reflected whenever the crowd looked upwards to consult the scoreboard. Wales were in touch for long periods. It was 10–9 at half-time.

If Neil Jenkins kicked three penalties by the interval, it was his opposite number, Stephen Larkham, who was enjoying the more astute game. He made sure his team did not tarry long in its own part of the field. He made Wales turn.

Four years prior to the tournament, Larkham was playing second-grade rugby in Canberra and doing so from the full-back position. Rod Macqueen turned him into a fly-half. Awkward of shape for the pivotal position, he is lanky and gawky-looking. There is no grace to his stride. To add to the gauche, unfinished look he sports a skull cap which, while drawing attention to himself, can hardly be said to be grand or rakish. Rather it persuades us of his lack of vanity, not the primping self-importance to which the occupier of the fly-half position is sometimes prone. Larkham sets a premium on practicality and that can only be of benefit to him and his team.

His variety of Garryowens, delicate chips and grubber kicks tormented Wales in the second half. This was after his first kick of the afternoon had been misjudged and drifted out of play over the dead-ball line. He then beat Shane Howarth to set Joe Roff free and to a near-score. He later sent the Welsh prop, Peter Rogers, reeling with an up-ending tackle. The game may change but the fly-half must remain the master of his domain. Larkham was for Australia but Jenkins, with Wilson in magnificent, wily, in-your-face form, was not for Wales.

Despite the superiority of Australia their margin lead remained a mere one point thirty minutes into the second half. With the fine rain falling and the surface slippery, Larkham sent the ball skidding along the ground for Ben Tune to chase and to give his team a converted try. Wales, for all their brave attempts, were unable to break down the stern Wallaby defence. They were to suffer the cruel fate, too, of the referee passing bad judgement when Horan's brilliance shone through to make a terrific break. When he was tackled the ball spilled out of his hand, which Colin Hawke failed to see, and the game moved on but, for Wales, only Dafydd James continued to run. The others stopped, expecting the referee to call a scrum. Unfortunately for Wales, Daniel Herbert kept running, as did Gregan who got to the ball first for the try. With Burke's conversion Australia stood 24–9 at the end. If the score flattered the Wallabies, the final outcome did not.

Wales had had a fine honeymoon under Graham Henry and as with all romantic notions of a prolonged, untrammelled and happy future a good deal of sentiment must play its part. There was the feeling that Wales's joy ride could not last. Australia provided the cold dose of reality. Their mental hardness and pace, quite simply, were significantly different.

This hardness was evident, too, in Paris when two mighty packs of forwards met, but, in the manner of an extraordinary game, the pace was not quite an obvious factor – although England's lack of pace meant that they were unable to close down the time and the space which allowed Jannie de Beer to demonstrate his kicking skills. The day's events belonged to the South African fly-half. In front of a disbelieving crowd, de Beer executed a bewildering series of kicks, more specifically an implausible five drop-goals, to scupper England's hopes of advance to the semi-final stage.

Once more, hearts bled for England. Even the most diehard debunker of what is perceived to be England's puffed-up assurance and much caricatured lordly strut, could not help but relent. They could only commiserate with them in their hour of exasperation and dumbfounded defeat. In 1995 they had been mesmerised and vanquished by an uncontrollable force of nature, of a kind hitherto unseen on rugby union's wing, in the form of Jonah Lomu. In 1999 they were transfixed and scuppered by the unforeseen de Beer's unique encore of drop-goals.

Famously, drop-goals have played a ritual role in World Cup rugby; moments which momentarily bring the game, hitherto full of rampant movement and chaotic chase, to a halt.

There is a pause in the hurly-burly as every eye turns to the flight and trajectory of the ball. Rob Andrew at Newlands sent Australia into an early exit in 1995. In the same year Joel Stransky, even more crucially, dropped a goal to elevate South Africa into greater glory.

With drop-goals in mind and to be reminded that they are not the sole preserve of fly-halves, we remember Jeremy Guscott's drop-goal to win the Lions series in South Africa in 1997. We would, sadly, have no more of his glittering talent to admire. Before this encounter in Paris, Guscott had announced his retirement from the game.

The result between England and South Africa at Stade de France was also settled by the use of rugby's sucker punch. Or, to put it another way, if much of rugby resembles a cavalry charge or an assault of storm troopers generating a momentum of attack, the drop-goal is rugby's version of the sniper's bullet. Everyone knows of the possibilities and where, generally, the sneaking ambush can be expected – although this is far from certain – but no one knows when exactly the deadly shot will come and who the executioner will be. It is done, by and large, on the hazard; a solitary figure chooses his moment when, usually, the tumult is at its highest and most intense.

For its drama and excitement and its potential for pulling the game out of the fire, the drop-goal is a great score. It is as someone said 'precision under pressure'.

For sure, if the blast comes once it may be duplicated another time but it can hardly be foreseen to be repeated five times, which is what the Springbok fly-half accomplished. No one until the afternoon of 24 October had succeeded with more than three in international rugby. Both Lomu's and de Beer's executions, therefore, were not of the ordinary. Furthermore, with his penalty shots at goal, the Springbok fly-half aimed at the goalposts twelve times in all and succeeded each time, to collect 34 points of his team's total of 44 which was a South African record and their biggest score against England. On both occasions, in 1995 and 1999, England could justifiably feel that the fates had conspired cruelly against them. Indeed, Jannie de Beer, a 28-year-old from Welkom in the Free State, was not even South Africa's first choice at fly-half. Henry Honiball was, but he had been unable to play because of injury.

Nick Mallett, the Springbok coach, had expected a tight game with the score low and chances rare. Mallett, with de Beer, had planned their strategy so that drop-goals were a practical option. Pieter Muller in the centre was to be the fall guy. He was to be in the vanguard to bulldoze his way down the middle of the field to commit England's centres and, in addition, to draw Neil Back into the resulting melée. The idea was that with the pace nullified, de Beer might have a modicum of freedom, of time and space, to aim for the posts.

The close encounter was reflected in the first half score: four penalties to Grayson; three to de Beer. The essential difference was supplied by a try by Joost van der Westhuizen, who managed to overcome the attentions of Greenwood and Hill but avoided – just – the corner post in the 36th minute. De Beer, presaging the kind of immaculate afternoon he was to enjoy, kicked the conversion from the touch-line. This gave them the edge by 16–12 at the interval.

England, aware of the kicking game both teams preferred and the cat and mouse game that ensued, were not tempted to break the monotonous pattern. Perry was engulfed, as were de Glanville and Dallaglio. Matt Dawson attempted a snipe or two around the scrum but the Springboks had the measure of him, as they did of others who tried to break free of the stranglehold. Space was at a premium. Grayson's penalty brought England a point short of their opponents.

Then, between the 43rd and the 74th minute, de Beer's repeated volleys destroyed England; their energy spent, their spirit evaporated. At each frustrating turn of the screw, as each player pulled up, turned to see how accurate the strike had been and to see the arm of referee Jim Fleming signal yet another true aim, the life visibly seeped out of England. Two more penalties also went de Beer's way. If Rossouw scored a try it was the fly-half who insisted on having the last word with his conversion.

England never did manage to cross the South African line. The other two scores had come from a Grayson penalty and when he was replaced in the 55th minute Wilkinson added one of his own.

Jannie de Beer's career changed. He had played for London Scottish. He was due to join Sale in the new season. But the Blue Bulls, formerly Northern Transvaal, beckoned and they persuaded him that their needs in South Africa should come first. Once the World Cup was over he did not play for South Africa again. Jannie de Beer had had his day in the sporting sun and he will, as the rest of us will, never forget what a phenomenal afternoon it had proved to be.

Points were raised afterwards concerning whether England's match against Fiji four days previously had had a tiring and detrimental effect on England's performance, as set against a team that were given eight days to recover from their series of first-round fixtures and time enough to prepare for the next one. South Africa, it was countered, had not had testing pool matches other than Scotland so they had not honed a fine enough edge to their game, while England were clearly battle-hardened. Where did the advantage lie? There was no settling the dispute.

Ireland would have simply been grateful to be still in the tournament at this stage. As it was, Dublin had prepared for their victorious return from Lens only to find that their calculations had been somewhat premature. Argentina had usurped their position. Nonetheless, Lansdowne Road, despite the re-arrangements of tickets and accommodation and the unanticipated loss of their own team, was almost full and, in the event, enjoyed a wonderfully exciting contest.

France were far from the purring machine which had won the grand slam on two consecutive seasons. Indeed, they had suffered a miserable year that followed. They had lost their two home games in the Five Nations Championship, the first time in 42 years, and to England at Twickenham.

After that they went on tour to the Southern Hemisphere and lost to Tonga, New Zealand 'A' and finally, and embarrassingly, to the All Blacks by 54–7. On the evidence of the World Cup so far they were a long way from capturing any of the form which might enamour their supporters, especially from the south of the country who had been enraptured by Fiji's exuberance.

They began hinting in this match of the level they might be capable of and which might restore their reputation. After 11 minutes they were 17 points in the lead. A collapsed scrum gave Christophe Lamaison his first of nine successful place kicks out of ten. This was immediately followed by a try by Xavier Garbajosa after Dourthe and Juillet had made the early running. If these points gave comfort, the next try gave rise to celebration and to a resounding 'Allez la France'. Benazzi and Magne in glorious mood ran from their own 22-metre line to set Philippe Bernat-Salles free to score under the posts. The tries were converted.

Argentina refused to lie down. Agustin Pichot, who was having a wonderful tournament, began the response with a try from a scrum. The metronomic Quesada added the extra points and kicked a penalty. They were back in the hunt. If Ntamack charged down a kick from Arbizu, the captain and centre, and scored a try with Lamaison converting and kicking another penalty, Argentina did not let them get too far ahead. By the end of a hectic and action-packed first half, the South Americans had pulled back to seven points when Arbizu made up for his error and scored a try himself with Quesada repeating his earlier pattern of conversion and penalty to make it 27–20. There was an exchange of penalties to make it 30–26 with fifteen minutes to go.

Argentina had given their all and had produced a fine challenge but fatigue set in. France had something extra to spare. Bernat-Salles and Garbajosa scored tries in the last ten minutes with Lamaison kicking the conversions and a last penalty to close an entertaining game at 47–26. The crowd, partisan and non-partisan alike, acknowledged a fine match. France alone remained in the tournament to represent the Northern Hemisphere.

No one truly felt that Scotland would join them, seeing the obvious power and comprehensive competence that distinguished the All Blacks. This was the third time Scotland had played New Zealand in the World Cup and the twenty-first in a series that stretched back to 1905. There had been two drawn matches in the previous twenty fixtures, which is the nearest Scotland had come to taking New Zealand's scalp.

This was the last of the day's quarter-finals and was played in the evening. A full house was guaranteed at Murrayfield for the first time in the tournament. The first half signs were ominous and signalled a heavy defeat for Scotland. While much of the debate inevitably centred around how it might be possible to corral Jonah Lomu, the players who made the early impact were Tana Umaga, Andrew Mehrtens, the fly-half, and Jeff Wilson at full-back.

Umaga had crossed for the first of his two first-half tries by the twelfth minute and two minutes later Wilson had crossed for his. Mehrtens had converted both of these as well as kicking two penalties, one before and one after these tries. To emphasise the constant threat, New Zealand's outside backs poised, Christian Cullen and Wilson master-minded the move with beautiful passing to conjure up Umaga's second try. Mehrtens was by this time off the field with injury. Once again, New Zealand's overall pace had been devastating. Scotland could only respond with a penalty by Logan and a drop-goal by Townsend.

There seemed to be no respite. Lomu, at the end of a long pass from the dynamic Kronfeld, extended the lead to 30–6. But their conquering style came to a halt. After showing glimpses of running in the first half, Scotland began to spread the ball themselves with confidence. After Lomu's score it was they who kept the scoreboard ticking over.

Indeed, Scotland outscored their opponents by 15 points to 5 in the second half. Budge Pountney scored the first try, converted by Logan, and, into injury time, Cameron Murray got the second. It had proved a terrific rearguard action by Scotland.

Following their exit from the tournament, both the coach, Jim Telfer, and the captain, Gary Armstrong, retired from their international commitments. Alan Tait, the centre, who was the only survivor of the 1987 contest, did likewise, as did Paul Burnell, the prop.

Thus, all roads led to London and to Twickenham where both semi-finals were to be played on consecutive days. The World Cup had only intermittently come alive. No great heights had yet been scaled. The two semi-finals in distinctly different fashion were to prove vivid and memorable. They were to 'make' the 1999 Rugby World Cup. If much else might be thought of as forgettable in the sense of a sporting occasion having aspirations of global significance but with standards which had as yet not been realised in 1999, then the semi-final matches cast aside such doubts and put those matters right. There was to be glory after all.

1999 SEMI-FINALS

So near and yet so far: therein lies the fate of losing semi-finalists.

Up to this point, the road has been long and tense and the competition fraught with frustration and nervous hopes. The journey is worth making and, since the destination remains a long way off, the defeats and the failures can be reasoned, not contentedly perhaps, but with a clear head and an acceptance of a kind. Before hopes are raised too far, before hints of great deeds have a chance of insinuating themselves into the heart, a player, a team, yield to the superiority of another without being struck sullen or dumb; exasperated maybe, but not with a resentment that rankles. Somebody, it is rationalised, has to lose.

This is not quite so at the semi-final stage. Failure depresses into impotence at the edge of rage: the rage that brings tears not blind fury. This is the Valhalla of broken dreams. This is also the moment of a heaven of freedom and of jubilation unconfined. This is the moment of extreme contrasts which not even the final itself endures. The joy of the successful semi-finalists is the joy that lasts for the days to come because the flame of hope remains alive; great as it may be so far, the greatest is yet to come. To strive for more, the chance of accomplishing what once might have seemed an unreachable goal is an intoxicating liberation. The trophy is in sight. There is no consolation for failing at the penultimate stage. Hopes have been tantalisingly raised; hopes are desperately dashed. Everything ends. Very few remember losing semi-finalists.

The team that fails at the final stage – even if there is a deep despondency – finds recompense in that it did, after all, reach the destination even if they were not to become the first.

It is a strange tale. For the winners even in their moment of great glory and accomplishment there is a brief sense of anti-climax; of time spent, of effort expended and of a mission accomplished…and then what? It is sport's equivalent, dare I say, of post-coital tristesse. Although the sense of satisfaction is immediate, appreciation of what was done and how it was done and with whom it was done comes later, in moments of tranquility and reflection.

At the moment of triumph, after the inner passion and the outer turbulence of the contest, there is a returning sense of reality when the tension evaporates. There is a hint that what had gone before were heightened passions, even of exaggeration. Having accomplished the deed, how was it that we thought so much about it? What was it all in aid of? To the outsider, unfamiliar with the contrasting and different emotions of sportsmen and the burdens which they bring upon themselves or have imposed on them by others, such a question sounds absurd. Nothing, however, is straightforward. It is the essence of sport's triviality. Our response is mixed; our emotions are uncertain.

For a brief time, in a life lived at an accelerated pace when the blood races at a gallop, a player, when the battle is done, can be overcome with immobility; a composure. Suddenly he can look upon the momentous occasion from a calmer vantage point. Amid the turmoil when the contest is over, created largely by those who did not play, the player in the dressing room is becalmed, as if spellbound. Later, the euphoria, in short sharp bursts, engulfs him.

That was to come. For the moment, the chorus of triumph or the swansong awaited the four semi-finalists.

Such a tumult of emotions was laid bare at Twickenham during the Saturday and Sunday of 30 and 31 October. On consecutive days, after its many trials and days of stagnation, the 1999 Rugby World Cup was brought spectacularly alive. The richness and diversity of rugby football was on view; the sudden impulse of an underdog team inspired by no more than a wing and a prayer against an inscrutable foe or the tournament favourite; or the strategy of carefully structured team work set against living life hazardously; of the irresistible force meeting the immovable object; of two teams standing toe to toe and neither giving an inch; of the chess game that was Australia and South Africa or the wheeler-dealing game of poker between France and New Zealand.

There had been much speculation about the 1999 World Cup needing an epic duel to lift the tournament. England and New Zealand had provided a fine contest, as indeed had England's match against South Africa and the bizarre five drop-goals. However, it could not truly be said to have contained anything as memorable as the Australia/France match in 1987 or Australia's encounter with New Zealand in 1991. As for 1995, there was much else apart from the rugby that made that tournament an unforgettable and unrestrained force.

The 1999 RWC needed a match to give an identity to the tournament as a whole and to pull it together. Neither the Springboks nor the Wallabies had sparkled, while the All Blacks had performed only fitfully. South Africa had not felt a part of the tournament with so little interest generated in Scotland, while Canada had felt isolated in France. For Gareth Rees, of Canada, the Rugby World Cup of 1999 always seemed to be happening somewhere else and never where he was.

Australia had conceded only one try throughout the tournament so far (in 1991 only three in six games), while South Africa had allowed three to pass through their defence. Australia had beaten the Springboks 32–6 in June but it was their only win in their last five meetings. This was to be first of the semi-finals.

Once again, the drop-goal was to play a role, a more tantalising role in its singular execution, than the amazing metronomic regularity of de Beer in Paris. In a strange and fatal narrative South Africa this time were to find themselves at the receiving end of rugby's version of the magician's trick of pulling the rabbit out of the hat. This was executed in the second period of extra time.

The game proved to be a mighty duel of hardness and power with few subtle nuances. If it was tough and uncompromising, it was never less than mesmerising in the way a judo bout can be. Which one of the contestants, in the confined space, is going to unsettle and unbalance the other? There is a kind of choreography; unscripted, yet the sequences are calculated. The players shift from toe to toe, they jostle for position, they heave and lunge, they flick and tap, a leg shoots out and the duelists lock again holding each other in a tight grip. There are moments of intense and quick mobility which almost immediately subside. Anchored to each other, it is a struggle of strength and endurance, and of timing. Such was the solid tableau on a wet day at Twickenham. Australia and South Africa parried with each other.

On this precarious edge the question was: who would falter and commit the fatal error at the end? Throughout the colossal contest only two names registered on the scoreboard: Burke and de Beer.

Gregan and van der Westhuizen may have battled heroically at scrum-half, Eales and Andrews reached high in the lines-out, Skinstad and Kefu (who had returned from a two-match suspension after his contretemps with Trevor Brennan of Ireland) challenged for supremacy at number 8, but it was Burke and de Beer who scored the points. Burke kicked seven penalties while de Beer kicked five and another of his drop-goals to give Australia a 21–18 lead eight minutes into injury time. This was a curiosity as the electronic board had signalled two minutes of added time.

There had been no tries, nor, for the first time in fixtures between the two countries, were there to be any. If there had been one player who might have risen to claim such a score then it would have been Tim Horan at centre, who supplied the cutting edge in a superior Australian midfield. As a centre, he was in a class of his own.

On Friday, he had been stricken low with a virus that caused vomiting and diarrhoea and which had kept him in bed throughout the day. Rod Kafer was on stand-by but Horan was just about declared fit enough to play. He lasted until the 74th minute, up to which time he gave a classical display of the centre-threequarter's art. Three times he succeeded in defying the attentions of the Springbok defence to create such havoc as tries might have resulted. This was undoubtedly a great performance from a player who ranks in the pantheon of the world's best centres.

The countdown to the game's end was tantalising. In the 79th minute Australia held a six-point lead. With his fifth penalty de Beer reduced it to three. Derek Bevan ignored the electronic clock, which said two minutes extra and followed his own judgment. In a prolonged and provocative period of added time, the suspense was at once emotive and agitating. Eight minutes of injury time had been played. On such occasions Rod Macqueen admitted that he tried not to get too emotional with time and the referee's decisions. Getting involved with the minute by minute issues means that the bigger picture gets ignored. 'We needed to concentrate on what was happening on the field,' he remarked. 'In that way we get to make more logical decisions.' It got worse for Australia. The Springboks struck another blow.

Pieter Muller, Stefan Terblanche and Joost van der Westhuizen first carried the ball into Australian territory. At the breakdown Owen Finegan, so often an unsung hero but harshly exposed as a villain here, prevented André Venter from releasing the ball, so that in the 88th minute de Beer ensured with his sixth penalty and the score at 21–21 that extra time would be necessary.

The deadlock remained. It remained with seven minutes to go in the second ten-minute period of extra time. Then Stephen Larkham, who had also been doubtful with ligament problems, dropped a goal from 45 metres. This was the fly-half's first ever drop-goal in his career and, whatever may come, none will ever be more significant. Not at any stage had there been more than a six-point difference to separate the two teams.

Even if Burke was to kick his eighth penalty, it was Larkham's impromptu drop-goal that provided not only the dramatic denouement to an heroic contest but also contributed so elegantly to South Africa's come-uppance. The drop-goal chimed ironically with what had gone before and what they had inflicted upon England. There was, for Twickenham's crowd, a sweet symmetry of a kind relished only on the wilder shores of romantic fiction; of the imaginative and improbable coincidence. Thankfully, sport as well as a fiction has the true capacity of transporting us to those unexpected places.

This was South Africa's first defeat in 11 World Cup matches while Australia were on their way to a second appearance in the World Cup final. The game had lasted for 107 minutes and had been a supreme test of mental and physical endurance. It had kept the crowd enthralled and, even without fluent movement, a testimony to rugby's capacity for dramatic tension.

'I was disappointed that the game had gone to extra time,' Macqueen remembers, 'but we had gone through every scenario. We knew what we needed to do. In other words, if it was still a draw at call time, after the final 20 minutes, I knew we would win. They had had a player sent off the field, we hadn't. This would be held against the Springboks which, as the rules states, meant we would then win. We shouldn't panic, not to give away penalties and to make sure that the game would be played in their half.'

If everyone held their breath as this gripping match unfolded gradually with an insistent beat growing into an irresistible crescendo, the game the following day, with another full crowd at Twickenham, left player and spectator alike breathless with its infinite variety of strange harmonies and discord, and induced a feverish energy. This was rugby's capacity to surprise. For many – realists probably, or the merely obstinate – rugby is a sport for big men, men of mighty muscle and bone. This is a game for Goliaths to subdue. For others, optimists and romancers, it is also a game for the swift and the fearless; those fleet of foot and agile of mind. This is rugby where the Davids of this world can dwell. The combat of rugby's dual personality met on neutral ground in the west of London.

Before his 69th cap for France, Abdelatif Benazzi, who had been on the winning side against New Zealand in three of the last five meetings, said: 'Let's face it, out of ten matches against New Zealand we would probably lose eight or nine times, but in the World Cup semi-final…you never know when you might be swept along by a superior force.'

The signs had not been auspicious. Three weeks before the tournament began France were simmering with frustration and dissatisfaction. They had lost six of their last seven matches. In March 1999 they had lost to Wales in Paris for the first time since 1975. That defeat had halted their run for an unprecedented third consecutive full house of victories in the European Championship and had triggered their inexplicable run of failure.

There lingered, however, the memories of a golden afternoon when Wembley was bathed in sunshine in April 1998. This was the time when, in the grandest possible style against Wales, France consummated their second grand slam. Their rugby was infused with balance and with the balletic touch of elegance and delicate movement of which they alone of all nations are capable. That afternoon's panache had been richly manifest in their fly-half, Thomas Castaignede. It is only they who, when they discover the inspirational mood, can turn rugby, so often with a beast at its core, into a game of beauty. The stimulus had come from the coaches Jean-Claude Skrela and Pierre Villepreux and their manager, Jo Maso. They were heroes of French rugby of the late '60s and '70s, players with the wind in their hair. The turnaround in their fortunes had been swift and cruel. There had been generous talk of France, but generous only in sympathy.

Under Raphael Ibanez, France had stumbled to a wooden spoon in 1999. Fabien Galthie was not in the original squad and was fourth choice originally, behind Philippe Carbonneau, Pierre Mignoni and Stephane Castaignede. Thomas Castaignede was no longer in the tournament. Christian Califano was not available at loose head prop after being banned for seven weeks for head-butting Joeli Veitayaki of Fiji. To epitomise the confusion which the French public felt and the French media expressed, Ntamack was unsure whether he played on the wing or in the centre. During the previous month of the competition, France's play had only served to confirm that they had failed to regain their *élan.*

New Zealand could look at their past record and scarcely feel any happier. Under Taine Randell, the captain, they had lost five games in a row the previous year. Nonetheless, they had shown during the tournament that they were powerful and were capable, if only fitfully, of playing magisterial rugby with speed and precision. France appeared not to have players like Wilson, Umaga and Cullen (with Lomu, the tournament's top try scorer to date with six) who collectively accounted for 104 international tries. Furthermore, in Kronfeld, New Zealand had the man who was challenging to be the player of the tournament. There was also the controlling influence of Mehrtens. He had been in superb form. However, for the first time in 27 tests together, he was to be without his partner Justin Marshall. Byron Kelleher played at scrum-half.

The consensus about the likely outcome was unmistakable and universal: France did not have a chance.

However – and there could never have been a bigger recanting 'however' in the history of the game – Twickenham, having had barely 24 hours respite from the nervous exhaustions of the previous day, was to witness one of the most scintillating reversals of all time.

At the end of the first half, Mehrtens had kicked four penalties and Lomu had scored a try against Christophe Lamaison's try, conversion and penalty. Soon after the interval Lomu struck again and Mehrtens converted to give the All Blacks what appeared from their dominance an insurmountable 24–10 lead. They were all of a piece, in harmony.

Then, with the All Blacks soaring away, France's miraculous journey to the World Cup final and the clipping of their opponent's wings began. In a devastating period of 13 minutes – between the 46th and the 59th minutes – France scored 26 points. Lamaison, in tune with the times, dropped two goals and then a couple of penalties. Galthie chipped the ball, Dominici re-gathered to slip past Mehrtens for a try which was soon followed by Lamaison's diagonal kick being picked up by Richard Dourthe to score their third try.

In the 74th minute a New Zealand attack broke down and the ubiquitous Lamaison kicked the ball forward. Olivier Magne was after it and with the All Blacks closing in on him, Philippe Bernat-Salles sped passed the flanker to reach the ball ahead of Wilson. In this time there had been 33 French points without reply from New Zealand. Lamaison's conversion to add to his three other conversions, a try, three penalties and two drop-goals meant that he collected 28 points in all. That Wilson, who had been hampered with a leg injury, scored in the 80th minute did not matter, but, with five altogether in the tournament, it did give him the New Zealand try-scoring record of 38 tries (beating John Kirwan's 35).

It had been an extraordinary contest. At 43–31, this was France's highest score against New Zealand. The All Blacks were stunned as, indeed, was everyone else at the sensational reversal of fortune. Amid all the jubilation, the Dax band played and in the overflow of powerful feeling the sight of Franck Tournaire, the French prop, carrying his daughter Laura-Marie aloft on his broad shoulders, was a poignant cameo of the immediacy of an uplifting victory; and of knowing, in all the pandemonium, where the heart lies.

This was France's second appearance in the final. Once more, after 1987, France's adventurous contribution and capacity for unsurpassable excitement at the semi-final stage had added immeasurably to the Rugby World Cup.

'Rugby is the product of the mind as well as the body,' concluded Pierre Villepreux. 'Rugby is about understanding – flexibility and adaptability, not organisation. To play with freedom and liberty you must be clever. Without the freedom to fail, how can you hope to be clever?'

At a time when rugby and the colourful variety of which it is tactically and technically capable seemed under threat and the homogeneity of thought was spreading, France alone suddenly appeared to prick the game's conscience. They are a team that can restore romantic notions of the freedom to run and illustrate also that the game does not always go to the mighty. This they achieved in 1999 when everything seemed to be at stake. For a week after this semi-final, the flame was alive.

1999 THIRD PLACE PLAY-OFF

A blissful aura encompassed the Rugby World Cup after the halcyon weekend of 30 and 31 October. After a recurring sense of scepticism and suspicion where rugby had been discredited with bouts of violence, doubts cast on the citing process, a lack of interest in Scotland, the uneven spread of fixtures which were concentrated at the end of the week, and the general absence of genuinely stimulating rugby, the tournament had failed to stir the imagination. Since before the tournament began, when they had been working against the clock to get the Millennium Stadium in Cardiff ready on time, the mood and spirits had not been moved to joyful celebration. Mostly it was muted, as if to say more with relief than joy: thank goodness, the tournament can go on.

The Rugby World Cup of 1999 will be remembered for the two great semi-final matches. Indeed, they might even break a habit: the two losers on this special occasion will not be forgotten and will be imprinted in the memory. To forget the losers would be, in this instance, to forget what made the two matches so memorable and to represent only half of a great story.

Indeed, let us go further. The one contest will not be remembered without recourse to recollect the other. The two matches are inseparable. The events of the Saturday and Sunday on that last weekend of October are a tidy whole representing rugby football in its infinite variety of play: the differing philosophies that can inform the game; how the high and the mighty confront each other and how, elsewhere, the well-organised can sometimes fall to the spontaneous and flighty genius.

France drew the most attention. For all their self-styled cynicism, sports journalists are romantic at heart. The sports pages were full of the twang of heart strings. A golden glow hung over every paragraph as they looked admiringly to France and their daring and opportunism, their flair and their insouciant, almost indulgent, sense of adventure. Benazzi's words, though, echoed in the background and were repeated by John Hart, New Zealand's coach. This was the one game out of ten to which France could lay claim. It was the one that mattered.

On that loss John Hart's future hung. A wonderfully imaginative and articulate coach, he had only a few days remaining in charge of the All Blacks. By Friday, after the third place play-off he resigned. For the third successive World Cup New Zealand had failed to win the title. Following in the footsteps of Alex Wyllie in 1991 and Laurie Mains in 1995, John Hart stood down. He had taken over from Mains in 1995. His record was 31 victories and nine defeats with one draw (26–26 against England in 1997).

His mind was made up before the match on Thursday to determine the third place. As every player testifies, very little can motivate a team when neither the gold nor the silver is on offer. To battle for the bronze can hardly have stimulated what must be regarded throughout the 20th century as the two mightiest rugby nations on the planet. They had not met on neutral ground before.

Yet van der Westhuizen said beforehand that no special motivation was necessary for the Springboks to play the All Blacks. Despite such musings the match proved to be disappointing; the teams showed that, with the main prize to be played for by others at another time, their hearts were not in it. They were neither the best nor the second best.

Jannie de Beer, charitably, made way for Henry Honiball, who had not played hitherto. He kicked three penalties, while Percy Montgomery, continuing the habit of the tournament, dropped two goals. He also converted the game's solitary try scored by Breyton Paulse, who chased his own kick and with balance and skill managed to avoid Cullen and control the touchdown. He, too, had not played in the tournament. This was to be the start of a fine rugby career, although he had yet to inaugurate his celebratory hand-spring and flik-flak behind the try-line after he had scored. This provided the brightest moment in an otherwise drab affair.

Andrew Mehrtens kicked six penalties for New Zealand. Little was seen of Umaga, Cullen, Ieremia and Lomu, the most potent threequarter line in the whole tournament. If attack was limited, both team's defences remained firm and largely unbroken.

Since 1921, when the series began between New Zealand and South Africa, honour and prestige had been at stake. Tradition grew to make this contest a clash of rugby's titans. The earth shook. Weak men trembled. Those were the days of Brand and Osler, of Scott and Allen, of Craven and Geffin, of Clarke and White, of Claassen and Malan, Meads and Tremain. They were supremely dynamic and often brutal affairs. What happened in 1999 in Cardiff was tame in comparison. Honour, by itself, was no longer enough. The prestige was in winning the cup. The great prize had eluded them both. It was a thoroughly emasculated affair.

1999 WORLD CUP FINAL

For all the expectation of a grand finale there was, nonetheless, a deep-rooted feeling which it was thought best – for those who were touched with it – to stifle or to ignore. This was the sense which overwhelms us that when something is so good it cannot possibly come to pass. After the two great semi-finals could the final game come anywhere near matching those extraordinary events? Furthermore, France had lit the touchpaper of flair and encouraged those in the Northern Hemisphere to believe in the possibility that at long last a team from their constituency might win. For others there was the longing that France might reverse the recent tactical trend that allowed defence to hold the game in a stranglehold and which thwarted the wider possibilities of attack. Defensive networks and tackling had come to dominate the game, even stifle it, at the expense of the freer rein to run and to find opportunities in the open spaces.

France at Twickenham had rekindled such hopes. It had not always been the case recently. They too had retreated into their shell and, despite the influence of Skrela, Villepreux and Maso, had chosen to ignore their heritage. Instead of leading the way, as they often had, and trying to improvise and to innovate, they attempted to imitate others. They had seen on the evidence of the Super 12 and the Tri Nations series how the rest of the world chose to play, and in their mountainous retreat in the Pyrenees where they had been preparing for the World Cup, had chosen to follow.

It was not difficult to draw the conclusion that modern rugby union was a hybrid sport born of the cross fertilisation of rugby league – set in two straight confrontational lines stretching across the pitch, for instance – and the aggressive blocking of American football which found expression around the fringes of the rucks, mauls and other loose situations. Both Richard Dourthe and Emile Ntamack were big men for the midfield at 6'2" and nearly 16st, and indicated in some respects France's retreat from subtlety at centre, even if they had the slight, but fleet of foot, Christophe Dominici on the wing.

By common consent, such a style is contrary to France's nature. For all their hostile tendencies in the forwards (and who is not prone to such habits in the maelstrom of the pack?), France enjoy running with freedom. As Franck Mesnel, centre or fly-half for France in 1987 and 1991, once said: 'The cliché is true. Inside the greatest French team the artist works alongside the butcher.' He and his colleagues at Racing Club once turned up, as legend has it, in pink bow ties for the final of the French championship at Parc des Princes, and were refreshed at half-time with champagne. Clearly, his inclination was towards the artist.

But there were claims made that it was the other trait that became evident in the final of the 1999 Rugby World Cup. What was inescapable for all to see was that France were unable to summon the stimulus which had so enraptured Twickenham the previous Saturday.

France's victory posed a dilemma for Australia. They, like everyone else, had been expecting to see New Zealand in Cardiff. The All Blacks were familiar.

It was the foe the Wallabies well knew. It was the opposition they had anticipated and planned for. But it was not the All Blacks who were waiting for them. Australia had swiftly had to revisit their intended strategy.

A new set of video recordings was urgently requested to be digested if they were to 'Bring Back Bill' – the William Webb Ellis Cup – as the team was exhorted to do by their supporters. France's progress had mostly been ignored or at least not considered of major consequence. The lessons were quickly absorbed so that on the day Australia held a referendum at home, which decided against the Republicans and for the Royalists, John Eales, an avowed Republican, received the cup from Her Majesty Queen Elizabeth. They became the first team to win the cup twice.

John Eales was the supreme line-out specialist and had a wonderful game, sharing the contest for Australian possession with Giffin and Cockbain. Not that Fabien Pelous, Abdel Benazzi and Christophe Juillet, who later came on for Olivier Brouzet, fell short for France. In a match which only rarely contained any continuous movement, two factors ensured that the Wallabies kept on top. France's recurring errors drew the attention of the referee, André Watson. In his 13th international, France hardly endeared themselves to him with their frequent transgressions and, it was later said, their more 'butchery' attentions.

There were accusations of several instances of eye gouging – Mike Foley, Richard Harry and George Gregan – to which at one stage Eales drew the referee's attentions. Raphael Ibanez was spoken to by the referee, while at one stage Eales, with a damaged cornea, was overheard threatening Watson that he would take his players off the field. Pieter de Villiers was stamped on, Magne was at the receiving end of a punch by Kefu.

The 'artist' was not so evident by his presence in a drab contest. Pelous was shown the yellow card and, to everyone's surprise, so was Eales, the epitome of rugby's ideal type. A gentleman who could play a rough and tumble game with skill, to rub shoulders with the best and the worst, he followed his competitive instincts without tarnishing either his character or the sport he played. Each time he parted the field he did so with a clear conscience and answered to the nickname 'Nobody' as in 'Nobody's perfect'.

There was no sin bin operating in the 1999 World Cup. These incidents did not overshadow the game in a way that other acts of violence in other matches do. Rather it was the sheer ordinariness of the game and the stagnant play that caused it to be less than memorable. This was not helped by a pitch surface which could hardly be described as lush. It looked as if it had suffered the wear and tear of a long season. It was not of the quality expected to stage a World Cup final.

The Wallaby half-back pair knew where to play the game and how. Larkham and Gregan had a better match than Lamaison and Galthie. Their clever choice of chips and kicks made certain that France could never run on their toes at any stage, apart from the opening quarter. They were largely in retreat and mostly uninspired. Much like 1987, France had reached their zenith in the semi-final and had little left to give in the final itself.

Australia were resolute. Tim Horan and Daniel Herbert closed down the midfield. Toutai Kefu and David Wilson snaffled any threat around the fringes of the scrum. Thus, there was no momentum to France's surges. Macqueen, the astute, determined and unblenching coach, had so outlined his strategy that there was nowhere left for France to go or for Ibanez, who was captain for the 21st time, to direct them. Australia were not going to allow them to cut loose in the manner of the All Blacks.

Yet after 15 minutes, the score stood at 6–6 and France had twice held the lead. They might have done so with a bigger margin when Magne, another magnificent forward, had been adjudged to have knocked on when leaping high to recover Lamaison's kick. His pass sent Benazzi over the line. However, he had to be called back.

Matt Burke, who was to miss with only two of his eleven kicks, ensured that his team went ahead 12–6 for the interval lead. By the end he was to pass the 500-point mark to establish a total of 509 points. This was to leave him a point short of the 102 points Quesada of Argentina scored to win the tournament's Golden Boot award.

Owen Finegan played a decisive role in both of Australia's tries in the second half. In the 66th minute, after Gregan and Horan had made the running, Finegan was on hand to link up with Ben Tune for the first try, and then in the fifth minute of injury time, after Eales had won the line-out possession, Gregan made the break and gave the sweetest of inside passes to the rampaging Finegan. The flanker scored and Burke converted both tries to add to his seven penalty goals. Lamaison had kicked two earlier penalties to make the final score 35–12. 'We didn't have the freshness or the frenzy,' was Ibanez's conclusion.

Australia, unlike the other winners of the tournaments since 1987, had achieved their goal away from home. Both New Zealand and South Africa had won the cup on home soil. This was a remarkable achievement for a nation who, unlike the other two winners, could not regard rugby union as a major sport for the nation's masses. Furthermore, the Wallabies had not for most of their rugby history been thought of as a major force in the way their counterparts in the Southern Hemisphere, the All Blacks and the Springboks, had been.

The transformation in their fortunes did not take place until the mid-1980s. As one indication of their rise to prominence it is worth noting that in eight fixtures with Wales between 1908 and 1975 they won only two. In the 13 fixtures since 1978, Australia have won 11 times. Wales can only record one victory at home in 1981 and their success in third place play-off in the 1987 Rugby World Cup.

In Wales, rugby union is judged to be the country's national sport. Such diminishing returns in the last two decades for Wales is in contrast to the parabola of Australian success. This reflects starkly the differing attitudes each country has to sporting success.

At the Millennium Stadium in Wales's capital city, two Australians took the major awards: John Eales lifted the cup and Tim Horan received the award for player of the tournament.

'ADVANCE AUSTRALIA FAIR'

The 1999 tournament was the triumph of defences. This was particularly so for the winners, Australia, whose success was testimony to the coaching skills of Rod Macqueen. Like other matters in the natural order of things there is so much that is elemental; the game is for the swift or the strong and sometimes for both; so much is born of survival instincts and primitive tendencies in the dark spots in the maul as well as in the light of open spaces.

Rugby union tactics have their seasons. From the time some bright spark thought in the very early days of the last century that there should be a division between backs and forwards and that players should have specialist skills in allocated positions, emphasis alters and shifts: the powerhouse scrummaging of the Springboks or the rucking techniques of the All Blacks; the flowing threequarter play of the Lions or the intermingling of forwards and backs of the French. Each style has had its day. Organised defence was the flavour in 1999 and of the immediate years that followed.

Rugby portrays many moods and views. 'We have the right to dream,' said the Toulon coach, Daniel Herrero in 1991. And in the same year Serge Blanco said before the game against England, 'The English are great gentlemen – after the game.' He also said, 'Rugby is a joy because it stems from friendship. It is pleasure because it is everything that unites man on the sporting field. You can only get results if you feel good together, if you appreciate each other. I would even say if you love each other.' It is the way they have in France.

There is another view, of course.

'Don't give 'em fuck all!' Brian Moore was heard saying when England played France the year before. His words were memorably picked up by the touch-line microphone.

Vive la difference! The difference is echoed in the tactics. The mood affects the play. Tactics, like the quixotic moods, come and go.

This period was dominated by a team's defence. Australia was simply the best. Only one try was scored against them. Attacking stratagems were not refined enough to overcome the comprehensive tentacles of Australia's defensive network.

Yet among them they had the outstanding threequarter not only of the 1999 tournament but of the era and, surely, of such abundant talent as to be worshipped in the pantheon of greatness of all time. Tim Horan was at the height of his prodigious gifts. Each game he played added another dimension to what we had seen before.

Indeed, it was remarkable that he should be playing at all. He had overcome a horrendous knee injury in the early '90s which was so severe that he might not have played again. 'There was a period,' he said, 'when all you hoped for was to be able to play football on the beach again and to lead a normal life. But, then, what is a normal life to someone like me? To me a normal life meant playing rugby. I was determined to get back. I had a huge amount of help from Greg Craig, the physiotherapist. But not only does a player need to get physically fit, he needs to be mentally in tune as well.'

At Ravenhill he had, after two minutes against the Romanians, scored the quickest try of the tournament, for which he received a cheque for £10,000 from Guinness for the charity of his choice. In an uncoordinated performance against Ireland at Lansdowne Road, Horan was the bright spark that lightened an otherwise dismal afternoon. In the 17th minute of the second half he opened and divided the Irish defence like a breeze bending and parting the reeds on a river bank. The defence seemed to lean out of his way. While others struggled in uncomfortable circumstances his class made the difference.

He was on equally commanding form in the quarter-finals against Wales. He always stood out. He demanded attention. And if by mischance his presence had somehow been passed by, his sublime play reached its apotheosis in the semi-final against South Africa, and placed it beyond all possible question.

In the increasingly congested midfield which every player believes it is his right to inhabit – from the prop forward who longs to escape from his chains to the back row forward who thinks he is the game's Everyman and can intervene at will and occupy any place he chooses – the centre-threequarter can be devoured by the selfishness or the unfulfilled desires of these upstarts. It is difficult to stand apart.

At Twickenham on 30 October, Tim Horan displayed the pivotal skills of his position. His accuracy was finely tuned, his judgement impeccable. And in this age of impregnable defences he broke the resistance and found his way clear on four separate occasions. It was as clear a statement as a sportsman would have wished to make about his own ability.

Yet, he suffered a painful few days leading up to the grand theatre of Twickenham. He had dinner with friends on Wednesday. Thursday was a day off and he felt a bit 'crook'. After seeing a doctor at 5:45am on Friday he remained in bed all day. He was still in the team but felt sick going to the game.

'I wanted to play,' he recollects, 'and I knew that once you're on the field there are no excuses. I wasn't nervous and then the adrenalin which comes with the big occasion kicked in. I felt superb. You only get to feel like that once or twice a season; when everything seems so right. I was "in the zone". It's a wonderful feeling.'

This was an expression of the kind that every sportsman dreams of. He knows he has the ability. He trains to give of his best. He believes he can do it. But will the moment, with all the vagaries that attend such competitive moments, will that moment ever come? Will others see you in the way you want them to see you? Will you ever get to rule your kingdom? Horan did on that overcast day against South Africa. There will have been other times of execution in his rugby career but none will surpass this in its 80-minute completeness – or in his case 74 minutes, which is when he came off the field.

'My energy had gone. There was nothing extra. What had happened the previous couple of days finally caught up with me. I was spent,' he concluded.

Rod Macqueen appreciated him in another way. 'The thing I noticed about Tim,' Macqueen recalls, 'was whereas other players who say they are going to play with such problems show it in some way, Tim was on the bus going to the game and he made an impact on all the other players. He's someone the team always looked up to. Nobody knew how sick he was. This showed to me how mentally strong he was. In that respect he is the hardest athlete I've ever come across.

'He had all-round ability. If you look across the board of attributes Tim would be nine all the way through in contrast, say, to someone like David Campese. Probably he might be lower down the scale on attitude and defence, but he would score ten on skill and natural ability. The greatest contribution that Horan made to Australia was on that day in the 1999 semi-final.'

There were other fine performances during the tournament. There was Josh Kronfeld of New Zealand, Jannie de Beer for South Africa, Christophe Dominici and Olivier Magne of France. But as with the tournament as a whole there was a lack of consistency, dominated by an Australian team who were tightly knit and focused. In John Eales they had one of the greatest of rugby captains.

For Macqueen, one of the wonderful things about his lock forward was he need not worry whether he was good enough for the team. 'It can be the case,' he says, 'that some captains are borderline cases as far as talent is concerned so that there is some debate as to his inclusion in the team. John was always first picked. That made life a lot easier for me as coach. He began as a good captain and ended a great captain. Some of that came from understanding that you have to make hard decisions when you are at the top. This was significant.'

He played 86 tests and was captain in 55 of them. If the World Cup victory ranks highest in his achievements he had also captained his country to three Bledisloe Cup series victories and was to enjoy successful Tri Nations campaigns in 2000 and 2001. Almost from the beginning of his career as a 21-year-old against Wales in 1991, he could be considered in the world rankings and remained there ten years later. As man and player there was, in the truest sense, greatness attached to Eales.

For Rod Macqueen the team had long been in preparation.

He had used the mantra of Phil Jackson of the Chicago Bulls: '*We*, not *me*.' This meant putting the team above everything else.

'We set ourselves a goal and the three parts which made up that goal,' explains Macqueen. 'There was the beginning, the journey and the destiny. We needed first of all to set standards that would make us successful, to get the type of fitness we felt the game needed in two years' time not the game as it was then. The game was not evolving. It was a revolution. The game had changed so quickly; we needed to pre-empt where the game would be and the type of fitness we needed to have.

'We talked about standards, not about the score, and the winning and the losing. In this way players became more critical of themselves and placed high emphasis on high standards. We had very critical sessions after winning games, which were so different from sessions after losing. If they lost they already knew where they had gone wrong.

'One of the best things we had worked out after studying and analysing the Super 12 series was the way the game had changed so dramatically. We looked at what was happening to the top teams and what the winning key performance indicators were of those sides. That, for instance, six phases or more on more than five occasions indicated that a team was more than likely to score; or if there were tackle completions of less than 80 per cent then this was a characteristic of a losing team; the number of line breaks and so on gave us a sound basis on where the game was going. The different performance indicators tell us how the game was changing. This was the beginning.'

The 'journey' commenced at the end of 1998. Australia had World Cup qualifiers against Fiji, Tonga and Samoa. These were more important than the Tri nations because it was essential to qualify as number one.

'Samoa was very close,' concludes Macqueen. 'We got through because we were so much better prepared physically and in terms of our superior fitness. It would have been harder otherwise.

'There was a good atmosphere at our base camp gatherings. The players' partners and children were invited along. This was a totally new experience for the players and was greatly appreciated. Wives were able to talk about the experience and gave us time to explain the many sacrifices that needed to be made.

'We kept everything at a professional level. There were no restrictions on drinking for instance. There was a huge expectation. Therefore there was no need for any restrictions. All the players knew what needed to be done. There were few disciplinary problems. There was a Chinese saying which I often quoted: "Know yourself and know your opposition and 1000 battles will never be in peril." We needed to respect the opposition at all times.

'When making decisions on selection we had to take into account the need for a leader in each group. We had John Eales as captain but he needed lieutenants on the field. If John called the line-outs generally we had Dave Giffin call the defensive ones. He would nominate where the oppositions would jump. We had David Wilson make the decisions at the kick-offs. By studying the strengths and weaknesses of the opposition he would determine the kick-offs. George Gregan made a lot of the defensive decisions. There were leaders in different groups with tasks appointed to them. A time came when they would be upset if they did not have such a responsibility. They did not look up to me in the grandstand to make the decisions for them.'

Then destiny was, of course, the World Cup itself.

'But we found that things had changed by the time we reached the tournament,' Macqueen says. 'For two years we had been training in a certain way and had analysed the way the game was being played. We had lived according to a certain code that if a team has possession and keeps it, chances are they'll win the match. We had developed skills therefore to retain possession.

'When we came to the World Cup several decisions were made by the IRB which changed the emphasis in the game. Supporting a player in the line-out and how much the referee would allow was re-defined, for instance, so that the way we had trained in the squad and the provinces had played in the Super 12 had to be reconsidered. They did away, too, with the sin bin.

'Also the referees had been instructed to watch the attacking team carefully at the point of the tackle. They were not watching the tackler to see that he was rolling away, they were instead watching the attacking team to ensure they did not come off their feet to fly in to secure the ball. That basically changed the entire game. The records our statisticians were giving us after two games of the World Cup were telling us that the team retaining possession were actually losing games. The more times you went into a breakdown situation in your own half, the greater the chance of a penalty against you. So we had to revise our two-year game plan and to kick the ball out of our own half because we were too concerned about the number of penalties we might give away.

'We also realised the number of deliberate fouls that were taking place so that whenever we looked like scoring a try, the opposition would lie on the ball. There would be a penalty decision, of course, but this meant the opportunity for three points not seven. There was no sin-binning. At that time a man suspended to the sin bin for 10 minutes meant a try or two would be scored against the guilty team. There were coaches and players who believed that was okay. The clear example of this was in the New Zealand–France game when the first-half penalty count was 16 to 3 in New Zealand's favour, but this destroyed New Zealand's continuity. In this way, two decisions by the IRB had a significant impact on the World Cup and on the way we played.

'We were a structured team with highly intelligent players. It hurt me when we were criticised for the way we played. We were well organised. We played it differently, but now everyone is playing that kind of rugby. But what we did was to analyse what the laws of the game allowed and the conditions in which the game was played. In fairness, if the laws had not been changed, if the sin bin had been in place and the referees concentrated on the defending team's illegalities we would have played a different game. Because there was no sin bin, for instance, teams transgressed repeatedly. They could not be sent off for 10 minutes. This favoured the negative team. If that had not been the case we might have scored more tries.'

As it was, he fashioned the team which secured the Rugby World Cup for the second time for Australia.

Chapter 8

2003 Rugby World Cup

Time brings everything – Plato

The Telstra Stadium in Sydney was a majestic setting. The evening of 22 November, though, was damp, with constant fine rain which came in the wake of the sweeping downpours of the previous two days. The match made in heaven of the game played in heaven, as it was referred to, seemed in no uncertain manner to have displeased, of all people, the resident Clerk of the Weather. He was the only sourpuss. Down he commanded the rain on the uncovered playing surface and upon the capacity crowd. If his intention was to disappoint and to cast a gloom on the proceedings, he failed. The rain neither dampened the spirits nor the welcoming mood.

In other circumstances it might have done, but the Rugby World Cup in Australia in 2003, played over a six-week period, beginning on Friday 10 October, was enjoyed in an unfailing mood of warmth and fun. If the Olympics were in Sydney, the World Cup embraced the whole of the continent. The fifth Rugby World Cup tournament would prove to be the best conceived and best implemented of the series; the culmination of which was to bring two old sporting foes together: Australia and England. For the tournament organisers, the Australian public and the comfortably seated television audience (whether tuning in at 8pm on Saturday in Sydney or 9am in England), this was perceived to be the ideal final for 2003.

Australia and England brought to the contest the baggage of a long and sometimes acrimonious history: the colonists and the colonised; the Empire-builders who brought with them the game of cricket which spawned the great Tests for the Ashes. This rivalry had begun in 1862 when 12 men from England set sail for Australia in a paddle-steamer to play cricket, thereby beginning a long and captivating tradition.

The history of the rivalry in rugby is relatively new. If the series between the two nations goes back to Blackheath in 1909, there was never the same intensity to these fixtures as was attached to cricket. Rugby is in its infancy in comparison. That the enterprise has become bolder between the two teams and the contests more earnest and impassioned is a relatively new phenomenon. This is due partly to the advent of Australian rugby from the doldrums, to become, since the 1980s, a major force; and partly to the number of times the two teams have faced each other across the half-way line in the World Cup.

If there was a famous match at Twickenham in 1958 when England were reduced to 14 men and the great deceptive maestro on the wing, Peter Jackson of Coventry, scored the try to win the match 9–6, the duel has since intensified as a result of the three meetings between them thus far in the Rugby World Cups of 1987, 1991 and 1995. They were rivals for the fourth time in 2003, thus enhancing the sporting tradition between them and so ensuring that each meeting henceforth will stimulate the settling of old and familiar scores.

There has always been a difference which separates the sporting sensibilities of the two nations. Neville Cardus once wrote: 'Absence of cant from Australian cricket can be very refreshing in a land where at times we no doubt incline towards sentimentality.' This might be said equally of rugby, too; the rugby of the old school, perhaps. The England of Clive Woodward and Martin Johnson in 2003 might have had cause to query Cardus' view of 73 years earlier as he set sail for Australia. This significant shift towards hardness of spirit and away from sentimentality was the hallmark of coach and captain; of knowing how much it meant to win.

Competition is a tough taskmaster and winning is an unshareable gift. Others can enjoy a sportsman or woman's success, celebrate a team's victory, partake in the fun, and so for a while live in the reflected glory. But to feel the sudden impact of being on the right side of that thin line which divides triumph from disaster; to come to recognise the sharp, almost electrical charge which comes upon the final blast of the referee's whistle and which calls the fury and the fear of the fray to an end is for the competitor alone. The supporter will jump and wriggle for joy but he will not know, cannot possibly know, the provocatively powerful dance of the soul and the rhythm of the heart when the duel finishes and all the favours and the prizes are yours. The ecstasy is swift.

Defeat in sport is not quite the same. You can only fall so low, the emotions frazzled only so much, before solace can be found. Afterall, it is *only* a game. There is the immediate agony to endure, and the demons may return, but there is no deep sorrow to suffer, nor is there human tragedy. There are perspectives of scale and importance. To win is to know briefly the uplifting joy of the spirit and to utter an uncontrollable and inspiring 'Ye-es !!' The wonder then fades, but at an uncertain hour the joy fleetingly returns. And so it will be for the victors for the rest of time; the flame will forever flicker and never fade. England and Australia had begun seven weeks earlier, along with 18 other teams in 48 matches, to go in search of that elusive feeling.

The path to each World Cup has not been one of untrammelled ease. For the first tournament in 1987 there was the uncertainty of putting into being a new concept for rugby union. There were the misgivings many administrators had about the consequences of a formal competition embracing 16 nations, more than half of whom were not in membership of the International Rugby Board, and which might lead to the professionalisation of the game. There was a clear and present danger which threatened the sport's guiding ethos. In 1991, there was the uncertainty which was attached to a tournament organised, not by two countries as in 1987 but, while hosted by England, shared among five nations of Europe. There was also, to begin with, the uncertainty about its financial success and the machinery which should be put in place to secure this. There was the internal squabbling about who was responsible for what. If there were those countries that stood their distance from the tournament in 1987, by 1991 everyone wanted stake in it and to have his share of the financial cake.

In 1995, there was the concern about South Africa's return to the fold, the reaction there might be to a large-scale event within the country itself and how the various communities, black and white, would respond. South Africa, culturally and politically, was in the process of dramatic transformation. Additionally, questions were raised as to whether the infrastructure of transport, accommodation, administration and so on could cope with the anticipated influx of thousands of visitors. Again, there was, inevitably, hard bargaining over the share of the financial spoils.

In 1999, when Wales were allocated host status, there was the nail-biting chase to get the Stadium in Cardiff completed in time. Completion was accomplished only by a whisker, but not without considerable trepidation.

Again, at the beginning of March 2002, the Rugby World Cup authorities were not at ease with themselves. Matters were coming to a head about the host and sub-host agreement, and the disagreement relating in the main to the issue of 'clean' stadia.

The IRB and RWCL had received a bid from Australia and New Zealand in 1998 to host and sub-host, respectively, the 2003 tournament. The bid was presented in accordance with known practice and standard requirements, including 'clean' venues, as drawn up by Keith Rowlands after the first event in 1987.

In April 1999, the terms were agreed. By November 2001, the Host Union Agreement (HUA) was signed between RWCL and Australia. New Zealand were expected to sign the Sub-Host Union Agreement (SHUA) the following month. From then on, the issue entered murky waters.

There were delays in signing the SHUA. New Zealand failed to accept terms which were markedly more favourable than those accepted by the Australian Rugby Union. When New Zealand indicated that it might have to reconsider its position because the financial forecast for its part of the tournament was negative, the Directors of the of RWCL persuaded the ARU to provide A$10 million to the NZRFU. However, the two unions agreed that each should pay their own costs and keep their own profits, or be responsible for their own losses.

New Zealand failed to accept terms which were consistent with their 1998 bid and failed to comply with what was meant in contractual and practical terms by the concept of 'clean' stadia, although, with a Director on the RWCL board, they had first-hand knowledge of it. There was further disagreement over the playing of New Zealand's domestic competition, the National Provincial Championship, during the period when 50 per cent of the Rugby World Cup fixtures were to be played in New Zealand.

By December 2001, New Zealand had signed a draft of the SHUA containing provisions relating to 'clean' stadia. By March, the New Zealand Rugby Football Union had declined to sign the agreement and reserved its position in respect of 'clean' venues. There was by this time dissent and acrimony in the air. New Zealand's position was unclear, yet the 'clean'-venue issue had been highlighted during the 1987 World Cup, after which 'all unions in membership of the IRFB [as it then was] were advised of the problems [relating to 'clean' venues] encountered in Australia and New Zealand. The Board urged the Five Nations in particular to ensure that in 1991 there would be no ground-advertising contracts which could cut across the commercial programme of the RWCL.' The point which was reiterated at the time was that, in a successful quest for sponsorship for the World Cup, long-term contractual commitments entered into by a host union in good faith could inhibit such commercial sponsorship.

Yet, after all these years, this remained an unresolved issue for New Zealand, the importance of which had not been fully recognised. The issue finally descended into a personal attack on Vernon Pugh, the Chairman of the RWCL and IRB. Murray McCaw, the NZRFU Chairman complained that Pugh had 'too much power'. David Rutherford, the Chief Executive, believed Pugh to be 'bloody-minded'. He was not, he was quoted as saying, 'prepared to mortgage the future of New Zealand rugby on the whims of Mr Pugh'. There was much more. New Zealand politicians entered the scene in an attempt to quell the tide of resentment as well as salvage what was left of an unpleasant episode in the history of the Rugby World Cup

On 18 April 2002, the Council of the IRB issued a statement saying that they had 'ratified recommendations from the Board of Rugby World Cup Limited that the finals of Rugby World Cup 2003 should be staged in Australia alone'. It continued, 'The recommendations from the Board of RWCL followed the refusal earlier this year by the New Zealand RFU to accept terms of the offer to host part of the tournament. RWCL subsequently requested and received an alternative bid for sole Host Union status from the Australian Rugby Union (ARU).'

The Board regretted the decision and the impact this might have on the game in New Zealand but said it was left with no alternative. 'Generous accommodations made by RWCL to meet the needs and problems of the NZRFU were repaid with consistent failures and wholly inappropriate behaviour,' the statement went on. As a result, there was an enquiry held in New Zealand into the whole shabby episode. The subsequent report by Sir Thomas Eichelbaum pointed the finger firmly at the NZRFU's council which, he concluded, was to blame for the loss of sub-host status. David Rutherford and Murray McCaw resigned as a result of the débâcle. Others, too, had to pass on. New Zealand's representatives on the IRB Executive Council were replaced by Jock Hobbs and Steve Tew.

Vernon Pugh concluded that the bottom line was that 'the difficulties had been caused by, at best, naivety followed by less than open explanation and, at worst, by arrogance and incompetence'. It was an unfortunate episode.

Therefore, like South Africa in 1995 the tournament in 2003 was held in one country. As a result of the great success of the Olympics in Sydney in 2000 there was vast optimism and expectation for the fifth Rugby World Cup in Australia. The tournament involved 20 nations, eight of whom pre-qualified by playing in the quarter-finals in 1999. Almost 90 nations went through the process of playing qualifying rounds, which began in September 2000, and from whom the other participating nations were drawn. The finals were staged in the six state capitals, as well as Townsville, Gosford, Launceston and Wollongong.

'Australia will embrace it wholeheartedly,' said Tim Horan, in anticipation of what was to come. 'As the Olympics showed, and the Lions tour a year later in 2001, the attitude will be entirely professional. It will be like a mini-Olympics. The Australian public will be a part of it – not just the matches themselves, but the whole celebration of sport." He was to be proved right.

The ARU and its Chief Executive, John O'Neill, was almost proved correct when he had confidently predicted that more than 2 million people would pass through the turnstiles. In the event, that number of tickets were sold, but those who ventured through turnstiles totalled 1.8 million. This was in comparison to the 600,000 who saw the first World Cup matches in 1987. Spread over 5 nations in 1999, there were 1.5 million spectators, while back in 1995, when it was in one country, there were 1 million.

16,000 tickets were sold for the Uruguay versus Georgia match in Pool C in Sydney. This fixture between two of rugby's emerging countries compares with the 18,600 crowd which turned up for the memorable Australia v France semi-final at the Concord Oval in 1987. The television audience came near to 4 billion in contrast to the 300 million in 1987.

If in the past Rugby World Cup finals had seen competing countries play their pool matches in one city or region, in 2003 most countries played matches in a number of Australian states.

'We want to demonstrate the full internationalism of rugby in a tangible way to the Australian community,' John O'Neill had said. 'This can be achieved by taking as many teams as possible to as many cities as possible so that the public can witness first-hand the teams in action. The Rugby World Cup is more than just the playing of rugby. It is a festival conducted every four years where the game's spirit is celebrated by the players on the pitch and by the thousands of fans off the pitch. This will be a player's tournament.'

In 1997, the ARU employed a staff of 30, with 2 working on marketing and sponsorship. By 2003, they employed 150 full-time staff with 18 responsible for marketing and sponsorship, working with commercial agents IMG. The five main sponsors were Heineken, Coca-Cola, Visa, Qantas and British Airways. The various forms of sponsorship and licensing brought in revenue between A$75 and A$100 million.

The ARU's direct revenue was, as it always has been, through ticket sales. All other official tournament income went to the IRB. The ARU income was capped at A$45 million. The first A$31 million in profit went to the ARU, while from A$31 and A$45 million the ARU received 70 cents in the dollar. The tournament added A$300 million to the New South Wales economy where most of the games were played.

While this was being settled, the process was underway to determine which nation or nations would host the 2007 tournament. It was no secret that, in line with what had been perceived in the past, if any one country would wish to go solo in Europe, then England and France would be the contenders. And so it turned out – both countries put in separate bids. France stuck to the formula of the previous tournaments, with 20 teams in four pools and using the stadia used for the Football World Cup in 1998. Ireland, Scotland and Wales would share some of the matches.

England, however, attempted something new.

England released their bid on 21 October 2002. This was both bold and imaginative, and it broke with the structure hitherto constructed for the tournament. Although they presented three choices in Dublin there was, in their view, a preferred option. This was the two-tier option in which 16 leading countries would contest for the Webb Ellis Cup, while there would be a parallel competition for 32 other countries to compete for a Rugby World Nations Cup. There would be 100 matches played over a 45-day period.

Francis Baron, the Chief Executive of the RFU, had said that he believed 'Australia 2003 will take the World Cup to new heights, but will exhaust the development possibilities of the current format'. There would be a pool stage of four pools with four teams in each. The top two teams in each pool would progress through to the Super 8 stage which would replace the knock-out quarter-finals. There would be eight games, before the best four teams, based on points for each game, reached the knock-out semi-final stage.

The 32 teams comprising the Rugby Nations Cup drawn from those in membership of the IRB and qualifying from regional tournaments would be played in venues throughout England, such as Bracknell, Clifton, Redruth, Stourbridge, Imber Court, Maidstone and so on. In this way, the two-tier system ensured that the professional and the amateur sides of rugby union were accommodated and might benefit each other. In this way, too, the system would do away with the numerous qualifying rounds played throughout the world to determine the teams to play in the finals. Expense could be saved. The RFU suggested that the tournament would be played in June and July and not in the autumn, as had happened in the previous two World Cups in the Northern Hemisphere. The RFU had assessed the net loss to the global game of playing the World Cup at specific times of the year and calculated that the net loss to be incurred in June/July would be £14.9 million. September and October would lose £59.4 million, and October/November £44.5 million. These figures were based on the loss of revenue from tours to the respective hemispheres and the effect all this would have on domestic rugby.

By January, after travelling to many parts of the world to sell their ideas, England revised their proposal to include Cardiff, Edinburgh and the new stadium in Wembley (due for completion in 2006) on the list of venues. Ireland was not included because of the uncertainty regarding any new development of a new stadium in Dublin to replace Lansdowne Road. A further change was in the Nations Cup, which would be reduced to include 20 teams. At every stage, England guaranteed the financial success of the format. The decision panel consisted of Syd Millar, acting Chairman of RWCL (in the absence of Vernon Pugh, who was then suffering from a serious and debilitating illness and which was to prove fatal); Mike Miller, the IRB Chief Executive; and Rian Oberholzer, Chief Executive of South Africa Rugby Football Union.

It was an intriguing conundrum: whether to play safe with France or take a radical move for change with England. There must have been those who wished they could base their decision having seen the outcome in Australia. It was believed that the tournament would succeed, at least in playing terms, but could the financial targets be met? The IRB needed approximately $80 million dollars to run their affairs over a four-year period. Since the Rugby World Cup was their only source of revenue, the tournament had to be a huge financial success in order to administer and develop the game worldwide; to fund their many other tournaments, none of which provided a profit; and to assist the developing countries with grants and donations.

It was during 2002, also, that the IRB were making serious overtures to the International Olympic Committee. They wanted rugby union to be included in the Olympic Games in Beijing. This would not only raise the profile of the sport but ensure that rugby union would be looked upon more sympathetically by governments who would only support a sport financially if it belonged to the Olympic movement and was included in the roster of events. Rugby union would benefit and might speed up the process of the sport's expansion. It was thought that the Sevens version of the game would prove to be the more suitable. This development was postponed to a later date.

In the Northern Hemisphere, autumn 2002 proved to be a hotbed of activity. All three of the major Southern Hemisphere countries were visiting Europe. England were to play all three, France would play New Zealand and South Africa, Wales had New Zealand, Scotland had South Africa and Ireland would play Australia. Italy would play Australia and Argentina. There were visits also from Canada, Fiji and Romania.

England were prepared like a spider to welcome the three Southern Hemisphere teams into their Twickenham web, from which nowadays rarely anyone finds release. When the time came, after all the expectation, England found that their three visitors were at less than full strength. New Zealand, in particular, had sent over a team which was perceived to be nothing more than their second string. This emasculated the potency of the contests, which many had interpreted as possibly justifying the world rankings and proving that England were indeed the best team in the world. England did march on to win the three matches: 31–28 against New Zealand, 32–31 against Australia and 55–3 against South Africa. Ireland defeated Australia 18–9 for the first time since 1979, after losing the previous 11 encounters. Scotland defeated the Springboks 21–6 for the first time since 1969. Wales, however, failed to stop the pattern of failure and lost 43–17 to make it 14 consecutive All Black victories since 1953. France drew 20–20 against the All Blacks and won 30–10 against South Africa.

In the Six Nations Championship that followed in February, there was the strong belief that the probable winners of the grand slam, England or France, would by unfortunate arrangement be meeting on the first weekend. The drama of the Championship, it was felt, was lost. The upshot, however, was different. A third horse entered in the shape of Ireland. The team from the Emerald Isle proved that rugby union was vastly improving. If in previous seasons the four Provinces had proved to be forces to be reckoned with in the Heineken Championship – Ulster having won the trophy in 1999, Munster having twice reached the final in 2000 and 2002 – the beneficial effects were observed on the International field. No more so than in 2003 when, under the captaincy of the brilliant Brian O' Driscoll, they looked set from the beginning to carve something for themselves during the Championship season.

England remained the team to beat. They had already set the high standards for the Six Nations Championship. Yet, to begin with they failed to show consistency throughout any of their games. Against France, Wales and Italy there were brief periods of power and concentration, adding up to no more than 20 minutes in each of the fixtures, when they secured their victories. It was enough.

France stuttered. They lost to England, defeated Scotland without impressing and then, in Lansdowne Road, they fell victim to a team which had rarely had the tag of favourites attached to them. Ireland remained on the road to their first grand slam since 1948. Italy were improving, whereas Scotland and Wales looked forlorn and helpless, stuck in a warp of ordinariness approaching impotence. In the Stadio Flaminio, where Scotland had lost to Italy in their first season in the Six nations Championship in 2000, Wales were to follow suit. Neither Scotland nor Wales looked to be able to exert any strong effect on the Six Nations Championship. Since the game at the highest level had become professional in 1995 and having failed to accommodate the new age, their influence seemed to have been negated.

There were many other fixtures to be played before the Rugby World Cup began. The various nations would cross north and south, east and west in June in a last ditch effort to put the final touches to their team's final preparations. The Tri Nations would be played in July and August before the Rugby World Cup began on 10 October in the Telstra Stadium, Sydney. Each player's eyes would be set on 22 November; fingers were crossed hoping that he and his team would rise above the common crowd to appear in the concluding line-up at the Telstra Stadium when the final would kick-off at 8:00 pm.

Each Rugby World Cup tournament has moved on steadily. Each one, every four years, has improved modestly on the last. With Australia's flair for showmanship, their inveterate love of sport, their extrovert pride in their country and their need to have their place in the world reinforced, the 2003 Rugby World Cup was always likely to take a vast leap forward. The extravaganza of the Olympics 2000 was still in people's minds. There was an overwhelming warmth to the welcome which was repeated a year later for those visitors who followed the Lions tour. The Rugby World Cup needed to be prepared to step out of its cocoon and to fly. In 2003 it did.

THE POOL STAGE

On Friday 10 October, the festival began with an A$5 million, 45-minute opening ceremony celebrating Australian culture and history in dance, song and mime. The centrepiece, to the accompaniment of the Sydney Symphony Orchestra, was the sight of 1,700 schoolchildren carrying different coloured banners, taking the formation of a giant rugby player carrying a ball. The ceremony was impressive in its staging and with the anthem 'World In Union', it tugged at the heart strings, as well as inspiring expectation of the excitement to come.

If the opening game between the host nation and Argentina demonstrated the typical nervousness of two teams starting out on their campaign, the first fixture

Roy Laidlaw of Scotland passes the ball from the base of the scrum during the 1987 Rugby World Cup match against New Zealand, played at Lancaster Park, New Zealand. The match finished in a 30–3 victory for the home team

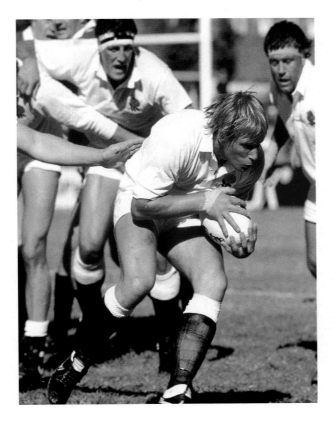

England's Peter Winterbottom charges forward during the 1987 Rugby World Cup match against the USA in Sydney. England won the match 34–6

Grant Fox of New Zealand in action during the 1987 tournament

John Kirwan of New Zealand evades a tackle and goes on to score during the 1987 Pool B
match against Fiji

France's Serge Blanco scores a dramatic try to beat the Wallabies at the Concord Oval in Sydney. France went on to lose 29–9 to New Zealand in the final

Robert Jones (centre right) of Wales clears the ball in the third place play-off against Australia at Rotorua in 1987

France's Pierre Berbizier prepares to offload the ball from the maul during the 1987 Rugby World Cup final against the All Blacks. The match finished in a 29–9 victory for the hosts, New Zealand

All Black captain David Kirk collects the Webb Ellis Cup after his team's victory over France in 1987

Gordon Hamilton of Ireland is mobbed after believing he had scored the winner against Australia in 1991. Australia had other ideas

Mick Skinner of England and Eric Champ of France square up in the 1991 quarter-final at the Parc des Princes, Paris

Point-scoring machine Michael Lynagh was the difference in the 1991 semi-final at Lansdowne Road, Dublin. Australia beat the All Blacks 16–6

Australia captain Nick Farr-Jones passes the ball out during the World Cup final against England at Twickenham, London. Australia won the match 12–6

Will Carling takes
on Tim Horan of
Australia during
the 1991 final at
Twickenham

Nick Farr-Jones and David Campese hold aloft the Webb Ellis Cup after Australia's victory
over England in 1991

Federico Mendez of Argentina exploded onto the international arena and figured strongly in the 1995 World Cup

Sean Fitzpatrick of New Zealand on the charge against Scotland in 1995

Gavin Hastings of Scotland clashes with France's Philippe Saint-Andre during their 1995 meeting in Pretoria. France won the match 22–19

The man for all seasons. France legend Philippe Sella would never quite reach the heights of World Cup winner, coming close in 1987 against New Zealand

Rob Andrew takes England into the 1995 semi-final with a winning drop kick against Australia

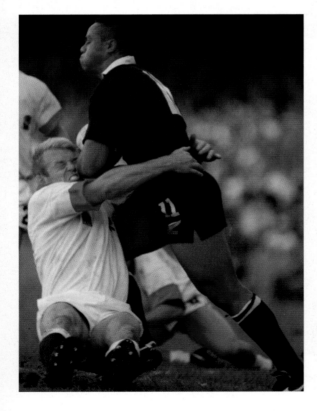

Flanker Tim Rodber attempts to put a stop to Jonah Lomu's run during the second semi-final of the 1995 World Cup at Newlands, Cape Town. New Zealand won the match 45–29 and went on to meet South Africa in the final

Zinzan Brooke kicks a drop goal during the All Blacks' 45–29 defeat of England

South Africa coach Kitch Christie is held aloft after his team's victory over New Zealand in the 1995 World Cup final

South Africa captain François Pienaar celebrates on Hennie le Roux's shoulders after their victorious defeat of New Zealand at Ellis Park, Johannesburg

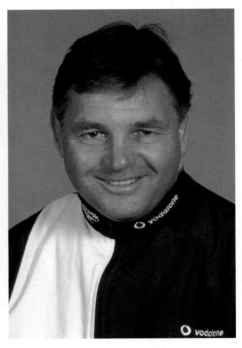

Rod Macqueen, Australia's head coach, in 1999

Jeremy Guscott in action during England's 67–7 victory over Italy in 1999

Joost van der Westhuizen feeds the ball from the base of the scrum during South Africa's 1999 Pool A match against Scotland. The game, played at Murrayfield, Edinburgh, finished in a 46–29 win for South Africa

Scott Gibbs of Wales is tackled by Samoa's George Leaupepe during the 1999 Pool D match at the Millennium Stadium, Cardiff. Samoa won a remarkable match 38–31

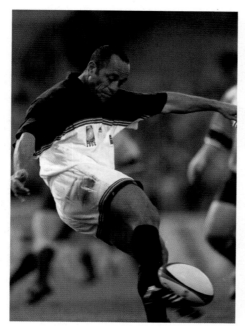

David Nin of the USA in action during the 1999 Pool E match at Thomond Park in Limerick, Ireland

Jonny Wilkinson of England kicks for goal in the 1999 quarter-final against the Springboks at the Stade de France, Paris

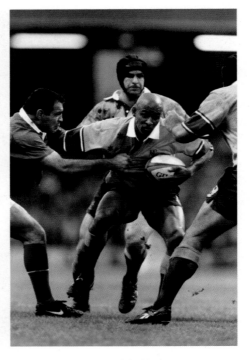

Jannie de Beer of South Africa kicks a world-record fifth drop goal in the 1999 quarter-final match against England

George Gregan is tackled by France's Raphael Ibanez during the 1999 final at the Millennium Stadium in Cardiff. Australia went on to lift the trophy after a 35–12 victory

Christophe Dominici of France can't escape from the clutches of New Zealand's Christian Cullen during the 1999 semi-final at Twickenham, London

Brian O'Driscoll of Ireland touches down against Australia. Having posted strong performances in the earlier stages of the 2003 tournament, Ireland were knocked out by France in the quarter-final

The Fiji wizard, Rupeni Caucaunibuca, dazzled briefly in the pool stage, as seen here against the Scots. Fiji would ultimately lose and fail to reach the quarter-finals

Mike Catt proved that age and experience is invaluable, as his timely arrival against Wales in the quarter-final proved to be the pivotal moment that swung the game England's way

France's stalwart leader Fabien Galthie in action in his team's victory over Ireland. Overlooked in previous World Cups, this would prove to be his swan song on the international stage

Australian captain George Gregan gives his team a pep talk as the Wallabies turned the form book on its head and beat the All Blacks convincingly in the semi-final

Over it goes! England's talismanic fly-half Jonny Wilkinson sends over the winning drop goal in the dramatic closing seconds of the final against Australia. Will his life ever be the same?

Despite a welter of severe pom-bashing running up to the final, the Australian newspapers were magnanimous in the defeat of their national side

Members of the England rugby squad make their way down Regent Street during the victory parade on 8 December 2003. 750,000 supporters lined the streets of London to welcome home the World Cup victors

England's victory parade culminated in a reception at Buckingham Palace, where members of the squad will return in 2004 to collect awards bestowed in the New Year's Honours list

was further undermined in Australia's sporting news headlines by the cricketer Matthew Hayden's record Test innings of 380 against Zimbabwe in Perth.

At any rate, the tournament was underway. Australia, having lost four of their last five matches, were glad to secure a win in front of 82,000 people in the Telstra Stadium. Wendell Sailor, Stephen Larkham, Mat Rogers and David Lyons were the pick of the Australians. Having nullified Argentina in the scrum, where the south Americans were persistently infringing, the Wallabies might have played more confidently, but uncertainty was to characterise their play almost throughout, other than in the very late stages of the competition. 24–8 would do for now in Pool A. There was a busy schedule for the next two days.

Four games the following day gave substantial victories to the favoured teams. In Pool A, Ireland scotched Romania's hopes 45–17, which gave evidence that this pool would ultimately provide intriguing and compulsive matches.

In Pool D, New Zealand dispatched Italy 70–7, the latter scoring only one point more than they did in 1987. Nonetheless, the win proved costly. Tana Umaga, the All Black vice captain and centre, left the field — and the competition as it was later to prove — with damaged cruciate ligaments of his left knee. His rugby intelligence and physical presence were going to be sorely missed. The All Blacks were never quite the same force without him.

France, playing the kind of fluid rugby which raised their profile and reputation, defeated Fiji 61–18 in Pool B. Rupeni Caucaunibuca is a player of brilliance, as he showed in the try he scored here, but not long after, the Fijian delivered another stunning blow. This time it was to Olivier Magne's head, and Caucau, as he was called, was suspended for two World Cup fixtures. Yannick Jauzion scored a hat-trick for France.

On the west coast, in the Subiaco Oval, Perth, South Africa opened their Pool C campaign against Uruguay with a thumping 72–6 victory.

There were three matches on Sunday. Wales, belying what was to come, were unconvincing against Canada. Down to 14 men without their captain, Colin Charvis, who had been sin-binned in the first half, they came out comfortably ahead, 41–10. While at the intriguingly named Dairy Farmers Stadium in Townsville, Japan played a fast and skilful game against Scotland and were only four points behind midway through the second half. Japan looked promising enough at that stage to provide an upset, but Scotland survived. No such fears attended England, who scored 12 tries against Georgia to give the biggest margin of victory so far.

By and large, the pattern remained of the minnows of the competition having a bag full of points scored against them. The closest game so far was that between the USA and Fiji, with only one point separating them (Mike Hercus missing a touchline conversion which would have stopped their run of nine successive losses since 1987). Argentina, Samoa and New Zealand scored over 60 points against Namibia, Uruguay and Canada, while Australia notched up 90 points against Romania. It was a familiar tale. If a couple of days later Samoa and Ireland were to establish substantial scores against Georgia and Namibia, in between, the tournament had its fist big test: England and South Africa, 'the critical Boer War replay', as was announced by one paper in a somewhat unsavoury manner.

The Springboks had left South Africa full of hope, but lacking in the confidence for which they were renowned. Draped outside a high building near the Convention Centre in Sandton, where a Gala dinner had been held to bid farewell to the team, was the legend proclaiming: 'Men who have achieved great things have been great dreamers.'

As the country anticipated the World Cup there was much talk of dreams. With their inability to recapture their former high place in the world rankings, the absence of good form in the Tri-Nations and the loss of key players, they needed to dream. There had also been accusations of a racist attitude inside the squad, which would be investigated. In rugby terms there had never been such self-doubt or a sense of insecurity. What South Africa hoped for was the spirit of *madiba*. Taken from the Xhosa language, this word had been applied to Nelson Mandela when he had emerged from his incarceration on Robben Island. Its meaning encompasses a profound sense of leadership, quiet power and the will to overcome overwhelming odds. 'South Africa is not a normal country when it comes to rugby,' Rudolf Straeuli said. The preparation for the English game was intense.

'We've got to recognise that this game is bigger, more intense than anything we've been involved in since the last World Cup,' said Martin Johnson. 'There's more anxiety, more nerves, more pressure.' Everyone was conscious of the ugly incidents of their previous meetings. Foul play are tactics of limitations. 'Teams don't get intimidated by foul play,' concluded Johnson. 'They get intimidated by good, fast, physical rugby.'

From the Springbok camp, Corne Krige, their captain, said, 'We have been working on our discipline. Habitual criminals have been spoken to.'

The England team was reputed to have received faxes and goodwill messages from the Queen, the Prime Minister and the leader of the Opposition, which raised the question of whether the Scottish and Welsh teams might be accorded the same courtesy in similar circumstances. Prince Harry, a devoted follower of the game, was said to be turning up for the England training sessions, to which Woodward's response, affecting humour for a change, was, 'I know we have injuries in the squad but they're not that bad.'

In the event, England won while under pressure for long periods and the Springboks felt at the end that they could take a lot of comfort from the loss. It meant, of course, that England would be top of the pool and that it was the Springboks who faced the prospect of meeting New Zealand in the quarter-finals. Corne Krige felt encouraged by his team's performance. He and his fellow back-row men had done much to shake England and, had Louis Koen not missed with four penalty shots at goal and a failed drop goal, it just might have been more serious for Johnson's men.

Will Greenwood, who had suffered personal difficulties during the week at the bedside of his wife, Caro, had a terrific game and it was his try which turned the nervousness of the 12–6 score-line into a well-cushioned 19–6. As ever, Jonny Wilkinson provided the large margin that separated the two teams at the end. To his conversion he added four penalties and two drop goals. Thus, England removed themselves from the shadow of a team which, to some extent, had the potential of upsetting their chase for glory.

'He who lives by the boot shall perish by the boot,' was the *New Zealand Herald*'s conclusion. 'Four years after Jannie de Beer drop-kicked England out of the quarter-finals of the World Cup, Jonny Wilkinson's left foot exacted revenge.'

There were signs for England to be ready for a media onslaught. They were not Australia's favourite team and the Pom-bashing was about to increase. Former captain John Eales had begun by complaining about the manner in which Neil Back was allowed to hold the ball at the back of the moving maul, with all the pack in front of him. According to the great Wallaby lock, this constituted obstruction. England were in for an uncomfortable time in the newspapers, but no doubt with their inner strength, garnered over several years, it would finally work in their favour.

Thus, the order in Pool C was settled. However, around the corner a small ambush was being planned. As has been their wont, Samoa, who can never be taken for granted, had a surprise in store before the first round closed.

In Pool D, everything was going to plan, too. Whereas Wales made things difficult for themselves against Italy, who were making substantial strides under

John Kirwan, their coach, and Tonga, against whom they scraped their way forward unconvincingly, the All Blacks were simply piling on the points.

In *The Times*, John Hopkins wrote: 'Wales seemed determined to give their supporters the fright of their lives before limping home with not an ounce of gas in the tank after another poor performance. Tonga outscored them by three tries to two.' This seemed to reflect the mood of the supporters, who could no longer look forward to any of their nation's games with any sense of confidence.

The All Blacks had scored 229 points with 20 points against in three matches. Wales's aim was to reach the quarter-final stage, upon which their mission, as it were, would be accomplished. They strove and, after a nail-biting moment or two, did so. But if they were destined to come second in the pool, they were not going to rest there so easily. They had their mark to make.

Pool A, too, was going as expected, in that the decisive game was to be the closing fixture of the pool against Australia. France would come top of Pool B, and Scotland, who were to suffer their worst World Cup campaign to date, would need to overcome Fiji to claim second spot. Not the foregone conclusion it might seem at first sight.

Among the emerging countries were some fascinating contests: Japan v USA marked the latter's first victory since 1987; Georgia against Uruguay, where the latter surprised everyone to win; Namibia and Romania pulled in a capacity crowd in the only game to be played in Launceston, Tasmania. To cheer both teams on, the crowd was divided according to their date of birth: odd numbers supported one side and the even numbers the other. It was a huge success.

On the same Sunday, the tournament had a taste of real conflict. In Adelaide Oval, the tension remained to the end of the game between Argentina and Ireland. The memories of Lens in 1999 haunted the Irish. There was one point in it at the interval (10–9); there was one point in it at the end (16–15). Alan Quinlan scored the decisive try in the 20th minute in a match dominated by the kicking of O'Gara and Humphreys for Ireland and Quesada and Corleto of Argentina. Quinlan, however, injured himself in the process of diving over a platform created by Keith Wood who, as captain and player, was on inspiring form for the Irish. This set up Ireland for the crucial contest with Australia.

England triumphed over Samoa, despite trailing by two points with a quarter of an hour to go. They had to survive a massive effort by the South Sea Islanders. Two brilliant tries at the end made the match their own. Vickery, with a swerve and hint of side step, scored a try, and the pin-point accuracy of Wilkinson's boot found Balshaw speeding wide out on the wing to score a scintillating try. Wilkinson himself bagged 15 points.

From the Samoa game there came the controversial incident when England had 16 men on the field. David Reddin, the England fitness coach, had ignored five requests from the fifth official, Brett Bowden, to wait for a break in play before sending Dan Luger onto the field to replace the injured Mike Tindall. In the subsequent inquiry into the incident it was judged that Reddin had been given specific instruction from Clive Woodward to ignore the instruction of the official not to send out a substitute. This was meat and drink to the Australian media, who thrived on accusations of English arrogance. The RFU were fined £10,000 and Reddin banned from the touchline for two games. Woodward and his team were clearly growing tense and in danger of losing their sense of proportion at this stage.

There had also been a side show to the main event. Steve Walsh, the New Zealand referee who was acting as the fourth official, was accused of misconduct against Reddin in the tunnel. Petulant display unworthy of playground behaviour: physical contact by Reddin, it was claimed, found Walsh responding by squirting water at the Englishman – kindergarten fun and games. Walsh was banned from running the line in the following game.

Having already qualified for the quarter-finals, it was rumoured that Ireland would choose a below-strength team for the fixture against Australia. Eddie O'Sullivan dispelled the gossip by picking his strongest available team, showing only three changes from the team who played against Argentina. Going against recent selection, Ronan O'Gara was preferred to David Humphreys at fly-half. Ireland wanted to finish top of Pool A, which would mean a match against Fiji or Scotland – on current form, a more amenable fixture at the quarter-final stage than France. 'If we did anything less than pick our best team, we would be capitulating a game we believe we can win,' said O'Sullivan. 'We should not leave anything in our locker at this stage of the World Cup.'

Keith Wood, the captain, felt that, 'There is a different mindset having qualified for the quarter-finals. I would hope the shackles are off. The pressures that were inherent against Argentina were absolutely colossal. I was shattered after the game, emotionally as much as physically.'

Of the fly-half position, the Irish coach said: 'Ronan came off the bench last week and did a good job. We try to pick the form guy because there is not much to choose between them. Ronan gets the nod. They are two very good players.'

While the other tough contest had been going on, Australia, in preparation for their encounter with Ireland, had recorded 142 points without reply against Namibia. This was a World Cup record and Australia's first century of points in their 104-year history. (Their previous highest had been 92 against Spain two years earlier.) New Zealand had scored 145 against Japan in 1995 but Japan had scored 17 points. The match at the Adelaide Oval provided the biggest margin of victory. Chris Latham scored 5 tries, the most scored by any Australian.

The game against Ireland proved to be different. The Wallabies could count themselves fortunate to get away with a single-point win against what was a rampant performance by the Irish team in the second half. In the final minutes, Humphreys struck the ball beautifully, it looking to be a score from the moment it left his boot, but he missed the target narrowly. Gregan's drop goal and Smith's try had opened an early eight-point advantage, but O'Driscoll, who had not been conspicuous on the score sheet of late, scored a try and drop goal, and O'Gara's two penalties brought Ireland back into the game. It was not enough. 'That's the best display from an Irish pack we have seen since I don't know when,' was O'Sullivan's verdict.

If the pool stage of the competition began by emphasising the discrepancies between nations, it was ending in glorious competition. There was one more match to go. A game that was thought a mere formality proved far from being the case. Indeed, it went so far as adding considerably to the lustre of the whole tournament.

Wales, who have made little memorable impression on the Rugby World Cup, apart from their third/fourth play-off game in 1987, were about to change the view that had been taken of them. They were about to be taken into the hearts of all who were at the Telstra Stadium. It was a game of sheer exhilaration, of ebb and flow and, from both teams, spontaneity and daring. Eight tries to New Zealand, four to Wales. It brought the house down and standing ovations for all; more to Wales, perhaps, because such movement and enterprise was least expected from them.

After 36 minutes it was four tries – two for Rokocoko, and one each for Leon MacDonald and Ali Williams – to Wales's one (Mark Taylor). Sonny Parker and Colin Charvis scored, and the lead was cut to four points. Six minutes into the second half and – beyond belief – Wales were actually ahead with a Shane Williams try. But, in the end, the All Blacks re-grouped and, after Stephen Jones, who had had his best game for Wales at fly-half, scored the last of Wales's points, half an hour remained for New Zealand to establish a 53–37 victory.

'We ran out of steam,' Steve Hansen , the Wales coach, concluded. 'We need to play at that intensity week in, week out. Our minimum goal here was to reach the quarter-finals. We do not have the money to have development squads and A-Teams. We just have to go back and train harder to keep climbing the ladder.'

The *Western Mail* in Wales declared: 'The Buzz Is Back In Welsh Rugby. We Must Set Our Goals High.' We wondered. We all wondered. After a couple of decades in the doldrums, every one from Wollongong to Waunarlwydd wondered whether the promise would ever be fulfilled.

2003 QUARTER-FINALS

The last eight of the 2003 Rugby World Cup involved the eight original countries of the International Rugby Board: the five European countries and the three from the Southern Hemisphere. After the debates over the pervious four weeks concerning the unchanging form of the rugby nations of the world and of the need, sooner rather later, for some of the emerging countries to find their regular place in the competitive hierarchy, the quarter-final line-up served to confirm that the eight major countries were still firmly in place. Afterall, in the past the pattern had been broken. In the absence of South Africa in 1987, Fiji had insinuated themselves into the last eight, as did Western Samoa and Canada in 1991. Western Samoa repeated their efforts in 1995, while Argentina upset the apple cart in 1999. In 2003, the old order remained.

There was the further feeling that, apart from the mighty tussle between New Zealand and South Africa, the other fixtures would be forgone conclusions. After the imperious progress of the All Blacks before and during the tournament, and their expected smooth progress to the final, the resurgent Springboks, after their displays against England and Samoa, were suddenly thought likely to cause these complacent perditions to be reconsidered. There was genuine feeling that their muscularity would more than test New Zealand in the tight phases and hinder their free-flowing style.

Elsewhere, Australia would prove too strong for a lightweight and somewhat directionless Scotland, who could no longer rely on strong players with confident flair in the backs, nor roaming terriers among the forwards. This was their least successful campaign in the series thus far. In the final analysis, the Scottish team as a whole lacked an overall identifiable personality. But then, neither could Australia have been said to set the tournament alight, despite their record 142–0 win against Namibia.

Ireland, who still went through, had given their all, it was felt, in their uncompromising games with Argentina and Australia, both of which went down to the wire. The unrelenting pressure they went through, physically and mentally, was illustrated by the fact that, in each game, only a point separated the teams at the end. They might have found that they did not have enough left to face a French team that was growing in confidence, playing some magnificent rugby and intent on correcting the impression that the last hurdle was beyond them, as suggested on the two occasions they had reached the final in the past. There was a new French resolve.

'This is the stage we're really looking forward to,' said Lawrence Dallaglio.

'You couldn't find a more excited bunch,' observed Will Greenwood. 'Wouldn't be anywhere else in the world at the moment.'

As for the old spectre of Wales and the evil eye it had cast on England over the years, Woodward observed: 'I would like to think that this England team has moved way beyond that era.'

These were the views, confident and unquestioning, before the match began. I wonder whether such calm perspective prevailed at half-time? This is when England were 10–3 down and in the kind of disarray that was foreign to them. Not even against Samoa had they appeared so out of control and at a loss as to what to do next. What the players and the coach felt also represented a consensus feeling among almost everyone else. England had so banished the fearful spectre of Wales, the bane of their past, to the extent that the only matter of judgement after so many resounding victories of late was how far beyond the 50-point marker they would settle. True, Wales had summoned up – from goodness knows where – some strange, hitherto absent, spirit against New Zealand and had strutted such exciting stuff as to make us believe that not all the uninhibited and natural talent, with which Welsh rugby players are fabled, had vanished. The nerves still jerked in a body which was thought to be have lain moribund for too long. The question, the only question, was whether Wales could summon up the spirit again against England and, if so, would it come the second time in a week?

The first fixture was the Southern Hemisphere contest between the All Blacks and the Springboks in Melbourne. The anticipation of a gladiatorial contest faded. Those who believed that the All Blacks lacked the necessary power at forward were soon disabused. For South Africa, the drive and application they showed against England disappeared. It was New Zealand who played with the kind of aggression that had been expected of the Springboks. It was New Zealand who held on to the ball and rarely gave it away. Keven Mealamu and Jerry Collins were on terrific form, popping up at all points to make the decisive tackle, to retrieve possession and to carry the game into the heart of the Springboks. It was Mealamu who scored the game-breaking try in the 60th minute, after the ubiquitous Richie McCaw's initial break, and which spelt it out that South Africa would be on their way home.

The cheekiest try was prompted inevitably by Carlos Spencer. With rare intuition, but which is of a kind that is characteristic of him, the fly-half passed the ball through his legs with his back to Joe Rokocoko for the winger to score the final try and his 16th this calendar year (one short of the record held by Daisuke Ohata of Japan), and which took New Zealand to 45 for the tournament. Spencer was full of such tricks. Mostly they came off but critically, as New Zealand were soon to find out, he sometimes dared too much.

In his 89th and final International, Joost van der Westhuizen nearly scored in the corner for the Springboks, but was bundled into touch. With a converted try by Leon MacDonald and two more penalties against Hougaard's two penalties, New Zealand held a 13–6 lead at half-time. They ended comfortably ahead, 29–9.

Scotland put in a fine performance against Australia and held them 9–9 at half-time, with some onlookers thinking they were not undeserving of the lead. This was their best performance to date. The Australians had come in for a good deal of criticism prior to the game. Eddie Jones, the coach, had been advised to 'get more width to the Aussie game' and to 'fix' his back line. Even Nick Farr-Jones, the former scrum-half and captain, had called for the axe to come down on his successor, George Gregan. As if to deflect attention away from him, Jones started attacking both Ian McGeechan, whose last match as Scotland's coach this was, and Clive Woodward. It was a touchy time.

At the Suncorp Stadium in Brisbane, the key for Scotland was the line-out. They put their opponents under a good deal of pressure, taking a substantial number of Australia's throw-ins. This was corrected when Matt Cockbain, at 6'6", replaced the 6' flanker George Smith, who had damaged his shoulder.

Australia remained unimpressive and, with more possession, were prone to handling errors in contrast to the better discipline of Scotland. Yet, for all this, Scotland failed to advance often beyond the gain-line. This was where Stirling Mortlock and Lote Tuqiri were impressive. The former scored the first try with a run from the half-way line in the 45th minute, followed by George

Gregan and David Lyons. If Scotland did not give way and were the team to score the last try (via Russell) a minute into injury time, the game had drifted away from them by that stage.

Matt Giteau had replaced the injured Stephen Larkham in the 54th minute, forcing most observers to feel that the Australian back line operated better with the youngster at fly-half. Even if Australia had brought the width to their game that was called for, the general impression remained that they would have to lift their game considerably if they were to give a good contest to the All Blacks. With this game, Ian McGeechan left the coaching arena after 20 years to take over the administrative position vacated by his companion-in-arms for so long, Jim Telfer, whose 40-year association with Scottish rugby had come to a close.

Rugby in these islands, and not just in Scotland, is immeasurably indebted to McGeechan. Without question he will go down as one of the great coaches of all time. He will have coached the cream while with the Lions but, without the luxury of such talent in his home country, he nonetheless could fashion a team which could offer the sternest of tests to the best of nations. He could make the most modest of club players feel and look the part of an International player. Under him they filled their jerseys and were encouraged to walk tall, to not feel out of place among those rugby players who might be thought of a higher calibre, and to oppose them without flinching and always to take a step forward. He himself was the best of men, a boon companion and one of the finest of coaches of this or any other generation.

After Australia (32) and England (47), Ireland had up to this moment conceded the least number of points: 56. But how much had been taken out of them after the previous two matches, where their defence had been so severely put to the test? If they were missing their swift men, Denis Hickie and Geordan Murphy, their line-out and sure possession was about the most successful of any team in the tournament. Keith Wood, the redoubtable captain, said, 'The kitchen sink can be thrown at this one because it doesn't matter. It is all or nothing. We can't hold anything back.' It was to be his last International game. A great hooker, jovial, and a giant of a personality.

France, it was felt, had not had the tough matches to get them battle-hardened, yet they had shown fine touches, especially with the young fly-half Frederic Michalak, who would remain the tournament's leading points scorer with 103, until overtaken by Jonny Wilkinson in the final.

This was to be Keith Wood's departure from International rugby. At 31 years of age and with 58 caps, he was about to have his last game in the green jersey. He was to leave as a much revered figure. Before he faced France, Wood said, 'We have to make certain we have the belief that we can win the game. We play France year in, year out, and they're always big games. This is the biggest game for the next four years. If for one minute some of the players don't think we are going to win, it becomes quite a struggle. Do you want to wait another four years to complain about "Oh, God, if only…"? There can't be any "if onlies". This is all or nothing.'

In the end, France took all the points on offer. Wood shed a tear in the arms of Fabien Galthie, who would also call it a day after the semi-final. Wood was given a standing ovation from the moment he entered the press conference until he left.

If France had dismantled Scotland, they were to do the same with Ireland. If there were misgivings about how they had been tested, they cast such doubts to the wind in Melbourne. They scored 37 points before their opponents had a chance of putting their mark on the scoreboard. They were in the best of French form: width to their attack, panache and daring in their minds. And every time Ireland had possession, there always seemed more Frenchmen around the ball and the tackler. Even the threat posed by Malcolm O'Kelly and Paul O'Connell was nullified in the line-out. Bernard Laporte, the French coach, had always emphasised the newfound discipline in his team and it was there for all to see. Magne, Betsen and Harinordoquy were on magnificent form; where one was, so were the other two. They were never far from each other.

Ireland were behind after three minutes when Michalak kicked to the right, Harinordoquy latched onto the tricky bounce, fed Marsh and then on to Magne for the first try. It was Magne who influenced the second try when he intercepted O'Gara's long pass. Ibanez and Betsen followed, and Dominici finished off the move. Magne won the line-out ball, allowing Galthie and Marconnet to pave the way for Harinordoquy to score. With Michalak on top form with his boot, France were 27 points ahead at half-time. Another ten points came swiftly after the interval. It was all over for the Irish. Late in the game, Maggs got a try and O'Driscoll scored two more.

And so to Brisbane for the last of the quarter-final matches. This was the surprise package that was to prove the best of the four. It was the best because at long last Wales made a contest in a fixture dominated by England for the last decade and more. During the summer before the World Cup began, England had gone to Cardiff with a second-string team and routed a Welsh team full of the first-choice players.

Wilkinson was out of sorts to begin with, unsure of himself and his kicking. He did, however, kick his team into the lead with a penalty in a match already overflowing with surprises. Wales were on maverick form, as they were against New Zealand, daring this and risking that against the powerful discipline of England. However, the tempo of the match changed into a major key and in the stadium the temperature rose in the 33rd minute when Wales scored the first of their three tries. It was Stephen Jones who scored, but the move, as earlier in the week, was inspired by the mercurial Shane Williams on the wing. He was supported by Gareth Cooper and Gareth Thomas. It was a devastating score; fleet of foot and a wink in the eye, a cock-a-snook try against the well-ordered England.

Indeed, at this stage England looked in disorder. There were times when the England forwards and backs were bunched together in one half of the width of the pitch, leaving the other half unattended, like children in the schoolyard all surrounding that area where the ball was. This is what happened before the try was scored, when Williams was faced in the open space with only Ben Kay to beat. Neither was England's line-out as commanding as it usually was: Colin Charvis scored the next from a line-out on England's line.

Wales led 10–3 at half-time. Mike Catt was brought on for the second half and his tactical kicking, with Wilkinson not quite having the eye or the temperament to read the game, saved England's beacon. The field positions gained by Catt's astute and accurate kicking ensured that Wilkinson had the chances to kick goals. In this respect, his temperament was fine, and between the 48th and 68th minute he kicked five penalty goals. If Martyn Williams scored the third try for Wales, the last word remained with Wilkinson, who dropped his customary goal in injury time to make it 28–17. As *The Times* headline thundered: 'The glory goes to Wales; England go to Sydney.'

It was a grand, enthralling game, full of noise and fury. In many ways, it was the day when a touch of individual flair struck against a monolith and very nearly brought it down. It was the day, in other words, when David turned on Goliath and all his mighty presumption and struck back unexpectedly. But whilst he succeeded with a few short, sharp and shocking strikes, he never quite managed this time to hit the bull's eye. Crucially, England regathered their resolve in the nick of time, and if Catt provided the stability, it was the running brilliance of Justin Robinson which provided the chance for the game-breaking score, only four minutes into the second half. Coming so soon after leaving the dressing room and its moments of thought and doubtless tetchiness, this revived and invigorated his team. Robinson made the devastating run. Greenwood scored. The game turned.

When the tantalising affair was over, the crowd stood still for some considerable time, the wonderful mingling of the red and white giving a standing ovation for what was the most colourful and intoxicating match so far. In the streets afterwards, 'Swing Low' vied with 'Cwm Rhondda', or perhaps 'Delilah', for primacy in the choral stakes. All this camaraderie and hail-fellow-well-met was in the mood of the 2003 tournament as a whole. Rugby's values, we could conclude, of hard play on the field and good fun off it remained healthily in place. All roads now led to Sydney for the penultimate round and to the end.

2003 SEMI-FINALS

The only matter that was certain was the fact that, come what may, the outcome of the two semi-finals meant that the Northern would meet the Southern Hemisphere in the last game.

Australia had only met the All Blacks once before in a World Cup fixture. This was in 1991 in Dublin. The score stood at 16–6 in the Wallabies' favour. In a devastating first half, they destroyed New Zealand, with David Campese enjoying a purple patch of shimmering brilliance, scoring a try and creating another. In 2003, Australia had shown no signs that they were capable of such exhilarating rugby as that which was so wondrously on show in Lansdowne Road, and coming from a team bursting with talent, from the shadows of the coal face of the scrum to the more rarefied air among the fancy-dans in the backs. Bob Dwyer, then coach, had not had to suffer, nor had he given cause for the kind of criticism levelled against the current coach, Eddie Jones. Nor had Nick Farr-Jones, the scrum-half and captain, known what it was to experience the disapproving words aimed at George Gregan, to which he himself had contributed. Pundits cavilled against the tactics, as well as the personnel. They did not have many friends even in their own country. Indeed, Australia was a team under pressure.

New Zealand, on the other hand, had forged many friends because of their freedom-to-run attitude to the game. They ran at will and scored a cart-load of tries. In Mils Muliaina, Joe Rokocoko and especially Doug Hewlett they had a back trio of exceptional talent who would choose to attack from every corner of the field. There were forwards like the straying hooker, Mealamu, McCaw, Collins and even Jack, locked in the depths of the middle of the scrum, who would happily support the adventure. In Carlos Spencer, New Zealand had the conjuring, sleight-of-hand gifts which could ensure that they kept others guessing. And if he failed to smell the way the game was moving, then Justin Marshall, inside him, could do so.

The difference between the two teams was that New Zealand had amply declared their intentions and their players had, time and again, displayed their many-faceted skills, whereas Australia clearly had not. New Zealand had qualities unique to them. They had declared them to the world. No one was at all sure what the strengths of Australia were. What evolving pattern was there? Admittedly, the talent of Wendell Sailor, Lote Tuqiri and Mat Rogers was recognised, but not so transparently as those of their All Black counterparts. If Australia remained largely an unknown quantity, it was their weaknesses that were highlighted, rather than the possibilities of potential strengths, the most potent of which was Australia's renowned determination, will to win and their national sporting pride.

From the first whistle to the last, these characteristics were blatantly on view. From the kick-off, they won the ball and kept it. They refused the All Blacks a touch of it. At one stage in the first 20 minutes, the statistics showed that the host nation had 82 per cent of the possession and that the All Blacks had 66 per cent of the territory. In other words, if the All Blacks had a major foothold in the Australian half for this period, they did so without having their hands on the ball. Their opponents refused to kick away the ball. Australia preferred the ball in their hands in their own half rather than kick themselves out of a defensive position. Without the ball, a team cannot play and they certainly cannot score. Committing no errors, Australia offered no opportunities for penalties at goal. It was a hugely disciplined tactical game. Even at the end, New Zealand had enjoyed most of the territorial advantage, while Australia had most of the ball. A further indication of this trend was that New Zealand had spent five minutes within the Australian 22-metre line to Australia's three minutes at the opposite end.

The delicate, if daring, skills of Spencer partly decided New Zealand's fate. The fly-half likes the large stage, is never overwhelmed by it nor allows himself to be restricted by it. Indeed, rugby would be immensely poorer for the absence of his genius. It is the way for attack to regain the ascendancy over defence; the individual and spontaneous spark which is hard to predict and to contain.

Yet, in the 11th minute, his penchant for the long, risky pass found its mark in a Wallaby, not an All Black. Muliaina had been muscled into touch by Tuqiri and, after two set pieces, Spencer sent a long pass to the left, missing out two players. The ball, taking the parabola it did, tarried too long in the air, which allowed Mortlock to time his intervention and to intercept the pass. He had 75 metres to go, which he covered without a hand being laid on him, allowing Elton Flatley to convert. If Spencer made amends in creating the space for Reuben Thorne to get a try for New Zealand, two more penalties by Flatley ensured that Australia went into the interval with a 13–7 lead.

Jones had done his homework comprehensively. He advised his players to close down Spencer's options, snuffled out the effectiveness of Mauger and MacDonald in midfield and so limited the options for the try-scoring trio of Hewlett, Rokocoko and Muliaina. And when it was necessary for a change of plan and to return to first principles of discipline and containment at forward, as they had done successfully against South Africa and Wales, the All Blacks were found wanting. They lacked the controlling presence of Justin Marshall at scrum-half, who had to retire with rib cartilage damage after a dubious tackle from George Smith in the 50th minute. They had opportunities to challenge more and to close the points gap but, lacking a consistent goal kicker in the team, they missed a couple of chances at goal which came their way. MacDonald only succeeded with one, while Flatley kicked three more.

As in 1999, a wonderful New Zealand team playing the best all-round game in the tournament left the competition, in some views, prematurely. Once more, they set standards of play which is beyond others. It is a marker for the future in terms of speed, invention and remarkable handling skills. Eddie Jones admitted as much. But his counterpart John Mitchell, despite the wonderful playing record of his team, returned to New Zealand with a question mark over his future. He had showed a different way of playing the game. But, like the prophet, he might not be celebrated in his own land and his voice will be as that in the wilderness. Like John Hart, the All Black coach in 1999, whose team also played with remarkable fluency and style, Mitchell may not remain in charge. Both coaches were courageous in that they believed in the attacking game, but failed at the crucial hurdle of the semi-final of the World Cup. With them the whiff of danger left the tournament. New Zealand had scored 46 tries, the most by any team, but these ultimately counted for nought when they lost what they most desired.

'Today was the day for the Dad's army,' said Frederic Michalak, after the French team had lost the following day to England. 'They have so much experience and played the conditions perfectly. I tried to continue my hot streak as a kicker, but I couldn't.' The rain came to spoil the French party and Michalak's in particular. He had had a brilliant tournament. But his opposite number, Wilkinson, was getting into his stride. They had plans to cover him.

'Somebody said he was dead,' said Bernard Laporte. 'He was not dead. He played a great match.'

'It is not Frederic's fault,' commentated Galthie. 'He is not a machine. He is human. It was a very difficult match for him.

'Personally I dreamt of a different outcome. It was great to have one last adventure. We all had our dreams, but what will be, will be. It is difficult to run after an objective and fall short. Minute after minute we were under pressure and most of the second half we played in our half. The result, therefore, is logic.'

The day brought together the ruling class of Europe and their shared dominance for a decade and more of the Northern Hemisphere. There was much to achieve and to prove. England had been at the final feast once and were found wanting in 1991. France had followed their uncertain path twice in 1987 and 1999, and still they failed, having given their all, in superbly scintillating fashion, in the penultimate game. They had played their final, as it were, in the semi-final. Glory had been theirs too soon, but was not to be resurrected thereafter. Each nation, therefore, wanted to correct their failures of the past.

There was a difference from the previous day. Saturday had been dry and warm. The rain, as had been predicted earlier in the week, came late in the day to affect the shape of Sunday's contest. In retrospect, after knowing of France's play later in the day, we might have drawn the conclusion that Fabien Galthie and his players, from their hotel in Bondi, must have cast their eyes at the grey skies that afternoon and the dismal prospect that lay ahead, and decided that if the weather was unkind, they would prefer not coming out to play. They hardly turned up. Their game not only faltered in the face of the resolute English, but disintegrated. Indeed, they might as well have stayed at home, so ineffectual was their play. For the team under Laporte which had prided itself on its discipline – three yellow cards in twenty matches – this was when the old habits returned. A penalty count of 13–7 against them and two yellow cards tells a story of weakness and of ill-directed and misguided tactics. Dominici and Betsen were the culprits, which meant that France only had an hour with a full complement in their team. This was a French performance so far from that which had created such a favourable view and which had made them, in the much-used phrase of the time, the 'the dark horses' of the tournament, that they resembled a motley crew of aimless travellers. The French pundits and journalists simply shrugged their Gallic shoulders to indicate a failure of understanding and to suggest how impossible the immobile performance was to analyse. France had promised so much more.

England, on the other hand, saw that the prize which they had long sought and which had once been but a speck on the distant horizon was now within reach. They were no longer looking as if it were through the wrong end of the telescope. The Webb Ellis Cup glinted close by. That evening against France they played knowing that, having come thus far, there was only one way to look and that was forward to the following Saturday and their return visit to clinch the deal. They walked tall and oozed confidence. They may not have had many defined moments in the World Cup where they were complete masters of their sphere – there had been too many errors of skill and of judgement – but against France in the semi-final no one could mistake their intent. While their opponents hesitated and scrambled for any form of coherence, England were clear-sighted and moved on to command the conditions – of the weather and of France's seeming impotence.

In microcosm, the game's success and failure was illustrated in the performances of the respective fly-halves, Wilkinson and Michalak. Wilkinson, not at his best, was still the main man, scoring all of his teams' 24 points, while the 21-year-old French fly-half was, from his first kick, which flew vertically in the air instead of a questioning threat to Josh Lewsey, nervously out of form. Gerald Merceron, who replaced him in the 65th minute, might have been called upon earlier, when Michalak was manifestly unable to bring together a semblance of his earlier form.

France's high point came early, when Betsen tore away from a line-out in which Hill was slow to react at the tail. The French flanker's score, which gave them the lead after ten minutes, was allowed to stand after the video referee had a prolonged look at the replay. Michalak converted. There was thereafter little that was threatening from France. It was to be their only score.

Two penalties and a brace of drop goals from the sure boot of Wilkinson gave England their interval lead. England then squeezed out what was left of the life in France. With the territorial advantage and their forwards in the ascendant, it was only a matter of time before Wilkinson hammered home the points. Three more penalties and a drop goal in the second half made certain that France would have to wait until 2007, when the tournament will be theirs to welcome to their soil, before they can get their hands on the trophy.

If England took away the honours, they also – or at least one in their midst – took a record away from a Frenchman. Jason Leonard, who went on the field as a replacement for Vickery, established a new record for International appearances. This was his 112th appearance, thereby overtaking Philippe Sella, the former centre. For his team, as every newspaper headline seemed to declare, 'Destiny beckoned'.

2003 WORLD CUP FINAL

'Hands Up If You Think We're Boring' read the newspaper headline over a photograph of the England team. It was representative of the kind of comment that had followed England around Australia. Another was the picture of Jonny Wilkinson with the catchphrase: 'Is That All You've Got?' Another, the droll comment of the English rugby player on being shown a chalk mark on the ground, and asked what it was. He shrugged. He didn't know.

'The try-line,' came the response.

'Haven't seen one in years,' was the English player's reply.

To the newspaper headlines, Clive Woodward responded by saying, 'I thought Sunday's game [against France] was incredibly exciting. If we want to play boring rugby, we'll really play boring rugby. Australians have seen nothing yet.'

Eddie Jones, Australia's coach, expressed his sense of duty: 'Our part of the responsibility is to play naturally and with freedom. And our natural game is attack. We'll be keeping our part of the bargain, I can assure you.' It was all fun and games.

Two England supporters standing outside a crowded pub, The Fortune Of War, on The Rocks, a small area near Circular Quay at the bottom end of George Street and Pitt Street, and sporting red judicial robes and white wigs, held up a banner which either threatened or promised: 'Judgement Day'. This was 22 November 2003. At 8:00pm, Australia would play England in the Rugby World Cup final at the Telstra Stadium, formerly the Olympic Stadium, in Sydney.

'Judgement Day' or 'Day Of Destiny', the hyperbole summed up the gathering over several years of overwhelming expectation and the sense of the nation's burden that England bore. The judge's regalia leavened the moment, as did the noise and the inevitable rendition of 'Swing Low, Sweet Chariot', which echoed across the harbour and beyond. Not that the team, had they been there to observe it, would have relished the reminder of how much this moment meant to so many people. Not that they, in fact, needed reminding.

It was a long road they had travelled: much time and money had been invested in pursuing a singular but treasured goal.

Clive Woodward's stern face, his demeanour, and his lean and hungry look told of his nervous obsession. He had borne the brunt of many accusations and only four years earlier might well have been banished as the national coach for his failure to deliver the cup in 1999. 'Judge me on the World Cup,' he had said. Hoist by his own petard, he was hounded to leave his post. Between the two tournaments, Woodward won 42 of the 46 games England played.

His colleagues and contemporaries since his playing days rallied around him at Twickenham, came to his defence and like a good pack of forwards shielded the gifted former centre threequarter from the rough trade and the slings and arrows that flew his way. The cry had gone out for Woodward to pass onto the other side and to let another take the reins. He survived as national coach to arrive at this juncture in his career, prepared to fulfil his and his Union's ambition which had been in England's sights since they realised, in 1987, the value of the World Cup as a global enterprise and the pinnacle of rugby ambition.

Woodward became the team coach in 1997 and his first game was against Australia on 15 November. It ended in a 15–15 draw. Lawrence Dallaglio was the captain and André Watson, the referee (who was also to be in charge of the 2003 final). There were no tries for England (five penalties from Catt), but two for Australia (Ben Tune and George Gregan). Even more promising was the game again New Zealand three weeks later, which they drew 26–26, with England outscoring their opponents by three tries to two. The back row was Back, Dallaglio and Hill.

In taking this step forward he and his team reeled backwards at speed in June when, on the 'tour from hell' to the Southern Hemisphere, his team, missing all the senior players, were destroyed 76–0 by Australia. Eleven tries were scored against Woodward's young team, among whom was Jonny Wilkinson and Phil Vickery. The New Zealand part of the disastrous tour was equally embarrassing, losing both tests by 64–22 and 40–10. They lost against South Africa, too, but less traumatically (18–0).

In December, they beat South Africa, who had won 17 successive victories. But by April 1999, a few months before the World Cup hosted by Wales, England, much against the run of play at Wembley, were delivered a devastating blow when they lost in the final minutes by Scott Gibbs' try and Neil Jenkins' conversion. From such hard and mortifying lessons Woodward's resolve must surely have grown. It is with such sticks he must have punished himself.

However, through the bad luck and sad misadventure of another, a new opportunity arose, which, it could be said, was the making of the team. This would prove to be the vital corner stone upon which England's great edifice would be built. Lawrence Dallaglio, the captain hitherto, was involved in an ugly episode of drug allegations. In the back row's moment of misfortune, Martin Johnson was elevated to the captaincy.

Martin Johnson was the rock of the team, so much so there would be continuous speculation in the years that followed as to what might happen were he not at any stage to play. Today, it seems that Johnson has been a permanent presence. In retrospect, however, it is but four short years – the span between two World Cups. Yet, his influence, presence and growing stature made him instantly recognisable. Wearing a perpetual frown, broken only rarely by a cracked smile, his lowering eyebrows made him an intimidating presence for opponents, questioning pundits and, I would guess, referees. Without him there was a sense of loss in the team. Although the question was asked, the chance never arose to find the answer to how England would respond in his absence.

Woodward found in his captain the single-mindedness which he himself possessed and which manifestly absorbed them both, almost to the point of distraction and to the exclusion of all else. The treasure they sought was as valuable and delicate as could be imagined in the realms of myth, as might be the quest for the Holy Grail. Could anyone from Europe ever lay their hands on the Webb Ellis Cup? The journey was long. The journey was tough. Woodward and Johnson set out to accomplish that which had never, in 16 years, been accomplished before.

Indeed, they had already achieved that which had not yet been achieved. In the length of this book, the record has changed. If it is shown at the beginning that no nation had succeeded in beating all the other nations – that is, the eight major nations of rugby – in any one 12-month period and so justify the title of World Champion, England did so in 2002/2003.

In the nine months leading up to the World Cup, England had beaten every team in the Southern and Northern Hemisphere. In autumn 2002, they had dispatched New Zealand, Australia and South Africa at Twickenham, and when the year turned, they went on, uninterruptedly, to win the grand slam in Europe (at Woodward's sixth time of asking), this time allowing neither the Celtic nor the Gallic nations to upset their party. England took it all in their stride. If Australia and New Zealand might protest that they had less than their full-strength teams in the autumn, then that is a problem *they* need to address, not England. But, so as to make certain that there would be no continued whingeing from the Southern Hemisphere, England went around almost all the houses once more. In June, they settled a few more scores by beating Australia and New Zealand in their own back yards. If they did not visit South Africa, then they did play the Springboks in the World Cup and won.

Woodward and Johnson had already accomplished a good deal, but... and there is always a 'but' or an 'if only' or a 'what-might-have-been'. It is the ghostly presence of those demon words that the sportsman and woman fear. All the fine victories achieved in the run-up to the main event in Sydney were worthy of celebration in their fashion, but if the English players could not drink freely, proudly and, perhaps, selfishly from an overflowing World Cup come midnight on 22 November, then all the midnights of the rest of their restless lives would provoke an unsuspecting visit from the shadows of those spectral words: 'but', 'if only', 'what-might-have-been'. The regrets and the recriminations would begin. Johnson was to say afterwards, 'If we had lost that game, I don't know what I would have done.' For sure, he would have had a lifetime contending with his demons.

For England, after all that had gone before, there had to be a crowing glory to vindicate their sustained success. It was no more than they deserved. The cup would lend authenticity to their reputation.

They had to win against their old rivals, Australia. This was a big stimulus for both teams. England knew that they had to overcome a team which belonged to a nation that not only expects success, but consider themselves hungrier and more resolute than any other. Australians, in their chosen sports, are tough of mind as well as body. They like to win, so much so that in saying as much they appear charmless and one-dimensional. It was a bit rich that they repeatedly condemned England for being boring. It had not escaped anyone's notice that if that is what it took to win a match, then Australia would more than happily comply.

It was an extraordinary game. For drama, heroism and knuckle-clinching tension this was the best yet. Once more, as in 1995, the game went into extra time. For such a close finish we should be thankful that the game did not require going into that period when a drop-goal competition between five players from either side would determine the winner. The high drama of the whole game would surely have descended into farce. Attempting a drop goal, however gracefully Wilkinson does so, requires timing and coordination which is beyond the majority of players, even seasoned Internationals. Thankfully, this was not necessary.

'Despite all this talk about England being boring, they are very, very professional,' was George Gregan's conclusion. 'They play to their strengths and that is why they are world champions. Hats off to them.'

'They played those last minutes very well,' remarked Jones. 'Champions' sides win close games and that is what they have done'.

Once more, the rain came for two days before Saturday and was set to continue during the game. If there was regret that these conditions would adversely affect the style of the game, it did not last long. Australia threw down the gauntlet in the seventh minute. A high kick from Larkham found Robinson out of position on the right wing. Too much in-field he had to run back to retrieve his position. Tuqiri, on the other hand, was running on to the accurate kick and could leap into the air. With the advantage of being taller, he got his hands to the ball first and fell over for the try.

If they ever needed it, this was England's wake-up call. Johnson's team seem to revel in the danger zone, when a big response is required of them. It is not something they wish, it is thrust upon them. This call-to-arms came earlier than usual. It galvanised their efforts. Woodman, Thompson and Vickery were immovable at the coal face. Behind them, the threequarters had a potential that was not often enough called upon in a game that only required so much from them. Lewsey was clear-sighted and strong at the back, and Cohen always a threat. Greenwood and Tindall might have done more if asked, but the threads of the game were drawn elsewhere.

Stirling Mortlock found little room in the midfield and was unlikely to find the kind of gifts New Zealand gave to him. Waugh and Smith were nullified by the seasoned Back, Hill and Dallaglio. Gregan at scrum-half, troublesome and sometimes querulous, found that Dawson was more than up to his challenges. The English scrum-half, aware of his own need to exert himself and make his name, was always protective, too, of his fly-half outside him.

Wilkinson was uncertain of himself. His scoring kicks were nigh-on perfect and his temperament to win matches unequalled in his generation, but his command of the game overall is open to question. The inclusion of Catt in the Welsh game (as here, although much later) is an indication that others are asking similar questions. As sacrilegious as it is to raise the point in the euphoria that has followed so successful a performance, Wilkinson needs to address the deficiency.

England grew into their game and commanded the tempo, wide or narrow. In wet conditions they were supremely confident. Wilkinson carried out the business he does so magnificently and kicked three penalty goals. Dawson in tandem with Dallaglio were instrumental in forging the path for Wilkinson to provide the telling pass for Robinson to score a glorious try. They were on song at 14–5. With the line at his mercy, Ben Kay spilt the ball. It might have been all over by half-time, such was England's dominance. Somehow they lost their touch and allowed their opponents back into the match. It made for a greater final, but an unnecessary white-knuckle ride for the white-jerseyed throng. Instead of a comfortable glide to the finish, which it could so easily have been, the England supporters were given instead a frenetic, bone-shaking slalom run to the wire.

Flatley, who had missed two chances in the first half, kicked two penalties to bring Australia three points short of a team which now looked to be surviving. Wilkinson, as part of the legend that will forever bind itself to the match, missed his third attempt at a drop goal. With seconds to go, the referee, André Watson, gave a contentious decision at a scrum against England. Where he himself has admitted in the past that what happens in the scrum is a mystery, as most people would agree, and which only the two props are party to, this was a decisive moment. Flatley, with nerves made of unyielding steel, found his mark to bring the score to 14–14. This brought the first part, excruciatingly so for all of England, to an end.

Within two minutes of extra time, Australia were penalised for an infringement on Johnson at a line-out. From 45 metres Wilkinson kicked a majestic goal. Catt came on to make inroads into Australia's defence, but the English tide was stemmed once more. Dallaglio in his best game of the tournament infringed to test the impassive Flatley once again. And once again he was true.

The player of the tournament, as well as of the season as a whole, was Jonny Wilkinson. In just over a minute's time he was to confirm his status as the figure which represented rugby union in a global context. He is rugby's superstar, taking over from Jonah Lomu as the most prominent and lionised player of rugby union on the world stage. Slim, fresh faced, yet mournful and tense, and broad of shoulder, he is the young man the mother wishes to knock on the door to take her daughter, not to the karaoke, but to share popcorn in the cinema. Professional rugby has been with us for eight years. Wilkinson, of all players, has come to the forefront to epitomise and to embrace the new ethos.

He was winning his 52nd International cap on 22 November, the first being against Ireland when he came on for Catt in April 1998. His first start was in the 76–0 humiliation in Brisbane. He had already made amends several times over for that defeat. It was time not to avenge anything, but simply to soar higher and to win the laurel wreath.

He had already scored 814 points, but the most momentous and the one destined to become the most celebrated was about to be struck. With the seconds ticking away, the sovereign moment awaited him.

The countdown began.

65 seconds to go

Thompson at the line-out to Moody at the back. To Dawson, to Wilkinson. Catt on the run, tackled by Flatley. Ball back to Dawson. Dawson snipes for 15 metres close to the forwards. Down again. Neil Back to Johnson. Johnson drives. Another tackle. Dawson now in position. So, behind him, was Wilkinson.

27 seconds to go.

All Australia knew was what was coming next. So did the whole world. Australia saw it coming but were useless to do anything about it, except to feel the fear of impending loss. And the hollow in the heart.

Wilkinson had been here so many times before. With his right foot he struck for home. Figures in the landscape stood still as so many years before in Cape Town, South Africa, they had done when Rob Andrew, his guardian at Newcastle, put Australia out of the competition. That was the 1995 quarter-final, with more heartache and soul-searching to come.

In slow motion, the ball glided through the posts and on to triumph, to fresh woods and pastures new.

This was the end. Wilkinson, with the rose of youth upon him, smiled the happy smile of the victor. The mournful face vanished. The World Cup belonged to England. They had accomplished the dream. Glory was theirs and immortality beckoned.

While all this was going on, 15 million viewers watched the match on television in the UK, the biggest ever audience for a rugby game. The RAC noted that 10 million cars were absent on the roads in the UK. The Australian Rugby Union were expected to net $45 million and the IRB £150 million.

'Jonny Gets His Kicks On Route 66'; 'Day Of Our Lives'; 'This Cup Was Touched By Magic'; 'Give 'Em A Gong'; 'Odds On, Sir Jonny'. These were a few of the headlines. 'I feel ecstatic', said Woodward, 'for every single person with a white shirt. It makes you feel proud to be English. We made many errors, but we won. We won the cup, that's it. It was massive. I am absolutely speechless. It was just fantastic, unbelievable. The whole team was brilliant. It was an awesome night.'

For the captain, he felt 'just happy for the players because they put so much into it. They put their hearts and soul into this campaign. We were frustrated in the second half, but we have got to give credit. They [Australia] are a very good team – with 20 minutes of extra time it could have gone any way. It couldn't have been closer and I'm just happy to be on the right side.'

And for the man who was to become the nation's sporting obsession, Jonny Wilkinson? 'I didn't want the game to go to a drop-goal competition. I just wanted to win so much for the other guys.' One for all and all – as they scrambled forward in the dying seconds, led by Johnson, to get to the right position – all for one. One man, one final sight of the posts, one deadly, accurate kick

And so the World Cup carnival passed on, the last cheer died away, the spare programme shifted in the breeze, the doors closed, the gates clanged to their rest and the great stadium assumed once more its silences and its echoes. The whispers will soon resume their discussion of the long road that needs to be travelled for the next tournament in France. In the quiet air of Sydney, where the ghosts of great players of the past hovered all day long, we can safely say, as we have been so lucky to say so many times before, that we were there again when, on the fields of praise, we saw the great game played and the making of new heroes. Our rich recollections will refresh our longing that rugby union will never lose its gifts for drama, for talent displayed, for friendships forged – yes, the camaraderie, for there is no better word – and for the laurel to go to the swift, the mighty and, we trust, to the honest. This tale has no end.

1987

Pool 1, First Match
Australia v England: 19-6
23 May 1987
Concord Oval, Sydney

Players

Australia

Prop	Andy McIntyre
Hooker	Tom Lawton
Prop	Topo Rodriguez
Lock	Bill Campbell
Lock	Steve Cutler
Flanker	Troy Coker
Flanker	Simon Poidevin
Number 8	Steve Tuynman
Scrum-half	Nick Farr-Jones
Fly-half	Michael Lynagh
Right Wing	David Campese
Centre	Brett Papworth
Centre	Andrew Slack (c)
Left Wing	Peter Grigg
Full-back	Roger Gould
Reserve	Steve James

England

Prop	Gary Pearce
Hooker	Brian Moore
Prop	Paul Rendall
Lock	Wade Dooley
Lock	Nigel Redman
Flanker	Gary Rees
Flanker	Peter Winterbottom
Number 8	Dean Richards
Scrum-half	Richard Harding
Fly-half	Peter Williams
Right Wing	Mike Harrison (c)
Centre	Jamie Salmon
Centre	Kevin Simms
Left Wing	Rory Underwood
Full-back	Marcus Rose
Reserve	Jon Webb
Referee	Lawrence KH

Points Scorers

Australia

	Tries	Conv	Pen K	Drop G	Points
Campese DI	1	0	0	0	4
Lynagh MP	0	1	3	0	11
Poidevin SP	1	0	0	0	4

England

	Tries	Conv	Pen K	Drop G	Points
Harrison ME	1	0	0	0	4
Webb JM	0	1	0	0	2

**Pool 1, Second Match
USA v Japan: 21–18
24 May 1987
Ballymore Stadium, Brisbane**

Players

USA

Prop	Rick Bailey
Hooker	John Everett
Prop	Fred Paoli
Lock	Ed Burlingham (c)
Lock	Kevin Swords
Flanker	Gary Lambert
Flanker	Blane Warhurst
Number 8	Brian Vizard
Scrum-half	Mike Saunders
Fly-half	Joe Clarkson
Right Wing	Gary Hein
Centre	Roy Helu
Centre	Kevin Higgins
Left Wing	Mike Purcell
Full-back	Ray Nelson

Japan

Prop	K Horaguchi
Hooker	Tsuyoshi Fujita
Prop	H Yasumi
Lock	Toshiyuki Hayashi (c)
Lock	Atsushi Oyagi
Flanker	Sinali-Tui Latu
Flanker	Katsufumi Miyamoto
Number 8	Michihito Chida
Scrum-half	H Ikuta
Fly-half	Seiji Hirao
Right Wing	S Onuki
Centre	Eiji Kutsuki
Centre	K Yoshinaga
Left Wing	Nofomuli Taumoefolau
Full-back	S Mukai
Referee	Maurette G

Points Scorers

USA

Name	Tries	Conv	Pen K	Drop G	Points
Lambert G	1	0	0	0	4
Nelson RB	1	3	1	0	13
Purcell M	1	0	0	0	4

Japan

Name	Tries	Conv	Pen K	Drop G	Points
Kutsuki E	0	0	1	0	3
Taumoefolau N	2	0	0	0	8
Yoshinaga K	1	0	1	0	7

Pool 1, Third Match
England v Japan: 60-7
30 May 1987
Concord Oval, Sydney

Players

England

Prop	Gareth Chilcott
Hooker	Brian Moore
Prop	Paul Rendall
Lock	Steve Bainbridge
Lock	Nigel Redman
Flanker	Gary Rees
Flanker	Peter Winterbottom
Number 8	Dean Richards
Scrum-half	Richard Harding
Fly-half	Peter Williams
Right Wing	Mike Harrison (c)
Centre	Jamie Salmon
Centre	Kevin Simms
Left Wing	Rory Underwood
Full-back	Jon Webb
Reserves	Rob Andrew, Fran Clough

Prop	K Horaguchi
Hooker	Tsuyoshi Fujita
Prop	T Kimura
Lock	S Kurihara
Lock	Atsushi Oyagi
Flanker	Toshiyuki Hayashi (c)
Flanker	Katsufumi Miyamoto
Number 8	Michihito Chida
Scrum-half	M Hagimoto
Fly-half	Seiji Hirao
Right Wing	S Onuki
Centre	Eiji Kutsuki
Centre	Katsuhiro Matsuo
Left Wing	Nofomuli Taumoefolau
Full-back	D Murai

Referee	Hourquet R

Points Scorers

England

Name	Tries	Conv	Pen K	Drop G	Points
Harrison ME	3	0	0	0	12
Redman NC	1	0	0	0	4
Rees GW	1	0	0	0	4
Richards D	1	0	0	0	4
Salmon JLB	1	0	0	0	4
Simms KG	1	0	0	0	4
Underwood R	2	0	0	0	8
Webb JM	0	7	2	0	20

Japan

Name	Tries	Conv	Pen K	Drop G	Points
Matsuo K	0	0	1	0	3
Miyamoto K	1	0	0	0	4

Pool 1, Fourth Match
Australia v USA: 47-12
31 May 1987
Ballymore Stadium, Brisbane

Players

Australia

Prop	Cameron Lillicrap
Hooker	Tom Lawton
Prop	Andy McIntyre
Lock	Bill Campbell
Lock	Troy Coker
Flanker	Jeff Miller
Flanker	Steve Tuynman
Number 8	David Codey
Scrum-half	Brian Smith
Fly-half	Michael Lynagh
Right Wing	Matthew Burke
Centre	Brett Papworth
Centre	Andrew Slack (c)
Left Wing	David Campese
Full-back	Andrew Leeds

USA

Prop	Butch Horwath
Hooker	Pat Johnson
Prop	Fred Paoli (c)
Lock	Bill Shiflet
Lock	Kevin Swords
Flanker	Stephen Finkel
Flanker	Tony Ridnell
Number 8	Brian Vizard
Scrum-half	Dave Dickson
Fly-half	Dave Horton
Right Wing	Gary Hein
Centre	Roy Helu
Centre	Tom Vinick
Left Wing	Kevin Higgins
Full-back	Ray Nelson
Reserves	Gary Lambert, Mike Saunders
Referee	Anderson JB

Points Scorers

Australia

Name	Tries	Conv	Pen K	Drop G	Points
Campese DI	1	0	0	0	4
Codey D	1	0	0	0	4
Leeds AJS	2	0	0	0	8
Lynagh MP	0	6	1	0	15
Papworth BW	1	0	0	0	4
Slack AG	1	0	0	0	4
Smith BA	1	0	0	0	4
Penalty Try	1	0	0	0	4

USA

Name	Tries	Conv	Pen K	Drop G	Points
Horton D	0	0	0	1	3
Nelson RB	1	1	1	0	9

Pool 1, Fifth Match
Australia v Japan: 42-23
3 June 1987
Concord Oval, Sydney

Players
Australia

Prop	Mark Hartill
Hooker	Mark McBain
Prop	Topo Rodriguez
Lock	Steve Cutler
Lock	Ross Reynolds
Flanker	Simon Poidevin (c)
Flanker	Steve Tuynman
Number 8	David Codey
Scrum-half	Brian Smith
Fly-half	Michael Lynagh
Right Wing	Matthew Burke
Centre	Michael Cook
Centre	Andrew Slack
Left Wing	Peter Grigg
Full-back	David Campese
Reserves	Bill Campbell, Brett Papworth

Japan

Prop	Magaharu Aizawa
Hooker	Tsuyoshi Fujita
Prop	T Kimura
Lock	Toshiyuki Hayashi (c)
Lock	Yoshihiko Sakuraba
Flanker	Y Kawasi
Flanker	Katsufumi Miyamoto
Number 8	Sinali-Tui Latu
Scrum-half	H Ikuta
Fly-half	Seiji Hirao
Right Wing	M Okidoi
Centre	Eiji Kutsuki
Centre	K Yoshinaga
Left Wing	Nofomuli Taumoefolau
Full-back	S Mukai
Referee	Fleming JM

Points Scorers
Australia

Name	Tries	Conv	Pen K	Drop G	Points
Burke MP	2	0	0	0	8
Campese DI	1	0	0	0	4
Grigg PC	1	0	0	0	4
Hartill MN	1	0	0	0	4
Lynagh MP	0	5	0	0	10
Slack AG	2	0	0	0	8
Tuynman SN	1	0	0	0	4

Japan

Name	Tries	Conv	Pen K	Drop G	Points
Fujita T	1	0	0	0	4
Kutsuki E	2	0	0	0	8
Okidoi M	0	1	2	1	11

Pool 1, Sixth Match
England v USA: 34-6
3 June 1987
Concord Oval, Sydney

Players

England

Prop	Gareth Chilcott
Hooker	Graham Dawe
Prop	Gary Pearce
Lock	Steve Bainbridge
Lock	Wade Dooley
Flanker	Gary Rees
Flanker	Peter Winterbottom
Number 8	Dean Richards
Scrum-half	Richard Hill
Fly-half	Rob Andrew
Right Wing	Mark Bailey
Centre	Fran Clough
Centre	Jamie Salmon
Left Wing	Mike Harrison (c)
Full-back	Jon Webb

USA

Prop	Rick Bailey
Hooker	John Everett
Prop	Neal Brendel
Lock	Ed Burlingham (c)
Lock	Bob Causey
Flanker	Stephen Finkel
Flanker	Gary Lambert
Number 8	Brian Vizard
Scrum-half	Mike Saunders
Fly-half	Joe Clarkson
Right Wing	Gary Hein
Centre	Kevin Higgins
Centre	Tom Vinick
Left Wing	Mike Purcell
Full-back	Ray Nelson
Referee	Fitzgerald KVJ

Points Scorers

England

Name	Tries	Conv	Pen K	Drop G	Points
Dooley WA	1	0	0	0	4
Harrison ME	1	0	0	0	4
Webb JM	0	3	4	0	18
Winterbottom PJ	2	0	0	0	8

USA

Name	Tries	Conv	Pen K	Drop G	Points
Nelson RB	0	1	0	0	2
Purcell M	1	0	0	0	4

Pool 2, First Match
Canada v Tonga: 37–4
24 May 1987
McLean Park, Napier

Players

Canada

Prop	Eddie Evans
Hooker	Mark Cardinal
Prop	Bill Handson
Lock	Hans de Goede (c)
Lock	Ron Vanden Brink
Flanker	RP Frame
Flanker	Roy Radu
Number 8	John Robertsen
Scrum-half	Ian Stuart
Fly-half	Gareth Rees
Right Wing	Pat Palmer
Centre	Spence McTavish
Centre	PC Vaesen
Left Wing	Tom Woods
Full-back	Mark Wyatt
Reserve	Glen Ennis

Tonga

Prop	Soakai Motu'apuaka
Hooker	'Amone Fungavaka
Prop	Hakatoa Tupou
Lock	Kasi Fine
Lock	Poluaiele Tuihalamaka
Flanker	Taipaleti Tu'uta Kakato
Flanker	Fakahau Valu (c)
Number 8	Kinisiliti Fotu
Scrum-half	Talai Fifita
Fly-half	'Alamoni Liava'a
Right Wing	Soane 'Asi
Centre	T Fukakitekei'aho
Centre	Samiu Mohi
Left Wing	Kutusi Fielea
Full-back	Tali Ete'aki
Reserves	Sione Tahaafe, Leaeki Vaipulu
Referee	Norling C

Points Scorers

Canada

Name	Tries	Conv	Pen K	Drop G	Points
Frame RP	1	0	0	0	4
Palmer P	2	0	0	0	8
Rees GL	0	1	1	0	5
Stuart IC	1	0	0	0	4
Vaesen PC	2	0	0	0	8
Wyatt MA	0	2	0	0	4
Penalty Try	1	0	0	0	4

Tonga

Name	Tries	Conv	Pen K	Drop G	Points
Valu F	1	0	0	0	4

Pool 2, Second Match
Ireland v Wales: 6-13
25 May 1987
Athletic Park, Wellington

Players

Ireland

Prop	Des Fitzgerald
Hooker	Terry Kingston
Prop	Phil Orr
Lock	Willie Anderson
Lock	Donal Lenihan (c)
Flanker	Philip Matthews
Flanker	Derek McGrath
Number 8	Brian Spillane
Scrum-half	Michael Bradley
Fly-half	Paul Dean
Right Wing	Keith Crossan
Centre	Michael Kiernan
Centre	Brendan Mullin
Left Wing	Trevor Ringland
Full-back	Hugo MacNeill

Wales

Prop	Stuart Evans
Hooker	Kevin Phillips
Prop	Jeff Whitefoot
Lock	Dick Moriarty (c)
Lock	Bob Norster
Flanker	Richie Collins
Flanker	Paul Moriarty
Number 8	Gareth Roberts
Scrum-half	Robert Jones
Fly-half	Jonathan Davies
Right Wing	Ieuan Evans
Centre	John Devereux
Centre	Mark Ring
Left Wing	Adrian Hadley
Full-back	Paul Thorburn
Referee	Fitzgerald KVJ

Points Scorers

Ireland

Name	Tries	Conv	Pen K	Drop G	Points
Kiernan MJ	0	0	2	0	6

Wales

Name	Tries	Conv	Pen K	Drop G	Points
Davies J	0	0	0	2	6
Ring MG	1	0	0	0	4
Thorburn PH	0	0	1	0	3

Pool 2, Third Match
Tonga v Wales: 16–29
29 May 1987
Showgrounds Oval, Palmerston North

Players

Tonga

Prop	Viliami Lutua
Hooker	'Amone Fungavaka
Prop	Hakatoa Tupou
Lock	Kasi Fine
Lock	Mofuike Tu'ungafasi
Flanker	Taipaleti Tu'uta Kakato
Flanker	Fakahau Valu (c)
Number 8	Maliu Filise
Scrum-half	Talai Fifita
Fly-half	'Aasaeli Amone
Right Wing	Kutusi Fielea
Centre	T Fukakitekei'aho
Centre	Samiu Mohi
Left Wing	Manu Vunipola
Full-back	Tali Ete'aki
Reserves	'Alamoni Liava'a, Latu Va'ene

Wales

Prop	Anthony Buchanan
Hooker	Kevin Phillips
Prop	Stuart Evans
Lock	Dick Moriarty (c)
Lock	Huw Richards
Flanker	Phil Davies
Flanker	Paul Moriarty
Number 8	Gareth Roberts
Scrum-half	Robert Jones
Fly-half	Malcolm Dacey
Right Wing	Adrian Hadley
Centre	Kevin Hopkins
Centre	Mark Ring
Left Wing	Glen Webbe
Full-back	Paul Thorburn
Reserves	Steven Blackmore, Jonathan Davies
Referee	Bishop DJ

Points Scorers

Tonga

Name	Tries	Conv	Pen K	Drop G	Points
Amone A	0	0	1	0	3
Fielea K	1	0	0	0	4
Fifita T	1	0	0	0	4
Liava'a A	0	1	1	0	5

Wales

Name	Tries	Conv	Pen K	Drop G	Points
Davies J	0	0	0	1	3
Hadley AM	1	0	0	0	4
Thorburn PH	0	2	2	0	10
Webbe GMC	3	0	0	0	12

Pool 2, Fourth Match
Canada v Ireland: 19-46
30 May 1987
Carisbrook Stadium, Dunedin

Players
Canada

Prop	Eddie Evans
Hooker	Mark Cardinal
Prop	Bill Handson
Lock	Hans de Goede (c)
Lock	Ro Hindson
Flanker	RP Frame
Flanker	Roy Radu
Number 8	Glen Ennis
Scrum-half	Ian Stuart
Fly-half	Gareth Rees
Right Wing	Pat Palmer
Centre	John Lecky
Centre	Spence McTavish
Left Wing	Tom Woods
Full-back	Mark Wyatt

Ireland

Prop	Des Fitzgerald
Hooker	John McDonald
Prop	Phil Orr
Lock	Willie Anderson
Lock	Donal Lenihan (c)
Flanker	Paul Collins
Flanker	Derek McGrath
Number 8	Brian Spillane
Scrum-half	Michael Bradley
Fly-half	Tony Ward
Right Wing	Keith Crossan
Centre	Michael Kiernan
Centre	Brendan Mullin
Left Wing	Trevor Ringland
Full-back	Hugo MacNeill
Reserve	Terry Kingston
Referee	Howard FA

Points Scorers
Canada

Name	Tries	Conv	Pen K	Drop G	Points
Cardinal ME	1	0	0	0	4
Rees GL	0	0	3	1	12
Wyatt MA	0	0	1	0	3

Ireland

Name	Tries	Conv	Pen K	Drop G	Points
Bradley MT	1	0	0	0	4
Crossan KD	2	0	0	0	8
Kiernan MJ	0	5	2	1	19
MacNeill HP	1	0	0	0	4
Ringland TM	1	0	0	0	4
Spillane BJ	1	0	0	0	4
Ward AJP	0	0	0	1	3

Pool 2, Fifth Match
Ireland v Tonga: 32–9
3 June 1987
Ballymore Stadium, Brisbane

Players

Ireland

Prop	JA Langbroek
Hooker	Terry Kingston
Prop	JJ McCoy
Lock	Willie Anderson
Lock	Donal Lenihan (c)
Flanker	Neil Francis
Flanker	Philip Matthews
Number 8	Derek McGrath
Scrum-half	Michael Bradley
Fly-half	Tony Ward
Right Wing	Keith Crossan
Centre	David Irwin
Centre	Brendan Mullin
Left Wing	Trevor Ringland
Full-back	Hugo MacNeill

Tonga

Prop	Viliami Lutua
Hooker	'Amone Fungavaka
Prop	Hakatoa Tupou
Lock	Kasi Fine
Lock	Mofuike Tu'ungafasi
Flanker	Taipaleti Tu'uta Kakato
Flanker	Fakahau Valu (c)
Number 8	Maliu Filise
Scrum-half	Talai Fifita
Fly-half	'Aasaeli Amone
Right Wing	Kutusi Fielea
Centre	'Alamoni Liava'a
Centre	Samiu Mohi
Left Wing	T Fukakitekei'aho
Full-back	Tali Ete'aki
Referee	Maurette G

Points Scorers

Ireland

Name	Tries	Conv	Pen K	Drop G	Points
MacNeill HP	2	0	0	0	8
Mullin BJ	3	0	0	0	12
Ward AJP	0	3	2	0	12

Tonga

Name	Tries	Conv	Pen K	Drop G	Points
Amone A	0	0	3	0	9

Pool 2, Sixth Match
Canada v Wales: 9-40
3 June 1987
Homestead Stadium, Invercargill

Players
Canada

Prop	Bill Handson
Hooker	Karl Svoboda
Prop	Randy McKellar
Lock	Hans de Goede (c)
Lock	Ro Hindson
Flanker	Bruce Breen
Flanker	RP Frame
Number 8	Glen Ennis
Scrum-half	Ian Stuart
Fly-half	Gareth Rees
Right Wing	Steve Gray
Centre	John Lecky
Centre	Tom Woods
Left Wing	Pat Palmer
Full-back	Mark Wyatt
Reserve	Dave Tucker

Wales

Prop	Steven Blackmore
Hooker	Allan Phillips
Prop	Jeff Whitefoot
Lock	Bob Norster
Lock	Steve Sutton
Flanker	Phil Davies
Flanker	Paul Moriarty
Number 8	Gareth Roberts
Scrum-half	Ray Giles
Fly-half	Jonathan Davies (c)
Right Wing	Ieuan Evans
Centre	Bleddyn Bowen
Centre	John Devereux
Left Wing	Adrian Hadley
Full-back	Paul Thorburn
Reserves	Kevin Hopkins, Dick Moriarty
Referee	Bishop DJ

Points Scorers
Canada

Name	Tries	Conv	Pen K	Drop G	Points
Rees GL	0	0	3	0	9

Wales

Name	Tries	Conv	Pen K	Drop G	Points
Bowen B	1	0	0	0	4
Devereux JA	1	0	0	0	4
Evans IC	4	0	0	0	16
Hadley AM	1	0	0	0	4
Phillips AJ	1	0	0	0	4
Thorburn PH	0	4	0	0	8

Pool 3, First Match
New Zealand v Italy: 70-6
22 May 1987
Eden Park, Auckland

Players
New Zealand

Prop	Richard Loe
Hooker	Sean Fitzpatrick
Prop	Steven McDowell
Lock	Murray Pierce
Lock	Gary Whetton
Flanker	Michael Jones
Flanker	Alan Whetton
Number 8	Buck Shelford
Scrum-half	David Kirk (c)
Fly-half	Grant Fox
Right Wing	Craig Green
Centre	Joe Stanley
Centre	Warwick Taylor
Left Wing	John Kirwan
Full-back	John Gallagher

Italy

Prop	Tito Lupini
Hooker	Giorgio Morelli
Prop	Guido Rossi
Lock	Franco Berni
Lock	Mauro Gardin
Flanker	Piergianni Farina
Flanker	Marzio Innocenti (c)
Number 8	Giuseppe Artuso
Scrum-half	Fulvio Lorigiola
Fly-half	Rodolfo Ambrosio
Right Wing	Marcello Cuttitta
Centre	Oscar Collodo
Centre	Fabio Gaetaniello
Left Wing	Massimo Mascioletti
Full-back	Serafino Ghizzoni
Referee	Fordham RJ

Points Scorers
New Zealand

Name	Tries	Conv	Pen K	Drop G	Points
Fox GJ	0	8	2	0	22
Green CI	2	0	0	0	8
Jones MN	1	0	0	0	4
Kirk DE	2	0	0	0	8
Kirwan JJ	2	0	0	0	8
McDowell SC	1	0	0	0	4
Stanley JT	1	0	0	0	4
Taylor WT	1	0	0	0	4
Whetton AJ	1	0	0	0	4
Penalty Try	1	0	0	0	4

Italy

Name	Tries	Conv	Pen K	Drop G	Points
Collodo O	0	0	1	1	6

Pool 3, Second Match
Fiji v Argentina: 28-9
24 May 1987
Rugby Park, Hamilton

Players
Fiji

Prop	Sairusi Naituku
Hooker	Salacieli Naivilawasa
Prop	Rusiate Namoro
Lock	Koli Rakoroi (c)
Lock	Laitia Savai
Flanker	Tekeli Gale
Flanker	Manasa Qoro
Number 8	John Sanday
Scrum-half	Pauliasi Tabulutu
Fly-half	E Rokowailoa
Right Wing	Kaveniki Nalaga
Centre	Tomasi Cama
Centre	E Naituku
Left Wing	Serupepeli Tuvula
Full-back	Severo Koroduadua
Reserves	Paolo Nawalu, Samu Vunivalu

Argentina

Prop	Luis Molina
Hooker	Diego Cash
Prop	Fernando Morel
Lock	Eliseo Branca
Lock	Gustavo Milano
Flanker	Jose Mostany
Flanker	Gabriel Travaglini
Number 8	Jorge Allen
Scrum-half	Fabio Gomez
Fly-half	Hugo Porta (c)
Right Wing	Marcelo Campo
Centre	Diego Cuesta Silva
Centre	Fabian Turnes
Left Wing	Juan Lanza
Full-back	Sebastian Salvat
Reserve	Alejandro Schiavio
Referee	Fleming JM

Points Scorers
Fiji

Name	Tries	Conv	Pen K	Drop G	Points
Gale T	1	0	0	0	4
Koroduadua S	0	2	2	0	10
Nalaga K	1	0	0	0	4
Rakoroi K	1	0	0	0	4
Rokowailoa E	0	1	0	0	2
Savai I	1	0	0	0	4

Argentina

Name	Tries	Conv	Pen K	Drop G	Points
Porta H	0	1	1	0	5
Travaglini G	1	0	0	0	4

Pool 3, Third Match
New Zealand v Fiji: 74-13
27 May 1987
Lancaster Park, Christchurch

Players

New Zealand

Prop	John Drake
Hooker	Sean Fitzpatrick
Prop	Steven McDowell
Lock	Albert Anderson
Lock	Gary Whetton
Flanker	Michael Jones
Flanker	Alan Whetton
Number 8	Buck Shelford
Scrum-half	David Kirk (c)
Fly-half	Grant Fox
Right Wing	Craig Green
Centre	Joe Stanley
Centre	Warwick Taylor
Left Wing	John Kirwan
Full-back	John Gallagher

Fiji

Prop	Mosese Taga
Hooker	Epeli Rakai
Prop	Peni Volavola
Lock	J Cama
Lock	Laitia Savai
Flanker	Lilvai Kididromo
Flanker	Samu Vunivalu
Number 8	Koli Rakoroi (c)
Scrum-half	Paolo Nawalu
Fly-half	E Rokowailoa
Right Wing	Tomasi Cama
Centre	Jone Kubu
Centre	Sirilo Lovokure
Left Wing	Serupepeli Tuvula
Full-back	Severo Koroduadua
Referee	Bevan WD

Points Scorers

New Zealand

Name	Tries	Conv	Pen K	Drop G	Points
Fox GJ	0	10	2	0	26
Gallagher JA	4	0	0	0	16
Green CI	4	0	0	0	16
Kirk DE	1	0	0	0	4
Kirwan JJ	1	0	0	0	4
Whetton AJ	1	0	0	0	4
Penalty Try	1	0	0	0	4

Fiji

Name	Tries	Conv	Pen K	Drop G	Points
Cama J	1	0	0	0	4
Koroduadua S	0	0	3	0	9

Pool 3, Fourth Match
Argentina v Italy: 25-16
28 May 1987
Lancaster Park, Christchurch

Players

Argentina

Prop	Serafin Denigra
Hooker	Diego Cash
Prop	Luis Molina
Lock	Eliseo Branca
Lock	Sergio Carrosio
Flanker	Alejandro Schiavio
Flanker	Gabriel Travaglini
Number 8	Jorge Allen
Scrum-half	Martin Yanguela
Fly-half	Hugo Porta (c)
Right Wing	Juan Lanza
Centre	Diego Cuesta Silva
Centre	Rafael Madero
Left Wing	Pedro Lanza
Full-back	Sebastian Salvat
Reserve	Fabio Gomez

Italy

Prop	Tito Lupini
Hooker	Antonio Galeazzo
Prop	Guido Rossi
Lock	Antonio Colella
Lock	Mauro Gardin
Flanker	Marzio Innocenti (c)
Flanker	Mario Pavin
Number 8	Gianni Zanon
Scrum-half	Fulvio Lorigiola
Fly-half	Oscar Collodo
Right Wing	Marcello Cuttitta
Centre	Stefano Barba
Centre	Fabio Gaetaniello
Left Wing	Massimo Mascioletti
Full-back	Daniele Tebaldi
Referee	Quittenton RC

Points Scorers

Argentina

Name	Tries	Conv	Pen K	Drop G	Points
Gomez EF	1	0	0	0	4
Lanza J	1	0	0	0	4
Porta H	0	1	5	0	17

Italy

Name	Tries	Conv	Pen K	Drop G	Points
Collodo O	0	1	2	0	8
Cuttitta M	1	0	0	0	4
Innocenti M	1	0	0	0	4

Pool 3, Fifth Match
Fiji v Italy: 15-18
31 May 1987
Carisbrook Stadium, Dunedin

Players
Fiji

Prop	Sairusi Naituku
Hooker	Salacieli Naivilawasa
Prop	Peni Volavola
Lock	W Nadolo
Lock	Laitia Savai
Flanker	Manasa Qoro
Flanker	John Sanday
Number 8	Koli Rakoroi (c)
Scrum-half	Paolo Nawalu
Fly-half	E Rokowailoa
Right Wing	Tomasi Cama
Centre	T Mitchell
Centre	Kaiava Salusalu
Left Wing	Serupepeli Tuvula
Full-back	Severo Koroduadua
Reserves	Jone Kubu, E Naituku

Italy

Prop	Giancarlo Cucchiella
Hooker	Stefano Romagnoli
Prop	Tito Lupini
Lock	Antonio Colella
Lock	Mauro Gardin
Flanker	Raffaele Dolfato
Flanker	Marzio Innocenti (c)
Number 8	Piergianni Farina
Scrum-half	Alessandro Ghini
Fly-half	Oscar Collodo
Right Wing	Marcello Cuttitta
Centre	Stefano Barba
Centre	Fabio Gaetaniello
Left Wing	Massimo Mascioletti
Full-back	Daniele Tebaldi
Referee	Lawrence KH

Points Scorers
Fiji

Name	Tries	Conv	Pen K	Drop G	Points
Koroduadua S	0	1	2	0	8
Naivilawasa S	1	0	0	0	4
Qoro M	0	0	0	1	3

Italy

Name	Tries	Conv	Pen K	Drop G	Points
Collodo O	0	0	1	1	6
Cuttitta M	1	0	0	0	4
Cucchiella G	1	0	0	0	4
Mascioletti M	1	0	0	0	4

Pool 3, Sixth Match
New Zealand v Argentina: 46-15
1 June 1987
Athletic Park, Wellington

Players

New Zealand

Prop	John Drake
Hooker	Sean Fitzpatrick
Prop	Richard Loe
Lock	Murray Pierce
Lock	Gary Whetton
Flanker	Zinzan Brooke
Flanker	Alan Whetton
Number 8	Andy Earl
Scrum-half	David Kirk (c)
Fly-half	Grant Fox
Right Wing	John Kirwan
Centre	Bernie McCahill
Centre	Joe Stanley
Left Wing	Terry Wright
Full-back	Kieran Crowley

Argentina

Prop	Serafin Denigra
Hooker	Diego Cash
Prop	Luis Molina
Lock	Eliseo Branca
Lock	Sergio Carrosio
Flanker	Jorge Allen
Flanker	Gabriel Travaglini
Number 8	Alejandro Schiavio
Scrum-half	Fabio Gomez
Fly-half	Hugo Porta (c)
Right Wing	Marcelo Campo
Centre	Rafael Madero
Centre	Fabian Turnes
Left Wing	Juan Lanza
Full-back	Guillermo Angaut
Reserves	Pedro Lanza, Jose Mostany
Referee	Quittenton RC

Points Scorers

New Zealand

Name	Tries	Conv	Pen K	Drop G	Points
Brooke ZV	1	0	0	0	4
Crowley KJ	1	0	0	0	4
Earl AT	1	0	0	0	4
Fox GJ	0	2	6	0	22
Kirk DE	1	0	0	0	4
Stanley JT	1	0	0	0	4
Whetton AJ	1	0	0	0	4

Argentina

Name	Tries	Conv	Pen K	Drop G	Points
Lanza J	1	0	0	0	4
Porta H	0	1	3	0	11

Pool 4, First Match
Romania v Zimbabwe: 21-20
23 May 1987
Eden Park, Auckland

Players

Romania

Prop	Ion Bucan
Hooker	E Grigore
Prop	Gheorghe Leonte
Lock	Stefan Constantin
Lock	Laurentiu Constantin
Flanker	Haralambie Dumitras
Flanker	Florica Murariu
Number 8	Christian Raducanu
Scrum-half	Mircea Paraschiv (c)
Fly-half	Dumitru Alexandru
Right Wing	V David
Centre	Adrian Lungu
Centre	Stefan Tofan
Left Wing	Alexandru Marin
Full-back	M Toader
Reserves	L Hodorca, Vasile Ion

Zimbabwe

Prop	George Elcome
Hooker	Lance Bray
Prop	Andy Tucker
Lock	Michael Martin
Lock	Tom Sawyer
Flanker	Dirk Buitendag
Flanker	Rod Gray
Number 8	Mark Neill
Scrum-half	Malcolm Jellicoe (c)
Fly-half	Craig Brown
Right Wing	Eric Barrett
Centre	Campbell Graham
Centre	Richard Tsimba
Left Wing	Peter Kaulback
Full-back	Andy Ferreira
Reserves	Errol Bredenkamp, Andre Buitendag
Referee	Hilditch SR

Points Scorers

Romania

Name	Tries	Conv	Pen K	Drop G	Points
Alexandru D	0	0	3	0	9
Hodorca L	1	0	0	0	4
Paraschiv M	1	0	0	0	4
Toader M	1	0	0	0	4

Zimbabwe

Name	Tries	Conv	Pen K	Drop G	Points
Ferreira AM	0	1	2	0	8
Neill M	1	0	0	0	4
Tsimba RU	2	0	0	0	8

Pool 4, Second Match
France v Scotland: 20-20
23 May 1987
Lancaster Park, Christchurch

Players
France

Prop	Jean-Pierre Garuet-Lempirou
Hooker	Daniel Dubroca (c)
Prop	Pascal Ondarts
Lock	Jean Condom
Lock	Alain Lorieux
Flanker	Eric Champ
Flanker	Dominique Erbani
Number 8	Laurent Rodriguez
Scrum-half	Pierre Berbizier
Fly-half	Franck Mesnel
Right Wing	Patrick Esteve
Centre	Denis Charvet
Centre	Philippe Sella
Left Wing	Patrice Lagisquet
Full-back	Serge Blanco

Scotland

Prop	Iain Milne
Hooker	Colin Deans (c)
Prop	David Sole
Lock	Alan Tomes
Lock	Derek White
Flanker	Finlay Calder
Flanker	John Jeffrey
Number 8	Iain Paxton
Scrum-half	Roy Laidlaw
Fly-half	John Rutherford
Right Wing	Matthew Duncan
Centre	Keith Robertson
Centre	Douglas Wyllie
Left Wing	Iwan Tukalo
Full-back	Gavin Hastings
Reserve	Alan Tait
Referee	Howard FA

Points Scorers
France

Name	Tries	Conv	Pen K	Drop G	Points
Berbizier P	1	0	0	0	4
Blanco S	1	1	2	0	12
Sella P	1	0	0	0	4

Scotland

Name	Tries	Conv	Pen K	Drop G	Points
Duncan MDF	1	0	0	0	4
Hastings AG	0	0	4	0	12
White DB	1	0	0	0	4

Pool 4, Third Match
France v Romania: 55-12
28 May 1987
Athletic Park, Wellington

Players

France

Prop	Louis Armary
Hooker	Philippe Dintrans (c)
Prop	Jean-Pierre Garuet-Lempirou
Lock	Jean Condom
Lock	Francis Haget
Flanker	Alain Carminati
Flanker	Eric Champ
Number 8	Dominique Erbani
Scrum-half	Pierre Berbizier
Fly-half	Guy Laporte
Right Wing	Marc Andrieu
Centre	Denis Charvet
Centre	Philippe Sella
Left Wing	Patrice Lagisquet
Full-back	Serge Blanco
Reserve	Didier Camberabero

Romania

Prop	F Opris
Hooker	V Ilca
Prop	V Pascu
Lock	Laurentiu Constantin
Lock	N Veres
Flanker	Gheorghie Dumitru
Flanker	E Necula
Number 8	Christian Raducanu
Scrum-half	Mircea Paraschiv (c)
Fly-half	R Bezuscu
Right Wing	Adrian Lungu
Centre	V David
Centre	Stefan Tofan
Left Wing	M Toader
Full-back	Vasile Ion
Reserve	E Grigore
Referee	Fordham RJ

Points Scorers

France

Name	Tries	Conv	Pen K	Drop G	Points
Andrieu M	1	0	0	0	4
Camberabero D	1	0	0	0	4
Charvet D	2	0	0	0	8
Erbani D	1	0	0	0	4
Lagisquet P	2	0	0	0	8
Laporte G	1	8	1	0	23
Sella P	1	0	0	0	4

Romania

Name	Tries	Conv	Pen K	Drop G	Points
Bezuscu R	0	0	4	0	12

Pool 4, Fourth Match
Scotland v Zimbabwe: 60-21
30 May 1987
Athletic Park, Wellington

Players

Scotland

Prop	Iain Milne
Hooker	Colin Deans (c)
Prop	David Sole
Lock	Jeremy Campbell-Lamerton
Lock	Alan Tomes
Flanker	Finlay Calder
Flanker	John Jeffrey
Number 8	Iain Paxton
Scrum-half	Greig Oliver
Fly-half	Douglas Wyllie
Right Wing	Matthew Duncan
Centre	Keith Robertson
Centre	Alan Tait
Left Wing	Iwan Tukalo
Full-back	Gavin Hastings

Zimbabwe

Prop	Alex Nicholls
Hooker	Lance Bray
Prop	Andy Tucker
Lock	Michael Martin
Lock	Tom Sawyer
Flanker	Dirk Buitendag
Flanker	Rod Gray
Number 8	Mark Neill
Scrum-half	Malcolm Jellicoe (c)
Fly-half	Marthinus Grobler
Right Wing	Eric Barrett
Centre	Andre Buitendag
Centre	Campbell Graham
Left Wing	Shawn Graham
Full-back	Andy Ferreira
Referee	Burnett DIH

Points Scorers

Scotland

Name	Tries	Conv	Pen K	Drop G	Points
Duncan MDF	2	0	0	0	8
Hastings AG	1	8	0	0	20
Jeffrey J	1	0	0	0	4
Oliver GH	1	0	0	0	4
Paxton IAMacL	2	0	0	0	8
Tait AV	2	0	0	0	8
Tukalo I	2	0	0	0	8

Zimbabwe

Name	Tries	Conv	Pen K	Drop G	Points
Buitendag D	1	0	0	0	4
Grobler M	0	1	5	0	17

Pool 4, Fifth Match
France v Zimbabwe: 70-12
2 June 1987
Eden Park, Auckland

Players

France

Prop	Pascal Ondarts
Hooker	Daniel Dubroca (c)
Prop	Jean-Louis Tolot
Lock	Jean Condom
Lock	Alain Lorieux
Flanker	Alain Carminati
Flanker	Jean-Luc Joinel
Number 8	Laurent Rodriguez
Scrum-half	Rodolphe Modin
Fly-half	Franck Mesnel
Right Wing	Marc Andrieu
Centre	Eric Bonneval
Centre	Denis Charvet
Left Wing	Patrick Esteve
Full-back	Didier Camberabero
Reserves	Guy Laporte, Philippe Sella

Zimbabwe

Prop	George Elcome
Hooker	Lance Bray
Prop	Andy Tucker
Lock	Michael Martin
Lock	Tom Sawyer
Flanker	Dirk Buitendag
Flanker	Rod Gray
Number 8	Mark Neill
Scrum-half	Malcolm Jellicoe (c)
Fly-half	Marthinus Grobler
Right Wing	Eric Barrett
Centre	Campbell Graham
Centre	Richard Tsimba
Left Wing	Peter Kaulback
Full-back	Andy Ferreira
Reserves	Neville Kloppers, Alex Nicholls
Referee	Bevan WD

Points Scorers

France

Name	Tries	Conv	Pen K	Drop G	Points
Camberabero D	3	9	0	0	30
Charvet D	2	0	0	0	8
Dubroca D	1	0	0	0	4
Esteve P	1	0	0	0	4
Laporte G	1	0	0	0	4
Modin R	3	0	0	0	12
Rodriguez L	2	0	0	0	8

Zimbabwe

Name	Tries	Conv	Pen K	Drop G	Points
Grobler M	0	1	2	0	8
Kaulback P	1	0	0	0	4

Pool 4, Sixth Match
Scotland v Romania: 55-28
2 June 1987
Carisbrook Stadium, Dunedin

Players

Scotland

Prop	Norrie Rowan
Hooker	Colin Deans (c)
Prop	David Sole
Lock	Alan Tomes
Lock	Derek White
Flanker	Finlay Calder
Flanker	John Jeffrey
Number 8	Iain Paxton
Scrum-half	Roy Laidlaw
Fly-half	Douglas Wyllie
Right Wing	Matthew Duncan
Centre	Scott Hastings
Centre	Alan Tait
Left Wing	Iwan Tukalo
Full-back	Gavin Hastings
Reserves	Jeremy Campbell-Lamerton, Richard Cramb

Romania

Prop	Ion Bucan
Hooker	E Grigore
Prop	Gheorghe Leonte
Lock	Stefan Constantin
Lock	Laurentiu Constantin
Flanker	Haralambie Dumitras
Flanker	Florica Murariu
Number 8	Christian Raducanu
Scrum-half	Mircea Paraschiv (c)
Fly-half	Dumitru Alexandru
Right Wing	A Pilotschi
Centre	Adrian Lungu
Centre	Stefan Tofan
Left Wing	M Toader
Full-back	Vasile Ion
Reserve	Gheorghie Dumitru
Referee	Hilditch SR

Points Scorers

Scotland

Name	Tries	Conv	Pen K	Drop G	Points
Duncan MDF	1	0	0	0	4
Hastings AG	2	8	1	0	27
Jeffrey J	3	0	0	0	12
Tait AV	2	0	0	0	8
Tukalo I	1	0	0	0	4

Romania

Name	Tries	Conv	Pen K	Drop G	Points
Alexandru D	0	1	3	0	11
Ion V	0	1	1	0	5
Murariu F	2	0	0	0	8
Toader M	1	0	0	0	4

First Quarter-Final
New Zealand v Scotland: 30-3
6 June 1987
Lancaster Park, Christchurch

Players
New Zealand

Prop	John Drake
Hooker	Sean Fitzpatrick
Prop	Steven McDowell
Lock	Murray Pierce
Lock	Gary Whetton
Flanker	Michael Jones
Flanker	Alan Whetton
Number 8	Buck Shelford
Scrum-half	David Kirk (c)
Fly-half	Grant Fox
Right Wing	Craig Green
Centre	Joe Stanley
Centre	Warwick Taylor
Left Wing	John Kirwan
Full-back	John Gallagher
Reserve	Bernie McCahill

Scotland

Prop	Iain Milne
Hooker	Colin Deans (c)
Prop	David Sole
Lock	Alan Tomes
Lock	Derek White
Flanker	Finlay Calder
Flanker	Derek Turnbull
Number 8	Iain Paxton
Scrum-half	Roy Laidlaw
Fly-half	Douglas Wyllie
Right Wing	Matthew Duncan
Centre	Keith Robertson
Centre	Alan Tait
Left Wing	Iwan Tukalo
Full-back	Gavin Hastings
Referee	Burnett DIH

Points Scorers
New Zealand

Name	Tries	Conv	Pen K	Drop G	Points
Fox GJ	0	2	6	0	22
Gallagher JA	1	0	0	0	4
Whetton AJ	1	0	0	0	4

Scotland

Name	Tries	Conv	Pen K	Drop G	Points
Hastings AG	0	0	1	0	3

Second Quarter-Final
Fiji v France: 16-31
7 June 1987
Eden Park, Auckland

Players
Fiji

Prop	Sairusi Naituku
Hooker	Epeli Rakai
Prop	Rusiate Namoro
Lock	Koli Rakoroi (c)
Lock	Laitia Savai
Flanker	Salacieli Naivilawasa
Flanker	Manasa Qoro
Number 8	Lilvai Kididromo
Scrum-half	Paolo Nawalu
Fly-half	Severo Koroduadua
Right Wing	J Damu
Centre	Tomasi Cama
Centre	Kaiava Salusalu
Left Wing	T Mitchell
Full-back	Jone Kubu
Reserves	W Nadolo, Samu Vunivalu

France

Prop	Jean-Pierre Garuet-Lempirou
Hooker	Daniel Dubroca (c)
Prop	Pascal Ondarts
Lock	Francis Haget
Lock	Alain Lorieux
Flanker	Eric Champ
Flanker	Dominique Erbani
Number 8	Laurent Rodriguez
Scrum-half	Pierre Berbizier
Fly-half	Guy Laporte
Right Wing	Denis Charvet
Centre	Franck Mesnel
Centre	Philippe Sella
Left Wing	Patrice Lagisquet
Full-back	Serge Blanco
Reserve	Didier Camberabero
Referee	Norling C

Points Scorers
Fiji

Name	Tries	Conv	Pen K	Drop G	Points
Damu JV	1	0	0	0	4
Koroduadua S	0	1	2	0	8
Qoro M	1	0	0	0	4

France

Name	Tries	Conv	Pen K	Drop G	Points
Lagisquet P	1	0	0	0	4
Laporte G	0	3	2	1	15
Lorieux A	1	0	0	0	4
Rodriguez L	2	0	0	0	8

Third Quarter-Final
Australia v Ireland: 33–15
7 June 1987
Concord Oval, Sydney

Players

Australia

Prop	Cameron Lillicrap
Hooker	Tom Lawton
Prop	Andy McIntyre
Lock	Bill Campbell
Lock	Steve Cutler
Flanker	Jeff Miller
Flanker	Simon Poidevin
Number 8	Steve Tuynman
Scrum-half	Nick Farr-Jones
Fly-half	Michael Lynagh
Right Wing	Matthew Burke
Centre	Brett Papworth
Centre	Andrew Slack (c)
Left Wing	Peter Grigg
Full-back	David Campese
Reserve	Brian Smith

Ireland

Prop	Des Fitzgerald
Hooker	Terry Kingston
Prop	Phil Orr
Lock	Willie Anderson
Lock	Donal Lenihan (c)
Flanker	Philip Matthews
Flanker	Derek McGrath
Number 8	Neil Francis
Scrum-half	Michael Bradley
Fly-half	Paul Dean
Right Wing	Keith Crossan
Centre	Michael Kiernan
Centre	Brendan Mullin
Left Wing	Trevor Ringland
Full-back	Hugo MacNeill
Reserves	David Irwin, Brian Spillane
Referee	Anderson JB

Points Scorers

Australia

Name	Tries	Conv	Pen K	Drop G	Points
Burke MP	2	0	0	0	8
Lynagh MP	0	4	3	0	17
McIntyre AJ	1	0	0	0	4
Smith BA	1	0	0	0	4

Ireland

Name	Tries	Conv	Pen K	Drop G	Points
Kiernan MJ	1	2	1	0	11
MacNeill HP	1	0	0	0	4

Fourth Quarter-Final
England v Wales: 3-16
8 June 1987
Ballymore Stadium, Brisbane

Players

England

Position	Player
Prop	Gary Pearce
Hooker	Brian Moore
Prop	Paul Rendall
Lock	Wade Dooley
Lock	Nigel Redman
Flanker	Gary Rees
Flanker	Peter Winterbottom
Number 8	Dean Richards
Scrum-half	Richard Harding
Fly-half	Peter Williams
Right Wing	Mike Harrison (c)
Centre	Jamie Salmon
Centre	Kevin Simms
Left Wing	Rory Underwood
Full-back	Jon Webb
Reserve	Gareth Chilcott

Wales

Prop	Anthony Buchanan
Hooker	Allan Phillips
Prop	Dai Young
Lock	Dick Moriarty (c)
Lock	Bob Norster
Flanker	Richie Collins
Flanker	Gareth Roberts
Number 8	Paul Moriarty
Scrum-half	Robert Jones
Fly-half	Jonathan Davies
Right Wing	Ieuan Evans
Centre	Bleddyn Bowen
Centre	John Devereux
Left Wing	Adrian Hadley
Full-back	Paul Thorburn
Reserve	Huw Richards
Referee	Hourquet R

Points Scorers

England

Name	Tries	Conv	Pen K	Drop G	Points
Webb JM	0	0	1	0	3

Wales

Name	Tries	Conv	Pen K	Drop G	Points
Devereux JA	1	0	0	0	4
Jones RN	1	0	0	0	4
Roberts GJ	1	0	0	0	4
Thorburn PH	0	2	0	0	4

First Semi-Final
Australia v France: 24-30
13 June 1987
Concord Oval, Sydney

Players

Australia

Prop	Cameron Lillicrap
Hooker	Tom Lawton
Prop	Andy McIntyre
Lock	Bill Campbell
Lock	Steve Cutler
Flanker	Jeff Miller
Flanker	Simon Poidevin
Number 8	Troy Coker
Scrum-half	Nick Farr-Jones
Fly-half	Michael Lynagh
Right Wing	Matthew Burke
Centre	Brett Papworth
Centre	Andrew Slack (c)
Left Wing	Peter Grigg
Full-back	David Campese
Reserves	David Codey, Anthony Herbert

France

Prop	Jean-Pierre Garuet-Lempirou
Hooker	Daniel Dubroca (c)
Prop	Pascal Ondarts
Lock	Jean Condom
Lock	Alain Lorieux
Flanker	Eric Champ
Flanker	Dominique Erbani
Number 8	Laurent Rodriguez
Scrum-half	Pierre Berbizier
Fly-half	Franck Mesnel
Right Wing	Didier Camberabero
Centre	Denis Charvet
Centre	Philippe Sella
Left Wing	Patrice Lagisquet
Full-back	Serge Blanco
Referee	Anderson JB

Points Scorers

Australia

Name	Tries	Conv	Pen K	Drop G	Points
Campese DI	1	0	0	0	4
Codey D	1	0	0	0	4
Lynagh MP	0	2	3	1	16

France

Name	Tries	Conv	Pen K	Drop G	Points
Blanco S	1	0	0	0	4
Camberabero D	0	4	2	0	14
Lagisquet P	1	0	0	0	4
Lorieux A	1	0	0	0	4
Sella P	1	0	0	0	4

Second Semi-Final
Wales v New Zealand: 6-49
14 June 1987
Ballymore Stadium, Brisbane

Players
Wales

Prop	Anthony Buchanan
Hooker	Kevin Phillips
Prop	Dai Young
Lock	Dick Moriarty (c)
Lock	Huw Richards
Flanker	Richie Collins
Flanker	Phil Davies
Number 8	Paul Moriarty
Scrum-half	Robert Jones
Fly-half	Jonathan Davies
Right Wing	Ieuan Evans
Centre	Bleddyn Bowen
Centre	John Devereux
Left Wing	Adrian Hadley
Full-back	Paul Thorburn
Reserve	Steve Sutton

New Zealand

Prop	John Drake
Hooker	Sean Fitzpatrick
Prop	Steven McDowell
Lock	Murray Pierce
Lock	Gary Whetton
Flanker	Mark Brooke-Cowden
Flanker	Alan Whetton
Number 8	Buck Shelford
Scrum-half	David Kirk (c)
Fly-half	Grant Fox
Right Wing	Craig Green
Centre	Joe Stanley
Centre	Warwick Taylor
Left Wing	John Kirwan
Full-back	John Gallagher
Reserve	Bernie McCahill
Referee	Fitzgerald KVJ

Points Scorers
New Zealand

Name	Tries	Conv	Pen K	Drop G	Points
Brooke-Cowden M	1	0	0	0	4
Drake JA	1	0	0	0	4
Fox GJ	0	7	1	0	17
Kirwan JJ	2	0	0	0	8
Shelford WT	2	0	0	0	8
Stanley JT	1	0	0	0	4
Whetton AJ	1	0	0	0	4

Wales

Name	Tries	Conv	Pen K	Drop G	Points
Devereux JA	1	0	0	0	4
Thorburn PH	0	1	0	0	2

Third Place Play-Off
Australia v Wales: 21-22
18 June 1987
Rotorua International Stadium

Players

Australia

Prop	Cameron Lillicrap
Hooker	Tom Lawton
Prop	Andy McIntyre
Lock	Troy Coker
Lock	Steve Cutler
Flanker	David Codey
Flanker	Simon Poidevin
Number 8	Steve Tuynman
Scrum-half	Brian Smith
Fly-half	Michael Lynagh
Right Wing	David Campese
Centre	Matthew Burke
Centre	Andrew Slack (c)
Left Wing	Peter Grigg
Full-back	Andrew Leeds
Reserves	Nick Farr-Jones, Topo Rodriguez

Wales

Prop	Steven Blackmore
Hooker	Allan Phillips
Prop	Anthony Buchanan
Lock	Dick Moriarty (c)
Lock	Steve Sutton
Flanker	Gareth Roberts
Flanker	Richard Webster
Number 8	Paul Moriarty
Scrum-half	Robert Jones
Fly-half	Jonathan Davies
Right Wing	Ieuan Evans
Centre	John Devereux
Centre	Mark Ring
Left Wing	Adrian Hadley
Full-back	Paul Thorburn
Referee	Howard FA

Points Scorers

Australia

Name	Tries	Conv	Pen K	Drop G	Points
Burke MP	1	0	0	0	4
Grigg PC	1	0	0	0	4
Lynagh MP	0	2	2	1	13

Wales

Name	Tries	Conv	Pen K	Drop G	Points
Hadley AM	1	0	0	0	4
Moriarty WP	1	0	0	0	4
Roberts GJ	1	0	0	0	4
Thorburn PH	0	2	2	0	10

Final
New Zealand v France: 29-9
20 June 1987
Eden Park, Auckland

Players
New Zealand

Prop	John Drake
Hooker	Sean Fitzpatrick
Prop	Steven McDowell
Lock	Murray Pierce
Lock	Gary Whetton
Flanker	Michael Jones
Flanker	Alan Whetton
Number 8	Buck Shelford
Scrum-half	David Kirk (c)
Fly-half	Grant Fox
Right Wing	Craig Green
Centre	Joe Stanley
Centre	Warwick Taylor
Left Wing	John Kirwan
Full-back	John Gallagher

France

Prop	Jean-Pierre Garuet-Lempirou
Hooker	Daniel Dubroca (c)
Prop	Pascal Ondarts
Lock	Jean Condom
Lock	Alain Lorieux
Flanker	Eric Champ
Flanker	Dominique Erbani
Number 8	Laurent Rodriguez
Scrum-half	Pierre Berbizier
Fly-half	Franck Mesnel
Right Wing	Didier Camberabero
Centre	Denis Charvet
Centre	Philippe Sella
Left Wing	Patrice Lagisquet
Full-back	Serge Blanco
Referee	Fitzgerald KVJ

Points Scorers
New Zealand

Name	Tries	Conv	Pen K	Drop G	Points
Fox GJ	0	1	4	1	17
Jones MN	1	0	0	0	4
Kirk DE	1	0	0	0	4
Kirwan JJ	1	0	0	0	4

France

Name	Tries	Conv	Pen K	Drop G	Points
Berbizier P	1	0	0	0	4
Camberabero D	0	1	1	0	5

1991

Pool 1, First Match
England v New Zealand: 12-18
3 October 1991
Twickenham, London

Players

England

Position	Player
Prop	Jason Leonard
Hooker	Brian Moore
Prop	Jeff Probyn
Lock	Paul Ackford
Lock	Wade Dooley
Flanker	Mike Teague
Flanker	Peter Winterbottom
Number 8	Dean Richards
Scrum-half	Richard Hill
Fly-half	Rob Andrew
Right Wing	Chris Oti
Centre	Will Carling (c)
Centre	Jerry Guscott
Left Wing	Rory Underwood
Full-back	Jon Webb

New Zealand

Position	Player
Prop	Richard Loe
Hooker	Sean Fitzpatrick
Prop	Steven McDowell
Lock	Ian Jones
Lock	Gary Whetton (c)
Flanker	Michael Jones
Flanker	Alan Whetton
Number 8	Zinzan Brooke
Scrum-half	Graeme Bachop
Fly-half	Grant Fox
Right Wing	John Kirwan
Centre	Craig Innes
Centre	Bernie McCahill
Left Wing	John Timu
Full-back	Terry Wright
Reserve	Andy Earl
Referee	Ieming JM

Points Scorers

England

Name	Tries	Conv	Pen K	Drop G	Points
Andrew CR	0	0	0	1	3
Webb JM	0	0	3	0	9

New Zealand

Name	Tries	Conv	Pen K	Drop G	Points
Fox GJ	0	1	4	0	14
Jones MN	1	0	0	0	4

Pool 1, Second Match
Italy v USA: 30-9
5 October 1991
Cross Green, Otley

Players

Italy

Prop	Massimo Cuttitta
Hooker	Giancarlo Pivetta
Prop	Franco Properzi-Curti
Lock	Giambattista Croci
Lock	Roberto Favaro
Flanker	Carlo Checchinato
Flanker	Roberto Saetti
Number 8	Gianni Zanon (c)
Scrum-half	Ivan Francescato
Fly-half	Diego Dominguez
Right Wing	Marcello Cuttitta
Centre	Stefano Barba
Centre	Fabio Gaetaniello
Left Wing	Paolo Vaccari
Full-back	Luigi Troiani

USA

Prop	Chris Lippert
Hooker	Tony Flay
Prop	Fred Paoli
Lock	Bill Leversee
Lock	Kevin Swords
Flanker	Rob Farley
Flanker	Brian Vizard (c)
Number 8	Tony Ridnell
Scrum-half	Barry Daily
Fly-half	Mike de Jong
Right Wing	Gary Hein
Centre	Kevin Higgins
Centre	Mark Williams
Left Wing	Eric Whitaker
Full-back	Ray Nelson
Reserve	Shawn Lipman
Referee	Doyle OE

Points Scorers

Italy

Name	Tries	Conv	Pen K	Drop G	Points
Barba S	1	0	0	0	4
Dominguez D	0	4	2	0	14
Francescato I	1	0	0	0	4
Gaetaniello F	1	0	0	0	4
Vaccari P	1	0	0	0	4

USA

Name	Tries	Conv	Pen K	Drop G	Points
Swords KR	1	0	0	0	4
Williams MA	0	1	1	0	5

Pool 1, Third Match
New Zealand v USA: 46-6
8 October 1991
Kingsholm, Gloucester

Players

New Zealand

Prop	Steven McDowell
Hooker	Sean Fitzpatrick
Prop	Graham Purvis
Lock	Ian Jones
Lock	Gary Whetton (c)
Flanker	Michael Jones
Flanker	Alan Whetton
Number 8	Andy Earl
Scrum-half	Graeme Bachop
Fly-half	Jon Preston
Right Wing	John Timu
Centre	Craig Innes
Centre	Bernie McCahill
Left Wing	Inga Tuigamala
Full-back	Terry Wright

USA

Prop	Chris Lippert
Hooker	Pat Johnson
Prop	Norm Mottram
Lock	Kevin Swords (c)
Lock	Chuck Tunnacliffe
Flanker	Shawn Lipman
Flanker	Mark Sawicki
Number 8	Tony Ridnell
Scrum-half	Mark Pidcock
Fly-half	Chris O'Brien
Right Wing	Gary Hein
Centre	Joe Burke
Centre	Mark Williams
Left Wing	Eric Whitaker
Full-back	Paul Sheehy
Reserve	Lance Manga
Referee	Sklar E

Points Scorers

New Zealand

Name	Tries	Conv	Pen K	Drop G	Points
Earl AT	1	0	0	0	4
Innes CR	1	0	0	0	4
Preston JP	0	4	2	0	14
Purvis GH	1	0	0	0	4
Timu JKR	1	0	0	0	4
Tuigamala VL	1	0	0	0	4
Wright TJ	3	0	0	0	12

USA

Name	Tries	Conv	Pen K	Drop G	Points
Williams MA	0	0	2	0	6

Pool 1, Fourth Match
England v Italy: 36-6
8 October 1991
Twickenham, London

Players
England

Prop	Jason Leonard
Hooker	Brian Moore
Prop	Jeff Probyn
Lock	Paul Ackford
Lock	Nigel Redman
Flanker	Mike Teague
Flanker	Peter Winterbottom
Number 8	Dean Richards
Scrum-half	Richard Hill
Fly-half	Rob Andrew
Right Wing	Chris Oti
Centre	Will Carling (c)
Centre	Jerry Guscott
Left Wing	Rory Underwood
Full-back	Jon Webb
Reserve	Paul Rendall

Italy

Prop	Massimo Cuttitta
Hooker	Giancarlo Pivetta
Prop	Franco Properzi-Curti
Lock	Giambattista Croci
Lock	Roberto Favaro
Flanker	Massimo Giovanelli
Flanker	Roberto Saetti
Number 8	Gianni Zanon (c)
Scrum-half	Ivan Francescato
Fly-half	Diego Dominguez
Right Wing	Marcello Cuttitta
Centre	Stefano Barba
Centre	Fabio Gaetaniello
Left Wing	Paolo Vaccari
Full-back	Luigi Troiani
Reserve	Massimo Bonomi
Referee	Anderson JB

Points Scorers
England

Name	Tries	Conv	Pen K	Drop G	Points
Guscott JC	2	0	0	0	8
Underwood R	1	0	0	0	4
Webb JM	1	4	4	0	24

Italy

Name	Tries	Conv	Pen K	Drop G	Points
Cuttitta M	1	0	0	0	4
Dominguez D	0	1	0	0	2

Pool 1, Fifth Match
England v USA: 37-9
11 October 1991
Twickenham, London

Players

England

Prop	Jason Leonard
Hooker	John Olver
Prop	Gary Pearce
Lock	Wade Dooley
Lock	Nigel Redman
Flanker	Gary Rees
Flanker	Mickey Skinner
Number 8	Dean Richards
Scrum-half	Richard Hill
Fly-half	Rob Andrew
Right Wing	Nigel Heslop
Centre	Will Carling (c)
Centre	Simon Halliday
Left Wing	Rory Underwood
Full-back	Simon Hodgkinson

USA

Prop	Lance Manga
Hooker	Tony Flay
Prop	Norm Mottram
Lock	Kevin Swords (c)
Lock	Chuck Tunnacliffe
Flanker	Rob Farley
Flanker	Shawn Lipman
Number 8	Tony Ridnell
Scrum-half	Mark Pidcock
Fly-half	Chris O'Brien
Right Wing	Gary Hein
Centre	Kevin Higgins
Centre	Mark Williams
Left Wing	Paul Sheehy
Full-back	Ray Nelson
Reserves	Mike de Jong, Jay Wilkerson
Referee	Peard LJ

Points Scorers

England

Name	Tries	Conv	Pen K	Drop G	Points
Carling WDC	1	0	0	0	4
Heslop NJ	1	0	0	0	4
Hodgkinson SD	0	4	3	0	17
Skinner MG	1	0	0	0	4
Underwood R	2	0	0	0	8

USA

Name	Tries	Conv	Pen K	Drop G	Points
Nelson RB	1	0	0	0	4
Williams MA	0	1	1	0	5

Pool 1, Sixth Match
Italy v New Zealand: 21–31
13 October 1991
Welford Road, Leicester

Players
Italy

Prop	Massimo Cuttitta
Hooker	Giancarlo Pivetta (c)
Prop	Franco Properzi-Curti
Lock	Giambattista Croci
Lock	Roberto Favaro
Flanker	Alessandro Bottacchiari
Flanker	Massimo Giovanelli
Number 8	Carlo Checchinato
Scrum-half	Ivan Francescato
Fly-half	Massimo Bonomi
Right Wing	Marcello Cuttitta
Centre	Diego Dominguez
Centre	Fabio Gaetaniello
Left Wing	Edgardo Venturi
Full-back	Paolo Vaccari
Reserve	Giovanni Grespan

New Zealand

Prop	Richard Loe
Hooker	Sean Fitzpatrick
Prop	Steven McDowell
Lock	Ian Jones
Lock	Gary Whetton (c)
Flanker	Mark Carter
Flanker	Alan Whetton
Number 8	Zinzan Brooke
Scrum-half	Jason Hewett
Fly-half	Grant Fox
Right Wing	John Kirwan
Centre	Craig Innes
Centre	Walter Little
Left Wing	Inga Tuigamala
Full-back	Terry Wright
Reserve	Shayne Philpott
Referee	Fitzgerald KVJ

Points Scorers
Italy

Name	Tries	Conv	Pen K	Drop G	Points
Bonomi M	1	0	0	0	4
Cuttitta M	1	0	0	0	4
Dominguez D	0	2	3	0	13

New Zealand

Name	Tries	Conv	Pen K	Drop G	Points
Brooke ZV	1	0	0	0	4
Fox GJ	0	3	3	0	15
Hewett JA	1	0	0	0	4
Innes CR	1	0	0	0	4
Tuigamala VL	1	0	0	0	4

Pool 2, First Match
Scotland v Japan: 47-9
5 October 1991
Murrayfield, Edinburgh

Players
Scotland

Prop	Paul Burnell
Hooker	John Allan
Prop	David Sole (c)
Lock	Chris Gray
Lock	Doddie Weir
Flanker	Finlay Calder
Flanker	John Jeffrey
Number 8	Derek White
Scrum-half	Gary Armstrong
Fly-half	Craig Chalmers
Right Wing	Tony Stanger
Centre	Scott Hastings
Centre	Sean Lineen
Left Wing	Iwan Tukalo
Full-back	Gavin Hastings
Reserves	David Milne, Douglas Wyllie

Japan

Prop	Osamu Ota
Hooker	Masahiro Kunda
Prop	Masanori Takura
Lock	Toshiyuki Hayashi
Lock	Ekeroma Tifaga
Flanker	Hiroyuki Kajihara
Flanker	Shuji Nakashima
Number 8	Sinali-Tui Latu
Scrum-half	Wataru Murata
Fly-half	Katsuhiro Matsuo
Right Wing	Terunori Masuho
Centre	Seiji Hirao (c)
Centre	Eiji Kutsuki
Left Wing	Yoshihito Yoshida
Full-back	Takahiro Hosokawa
Referee	Morrison EF

Points Scorers
Scotland

Name	Tries	Conv	Pen K	Drop G	Points
Penalty Try	1	0	0	0	4
Chalmers CM	1	0	1	0	7
Hastings AG	1	5	2	0	20
Hastings S	1	0	0	0	4
Stanger AG	1	0	0	0	4
Tukalo I	1	0	0	0	4
White DB	1	0	0	0	4

Japan

Name	Tries	Conv	Pen K	Drop G	Points
Hosokawa T	1	1	0	1	9

Pool 2, Second Match
Ireland v Zimbabwe: 55–11
6 October 1991
Lansdowne Road, Dublin

Players

Ireland

Prop	Des Fitzgerald
Hooker	Steve Smith
Prop	Nick Popplewell
Lock	Neil Francis
Lock	Donal Lenihan
Flanker	Gordon Hamilton
Flanker	Philip Matthews (c)
Number 8	Brian Robinson
Scrum-half	Rob Saunders
Fly-half	Ralph Keyes
Right Wing	Keith Crossan
Centre	David Curtis
Centre	Vince Cunningham
Left Wing	Simon Geoghegan
Full-back	Jim Staples

Zimbabwe

Prop	Adrian Garvey
Hooker	Brian Beattie
Prop	Robin Hunter
Lock	Rob Demblon
Lock	Michael Martin
Flanker	Chris Botha
Flanker	Brendon Dawson
Number 8	Brenton Catterall
Scrum-half	Andy Ferreira
Fly-half	Ralph Kuhn
Right Wing	Craig Brown
Centre	Mark Letcher
Centre	Richard Tsimba
Left Wing	David Walters
Full-back	Brian Currin (c)
Reserve	William Schultz
Referee	Lawrence KH

Points Scorers

Ireland

Name	Tries	Conv	Pen K	Drop G	Points
Curtis DM	1	0	0	0	4
Geoghegan SP	1	0	0	0	4
Keyes RP	0	4	5	0	23
Popplewell NJ	2	0	0	0	8
Robinson BF	4	0	0	0	16

Zimbabwe

Name	Tries	Conv	Pen K	Drop G	Points
Dawson BN	1	0	0	0	4
Ferreira AM	0	0	1	0	3
Schultz WH	1	0	0	0	4

Pool 2, Third Match
Ireland v Japan: 21-16
9 October 1991
Lansdowne Road, Dublin

Players
Ireland

Prop	John Fitzgerald
Hooker	Terry Kingston (c)
Prop	Gary Halpin
Lock	Neil Francis
Lock	Mick Galwey
Flanker	Gordon Hamilton
Flanker	Pat O'Hara
Number 8	Noel Mannion
Scrum-half	Rob Saunders
Fly-half	Ralph Keyes
Right Wing	Jack Clarke
Centre	David Curtis
Centre	Brendan Mullin
Left Wing	Keith Crossan
Full-back	Jim Staples
Reserve	Vince Cunningham

Japan

Prop	Osamu Ota
Hooker	Tsuyoshi Fujita
Prop	Masanori Takura
Lock	Toshiyuki Hayashi
Lock	Atsushi Oyagi
Flanker	Hiroyuki Kajihara
Flanker	Ekeroma Tifaga
Number 8	Sinali-Tui Latu
Scrum-half	Masami Horikoshi
Fly-half	Katsuhiro Matsuo
Right Wing	Terunori Masuho
Centre	Seiji Hirao (c)
Centre	Eiji Kutsuki
Left Wing	Yoshihito Yoshida
Full-back	Takahiro Hosokawa
Reserves	Masahiro Kunda, Katsufumi Miyamoto
Referee	Colati L

Points Scorers
Ireland

Name	Tries	Conv	Pen K	Drop G	Points
Keyes RP	0	2	4	0	16
Mannion NPS	2	0	0	0	8
O'Hara PT	1	0	0	0	4
Staples JE	1	0	0	0	4

Japan

Name	Tries	Conv	Pen K	Drop G	Points
Hayashi T	1	0	0	0	4
Hosokawa T	0	2	0	0	4
Kajihara H	1	0	0	0	4
Yoshida Y	1	0	0	0	4

Pool 2, Fourth Match
Scotland v Zimbabwe: 51–12
9 October 1991
Murrayfield, Edinburgh

Players

Scotland

Prop	Paul Burnell
Hooker	Kenny Milne
Prop	Alan Watt
Lock	Damian Cronin
Lock	Doddie Weir
Flanker	Graham Marshall
Flanker	Derek Turnbull
Number 8	Derek White
Scrum-half	Greig Oliver
Fly-half	Douglas Wyllie
Right Wing	Tony Stanger
Centre	Scott Hastings
Centre	Sean Lineen
Left Wing	Iwan Tukalo
Full-back	Peter Dods (c)
Reserve	Craig Chalmers

Zimbabwe

Prop	Adrian Garvey
Hooker	Brian Beattie
Prop	Alex Nicholls
Lock	Michael Martin
Lock	Honeywell Nguruve
Flanker	Brendon Dawson
Flanker	Darren Muirhead
Number 8	Brenton Catterall
Scrum-half	Ewan MacMillan
Fly-half	Craig Brown
Right Wing	William Schultz
Centre	Mark Letcher
Centre	Richard Tsimba
Left Wing	David Walters
Full-back	Brian Currin (c)
Reserve	Elimon Chimbima
	Robin Hunter
	Chris Roberts
Referee	Reordan D

Points Scorers

Scotland

Name	Tries	Conv	Pen K	Drop G	Points
Dods PW	0	5	2	0	16
Hastings S	1	0	0	0	4
Stanger AG	1	0	0	0	4
Tukalo I	3	0	0	0	12
Turnbull DJ	1	0	0	0	4
Weir GW	1	0	0	0	4
White DB	1	0	0	0	4
Wyllie DS	0	0	0	1	3

Zimbabwe

Name	Tries	Conv	Pen K	Drop G	Points
Currin BS	0	2	0	0	4
Garvey AC	2	0	0	0	8

Pool 2, Fifth Match
Scotland v Ireland: 24-15
12 October 1991
Murrayfield, Edinburgh

Players
Scotland

Prop	Paul Burnell
Hooker	John Allan
Prop	David Sole (c)
Lock	Chris Gray
Lock	Doddie Weir
Flanker	Finlay Calder
Flanker	John Jeffrey
Number 8	Derek White
Scrum-half	Gary Armstrong
Fly-half	Craig Chalmers
Right Wing	Tony Stanger
Centre	Scott Hastings
Centre	Sean Lineen
Left Wing	Iwan Tukalo
Full-back	Gavin Hastings
Reserve	Graham Shiel

Ireland

Prop	Des Fitzgerald
Hooker	Steve Smith
Prop	Nick Popplewell
Lock	Neil Francis
Lock	Donal Lenihan
Flanker	Gordon Hamilton
Flanker	Philip Matthews (c)
Number 8	Brian Robinson
Scrum-half	Rob Saunders
Fly-half	Ralph Keyes
Right Wing	Keith Crossan
Centre	David Curtis
Centre	Brendan Mullin
Left Wing	Simon Geoghegan
Full-back	Jim Staples
Referee	Howard FA

Points Scorers
Scotland

Name	Tries	Conv	Pen K	Drop G	Points
Armstrong G	1	0	0	0	4
Chalmers CM	0	0	0	1	3
Hastings AG	0	2	3	0	13
Shiel AG	1	0	0	0	4

Ireland

Name	Tries	Conv	Pen K	Drop G	Points
Keyes RP	0	0	4	1	15

Pool 2, Sixth Match
Japan v Zimbabwe: 52-8
14 October 1991
Ravenhill Park, Belfast

Players
Japan

Prop	Osamu Ota
Hooker	Masahiro Kunda
Prop	Masanori Takura
Lock	Toshiyuki Hayashi
Lock	Atsushi Oyagi
Flanker	Hiroyuki Kajihara
Flanker	Ekeroma Tifaga
Number 8	Sinali-Tui Latu
Scrum-half	Masami Horikoshi
Fly-half	Katsuhiro Matsuo
Right Wing	Terunori Masuho
Centre	Seiji Hirao (c)
Centre	Eiji Kutsuki
Left Wing	Yoshihito Yoshida
Full-back	Takahiro Hosokawa

Zimbabwe

Prop	Adrian Garvey
Hooker	Brian Beattie
Prop	Alex Nicholls
Lock	Chris Botha
Lock	Michael Martin
Flanker	Brendon Dawson
Flanker	Honeywell Nguruve
Number 8	Brenton Catterall
Scrum-half	Ewan MacMillan
Fly-half	Craig Brown
Right Wing	William Schultz
Centre	Mark Letcher
Centre	Richard Tsimba
Left Wing	David Walters
Full-back	Brian Currin (c)
Reserve	Gary Snyder
Referee	Hourquet R

Points Scorers
Japan

Name	Tries	Conv	Pen K	Drop G	Points
Horikoshi M	1	0	0	0	4
Hosokawa T	0	5	2	0	16
Kutsuki E	2	0	0	0	8
Masuho T	2	0	0	0	8
Matsuo K	1	0	0	0	4
Tifaga E	1	0	0	0	4
Yoshida Y	2	0	0	0	8

Zimbabwe

Name	Tries	Conv	Pen K	Drop G	Points
Nguruve H	1	0	0	0	4
Tsimba RU	1	0	0	0	4

Pool 3, First Match
Argentina v Australia: 19-32
4 October 1991
Stradey Park, Llanelli

Players

Argentina

Prop	Diego Cash
Hooker	Ricardo leFort
Prop	Federico Mendez
Lock	German Llanes
Lock	Pedro Sporleder
Flanker	Mario Carreras
Flanker	Pablo Garreton (c)
Number 8	Jose Santamarina
Scrum-half	Gonzalo Camardon
Fly-half	Lisandro Arbizu
Right Wing	Diego Cuesta Silva
Centre	Hernan Garcia Simon
Centre	Eduardo Laborde
Left Wing	Martin Teran Nougues
Full-back	Guillermo Del Castillo
Reserve	Mariano Bosch

Australia

Prop	Tony Daly
Hooker	Phil Kearns
Prop	Ewen McKenzie
Lock	Troy Coker
Lock	Rod McCall
Flanker	Willie Ofahengaue
Flanker	Simon Poidevin
Number 8	John Eales
Scrum-half	Nick Farr-Jones (c)
Fly-half	Michael Lynagh
Right Wing	David Campese
Centre	Tim Horan
Centre	Jason Little
Left Wing	Bob Egerton
Full-back	Marty Roebuck
Reserve	David Nucifora
Referee	Bishop DJ

Points Scorers

Argentina

Name	Tries	Conv	Pen K	Drop G	Points
Arbizu L	0	0	0	2	6
Del Castillo GJ	0	1	1	0	5
Teran Nougues MJ	2	0	0	0	8

Australia

Name	Tries	Conv	Pen K	Drop G	Points
Campese DI	2	0	0	0	8
Horan TJ	2	0	0	0	8
Kearns PN	1	0	0	0	4
Lynagh MP	0	3	2	0	12

Pool 3, Second Match
Wales v Western Samoa: 13-16
6 October 1991
Cardiff Arms Park, Cardiff

Players

Wales

Prop	Laurance Delaney
Hooker	Ken Waters
Prop	Mike Griffiths
Lock	Phil May
Lock	Kevin Moseley
Flanker	Richie Collins
Flanker	Emyr Lewis
Number 8	Phil Davies
Scrum-half	Robert Jones
Fly-half	Mark Ring
Right Wing	Ieuan Evans (c)
Centre	Scott Gibbs
Centre	Mike Hall
Left Wing	Arthur Emyr
Full-back	Tony Clement
Reserves	Garin Jenkins, Martyn Morris, Mike Rayer

Western Samoa

Prop	Vili Alalatoa
Hooker	Stan To'omalatai
Prop	Peter Fatialofa (c)
Lock	Mark Birtwistle
Lock	Mat Keenan
Flanker	Apollo Perelini
Flanker	Sila Vaifale
Number 8	Pat Lam
Scrum-half	Mathew Vaea
Fly-half	Stephen Bachop
Right Wing	Brian Lima
Centre	Frank Bunce
Centre	To'o Vaega
Left Wing	Timo Tagaloa
Full-back	Andrew Aiolupo
Referee	Robin P

Points Scorers

Wales

Name	Tries	Conv	Pen K	Drop G	Points
Evans IC	1	0	0	0	4
Jones AE	1	0	0	0	4
Ring MG	0	1	1	0	5

Western Samoa

Name	Tries	Conv	Pen K	Drop G	Points
Vaega TM	1	0	0	0	4
Vaifale SL	1	0	0	0	4
Vaea M	0	1	2	0	8

Pool 3, Third Match
Wales v Argentina: 16-7
9 October 1991
Cardiff Arms Park, Cardiff

Players

Wales

Prop	Laurance Delaney
Hooker	Garin Jenkins
Prop	Mike Griffiths
Lock	Paul Arnold
Lock	Kevin Moseley
Flanker	Emyr Lewis
Flanker	Richard Webster
Number 8	Phil Davies
Scrum-half	Robert Jones
Fly-half	Mark Ring
Right Wing	Ieuan Evans (c)
Centre	Scott Gibbs
Centre	Mike Hall
Left Wing	Arthur Emyr
Full-back	Mike Rayer

Argentina

Prop	Federico Mendez
Hooker	Ricardo leFort
Prop	Luis Molina
Lock	German Llanes
Lock	Pedro Sporleder
Flanker	Mario Carreras
Flanker	Pablo Garreton (c)
Number 8	Jose Santamarina
Scrum-half	Gonzalo Camardon
Fly-half	Lisandro Arbizu
Right Wing	Diego Cuesta Silva
Centre	Hernan Garcia Simon
Centre	Eduardo Laborde
Left Wing	Martin Teran Nougues
Full-back	Guillermo Del Castillo
Referee	Hourquet R

Points Scorers

Wales

Name	Tries	Conv	Pen K	Drop G	Points
Arnold P	1	0	0	0	4
Rayer MA	0	0	1	0	3
Ring MG	0	0	3	0	9

Argentina

Name	Tries	Conv	Pen K	Drop G	Points
Del Castillo GJ	0	0	1	0	3
Garcia Simon HM	1	0	0	0	4

Pool 3, Fourth Match
Australia v Western Samoa: 9-3
9 October 1991
Pontypool Park

Players

Australia

Prop	Dan Crowley
Hooker	Phil Kearns
Prop	Cameron Lillicrap
Lock	Troy Coker
Lock	Steve Cutler
Flanker	Jeff Miller
Flanker	Brendon Nasser
Number 8	John Eales
Scrum-half	Nick Farr-Jones (c)
Fly-half	Michael Lynagh
Right Wing	David Campese
Centre	Anthony Herbert
Centre	Tim Horan
Left Wing	John Flett
Full-back	Marty Roebuck
Reserve	Peter Slattery

Western Samoa

Prop	Vili Alalatoa
Hooker	Stan To'omalatai
Prop	Peter Fatialofa (c)
Lock	Mark Birtwistle
Lock	Mat Keenan
Flanker	Danny Kaleopa
Flanker	Junior Paramore
Number 8	Apollo Perelini
Scrum-half	Mathew Vaea
Fly-half	Stephen Bachop
Right Wing	Tupo Fa'amasino
Centre	Frank Bunce
Centre	To'o Vaega
Left Wing	Brian Lima
Full-back	Andrew Aiolupo
Reserve	Timo Tagaloa

Referee	Morrison EF

Points Scorers

Australia

Name	Tries	Conv	Pen K	Drop G	Points
Lynagh MP	0	0	3	0	9

Western Samoa

Name	Tries	Conv	Pen K	Drop G	Points
Vaea M	0	0	1	0	3

Pool 3, Fifth Match
Wales v Australia: 3-38
12 October 1991
Cardiff Arms Park, Cardiff

Players
Wales

Prop	Laurance Delaney
Hooker	Garin Jenkins
Prop	Mike Griffiths
Lock	Paul Arnold
Lock	Kevin Moseley
Flanker	Emyr Lewis
Flanker	Richard Webster
Number 8	Phil Davies
Scrum-half	Robert Jones
Fly-half	Mark Ring
Right Wing	Ieuan Evans (c)
Centre	Scott Gibbs
Centre	Mike Hall
Left Wing	Arthur Jones
Full-back	Tony Clement
Reserves	David Evans, Mike Rayer

Australia

Prop	Tony Daly
Hooker	Phil Kearns
Prop	Ewen McKenzie
Lock	John Eales
Lock	Rod McCall
Flanker	Jeff Miller
Flanker	Simon Poidevin
Number 8	Willie Ofahengaue
Scrum-half	Peter Slattery
Fly-half	Michael Lynagh (c)
Right Wing	David Campese
Centre	Tim Horan
Centre	Jason Little
Left Wing	Bob Egerton
Full-back	Marty Roebuck
Referee	Lawrence KH

Points Scorers
Wales

Name	Tries	Conv	Pen K	Drop G	Points
Ring MG	0	0	1	0	3

Australia

Name	Tries	Conv	Pen K	Drop G	Points
Campese DI	1	0	0	0	4
Horan TJ	1	0	0	0	4
Lynagh MP	1	4	2	0	18
Roebuck MC	2	0	0	0	8
Slattery PJ	1	0	0	0	4

Pool 3, Sixth Match
Argentina v Western Samoa: 12-35
13 October 1991
Pontypridd

Players
Argentina

Prop	Manuel Aguirre
Hooker	Mariano Bosch
Prop	Diego Cash
Lock	Fernando Buabse
Lock	Pedro Sporleder
Flanker	Pablo Garreton (c)
Flanker	Francisco Irarrazaval
Number 8	Jose Santamarina
Scrum-half	Gonzalo Camardon
Fly-half	Lisandro Arbizu
Right Wing	Diego Cuesta Silva
Centre	Hernan Garcia Simon
Centre	Eduardo Laborde
Left Wing	Martin Teran Nougues
Full-back	Guillermo Angaut
Reserves	Mario Carreras, Santiago Meson

Western Samoa

Prop	Vili Alalatoa
Hooker	Stan To'omalatai
Prop	Peter Fatialofa (c)
Lock	Mark Birtwistle
Lock	Mat Keenan
Flanker	Apollo Perelini
Flanker	Sila Vaifale
Number 8	Pat Lam
Scrum-half	Mathew Vaea
Fly-half	Stephen Bachop
Right Wing	Brian Lima
Centre	Frank Bunce
Centre	To'o Vaega
Left Wing	Timo Tagaloa
Full-back	Andrew Aiolupo
Referee	Anderson/Fleming

Points Scorers
Argentina

Name	Tries	Conv	Pen K	Drop G	Points
Arbizu L	0	1	1	0	5
Laborde EH	0	0	1	0	3
Teran Nougues MJ	1	0	0	0	4

Western Samoa

Name	Tries	Conv	Pen K	Drop G	Points
Bachop SJ	1	0	0	0	4
Bunce FE	1	0	0	0	4
Lima BP	2	0	0	0	8
Tagaloa TDL	2	0	0	0	8
Vaea M	0	4	1	0	11

Pool 4, First Match
France v Romania: 30-3
4 October 1991
Stade de la Méditerranée, Béziers

Players
France

Prop	Gregoire Lascube
Hooker	Philippe Marocco
Prop	Pascal Ondarts
Lock	Jean-Marie Cadieu
Lock	Olivier Roumat
Flanker	Laurent Cabannes
Flanker	Eric Champ
Number 8	Abdelatif Benazzi
Scrum-half	Fabien Galthie
Fly-half	Didier Camberabero
Right Wing	Patrice Lagisquet
Centre	Thierry Lacroix
Centre	Franck Mesnel
Left Wing	Philippe Saint-Andre
Full-back	Serge Blanco (c)
Reserve	Jean-Baptiste Lafond

Romania

Prop	Gheorghe Leonte
Hooker	Gheorghe Ion
Prop	Constantin Stan
Lock	Sandu Ciorascu
Lock	Constantin Cojocariu
Flanker	Gheorghe Dinu
Flanker	Andrei Guranescu
Number 8	Haralambie Dumitras (c)
Scrum-half	Daniel Neaga
Fly-half	Neculai Nichitean
Right Wing	Nicolae Racean
Centre	Adrian Lungu
Centre	George Sava
Left Wing	Catalin Sasu
Full-back	Marian Dumitru
Referee	Peard LJ

Points Scorers
France

Name	Tries	Conv	Pen K	Drop G	Points
Camberabero D	0	1	4	0	14
Lafond J-B	1	0	0	0	4
Roumat O	1	0	0	0	4
Saint-Andre PG	1	0	0	0	4
Penalty Try	1	0	0	0	4

Romania

Name	Tries	Conv	Pen K	Drop G	Points
Nichitean N	0	0	1	0	3

**Pool 4, Second Match
Canada v Fiji: 13-3
5 October 1991
Stade Jean Dauger, Bayonne**

Players
Canada

Prop	Eddie Evans
Hooker	David Speirs
Prop	Dan Jackart
Lock	Norm Hadley
Lock	John Robertsen
Flanker	Alan Charron
Flanker	Gord MacKinnon
Number 8	Glen Ennis (c)
Scrum-half	Chris Tynan
Fly-half	Gareth Rees
Right Wing	Steve Gray
Centre	John Lecky
Centre	Christian Stewart
Left Wing	Pat Palmer
Full-back	Scott Stewart

Fiji

Prop	Epeli Naituvau
Hooker	Salacieli Naivilawasa
Prop	Mosese Taga (c)
Lock	Samuela Domoni
Lock	Laitia Savai
Flanker	Alifereti Dere
Flanker	Laisenia Katonawale
Number 8	Tamovutoakula
Scrum-half	Pauliasi Tabulutu
Fly-half	Waisale Serevi
Right Wing	Tomasi Lovo
Centre	Savenaca Aria
Centre	Noa Nadruku
Left Wing	Filimoni Seru
Full-back	Severo Koroduadua
Reserve	Dranivesi Baleiwei
Referee	Fitzgerald KVJ

Points Scorers
Canada

Name	Tries	Conv	Pen K	Drop G	Points
Rees GL	0	0	3	0	9
Stewart DS	1	0	0	0	4

Fiji

Name	Tries	Conv	Pen K	Drop G	Points
Serevi WT	0	0	0	1	3

Pool 4, Third Match
France v Fiji: 33-9
8 October 1991
Stade les Diguieres, Grenoble

Players

France

Prop	Gregoire Lascube
Hooker	Philippe Marocco
Prop	Pascal Ondarts
Lock	Jean-Marie Cadieu
Lock	Olivier Roumat
Flanker	Laurent Cabannes
Flanker	Eric Champ
Number 8	Abdelatif Benazzi
Scrum-half	Fabien Galthie
Fly-half	Didier Camberabero
Right Wing	Jean-Baptiste Lafond
Centre	Franck Mesnel
Centre	Philippe Sella
Left Wing	Philippe Saint-Andre
Full-back	Serge Blanco (c)

Prop	Mosese Taga (c)
Hooker	Dranivesi Baleiwei
Prop	Naibuka Vuli
Lock	Samuela Domoni
Lock	Laitia Savai
Flanker	Alifereti Dere
Flanker	Pita Naruma
Number 8	Tamovutoakula
Scrum-half	Mosese Vosanibole
Fly-half	Waisale Serevi
Right Wing	Tomasi Lovo
Centre	Savenaca Aria
Centre	Kalaveti Naisoro
Left Wing	Filimoni Seru
Full-back	Severo Koroduadua
Reserves	Laisenia Katonawale, Pauliasi Tabulutu, Peni Volavola

Referee	Bevan WD

Points Scorers

France

Name	Tries	Conv	Pen K	Drop G	Points
Camberabero D	1	3	1	0	13
Lafond J-B	3	0	0	0	12
Sella P	2	0	0	0	8

Fiji

Name	Tries	Conv	Pen K	Drop G	Points
Koroduadua S	0	1	1	0	5
Naruma P	1	0	0	0	4

Pool 4, Fourth Match
Canada v Romania: 19-11
9 October 1991
Stade Municipal, Toulouse

Players

Canada

Prop	Eddie Evans
Hooker	Karl Svoboda
Prop	Dan Jackart
Lock	Norm Hadley
Lock	Ron Vanden Brink
Flanker	Bruce Breen
Flanker	Gord MacKinnon
Number 8	Glen Ennis
Scrum-half	John Graf
Fly-half	Gareth Rees
Right Wing	Pat Palmer
Centre	John Lecky
Centre	Christian Stewart
Left Wing	Scott Stewart
Full-back	Mark Wyatt (c)

Romania

Prop	Gheorghe Leonte
Hooker	Gheorghe Ion
Prop	Constantin Stan
Lock	Sandu Ciorascu
Lock	Constantin Cojocariu
Flanker	Gheorghe Dinu
Flanker	Ioan Doja
Number 8	Haralambie Dumitras (c)
Scrum-half	Daniel Neaga
Fly-half	Neculai Nichitean
Right Wing	Nicolae Racean
Centre	Nicolae Fulina
Centre	Adrian Lungu
Left Wing	Catalin Sasu
Full-back	Marian Dumitru
Reserves	Tiberiu Brinza, George Sava, Gabriel Vlad
Referee	Macneill AR

Points Scorers

Canada

Name	Tries	Conv	Pen K	Drop G	Points
Ennis GD	1	0	0	0	4
MacKinnon GI	1	0	0	0	4
Rees GL	0	0	0	1	3
Wyatt MA	0	1	2	0	8

Romania

Name	Tries	Conv	Pen K	Drop G	Points
Lungu A	1	0	0	0	4
Nichitean N	0	0	1	0	3
Sasu C	1	0	0	0	4

Pool 4, Fifth Match
Romania v Fiji: 17-15
12 October 1991
Stade Municipal des Sports, Brive

Players
Romania
Prop	Constantin Stan
Hooker	Gheorghe Ion
Prop	Gabriel Vlad
Lock	Sandu Ciorascu
Lock	Constantin Cojocariu
Flanker	Gheorghe Dinu
Flanker	Micusor Marin
Number 8	Haralambie Dumitras (c)
Scrum-half	Daniel Neaga
Fly-half	Neculai Nichitean
Right Wing	Lician Colceriu
Centre	Nicolae Fulina
Centre	Adrian Lungu
Left Wing	Catalin Sasu
Full-back	Nicolae Racean
Reserve	Ilie Ivancuic

Fiji
Prop	Peni Volavola
Hooker	Dranivesi Baleiwei
Prop	Naibuka Vuli
Lock	Aisake Nadolo
Lock	Laitia Savai
Flanker	Alifereti Dere (c)
Flanker	Tamovutoakula
Number 8	Max Olsson
Scrum-half	Pauliasi Tabulutu
Fly-half	Tomasi Rabaka
Right Wing	Filimoni Seru
Centre	Kalaveti Naisoro
Centre	Noa Nadruku
Left Wing	Tevita Vonolagi
Full-back	Opeti Turuva
Reserves	Epeli Naituvau, Pita Naruma
Referee	Doyle OE

Points Scorers
Romania
Name	Tries	Conv	Pen K	Drop G	Points
Dumitras HT	1	0	0	0	4
Ion G	1	0	0	0	4
Nichitean N	0	0	1	0	3
Racean N	0	1	0	0	2
Sasu C	1	0	0	0	4

Fiji
Name	Tries	Conv	Pen K	Drop G	Points
Rabaka TM	0	0	0	2	6
Turuva O	0	0	2	1	9

Pool 4, Sixth Match
France v Canada: 19-13
13 October 1991
Stade Armandie, Agen

Players

France

Prop	Gregoire Lascube
Hooker	Philippe Marocco
Prop	Pascal Ondarts
Lock	Jean-Marie Cadieu
Lock	Olivier Roumat
Flanker	Laurent Cabannes
Flanker	Eric Champ
Number 8	Abdelatif Benazzi
Scrum-half	Fabien Galthie
Fly-half	Didier Camberabero
Right Wing	Jean-Baptiste Lafond
Centre	Franck Mesnel
Centre	Philippe Sella
Left Wing	Philippe Saint-Andre
Full-back	Serge Blanco (c)
Reserves	Thierry Lacroix, Jean-Luc Sadourny

Canada

Prop	Eddie Evans
Hooker	Karl Svoboda
Prop	Dan Jackart
Lock	Norm Hadley
Lock	John Robertsen
Flanker	Alan Charron
Flanker	Gord MacKinnon
Number 8	Glen Ennis
Scrum-half	Chris Tynan
Fly-half	Gareth Rees
Right Wing	Steve Gray
Centre	Christian Stewart
Centre	Tom Woods
Left Wing	Pat Palmer
Full-back	Mark Wyatt (c)
Reserves	Scott Stewart, Ron Vanden Brink
Referee	Hilditch SR

Points Scorers

France

Name	Tries	Conv	Pen K	Drop G	Points
Camberabero D	0	1	1	0	5
Lafond J-B	1	0	0	0	4
Lacroix T	0	0	2	0	6
Saint-Andre PG	1	0	0	0	4

Canada

Name	Tries	Conv	Pen K	Drop G	Points
Rees GL	0	0	1	1	6
Wyatt MA	1	0	1	0	7

First Quarter-Final
Scotland v Western Samoa: 28-6
19 October 1991
Murrayfield, Edinburgh

Players

Scotland

Prop	Paul Burnell
Hooker	John Allan
Prop	David Sole (c)
Lock	Chris Gray
Lock	Doddie Weir
Flanker	Finlay Calder
Flanker	John Jeffrey
Number 8	Derek White
Scrum-half	Gary Armstrong
Fly-half	Craig Chalmers
Right Wing	Tony Stanger
Centre	Scott Hastings
Centre	Graham Shiel
Left Wing	Iwan Tukalo
Full-back	Gavin Hastings

Western Samoa

Prop	Vili Alalatoa
Hooker	Stan To'omalatai
Prop	Peter Fatialofa (c)
Lock	Mark Birtwistle
Lock	Eddie Ioane
Flanker	Apollo Perelini
Flanker	Sila Vaifale
Number 8	Pat Lam
Scrum-half	Mathew Vaea
Fly-half	Stephen Bachop
Right Wing	Brian Lima
Centre	Frank Bunce
Centre	To'o Vaega
Left Wing	Timo Tagaloa
Full-back	Andrew Aiolupo
Referee	Bevan WD

Points Scorers

Scotland

Name	Tries	Conv	Pen K	Drop G	Points
Hastings AG	0	2	4	0	16
Jeffrey J	2	0	0	0	8
Stanger AG	1	0	0	0	4

Western Samoa

Name	Tries	Conv	Pen K	Drop G	Points
Bachop SJ	0	0	0	1	3
Vaea M	0	0	1	0	3

Second Quarter-Final
France v England: 10-19
19 October 1991
Parc des Princes, Paris

Players
France

Prop	Gregoire Lascube
Hooker	Philippe Marocco
Prop	Pascal Ondarts
Lock	Jean-Marie Cadieu
Lock	Olivier Roumat
Flanker	Laurent Cabannes
Flanker	Eric Champ
Number 8	Marc Cecillon
Scrum-half	Fabien Galthie
Fly-half	Thierry Lacroix
Right Wing	Jean-Baptiste Lafond
Centre	Franck Mesnel
Centre	Philippe Sella
Left Wing	Philippe Saint-Andre
Full-back	Serge Blanco (c)

England

Prop	Jason Leonard
Hooker	Brian Moore
Prop	Jeff Probyn
Lock	Paul Ackford
Lock	Wade Dooley
Flanker	Mickey Skinner
Flanker	Peter Winterbottom
Number 8	Mike Teague
Scrum-half	Richard Hill
Fly-half	Rob Andrew
Right Wing	Nigel Heslop
Centre	Will Carling (c)
Centre	Jerry Guscott
Left Wing	Rory Underwood
Full-back	Jon Webb
Referee	Bishop DJ

Points Scorers
France

Name	Tries	Conv	Pen K	Drop G	Points
Lafond J-B	1	0	0	0	4
Lacroix T	0	0	2	0	6

England

Name	Tries	Conv	Pen K	Drop G	Points
Carling WDC	1	0	0	0	4
Underwood R	1	0	0	0	4
Webb JM	0	1	3	0	11

Third Quarter-Final
Ireland v Australia: 18-19
20 October 1991
Lansdowne Road, Dublin

Players

Ireland

Prop	Des Fitzgerald
Hooker	Steve Smith
Prop	Nick Popplewell
Lock	Neil Francis
Lock	Donal Lenihan
Flanker	Gordon Hamilton
Flanker	Philip Matthews (c)
Number 8	Brian Robinson
Scrum-half	Rob Saunders
Fly-half	Ralph Keyes
Right Wing	Jack Clarke
Centre	David Curtis
Centre	Brendan Mullin
Left Wing	Simon Geoghegan
Full-back	Jim Staples

Australia

Prop	Tony Daly
Hooker	Phil Kearns
Prop	Ewen McKenzie
Lock	John Eales
Lock	Rod McCall
Flanker	Jeff Miller
Flanker	Simon Poidevin
Number 8	Willie Ofahengaue
Scrum-half	Nick Farr-Jones (c)
Fly-half	Michael Lynagh
Right Wing	David Campese
Centre	Tim Horan
Centre	Jason Little
Left Wing	Bob Egerton
Full-back	Marty Roebuck
Reserve	Peter Slattery
Referee	Fleming JM

Points Scorers

Ireland

Name	Tries	Conv	Pen K	Drop G	Points
Hamilton GF	1	0	0	0	4
Keyes RP	0	1	3	1	14

Australia

Name	Tries	Conv	Pen K	Drop G	Points
Campese DI	2	0	0	0	8
Lynagh MP	1	2	1	0	11

Fourth Quarter-Final
Canada v New Zealand: 13-29
20 October 1991
Lille

Players
Canada

Prop	Eddie Evans
Hooker	David Speirs
Prop	Paul Szabo
Lock	Norm Hadley
Lock	Ron Vanden Brink
Flanker	Alan Charron
Flanker	Gord MacKinnon
Number 8	Glen Ennis
Scrum-half	Chris Tynan
Fly-half	Gareth Rees
Right Wing	Steve Gray
Centre	Christian Stewart
Centre	Tom Woods
Left Wing	Scott Stewart
Full-back	Mark Wyatt (c)

New Zealand

Prop	Richard Loe
Hooker	Sean Fitzpatrick
Prop	Steven McDowell
Lock	Ian Jones
Lock	Gary Whetton (c)
Flanker	Paul Henderson
Flanker	Alan Whetton
Number 8	Zinzan Brooke
Scrum-half	Graeme Bachop
Fly-half	Grant Fox
Right Wing	John Kirwan
Centre	Craig Innes
Centre	Bernie McCahill
Left Wing	Inga Tuigamala
Full-back	John Timu
Referee	Howard FA

Points Scorers
Canada

Name	Tries	Conv	Pen K	Drop G	Points
Charron AJ	1	0	0	0	4
Rees GL	0	1	0	0	2
Tynan CJC	1	0	0	0	4
Wyatt MA	0	0	1	0	3

New Zealand

Name	Tries	Conv	Pen K	Drop G	Points
Brooke ZV	1	0	0	0	4
Fox GJ	0	3	1	0	9
Kirwan JJ	1	0	0	0	4
McCahill BJ	1	0	0	0	4
Timu JKR	2	0	0	0	8

First Semi-Final
Scotland v England: 6-9
26 October 1991
Murrayfield, Edinburgh

Players
Scotland

Position	Player
Prop	Paul Burnell
Hooker	John Allan
Prop	David Sole (c)
Lock	Chris Gray
Lock	Doddie Weir
Flanker	Finlay Calder
Flanker	John Jeffrey
Number 8	Derek White
Scrum-half	Gary Armstrong
Fly-half	Craig Chalmers
Right Wing	Tony Stanger
Centre	Scott Hastings
Centre	Sean Lineen
Left Wing	Iwan Tukalo
Full-back	Gavin Hastings

England

Position	Player
Prop	Jason Leonard
Hooker	Brian Moore
Prop	Jeff Probyn
Lock	Paul Ackford
Lock	Wade Dooley
Flanker	Mickey Skinner
Flanker	Peter Winterbottom
Number 8	Mike Teague
Scrum-half	Richard Hill
Fly-half	Rob Andrew
Right Wing	Simon Halliday
Centre	Will Carling (c)
Centre	Jerry Guscott
Left Wing	Rory Underwood
Full-back	Jon Webb
Referee	Fitzgerald KVJ

Points Scorers
Scotland

Name	Tries	Conv	Pen K	Drop G	Points
Hastings AG	0	0	2	0	6

England

Name	Tries	Conv	Pen K	Drop G	Points
Andrew CR	0	0	0	1	3
Webb JM	0	0	2	0	6

Second Semi-Final
Australia v New Zealand: 16-6
27 October 1991
Lansdowne Road, Dublin

Players

Australia

Prop	Tony Daly
Hooker	Phil Kearns
Prop	Ewen McKenzie
Lock	John Eales
Lock	Rod McCall
Flanker	Willie Ofahengaue
Flanker	Simon Poidevin
Number 8	Troy Coker
Scrum-half	Nick Farr-Jones (c)
Fly-half	Michael Lynagh
Right Wing	David Campese
Centre	Tim Horan
Centre	Jason Little
Left Wing	Bob Egerton
Full-back	Marty Roebuck

New Zealand

Prop	Richard Loe
Hooker	Sean Fitzpatrick
Prop	Steven McDowell
Lock	Ian Jones
Lock	Gary Whetton (c)
Flanker	Mark Carter
Flanker	Alan Whetton
Number 8	Zinzan Brooke
Scrum-half	Graeme Bachop
Fly-half	Grant Fox
Right Wing	John Kirwan
Centre	Craig Innes
Centre	Bernie McCahill
Left Wing	John Timu
Full-back	Kieran Crowley
Referee	Fleming JM

Points Scorers

Australia

Name	Tries	Conv	Pen K	Drop G	Points
Campese DI	1	0	0	0	4
Horan TJ	1	0	0	0	4
Lynagh MP	0	1	2	0	8

New Zealand

Name	Tries	Conv	Pen K	Drop G	Points
Fox GJ	0	0	2	0	6

Third Place Play-Off
New Zealand v Scotland: 13-6
30 October 1991
Cardiff Arms Park, Cardiff

Players

New Zealand

Position	Player
Prop	Richard Loe
Hooker	Sean Fitzpatrick
Prop	Steven McDowell
Lock	Ian Jones
Lock	Gary Whetton (c)
Flanker	Andy Earl
Flanker	Michael Jones
Number 8	Zinzan Brooke
Scrum-half	Graeme Bachop
Fly-half	Jon Preston
Right Wing	John Kirwan
Centre	Craig Innes
Centre	Walter Little
Left Wing	Inga Tuigamala
Full-back	Terry Wright
Reserve	Shayne Philpott

Scotland

Position	Player
Prop	Paul Burnell
Hooker	John Allan
Prop	David Sole (c)
Lock	Chris Gray
Lock	Doddie Weir
Flanker	Finlay Calder
Flanker	John Jeffrey
Number 8	Derek White
Scrum-half	Gary Armstrong
Fly-half	Craig Chalmers
Right Wing	Tony Stanger
Centre	Scott Hastings
Centre	Sean Lineen
Left Wing	Iwan Tukalo
Full-back	Gavin Hastings
Reserve	Peter Dods
Referee	Hilditch SR

Points Scorers

New Zealand

Name	Tries	Conv	Pen K	Drop G	Points
Little WK	1	0	0	0	4
Preston JP	0	0	3	0	9

Scotland

Name	Tries	Conv	Pen K	Drop G	Points
Hastings AG	0	0	2	0	6

Final
England v Australia: 6-12
2 November 1991
Twickenham, London

Players

England

Prop	Jason Leonard
Hooker	Brian Moore
Prop	Jeff Probyn
Lock	Paul Ackford
Lock	Wade Dooley
Flanker	Mickey Skinner
Flanker	Peter Winterbottom
Number 8	Mike Teague
Scrum-half	Richard Hill
Fly-half	Rob Andrew
Right Wing	Simon Halliday
Centre	Will Carling (c)
Centre	Jerry Guscott
Left Wing	Rory Underwood
Full-back	Jon Webb

Australia

Prop	Tony Daly
Hooker	Phil Kearns
Prop	Ewen McKenzie
Lock	John Eales
Lock	Rod McCall
Flanker	Willie Ofahengaue
Flanker	Simon Poidevin
Number 8	Troy Coker
Scrum-half	Nick Farr-Jones (c)
Fly-half	Michael Lynagh
Right Wing	David Campese
Centre	Tim Horan
Centre	Jason Little
Left Wing	Bob Egerton
Full-back	Marty Roebuck
Referee	Bevan WD

Points Scorers

England

Name	Tries	Conv	Pen K	Drop G	Points
Webb JM	0	0	2	0	6

Australia

Name	Tries	Conv	Pen K	Drop G	Points
Daly AJ	1	0	0	0	4
Lynagh MP	0	1	2	0	8

1995

Pool A, First Match
South Africa v Australia: 27-18
25 May 1995
Newlands, Cape Town

Players

South Africa

Prop	Os Du Randt
Hooker	James Dalton
Prop	Balie Swart
Lock	Mark Andrews
Lock	Hannes Strydom
Flanker	Ruben Kruger
Flanker	François Pienaar (c)
Number 8	Rudolf Straeuli
Scrum-half	Joost van der Westhuizen
Fly-half	Joel Stransky
Right Wing	Pieter Hendriks
Centre	Hennie le Roux
Centre	Japie Mulder
Left Wing	James Small
Full-back	Andre Joubert
Reserve	Garry Pagel

Australia

Prop	Dan Crowley
Hooker	Phil Kearns
Prop	Ewen McKenzie
Lock	John Eales
Lock	Rod McCall
Flanker	Willie Ofahengaue
Flanker	David Wilson
Number 8	Tim Gavin
Scrum-half	George Gregan
Fly-half	Michael Lynagh (c)
Right Wing	David Campese
Centre	Dan Herbert
Centre	Jason Little
Left Wing	Damian Smith
Full-back	Matt Pini
Referee	Bevan WD

Points Scorers

South Africa

Name	Tries	Conv	Pen K	Drop G	Points
Hendriks P	1	0	0	0	5
Stransky JT	1	1	4	1	22

Australia

Name	Tries	Conv	Pen K	Drop G	Points
Kearns PN	1	0	0	0	5
Lynagh MP	1	1	2	0	13

Pool A, Second Match
Canada v Romania: 34-3
26 May 1995
Boet Erasmus Stadium, Port Elizabeth

Players

Canada

Prop	Eddie Evans
Hooker	Mark Cardinal
Prop	Rod Snow
Lock	Glen Ennis
Lock	Mike James
Flanker	Alan Charron
Flanker	Ian Gordon
Number 8	Colin McKenzie
Scrum-half	John Graf
Fly-half	Gareth Rees (c)
Right Wing	Dave Lougheed
Centre	Steve Gray
Centre	Christian Stewart
Left Wing	Winston Stanley
Full-back	Scott Stewart

Romania

Prop	Gheorghe Leonte
Hooker	Ionel Negreci
Prop	Gabriel Vlad
Lock	Sandu Ciorascu (c)
Lock	Constantin Cojocariu
Flanker	Alexandru Gealapu
Flanker	Traian Oroian
Number 8	Ovidiu Slusariuc
Scrum-half	Daniel Neaga
Fly-half	Neculai Nichitean
Right Wing	Lician Colceriu
Centre	Romeo Gontineac
Centre	Nicolae Racean
Left Wing	Ionel Rotaru
Full-back	Gheorghe Solomie
Reserves	Vasile Flutur, Ilie Ivancuic
Referee	Hawke CJ

Points Scorers

Canada

Name	Tries	Conv	Pen K	Drop G	Points
Charron AJ	1	0	0	0	5
McKenzie JC	1	0	0	0	5
Rees GL	0	2	4	1	19
Snow RGA	1	0	0	0	5

Romania

Name	Tries	Conv	Pen K	Drop G	Points
Nichitean N	0	0	1	0	3

Pool A, Third Match
South Africa v Romania: 21-8
30 May 1995
Newlands, Cape Town

Players

South Africa

Prop	Marius Hurter
Hooker	Chris Rossouw
Prop	Garry Pagel
Lock	Krynauw Otto
Lock	Kobus Wiese
Flanker	Robbie Brink
Flanker	Ruben Kruger
Number 8	Adriaan Richter (c)
Scrum-half	Johan Roux
Fly-half	Hennie le Roux
Right Wing	Pieter Hendriks
Centre	Christiaan Scholtz
Centre	Brendan Venter
Left Wing	James Small
Full-back	Gavin Johnson
Reserve	Joel Stransky

Romania

Prop	Gheorghe Leonte
Hooker	Ionel Negreci
Prop	Gabriel Vlad
Lock	Sandu Ciorascu
Lock	Constantin Cojocariu
Flanker	Alexandru Gealapu
Flanker	Andrei Guranescu
Number 8	Tiberiu Brinza (c)
Scrum-half	Vasile Flutur
Fly-half	Ilie Ivancuic
Right Wing	Lician Colceriu
Centre	Romeo Gontineac
Centre	Nicolae Racean
Left Wing	Gheorghe Solomie
Full-back	Vasile Brici
Reserve	Valere Tufa
Referee	McCartney KW

Points Scorers

South Africa

Name	Tries	Conv	Pen K	Drop G	Points
Johnson GK	0	1	3	0	11
Richter AH	2	0	0	0	10

Romania

Name	Tries	Conv	Pen K	Drop G	Points
Guranescu A	1	0	0	0	5
Ivancuic I	0	0	1	0	3

Pool A, Fourth Match
Australia v Canada: 27-11
31 May 1995
Boet Erasmus Stadium, Port Elizabeth

Players

Australia

Prop	Tony Daly
Hooker	Phil Kearns
Prop	Mark Hartill
Lock	John Eales
Lock	Warwick Waugh
Flanker	Willie Ofahengaue
Flanker	Ilie Tabua Tamanivalu
Number 8	Tim Gavin
Scrum-half	Peter Slattery
Fly-half	Michael Lynagh (c)
Right Wing	David Campese
Centre	Tim Horan
Centre	Jason Little
Left Wing	Joe Roff
Full-back	Matthew Burke
Reserves	Michael Foley, George Gregan, Ewen McKenzie

Canada

Prop	Eddie Evans
Hooker	Karl Svoboda
Prop	Rod Snow
Lock	Mike James
Lock	Gareth Rowlands
Flanker	John Hutchinson
Flanker	Gord MacKinnon
Number 8	Alan Charron
Scrum-half	John Graf
Fly-half	Gareth Rees (c)
Right Wing	Dave Lougheed
Centre	Steve Gray
Centre	Christian Stewart
Left Wing	Winston Stanley
Full-back	Scott Stewart
Reserve	Glen Ennis
Referee	Robin P

Points Scorers

Australia

Name	Tries	Conv	Pen K	Drop G	Points
Lynagh MP	1	3	2	0	17
Roff JWC	1	0	0	0	5
Tabua Tamanivalu T	1	0	0	0	5

Canada

Name	Tries	Conv	Pen K	Drop G	Points
Charron AJ	1	0	0	0	5
Rees GL	0	0	2	0	6

Pool A, Fifth Match
South Africa v Canada: 20-0
3 June 1995
Boet Erasmus Stadium, Port Elizabeth

Players

South Africa

Prop	Marius Hurter
Hooker	James Dalton
Prop	Garry Pagel
Lock	Hannes Strydom
Lock	Kobus Wiese
Flanker	Robbie Brink
Flanker	François Pienaar (c)
Number 8	Adriaan Richter
Scrum-half	Johan Roux
Fly-half	Joel Stransky
Right Wing	Pieter Hendriks
Centre	Christiaan Scholtz
Centre	Brendan Venter
Left Wing	Gavin Johnson
Full-back	Andre Joubert
Reserves	Hennie le Roux, Krynauw Otto, Joost van der Westhuizen

Canada

Prop	Eddie Evans
Hooker	Mark Cardinal
Prop	Rod Snow
Lock	Alan Charron
Lock	Glen Ennis
Flanker	Ian Gordon
Flanker	Gord MacKinnon
Number 8	Colin McKenzie
Scrum-half	John Graf
Fly-half	Gareth Rees (c)
Right Wing	Dave Lougheed
Centre	Steve Gray
Centre	Christian Stewart
Left Wing	Winston Stanley
Full-back	Scott Stewart
Reserves	John Hutchinson, Chris Michaluk
Referee	McHugh DTM

Points Scorers

South Africa

Name	Tries	Conv	Pen K	Drop G	Points
Richter AH	2	0	0	0	10
Stransky JT	0	2	2	0	10

Pool A, Sixth Match
Australia v Romania: 42-3
3 June 1995
Danie Craven Stadium, Stellenbosch

Players

Australia

Prop	Tony Daly
Hooker	Michael Foley
Prop	Ewen McKenzie
Lock	John Eales
Lock	Rod McCall (c)
Flanker	Ilie Tabua Tamanivalu
Flanker	David Wilson
Number 8	Tim Gavin
Scrum-half	George Gregan
Fly-half	Scott Bowen
Right Wing	Joe Roff
Centre	Dan Herbert
Centre	Tim Horan
Left Wing	Damian Smith
Full-back	Matthew Burke
Reserves	Daniel Manu, Matt Pini, Peter Slattery

Romania

Prop	Gheorghe Leonte
Hooker	Ionel Negreci
Prop	Gabriel Vlad
Lock	Sandu Ciorascu
Lock	Constantin Cojocariu
Flanker	Alexandru Gealapu
Flanker	Andrei Guranescu
Number 8	Tiberiu Brinza (c)
Scrum-half	Vasile Flutur
Fly-half	Ilie Ivancuic
Right Wing	Lician Colceriu
Centre	Romeo Gontineac
Centre	Nicolae Racean
Left Wing	Gheorghe Solomie
Full-back	Vasile Brici
Reserves	Adrian Lungu, Valere Tufa
Referee	Saito N

Points Scorers

Australia

Name	Tries	Conv	Pen K	Drop G	Points
Burke MC	1	2	0	0	9
Eales JA	0	4	0	0	8
Foley MA	1	0	0	0	5
Roff JWC	2	0	0	0	10
Smith DPP	1	0	0	0	5
Wilson DJ	1	0	0	0	5

Romania

Name	Tries	Conv	Pen K	Drop G	Points
Ivancuic I	0	0	0	1	3

Pool B, First Match
Argentina v England: 18-24
27 May 1995
King's Park, Durban

Players

Argentina

Prop	Matias Corral
Hooker	Federico Mendez
Prop	Patricio Noriega
Lock	German Llanes
Lock	Pedro Sporleder
Flanker	Rolando Martin
Flanker	Cristian Viel Temperley
Number 8	Jose Santamarina
Scrum-half	Rodrigo Crexell
Fly-half	Lisandro Arbizu
Right Wing	Diego Albanese
Centre	Diego Cuesta Silva
Centre	Sebastian Salvat (c)
Left Wing	Martin Teran Nougues
Full-back	Ezequiel Jurado
Reserve	Sebastian Irazoqui

England

Prop	Jason Leonard
Hooker	Brian Moore
Prop	Victor Ubogu
Lock	Martin Bayfield
Lock	Martin Johnson
Flanker	Ben Clarke
Flanker	Tim Rodber
Number 8	Steve Ojomoh
Scrum-half	Dewi Morris
Fly-half	Rob Andrew
Right Wing	Rory Underwood
Centre	Will Carling (c)
Centre	Jerry Guscott
Left Wing	Tony Underwood
Full-back	Mike Catt
Reserves	Neil Back, Phil de Glanville
Referee	Fleming JM

Points Scorers

Argentina

Name	Tries	Conv	Pen K	Drop G	Points
Arbizu L	1	1	2	0	13
Noriega EP	1	0	0	0	5

England

Name	Tries	Conv	Pen K	Drop G	Points
Andrew CR	0	0	6	2	24

Pool B, Second Match
Italy v Western Samoa: 18-42
27 May 1995
Basil Kenyon Stadium, East London

Players
Italy

Prop	Massimo Cuttitta (c)
Hooker	Carlo Orlandi
Prop	Franco Properzi-Curti
Lock	Roberto Favaro
Lock	Pierpaolo Pedroni
Flanker	Orazio Arancio
Flanker	Julian Gardner
Number 8	Carlo Checchinato
Scrum-half	Alessandro Troncon
Fly-half	Diego Dominguez
Right Wing	Marcello Cuttitta
Centre	Massimo Bonomi
Centre	Ivan Francescato
Left Wing	Massimo Ravazzolo
Full-back	Paolo Vaccari

Western Samoa

Prop	Peter Fatialofa (c)
Hooker	Tala Leiasamaiva'o
Prop	Mike Mika
Lock	Lio Falaniko
Lock	Daryl Williams
Flanker	Junior Paramore
Flanker	Sila Vaifale
Number 8	Shem Tatupu
Scrum-half	Tu Nu'uali'itia
Fly-half	Darren Kellett
Right Wing	George Harder
Centre	Tupo Fa'amasino
Centre	To'o Vaega
Left Wing	Brian Lima
Full-back	Mike Umaga
Reserve	Potu Leavasa
Referee	Dume J

Points Scorers
Italy

Name	Tries	Conv	Pen K	Drop G	Points
Cuttitta M	1	0	0	0	5
Dominguez D	0	1	1	1	8
Vaccari P	1	0	0	0	5

Western Samoa

Name	Tries	Conv	Pen K	Drop G	Points
Harder G	2	0	0	0	10
Kellett DJ	1	3	2	0	17
Lima BP	2	0	0	0	10
Tatupu SJ	1	0	0	0	5

Pool B, Third Match
Western Samoa v Argentina: 32-26
30 May 1995
Basil Kenyon Stadium, East London

Players

Western Samoa

Prop	George Latu
Hooker	Tala Leiasamaiva'o
Prop	Mike Mika
Lock	Lio Falaniko
Lock	Potu Leavasa
Flanker	Junior Paramore
Flanker	Shem Tatupu
Number 8	Pat Lam (c)
Scrum-half	Tu Nu'uali'itia
Fly-half	Darren Kellett
Right Wing	George Harder
Centre	Tupo Fa'amasino
Centre	To'o Vaega
Left Wing	Brian Lima
Full-back	Mike Umaga
Reserves	Peter Fatialofa, George Leaupepe, Fata Sini

Argentina

Prop	Matias Corral
Hooker	Federico Mendez
Prop	Patricio Noriega
Lock	German Llanes
Lock	Pedro Sporleder
Flanker	Rolando Martin
Flanker	Cristian Viel Temperley
Number 8	Jose Santamarina
Scrum-half	Rodrigo Crexell
Fly-half	Jose Cilley
Right Wing	Diego Cuesta Silva
Centre	Lisandro Arbizu
Centre	Sebastian Salvat (c)
Left Wing	Martin Teran Nougues
Full-back	Ezequiel Jurado
Referee	Bishop DJ

Points Scorers

Western Samoa

Name	Tries	Conv	Pen K	Drop G	Points
Harder G	1	0	0	0	5
Kellett DJ	0	1	5	0	17
Lam PR	1	0	0	0	5
Leaupepe GE	1	0	0	0	5

Argentina

Name	Tries	Conv	Pen K	Drop G	Points
Cilley JL	0	2	4	0	16
Crexell RH	1	0	0	0	5
Penalty Try	1	0	0	0	5

Pool B, Fourth Match
England v Italy: 27-20
31 May 1995
King's Park, Durban

Players

England

Prop	Jason Leonard
Hooker	Brian Moore
Prop	Graham Rowntree
Lock	Martin Bayfield
Lock	Martin Johnson
Flanker	Neil Back
Flanker	Tim Rodber
Number 8	Ben Clarke
Scrum-half	Kyran Bracken
Fly-half	Rob Andrew (c)
Right Wing	Rory Underwood
Centre	Phil de Glanville
Centre	Jerry Guscott
Left Wing	Tony Underwood
Full-back	Mike Catt

Italy

Prop	Massimo Cuttitta (c)
Hooker	Carlo Orlandi
Prop	Franco Properzi-Curti
Lock	Mark Giacheri
Lock	Pierpaolo Pedroni
Flanker	Orazio Arancio
Flanker	Andrea Sgorlon
Number 8	Julian Gardner
Scrum-half	Alessandro Troncon
Fly-half	Diego Dominguez
Right Wing	Mario Gerosa
Centre	Stefano Bordon
Centre	Ivan Francescato
Left Wing	Paolo Vaccari
Full-back	Luigi Troiani
Referee	Hilditch SR

Points Scorers

England

Name	Tries	Conv	Pen K	Drop G	Points
Andrew CR	0	1	5	0	17
Underwood R	1	0	0	0	5
Underwood T	1	0	0	0	5

Italy

Name	Tries	Conv	Pen K	Drop G	Points
Cuttitta M	1	0	0	0	5
Dominguez D	0	2	2	0	10
Vaccari P	1	0	0	0	5

Pool B, Fifth Match
England v Western Samoa: 44-22
4 June 1995
King's Park, Durban

Players
England

Prop	Graham Rowntree
Hooker	Graham Dawe
Prop	Victor Ubogu
Lock	Martin Johnson
Lock	Richard West
Flanker	Neil Back
Flanker	Steve Ojomoh
Number 8	Dean Richards
Scrum-half	Dewi Morris
Fly-half	Mike Catt
Right Wing	Ian Hunter
Centre	Will Carling (c)
Centre	Phil de Glanville
Left Wing	Rory Underwood
Full-back	Jon Callard
Reserves	Kyran Bracken, Damian Hopley, John Mallett, Brian Moore, Tim Rodber

Western Samoa

Prop	George Latu
Hooker	Tala Leiasamaiva'o
Prop	Mike Mika
Lock	Lio Falaniko
Lock	Daryl Williams
Flanker	Malaki Iupeli
Flanker	Potu Leavasa
Number 8	Pat Lam (c)
Scrum-half	Tu Nu'uali'itia
Fly-half	Esera Puleitu
Right Wing	George Leaupepe
Centre	Tupo Fa'amasino
Centre	To'o Vaega
Left Wing	Brian Lima
Full-back	Mike Umaga
Reserves	Peter Fatialofa, Saini Lemamea, Fata Sini, Shem Tatupu
Referee	Robin P

Points Scorers
England

Name	Tries	Conv	Pen K	Drop G	Points
Back NA	1	0	0	0	5
Callard JEB	0	3	5	0	21
Catt MJ	0	0	0	1	3
Underwood R	2	0	0	0	10
Penalty Try	1	0	0	0	5

Western Samoa

Name	Tries	Conv	Pen K	Drop G	Points
Fa'amasino T	0	2	1	0	7
Sini J	2	0	0	0	10
Umaga MT	1	0	0	0	5

Pool B, Sixth Match
Italy v Argentina: 31-25
4 June 1995
Basil Kenyon Stadium, East London

Players
Italy

Prop	Matias Corral
Hooker	Federico Mendez
Prop	Patricio Noriega
Lock	German Llanes
Lock	Pedro Sporleder
Flanker	Rolando Martin
Flanker	Cristian Viel Temperley
Number 8	Jose Santamarina
Scrum-half	Rodrigo Crexell
Fly-half	Jose Cilley
Right Wing	Diego Cuesta Silva
Centre	Lisandro Arbizu
Centre	Sebastian Salvat (c)
Left Wing	Martin Teran Nougues
Full-back	Ezequiel Jurado

Argentina

Prop	Massimo Cuttitta (c)
Hooker	Carlo Orlandi
Prop	Franco Properzi-Curti
Lock	Mark Giacheri
Lock	Pierpaolo Pedroni
Flanker	Orazio Arancio
Flanker	Andrea Sgorlon
Number 8	Julian Gardner
Scrum-half	Alessandro Troncon
Fly-half	Diego Dominguez
Right Wing	Mario Gerosa
Centre	Stefano Bordon
Centre	Ivan Francescato
Left Wing	Paolo Vaccari
Full-back	Luigi Troiani
Referee	Thomas C

Points Scorers
Italy

Name	Tries	Conv	Pen K	Drop G	Points
Dominguez D	1	2	4	0	21
Gerosa MO	1	0	0	0	5
Vaccari P	1	0	0	0	5

Argentina

Name	Tries	Conv	Pen K	Drop G	Points
Cilley JL	1	1	1	0	10
Corral ME	1	0	0	0	5
Martin RA	1	0	0	0	5
Penalty Try	1	0	0	0	5

Pool C, First Match
Wales v Japan: 57–10
27 May 1995
Free State Stadium, Bloemfontein

Players

Wales

Prop	John Davies
Hooker	Garin Jenkins
Prop	Mike Griffiths
Lock	Derwyn Jones
Lock	Gareth Llewellyn
Flanker	Stuart Davies
Flanker	Hemi Taylor
Number 8	Emyr Lewis
Scrum-half	Andrew Moore
Fly-half	Adrian Davies
Right Wing	Ieuan Evans
Centre	Mike Hall (c)
Centre	Neil Jenkins
Left Wing	Gareth Thomas
Full-back	Tony Clement
Reserves	David Evans, Stuart Roy

Japan

Prop	Osamu Ota
Hooker	Masahiro Kunda (c)
Prop	Kazuaki Takahashi
Lock	Bruce Ferguson
Lock	Yoshihiko Sakuraba
Flanker	Hiroyuki Kajihara
Flanker	Sinali-Tui Latu
Number 8	Sione-Tupo Latu Mailangi
Scrum-half	Masami Horikoshi
Fly-half	Seiji Hirao
Right Wing	Terunori Masuho
Centre	Yukio Motoki
Centre	Akira Yoshida
Left Wing	Lopeti Oto
Full-back	Tsutomu Matsuda
Referee	Sklar E

Points Scorers

Wales

Name	Tries	Conv	Pen K	Drop G	Points
Evans IC	2	0	0	0	10
Jenkins NR	0	5	4	0	22
Moore AP	1	0	0	0	5
Taylor HT	1	0	0	0	5
Thomas G	3	0	0	0	15

Japan

Name	Tries	Conv	Pen K	Drop G	Points
Oto L	2	0	0	0	10

Pool C, Second Match
Ireland v New Zealand: 19-43
27 May 1995
Ellis Park, Johannesburg

Players
Ireland

Prop	Gary Halpin
Hooker	Terry Kingston (c)
Prop	Nick Popplewell
Lock	Neil Francis
Lock	Gabriel Fulcher
Flanker	David Corkery
Flanker	Denis McBride
Number 8	Paddy Johns
Scrum-half	Michael Bradley
Fly-half	Eric Elwood
Right Wing	Simon Geoghegan
Centre	Jonathan Bell
Centre	Brendan Mullin
Left Wing	Richard Wallace
Full-back	Jim Staples
Reserve	Maurice Field

New Zealand

Prop	Olo Brown
Hooker	Sean Fitzpatrick (c)
Prop	Craig Dowd
Lock	Ian Jones
Lock	Blair Larsen
Flanker	Jamie Joseph
Flanker	Josh Kronfeld
Number 8	Mike Brewer
Scrum-half	Graeme Bachop
Fly-half	Andrew Mehrtens
Right Wing	Jonah Lomu
Centre	Frank Bunce
Centre	Walter Little
Left Wing	Jeff Wilson
Full-back	Glen Osborne
Reserves	Marc Ellis, Norm Hewitt, Kevin Schuler
Referee	Erickson WJ

Points Scorers
Ireland

Name	Tries	Conv	Pen K	Drop G	Points
Corkery SD	1	0	0	0	5
Elwood EP	0	2	0	0	4
Halpin GF	1	0	0	0	5
McBride WD	1	0	0	0	5

New Zealand

Name	Tries	Conv	Pen K	Drop G	Points
Bunce FE	1	0	0	0	5
Kronfeld JA	1	0	0	0	5
Lomu JT	2	0	0	0	10
Mehrtens AP	0	3	4	0	18
Osborne GM	1	0	0	0	5

Pool C, Third Match
Ireland v Japan: 50-28
31 May 1995
Free State Stadium, Bloemfontein

Players
Ireland

Prop	Nick Popplewell (c)
Hooker	Keith Wood
Prop	Paul Wallace
Lock	Neil Francis
Lock	Davy Tweed
Flanker	David Corkery
Flanker	Eddie Halvey
Number 8	Paddy Johns
Scrum-half	Niall Hogan
Fly-half	Paul Burke
Right Wing	Simon Geoghegan
Centre	Maurice Field
Centre	Brendan Mullin
Left Wing	Richard Wallace
Full-back	Conor O'Shea
Reserves	Anthony Foley, Terry Kingston

Japan

Prop	Osamu Ota
Hooker	Masahiro Kunda (c)
Prop	Masanori Takura
Lock	Bruce Ferguson
Lock	Yoshihiko Sakuraba
Flanker	Hiroyuki Kajihara
Flanker	Sinali-Tui Latu
Number 8	Sione-Tupo Latu Mailangi
Scrum-half	Masami Horikoshi
Fly-half	Seiji Hirao
Right Wing	Lopeti Oto
Centre	Yukio Motoki
Centre	Akira Yoshida
Left Wing	Yoshihito Yoshida
Full-back	Tsutomu Matsuda
Reserve	Ko Izawa
Referee	Neethling S

Points Scorers
Ireland

Name	Tries	Conv	Pen K	Drop G	Points
Burke PA	0	6	1	0	15
Corkery SD	1	0	0	0	5
Francis NP	1	0	0	0	5
Geoghegan SP	1	0	0	0	5
Halvey EO	1	0	0	0	5
Hogan NA	1	0	0	0	5
Penalty Try	2	0	0	0	10

Japan

Name	Tries	Conv	Pen K	Drop G	Points
Hirao S	1	0	0	0	5
Izawa K	1	0	0	0	5
Latu S-T	1	0	0	0	5
Takura M	1	0	0	0	5
Yoshida Y	0	4	0	0	8

Pool C, Fourth Match
New Zealand v Wales: 34-9
31 May 1995
Ellis Park, Johannesburg

Players

New Zealand

Prop	Olo Brown
Hooker	Sean Fitzpatrick (c)
Prop	Craig Dowd
Lock	Ian Jones
Lock	Blair Larsen
Flanker	Jamie Joseph
Flanker	Josh Kronfeld
Number 8	Mike Brewer
Scrum-half	Graeme Bachop
Fly-half	Andrew Mehrtens
Right Wing	Marc Ellis
Centre	Frank Bunce
Centre	Walter Little
Left Wing	Jonah Lomu
Full-back	Glen Osborne
Reserve	Eric Rush

Wales

Prop	John Davies
Hooker	Jonathan Humphreys
Prop	Ricky Evans
Lock	Derwyn Jones
Lock	Greg Prosser
Flanker	Mark Bennett
Flanker	Gareth Llewellyn
Number 8	Hemi Taylor
Scrum-half	Robert Jones
Fly-half	Neil Jenkins
Right Wing	Ieuan Evans
Centre	Mike Hall (c)
Centre	Gareth Thomas
Left Wing	Wayne Proctor
Full-back	Tony Clement
Referee	Morrison EF

Points Scorers

New Zealand

Name	Tries	Conv	Pen K	Drop G	Points
Ellis MCG	1	0	0	0	5
Kronfeld JA	1	0	0	0	5
Little WK	1	0	0	0	5
Mehrtens AP	0	2	4	1	19

Wales

Name	Tries	Conv	Pen K	Drop G	Points
Jenkins NR	0	0	2	1	9

Pool C, Fifth Match
Japan v New Zealand: 17-145
4 June 1995
Free State Stadium, Bloemfontein

Players

Japan

Prop	Osamu Ota
Hooker	Masahiro Kunda (c)
Prop	Kazuaki Takahashi
Lock	Bruce Ferguson
Lock	Yoshihiko Sakuraba
Flanker	Ko Izawa
Flanker	Hiroyuki Kajihara
Number 8	Sinali-Tui Latu
Scrum-half	Wataru Murata
Fly-half	Keiji Hirose
Right Wing	Lopeti Oto
Centre	Yukio Motoki
Centre	Akira Yoshida
Left Wing	Yoshihito Yoshida
Full-back	Tsutomu Matsuda
Reserve	Takashi Akatsuka

New Zealand

Prop	Craig Dowd
Hooker	Norm Hewitt
Prop	Richard Loe
Lock	Robin Brooke
Lock	Blair Larsen
Flanker	Paul Henderson (c)
Flanker	Kevin Schuler
Number 8	Zinzan Brooke
Scrum-half	Ant Strachan
Fly-half	Simon Culhane
Right Wing	Eric Rush
Centre	Marc Ellis
Centre	Alama Ieremia
Left Wing	Jeff Wilson
Full-back	Glen Osborne
Reserve	Jamie Joseph
Referee	Gadjovich G

Points Scorers

Japan

Name	Tries	Conv	Pen K	Drop G	Points
Hirose K	0	2	1	0	7
Kajihara H	2	0	0	0	10

New Zealand

Name	Tries	Conv	Pen K	Drop G	Points
Brooke RM	2	0	0	0	10
Culhane SD	1	20	0	0	45
Dowd CW	1	0	0	0	5
Ellis MCG	6	0	0	0	30
Henderson PW	1	0	0	0	5
Ieremia AI	1	0	0	0	5
Loe RW	1	0	0	0	5
Osborne GM	2	0	0	0	10
Rush EJ	3	0	0	0	15
Wilson JW	3	0	0	0	15

Pool C, Sixth Match
Ireland v Wales: 24-23
4 June 1995
Ellis Park, Johannesburg

Players
Ireland

Prop	Gary Halpin
Hooker	Terry Kingston (c)
Prop	Nick Popplewell
Lock	Neil Francis
Lock	Gabriel Fulcher
Flanker	David Corkery
Flanker	Denis McBride
Number 8	Paddy Johns
Scrum-half	Niall Hogan
Fly-half	Eric Elwood
Right Wing	Simon Geoghegan
Centre	Jonathan Bell
Centre	Brendan Mullin
Left Wing	Richard Wallace
Full-back	Conor O'Shea
Reserve	Eddie Halvey

Wales

Prop	John Davies
Hooker	Jonathan Humphreys
Prop	Mike Griffiths
Lock	Derwyn Jones
Lock	Gareth Llewellyn
Flanker	Stuart Davies
Flanker	Hemi Taylor
Number 8	Emyr Lewis
Scrum-half	Robert Jones
Fly-half	Adrian Davies
Right Wing	Ieuan Evans
Centre	Mike Hall (c)
Centre	Neil Jenkins
Left Wing	Gareth Thomas
Full-back	Tony Clement
Reserve	Ricky Evans
Referee	Rogers I

Points Scorers
Ireland

Name	Tries	Conv	Pen K	Drop G	Points
Elwood EP	0	3	1	0	9
Halvey EO	1	0	0	0	5
McBride WD	1	0	0	0	5
Popplewell NJ	1	0	0	0	5

Wales

Name	Tries	Conv	Pen K	Drop G	Points
Davies A	0	0	0	1	3
Humphreys JM	1	0	0	0	5
Jenkins NR	0	2	2	0	10
Taylor HT	1	0	0	0	5

Pool D, First Match
France v Tonga: 38-10
26 May 1995
Loftus Versfeld, Pretoria

Players

France

Prop	Louis Armary
Hooker	Jean-Michel Gonzales
Prop	Philippe Gallart
Lock	Olivier Brouzet
Lock	Olivier Merle
Flanker	Abdelatif Benazzi
Flanker	Philippe Benetton
Number 8	Marc Cecillon
Scrum-half	Aubin Hueber
Fly-half	Yann Delaigue
Right Wing	Emile Ntamack
Centre	Thierry Lacroix
Centre	Philippe Sella
Left Wing	Philippe Saint-Andre (c)
Full-back	Jean-Luc Sadourny
Reserve	Laurent Cabannes

Tonga

Prop	Saili Feao
Hooker	Fololisi Masila
Prop	Tu'akalua Fukofuka
Lock	Willie Lose
Lock	Falamani Mafi
Flanker	'Ipolito Fenukitau
Flanker	Feleti Mahoni
Number 8	Mana 'Otai (c)
Scrum-half	Manu Vunipola
Fly-half	'Elisi Vunipola
Right Wing	Alaska Taufa
Centre	Peneili Latu
Centre	Unuoi Va'enuku
Left Wing	Tevita Va'enuku
Full-back	Sateki Tuipulotu
Reserves	'Inoke Afeaki, Fe'ao Vunipola
Referee	Lander S

Points Scorers

France

Name	Tries	Conv	Pen K	Drop G	Points
Delaigue Y	0	0	0	1	3
Hueber A	1	0	0	0	5
Lacroix T	2	3	3	0	25
Saint-Andre PG	1	0	0	0	5

Tonga

Name	Tries	Conv	Pen K	Drop G	Points
Tuipulotu S	0	1	1	0	5
Va'enuku T	1	0	0	0	5

Pool D, Second Match
Scotland v Ivory Coast: 89-0
26 May 1995
Olympia Park, Rustenburg

Players
Scotland

Prop	Paul Burnell
Hooker	Kevin McKenzie
Prop	Peter Wright
Lock	Stewart Campbell
Lock	Doddie Weir
Flanker	Ian Smith
Flanker	Peter Walton
Number 8	Rob Wainwright
Scrum-half	Bryan Redpath
Fly-half	Craig Chalmers
Right Wing	Craig Joiner
Centre	Graham Shiel
Centre	Tony Stanger
Left Wing	Kenny Logan
Full-back	Gavin Hastings (c)

Ivory Coast

Prop	Ernest Bley
Hooker	Eduard Angoran
Prop	Toussaint Djehi
Lock	Gilbert Bado
Lock	Amidou Kone
Flanker	Isimaila Lassissi
Flanker	Patrice Pere
Number 8	Djakaria Sanoko
Scrum-half	Frederic Dupont
Fly-half	Athanase Dali (c)
Right Wing	Paulin Bouazo
Centre	Lucien Niakou
Centre	Jean Sathiq
Left Wing	Celestin N'Gabala
Full-back	Victor Kouassi
Reserves	Max Brito, Abubacar Camara, Alfred Okou

Points Scorers
Scotland

Name	Tries	Conv	Pen K	Drop G	Points
Hastings G	4	9	2	0	44
Logan K	2	0	0	0	10
Walton P	2	0	0	0	10
Chalmers C	1	0	0	0	5
Stanger T	1	0	0	0	5
Burnell P	1	0	0	0	5
Wright P	1	0	0	0	5
Shiel G	1	0	0	0	5

Pool D, Third Match
Scotland v Tonga: 41-5
30 May 1995
Loftus Versfeld, Pretoria

Players
Scotland

Prop	Dave Hilton
Hooker	Kenny Milne
Prop	Peter Wright
Lock	Damian Cronin
Lock	Doddie Weir
Flanker	Iain Morrison
Flanker	Rob Wainwright
Number 8	Eric Peters
Scrum-half	Derrick Patterson
Fly-half	Craig Chalmers
Right Wing	Craig Joiner
Centre	Scott Hastings
Centre	Ian Jardine
Left Wing	Kenny Logan
Full-back	Gavin Hastings (c)
Reserve	Paul Burnell

Tonga

Prop	Saili Feao
Hooker	Fe'ao Vunipola
Prop	Tu'akalua Fukofuka
Lock	Pouvalu Latukefu
Lock	Willie Lose
Flanker	'Inoke Afeaki
Flanker	'Ipolito Fenukitau
Number 8	Mana 'Otai (c)
Scrum-half	Manu Vunipola
Fly-half	'Elisi Vunipola
Right Wing	Alaska Taufa
Centre	Peneili Latu
Centre	Unuoi Va'enuku
Left Wing	Tevita Va'enuku
Full-back	Sateki Tuipulotu
Reserves	Nafe Tufui, Etuini Talakai
Referee	Leask B

Points Scorers
Scotland

Name	Tries	Conv	Pen K	Drop G	Points
Hastings G	1	1	8	0	31
Hastings S	1	0	0	0	5
Peters EW	1	0	0	0	5

Tonga

Name	Tries	Conv	Pen K	Drop G	Points
Fenukitau I	1	0	0	0	5

Pool D, Fourth Match
France v Ivory Coast: 54-18
30 May 1995
Olympia Park, Rustenburg

Players
France

Prop	Laurent Benezech
Hooker	Marc de Rougemont
Prop	Christian Califano
Lock	Olivier Brouzet
Lock	Olivier Roumat
Flanker	Laurent Cabannes
Flanker	Arnaud Costes
Number 8	Abdelatif Benazzi
Scrum-half	Guy Accoceberry
Fly-half	Yann Delaigue
Right Wing	Philippe Saint-Andre (c)
Centre	Thierry Lacroix
Centre	Franck Mesnel
Left Wing	William Techoueyres
Full-back	Sebastien Viars
Reserves	Philippe Benetton, Christophe Deylaud

Ivory Coast

Prop	Toussaint Djehi
Hooker	Achille Niamien
Prop	Jean-Pasca Ezoua
Lock	Djakaria Sanoko
Lock	Ble Aka
Flanker	Alfred Okou
Flanker	Patrice Pere
Number 8	Isimaila Lassissi
Scrum-half	Frederic Dupont
Fly-half	Abubacar Camara
Right Wing	Max Brito
Centre	Lucien Niakou
Centre	Jean Sathiq (c)
Left Wing	ASoulama
Full-back	Victor Kouassi
Reserves	Eduard Angoran, Ernest Bley, Paulin Bouazo, Amidou Kone
Referee	Han M

Points Scorers
France

Name	Tries	Conv	Pen K	Drop G	Points
Accoceberry G	1	0	0	0	5
Benazzi A	1	0	0	0	5
Costes A	1	0	0	0	5
Deylaud C	0	2	0	0	4
Lacroix T	2	2	2	0	20
Saint-Andre PG	1	0	0	0	5
Techoueyres W	1	0	0	0	5
Viars S	1	0	0	0	5

Ivory Coast

Name	Tries	Conv	Pen K	Drop G	Points
Camara A	1	0	0	0	5
Kouassi V	0	1	2	0	8
Soulama A	1	0	0	0	5

Pool D, Fifth Match
France v Scotland: 22-19
3 June 1995
Loftus Versfeld, Pretoria

Players

France

Prop	Laurent Benezech
Hooker	Jean-Michel Gonzales
Prop	Christian Califano
Lock	Olivier Merle
Lock	Olivier Roumat
Flanker	Abdelatif Benazzi
Flanker	Laurent Cabannes
Number 8	Philippe Benetton
Scrum-half	Guy Accoceberry
Fly-half	Christophe Deylaud
Right Wing	Emile Ntamack
Centre	Thierry Lacroix
Centre	Philippe Sella
Left Wing	Philippe Saint-Andre (c)
Full-back	Jean-Luc Sadourny
Reserves	Marc Cecillon, Aubin Hueber

Scotland

Prop	Dave Hilton
Hooker	Kenny Milne
Prop	Peter Wright
Lock	Damian Cronin
Lock	Doddie Weir
Flanker	Iain Morrison
Flanker	Rob Wainwright
Number 8	Eric Peters
Scrum-half	Bryan Redpath
Fly-half	Craig Chalmers
Right Wing	Craig Joiner
Centre	Scott Hastings
Centre	Graham Shiel
Left Wing	Kenny Logan
Full-back	Gavin Hastings (c)
Reserves	Paul Burnell, Ian Jardine
Referee	Erickson WJ

Points Scorers

France

Name	Tries	Conv	Pen K	Drop G	Points
Lacroix T	0	1	5	0	17
Ntamack E	1	0	0	0	5

Scotland

Name	Tries	Conv	Pen K	Drop G	Points
Hastings AG	0	1	4	0	14
Wainwright RI	1	0	0	0	5

Pool D, Sixth Match
Tonga v Ivory Coast: 29-11
3 June 1995
Olympia Park, Rustenburg

Players

Tonga

Prop	Tu'akalua Fukofuka
Hooker	Fe'ao Vunipola
Prop	Etuini Talakai
Lock	Pouvalu Latukefu
Lock	Falamani Mafi
Flanker	'Inoke Afeaki
Flanker	Willie Lose
Number 8	Mana 'Otai (c)
Scrum-half	Nafe Tufui
Fly-half	'Elisi Vunipola
Right Wing	Peneili Latu
Centre	Simana Mafile'o
Centre	Unuoi Va'enuku
Left Wing	Tevita Va'enuku
Full-back	Sateki Tuipulotu
Reserves	Taipa Isitolo, Takau Lutua, Feleti Fakaongo

Ivory Coast

Prop	Ernest Bley
Hooker	Eduard Angoran
Prop	Toussaint Djehi
Lock	Gilbert Bado
Lock	Soumalia Kone
Flanker	Alfred Okou
Flanker	Patrice Pere
Number 8	Isimaila Lassissi
Scrum-half	Frederic Dupont
Fly-half	Abubacar Camara
Right Wing	Max Brito
Centre	Lucien Niakou
Centre	Jean Sathiq (c)
Left Wing	ASoulama
Full-back	Victor Kouassi
Reserves	Djakaria Sanoko, Athanase Dali, Thierry Kouame, Daniel Quansah
Referee	Reordan D

Points Scorers

Tonga

Name	Tries	Conv	Pen K	Drop G	Points
Penalty Try	1	0	0	0	5
Latukefu P	1	0	0	0	5
'Otai M	1	0	0	0	5
Tuipulotu S	1	3	1	0	14

Ivory Coast

Name	Tries	Conv	Pen K	Drop G	Points
Okou A	1	0	0	0	5
Dali A	0	0	2	0	6

First Quarter-Final
France v Ireland: 36-12
10 June 1995
King's Park, Durban

Players
France

Prop	Louis Armary
Hooker	Jean-Michel Gonzales
Prop	Christian Califano
Lock	Olivier Merle
Lock	Olivier Roumat
Flanker	Abdelatif Benazzi
Flanker	Laurent Cabannes
Number 8	Marc Cecillon
Scrum-half	Aubin Hueber
Fly-half	Christophe Deylaud
Right Wing	Emile Ntamack
Centre	Thierry Lacroix
Centre	Philippe Sella
Left Wing	Philippe Saint-Andre (c)
Full-back	Jean-Luc Sadourny

Ireland

Prop	Gary Halpin
Hooker	Terry Kingston (c)
Prop	Nick Popplewell
Lock	Neil Francis
Lock	Gabriel Fulcher
Flanker	David Corkery
Flanker	Denis McBride
Number 8	Paddy Johns
Scrum-half	Niall Hogan
Fly-half	Eric Elwood
Right Wing	Simon Geoghegan
Centre	Jonathan Bell
Centre	Brendan Mullin
Left Wing	Darragh O'Mahony
Full-back	Conor O'Shea
Reserve	Eddie Halvey
Referee	Morrison EF

Points Scorers
France

Name	Tries	Conv	Pen K	Drop G	Points
Lacroix T	0	1	8	0	26
Ntamack E	1	0	0	0	5
Saint-Andre PG	1	0	0	0	5

Ireland

Name	Tries	Conv	Pen K	Drop G	Points
Elwood EP	0	0	4	0	12

Second Quarter-Final
South Africa v Western Samoa: 42-14
10 June 1995
Ellis Park, Johannesburg

Players
South Africa

Prop	Os Du Randt
Hooker	Chris Rossouw
Prop	Balie Swart
Lock	Mark Andrews
Lock	Kobus Wiese
Flanker	Ruben Kruger
Flanker	François Pienaar (c)
Number 8	Rudolf Straeuli
Scrum-half	Joost van der Westhuizen
Fly-half	Hennie le Roux
Right Wing	Gavin Johnson
Centre	Japie Mulder
Centre	Christiaan Scholtz
Left Wing	Chester Williams
Full-back	Andre Joubert
Reserves	Naka Drotske, Krynauw Otto, Adriaan Richter, Brendan Venter

Western Samoa

Prop	George Latu
Hooker	Tala Leiasamaiva'o
Prop	Mike Mika
Lock	Lio Falaniko
Lock	Saini Lemamea
Flanker	Junior Paramore
Flanker	Shem Tatupu
Number 8	Pat Lam (c)
Scrum-half	Tu Nu'uali'itia
Fly-half	Fata Sini
Right Wing	George Harder
Centre	Tupo Fa'amasino
Centre	To'o Vaega
Left Wing	Brian Lima
Full-back	Mike Umaga
Reserves	Peter Fatialofa, Brendan Reidy, Fereti Tuilagi, Sila Vaifale
Referee	Fleming JM

Points Scorers
South Africa

Name	Tries	Conv	Pen K	Drop G	Points
Andrews MG	1	0	0	0	5
Johnson GK	0	3	2	0	12
Rossouw CleC	1	0	0	0	5
Williams CM	4	0	0	0	20

Western Samoa

Name	Tries	Conv	Pen K	Drop G	Points
Fa'amasino T	0	2	0	0	4
Nu'uali'itia T	1	0	0	0	5
Tatupu SJ	1	0	0	0	5

Third Quarter-Final
Australia v England: 22-25
11 June 1995
Newlands, Cape Town

Players
Australia

Prop	Dan Crowley
Hooker	Phil Kearns
Prop	Ewen McKenzie
Lock	John Eales
Lock	Rod McCall
Flanker	Willie Ofahengaue
Flanker	David Wilson
Number 8	Tim Gavin
Scrum-half	George Gregan
Fly-half	Michael Lynagh (c)
Right Wing	David Campese
Centre	Tim Horan
Centre	Jason Little
Left Wing	Damian Smith
Full-back	Matthew Burke

England

Prop	Jason Leonard
Hooker	Brian Moore
Prop	Victor Ubogu
Lock	Martin Bayfield
Lock	Martin Johnson
Flanker	Ben Clarke
Flanker	Tim Rodber
Number 8	Dean Richards
Scrum-half	Dewi Morris
Fly-half	Rob Andrew
Right Wing	Rory Underwood
Centre	Will Carling (c)
Centre	Jerry Guscott
Left Wing	Tony Underwood
Full-back	Mike Catt
Reserve	Steve Ojomoh
Referee	Bishop DJ

Points Scorers
Australia

Name	Tries	Conv	Pen K	Drop G	Points
Lynagh MP	0	1	5	0	17
Smith DPP	1	0	0	0	5

England

Name	Tries	Conv	Pen K	Drop G	Points
Andrew CR	0	1	5	1	20
Underwood T	1	0	0	0	5

Fourth Quarter-Final
New Zealand v Scotland: 48-30
11 June 1995
Loftus Versfeld, Pretoria

Players
New Zealand
Prop	Olo Brown
Hooker	Sean Fitzpatrick (c)
Prop	Richard Loe
Lock	Robin Brooke
Lock	Ian Jones
Flanker	Jamie Joseph
Flanker	Josh Kronfeld
Number 8	Zinzan Brooke
Scrum-half	Graeme Bachop
Fly-half	Andrew Mehrtens
Right Wing	Marc Ellis
Centre	Frank Bunce
Centre	Walter Little
Left Wing	Jonah Lomu
Full-back	Jeff Wilson

Scotland
Prop	Dave Hilton
Hooker	Kenny Milne
Prop	Peter Wright
Lock	Damian Cronin
Lock	Doddie Weir
Flanker	Iain Morrison
Flanker	Rob Wainwright
Number 8	Eric Peters
Scrum-half	Bryan Redpath
Fly-half	Craig Chalmers
Right Wing	Craig Joiner
Centre	Scott Hastings
Centre	Graham Shiel
Left Wing	Kenny Logan
Full-back	Gavin Hastings (c)
Reserves	Stewart Campbell, Ian Jardine
Referee	Bevan WD

Points Scorers
New Zealand
Name	Tries	Conv	Pen K	Drop G	Points
Bunce FE	1	0	0	0	5
Fitzpatrick SBT	1	0	0	0	5
Little WK	2	0	0	0	10
Lomu JT	1	0	0	0	5
Mehrtens AP	1	6	2	0	23

Scotland
Name	Tries	Conv	Pen K	Drop G	Points
Hastings AG	0	3	3	0	15
Hastings S	1	0	0	0	5
Weir GW	2	0	0	0	10

First Semi-Final
South Africa v France: 19-15
17 June 1995
King's Park, Durban

Players
South Africa

Prop	Os Du Randt
Hooker	Chris Rossouw
Prop	Balie Swart
Lock	Hannes Strydom
Lock	Kobus Wiese
Flanker	Ruben Kruger
Flanker	François Pienaar (c)
Number 8	Mark Andrews
Scrum-half	Joost van der Westhuizen
Fly-half	Joel Stransky
Right Wing	James Small
Centre	Hennie le Roux
Centre	Japie Mulder
Left Wing	Chester Williams
Full-back	Andre Joubert
Reserve	Johan Roux

France

Prop	Louis Armary
Hooker	Jean-Michel Gonzales
Prop	Christian Califano
Lock	Olivier Merle
Lock	Olivier Roumat
Flanker	Abdelatif Benazzi
Flanker	Laurent Cabannes
Number 8	Marc Cecillon
Scrum-half	Fabien Galthie
Fly-half	Christophe Deylaud
Right Wing	Emile Ntamack
Centre	Thierry Lacroix
Centre	Philippe Sella
Left Wing	Philippe Saint-Andre (c)
Full-back	Jean-Luc Sadourny
Referee	Bevan WD

Points Scorers
South Africa

Name	Tries	Conv	Pen K	Drop G	Points
Kruger RJ	1	0	0	0	5
Stransky JT	0	1	4	0	14

France

Name	Tries	Conv	Pen K	Drop G	Points
Lacroix T	0	0	5	0	15

Second Semi-Final
England v New Zealand: 29-45
18 June 1995
Newlands, Cape Town

Players
England

Prop	Jason Leonard
Hooker	Brian Moore
Prop	Victor Ubogu
Lock	Martin Bayfield
Lock	Martin Johnson
Flanker	Ben Clarke
Flanker	Tim Rodber
Number 8	Dean Richards
Scrum-half	Dewi Morris
Fly-half	Rob Andrew
Right Wing	Rory Underwood
Centre	Will Carling (c)
Centre	Jerry Guscott
Left Wing	Tony Underwood
Full-back	Mike Catt

New Zealand

Prop	Olo Brown
Hooker	Sean Fitzpatrick (c)
Prop	Craig Dowd
Lock	Robin Brooke
Lock	Ian Jones
Flanker	Mike Brewer
Flanker	Josh Kronfeld
Number 8	Zinzan Brooke
Scrum-half	Graeme Bachop
Fly-half	Andrew Mehrtens
Right Wing	Jonah Lomu
Centre	Frank Bunce
Centre	Walter Little
Left Wing	Jeff Wilson
Full-back	Glen Osborne
Reserve	Blair Larsen
Referee	Hilditch SR

Points Scorers
England

Name	Tries	Conv	Pen K	Drop G	Points
Andrew CR	0	3	1	0	9
Carling WDC	2	0	0	0	10
Underwood R	2	0	0	0	10

New Zealand

Name	Tries	Conv	Pen K	Drop G	Points
Bachop GTM	1	0	0	0	5
Brooke ZV	0	0	0	1	3
Kronfeld JA	1	0	0	0	5
Lomu JT	4	0	0	0	20
Mehrtens AP	0	3	1	1	12

Third Place Play-Off
England v France: 9-19
22 June 1995
Loftus Versfeld, Pretoria

Players
England

Prop	Jason Leonard
Hooker	Brian Moore
Prop	Victor Ubogu
Lock	Martin Bayfield
Lock	Martin Johnson
Flanker	Ben Clarke
Flanker	Tim Rodber
Number 8	Steve Ojomoh
Scrum-half	Dewi Morris
Fly-half	Rob Andrew
Right Wing	Ian Hunter
Centre	Will Carling (c)
Centre	Jerry Guscott
Left Wing	Rory Underwood
Full-back	Mike Catt

France

Prop	Laurent Benezech
Hooker	Jean-Michel Gonzales
Prop	Christian Califano
Lock	Olivier Merle
Lock	Olivier Roumat
Flanker	Abdelatif Benazzi
Flanker	Laurent Cabannes
Number 8	Albert Cigagna
Scrum-half	Fabien Galthie
Fly-half	Franck Mesnel
Right Wing	Emile Ntamack
Centre	Thierry Lacroix
Centre	Philippe Sella
Left Wing	Philippe Saint-Andre (c)
Full-back	Jean-Luc Sadourny
Reserve	Olivier Brouzet
Referee	Bishop DJ

Points Scorers
England

Name	Tries	Conv	Pen K	Drop G	Points
Andrew CR	0	0	3	0	9

France

Name	Tries	Conv	Pen K	Drop G	Points
Lacroix T	0	0	3	0	9
Ntamack E	1	0	0	0	5
Roumat O	1	0	0	0	5

349

Final
South Africa v New Zealand: 15-12
24 June 1995
Ellis Park, Johannesburg

Players

South Africa

Prop	Os Du Randt
Hooker	Chris Rossouw
Prop	Balie Swart
Lock	Hannes Strydom
Lock	Kobus Wiese
Flanker	Ruben Kruger
Flanker	François Pienaar (c)
Number 8	Mark Andrews
Scrum-half	Joost van der Westhuizen
Fly-half	Joel Stransky
Right Wing	James Small
Centre	Hennie le Roux
Centre	Japie Mulder
Left Wing	Chester Williams
Full-back	Andre Joubert
Reserves	Garry Pagel, Rudolf Straeuli, Brendan Venter

New Zealand

Prop	Olo Brown
Hooker	Sean Fitzpatrick (c)
Prop	Craig Dowd
Lock	Robin Brooke
Lock	Ian Jones
Flanker	Mike Brewer
Flanker	Josh Kronfeld
Number 8	Zinzan Brooke
Scrum-half	Graeme Bachop
Fly-half	Andrew Mehrtens
Right Wing	Jonah Lomu
Centre	Frank Bunce
Centre	Walter Little
Left Wing	Jeff Wilson
Full-back	Glen Osborne
Reserves	Marc Ellis, Jamie Joseph, Richard Loe, Ant Strachan

Referee	Morrison EF

Points Scorers

South Africa

Name	Tries	Conv	Pen K	Drop G	Points
Stransky JT	0	0	3	2	15

New Zealand

Name	Tries	Conv	Pen K	Drop G	Points
Mehrtens AP	0	0	3	1	12

1999

Pool A, First Match
Spain v Uruguay: 15-12
2 October 1999
Netherdale, Galashiels

Players
Spain

Prop	Jordi Camps Riba
Hooker	Fernando de la Calle Pozo
Prop	Jose Ignacio Zapatero Ferreras
Lock	Sergio Souto Vidal
Lock	Jose Miguel Villau Cabeza
Flanker	Jose Diaz
Flanker	Carlos Souto Vidal
Number 8	Alberto Malo Navio (c)
Scrum-half	Jaime Alonso Lasheras
Fly-half	Andrei Kovalenco
Right Wing	Rafael Bastide Gutierrez
Centre	Alvar Enciso Fernandez-Valderam
Centre	Sebastien Loubsens
Left Wing	Oriol Ripol Fortuny
Full-back	Miguel Angel Frechilla Manrique
Reserves	Oscar Astarloa Uriarte, Alfonso Mata Suarez, Diego Zarzosa Pena

Uruguay

Prop	Pablo Lemoine
Hooker	Diego Lamelas
Prop	Rodrigo Sanchez
Lock	Juan Carlos Bado
Lock	Mario Lame
Flanker	Nicolas Brignoni
Flanker	Martin Panizza
Number 8	Diego Ormachea (c)
Scrum-half	Federico Sciarra
Fly-half	Diego Aguirre
Right Wing	Pablo Costabile
Centre	Martin Mendaro
Centre	Pedro Vecino
Left Wing	Martin Ferres
Full-back	Alfonso Cardoso
Reserves	Francisco de los Santos, Nicolas Grille, Juan Menchaca, Agustin Ponce de Leon, Fernando Sosa Diaz, Guillermo Storace
Referee	White C

Points Scorers
Spain

Name	Tries	Conv	Pen K	Drop G	Points
Kovalenco A	0	0	5	0	15

Uruguay

Name	Tries	Conv	Pen K	Drop G	Points
Aguirre D	0	1	1	0	5
Cardoso A	1	0	0	0	5
Menchaca J	1	0	0	0	5
Ormachea D	1	0	0	0	5
Sciarra F	0	1	0	0	2
Penalty Try	1	0	0	0	5

Pool A, Second Match
Scotland v South Africa: 29-46
3 October 1999
Murrayfield, Edinburgh

Players
Scotland

Prop	George Graham
Hooker	Gordon Bulloch
Prop	Tom Smith
Lock	Stuart Grimes
Lock	Scott Murray
Flanker	Budge Pountney
Flanker	Martin Leslie
Number 8	Gordon Simpson
Scrum-half	Gary Armstrong (c)
Fly-half	Gregor Townsend
Right Wing	Kenny Logan
Centre	John Leslie
Centre	Alan Tait
Left Wing	Cammie Murray
Full-back	Glenn Metcalfe
Reserves	Dave Hilton, Jamie Mayer, Peter Walton, Doddie Weir

South Africa

Prop	Os Du Randt
Hooker	Naka Drotske
Prop	Cobus Visagie
Lock	Mark Andrews
Lock	Albert van den Bergh
Flanker	Johan Erasmus
Flanker	Andre Venter
Number 8	Bobby Skinstad
Scrum-half	Joost van der Westhuizen (c)
Fly-half	Jannie de Beer
Right Wing	Deon Kayser
Centre	Robbie Fleck
Centre	Brendan Venter
Left Wing	Pieter Rossouw
Full-back	Percy Montgomery
Reserves	Ollie le Roux, Krynauw Otto, Breyton Paulse
Referee	Hawke C

Points Scorers
Scotland

Name	Tries	Conv	Pen K	Drop G	Points
Leslie MD	1	0	0	0	5
Logan KMcK	0	2	4	0	16
Tait AV	1	0	0	0	5
Townsend GPJ	0	0	0	1	3

South Africa

Name	Tries	Conv	Pen K	Drop G	Points
de Beer JH	0	5	2	0	16
Fleck RF	1	0	0	0	5
Kayser DJ	1	0	0	0	5
le Roux A-H	1	0	0	0	5
van der Westhuizen J	1	0	0	0	5
Venter B	1	0	0	0	5
Venter AG	1	0	0	0	5

Pool A, Third Match
Scotland v Uruguay: 43-12
8 October 1999
Murrayfield, Edinburgh

Players
Scotland

Prop	George Graham
Hooker	Gordon Bulloch
Prop	Tom Smith
Lock	Stuart Grimes
Lock	Scott Murray
Flanker	Budge Pountney
Flanker	Martin Leslie
Number 8	Gordon Simpson
Scrum-half	Gary Armstrong (c)
Fly-half	Gregor Townsend
Right Wing	Kenny Logan
Centre	Jamie Mayer
Centre	Alan Tait
Left Wing	Cammie Murray
Full-back	Glenn Metcalfe
Reserves	Shaun Longstaff, Dave Hilton, Bryan Redpath, Robbie Russell, Peter Walton

Uruguay

Prop	Pablo Lemoine
Hooker	Diego Lamelas
Prop	Rodrigo Sanchez
Lock	Juan Carlos Bado
Lock	Mario Lame
Flanker	Nicolas Brignoni
Flanker	Martin Panizza
Number 8	Diego Ormachea (c)
Scrum-half	Federico Sciarra
Fly-half	Diego Aguirre
Right Wing	Pablo Costabile
Centre	Martin Mendaro
Centre	Pedro Vecino
Left Wing	Juan Menchaca
Full-back	Alfonso Cardoso
Reserves	Eduardo Berruti, Francisco de los Santos, Nicolas Grille, Agustin Ponce de Leon, Fernando Sosa Diaz, Guillermo Storace, Jose Viana

Referee	Dickinson S

Points Scorers
Scotland

Name	Tries	Conv	Pen K	Drop G	Points
Metcalfe GH	1	0	0	0	5
Armstrong G	1	0	0	0	5
Leslie MD	1	0	0	0	5
Logan KMcK	0	5	1	0	13
Russell RR	1	0	0	0	5
Simpson GL	1	0	0	0	5
Townsend GPJ	1	0	0	0	5

Uruguay

Name	Tries	Conv	Pen K	Drop G	Points
Aguirre D	0	0	3	0	9
Sciarra F	0	0	1	0	3

Pool A, Fourth Match
South Africa v Spain: 47-3
10 October 1999
Murrayfield, Edinburgh

Players
South Africa

Prop	Adrian Garvey
Hooker	Chris Rossouw
Prop	Ollie le Roux
Lock	Krynauw Otto
Lock	Fritz van Heerden
Flanker	Ruben Kruger
Flanker	Andre Vos (c)
Number 8	Anton Leonard
Scrum-half	Werner Swanepoel
Fly-half	Jannie de Beer
Right Wing	Kaya Malotana
Centre	Wayne Julies
Centre	Pieter Muller
Left Wing	Stefan Terblanche
Full-back	Breyton Paulse
Reserves	Naka Drotske, Os Du Randt, Deon Kayser, Bobby Skinstad, Joost van der Westhuizen

Spain

Prop	Jordi Camps Riba
Hooker	Diego Zarzosa Pena
Prop	Jose Ignacio Zapatero Ferreras
Lock	Oscar Astarloa Uriarte
Lock	Jose Miguel Villau Cabeza
Flanker	Jose Diaz
Flanker	Carlos Souto Vidal
Number 8	Alberto Malo Navio (c)
Scrum-half	Aratz Gallastegui Sodupe
Fly-half	Aitor Etxeberria de la Rosa
Right Wing	Miguel Angel Frechilla Manrique
Centre	Fernando Diez Molina
Centre	Alberto Socias Olmos
Left Wing	Jose Ignacio Inchausti Bravo
Full-back	Francisco Puertas Soto
Reserves	Fernando de la Calle Pozo, Luis Javier Martinez Villanueva, Alfonso Mata Suarez, Victor Torres Funes, Ferran Velazco Querol
Referee	Honiss P

Points Scorers
South Africa

Name	Tries	Conv	Pen K	Drop G	Points
Penalty Try	1	0	0	0	5
de Beer JH	0	6	0	0	12
Leonard A	1	0	0	0	5
Muller PG	1	0	0	0	5
Skinstad RB	1	0	0	0	5
Swanepoel W	1	0	0	0	5
Vos AN	2	0	0	0	10

Spain

Name	Tries	Conv	Pen K	Drop G	Points
Velazco Querol F	0	0	1	0	3

Pool A, Fifth Match
South Africa v Uruguay: 39-3
15 October 1999
Hampden Park, Glasgow

Players

South Africa

Prop	Os Du Randt
Hooker	Naka Drotske
Prop	Cobus Visagie
Lock	Mark Andrews
Lock	Krynauw Otto
Flanker	Johan Erasmus
Flanker	Andre Venter
Number 8	Bobby Skinstad
Scrum-half	Joost van der Westhuizen (c)
Fly-half	Jannie de Beer
Right Wing	Deon Kayser
Centre	Robbie Fleck
Centre	Brendan Venter
Left Wing	Pieter Rossouw
Full-back	Percy Montgomery
Reserves	Ollie le Roux, Albert van den Bergh

Uruguay

Prop	Pablo Lemoine
Hooker	Diego Lamelas
Prop	Rodrigo Sanchez
Lock	Juan Carlos Bado
Lock	Mario Lame
Flanker	Nicolas Grille
Flanker	Martin Panizza
Number 8	Diego Ormachea (c)
Scrum-half	Fernando Sosa Diaz
Fly-half	Diego Aguirre
Right Wing	Pablo Costabile
Centre	Fernando Paullier
Centre	Pedro Vecino
Left Wing	Juan Menchaca
Full-back	Alfonso Cardoso
Reserves	Sebastian Aguirre, Juan Alzueta, Eduardo Berruti, Nicolas Brignoni, Guillermo Storace, Jose Viana
Referee	Marshall P

Points Scorers

South Africa

Name	Tries	Conv	Pen K	Drop G	Points
de Beer JH	0	4	2	0	14
Fleck RF	1	0	0	0	5
Kayser DJ	1	0	0	0	5
van der Westhuizen J	1	0	0	0	5
van den Bergh PA	2	0	0	0	10

Uruguay

Name	Tries	Conv	Pen K	Drop G	Points
Aguirre D	0	0	1	0	3

Pool A, Sixth Match
Scotland v Spain: 48-0
16 October 1999
Murrayfield, Edinburgh

Players

Scotland

Prop	Paul Burnell
Hooker	Robbie Russell
Prop	Dave Hilton
Lock	Andy Reed
Lock	Doddie Weir
Flanker	Cameron Mather
Flanker	Peter Walton
Number 8	Stuart Reid
Scrum-half	Bryan Redpath (c)
Fly-half	Duncan Hodge
Right Wing	Shaun Longstaff
Centre	Jamie Mayer
Centre	James McLaren
Left Wing	Cammie Murray
Full-back	Chris Paterson
Reserves	Iain Fairley, Gregor Townsend

Spain

Prop	Victor Torres Funes
Hooker	Diego Zarzosa Pena
Prop	Jose Ignacio Zapatero Ferreras
Lock	Oscar Astarloa Uriarte
Lock	Jose Miguel Villau Cabeza
Flanker	Jose Diaz
Flanker	Carlos Souto Vidal
Number 8	Alfonso Mata Suarez
Scrum-half	Aratz Gallastegui Sodupe
Fly-half	Andrei Kovalenco
Right Wing	Miguel Angel Frechilla Manrique
Centre	Alvar Enciso Fernandez-Valderam (c)
Centre	Sebastien Loubsens
Left Wing	Jose Ignacio Inchausti Bravo
Full-back	Francisco Puertas Soto
Reserves	Fernando de la Calle Pozo, Luis Javier Martinez Villanueva, Agustin Malet Raga, Alberto Socias Olmos, Steve Tuineau Iloa, Ferran Velazco Querol

Referee	Thomas C

Points Scorers

Scotland

Name	Tries	Conv	Pen K	Drop G	Points
Longstaff SL	1	0	0	0	5
Penalty Try	1	0	0	0	5
Hodge DW	1	5	1	0	18
Mather CG	2	0	0	0	10
McLaren JG	1	0	0	0	5
Murray CA	1	0	0	0	5

Pool B, First Match
England v Italy: 67-7
2 October 1999
Twickenham, London

Players
England

Prop	Jason Leonard
Hooker	Richard Cockerill
Prop	Phil Vickery
Lock	Danny Grewcock
Lock	Martin Johnson (c)
Flanker	Neil Back
Flanker	Richard Hill
Number 8	Lawrence Dallaglio
Scrum-half	Matt Dawson
Fly-half	Jonny Wilkinson
Right Wing	Austin Healey
Centre	Phil de Glanville
Centre	Will Greenwood
Left Wing	Dan Luger
Full-back	Matt Perry
Reserves	Nick Beal, Martin Corry, Darren Garforth, Phil Greening, Jerry Guscott, Graham Rowntree

Italy

Prop	Franco Properzi-Curti
Hooker	Alessandro Moscardi
Prop	Federico Pucciariello
Lock	Walter Cristofoletto
Lock	Mark Giacheri
Flanker	Mauro Bergamasco
Flanker	Massimo Giovanelli (c)
Number 8	Orazio Arancio
Scrum-half	Alessandro Troncon
Fly-half	Diego Dominguez
Right Wing	Paolo Vaccari
Centre	Luca Martin
Centre	Cristian Stoica
Left Wing	Nicolas Zisti
Full-back	Matt Pini
Reserves	Carlo Checchinato, Andrea de Rossi, Francesco Mazzariol, Nicola Mazzucato
Referee	Watson A

Points Scorers
England

Name	Tries	Conv	Pen K	Drop G	Points
Back NA	1	0	0	0	5
Corry ME	1	0	0	0	5
Dawson MJS	1	0	0	0	5
de Glanville PR	1	0	0	0	5
Hill RA	1	0	0	0	5
Luger DD	1	0	0	0	5
Perry MB	1	0	0	0	5
Wilkinson JP	1	6	5	0	32

Italy

Name	Tries	Conv	Pen K	Drop G	Points
Dominguez D	1	1	0	0	7

Pool B, Second Match
New Zealand v Tonga: 45-9
3 October 1999
Ashton Gate, Bristol

Players
New Zealand

Prop	Carl Hoeft
Hooker	Anton Oliver
Prop	Kees Meeuws
Lock	Robin Brooke
Lock	Norm Maxwell
Flanker	Josh Kronfeld
Flanker	Reuben Thorne
Number 8	Taine Randell (c)
Scrum-half	Justin Marshall
Fly-half	Andrew Mehrtens
Right Wing	Jonah Lomu
Centre	Christian Cullen
Centre	Alama Ieremia
Left Wing	Tana Umaga
Full-back	Jeff Wilson
Reserves	Craig Dowd, Daryl Gibson, Byron Kelleher, Royce Willis

Tonga

Prop	Ta'u Fainga'anuku
Hooker	Fe'ao Vunipola
Prop	Tevita Taumoepeau
Lock	Isi Fatani
Lock	Ben Hur Kivalu
Flanker	Hese Fakatou
Flanker	Jonathan Koloi
Number 8	Va'a Toloke
Scrum-half	Sililo Martens
Fly-half	'Elisi Vunipola
Right Wing	Tauna'holo Taufahema
Centre	David Tiueti
Centre	Semi Taupeaafe
Left Wing	Fepiko Tatafu
Full-back	Siua Taumalolo
Reserves	David Edwards, Latiume Maka, Falamani Mafi, Ngalu Taufo'ou, Isi Tapueluelu, Matt Te Pou, Sione Tuipulotu
Referee	Bevan D

Points Scorers
New Zealand

Name	Tries	Conv	Pen K	Drop G	Points
Kelleher BT	1	0	0	0	5
Kronfeld JA	1	0	0	0	5
Lomu JT	2	0	0	0	10
Maxwell NM	1	0	0	0	5
Mehrtens AP	0	4	4	0	20

Tonga

Name	Tries	Conv	Pen K	Drop G	Points
Taumalolo S	0	0	3	0	9

Pool B, Third Match
England v New Zealand: 16-30
9 October 1999
Twickenham, London

Players

England

Prop	Jason Leonard
Hooker	Richard Cockerill
Prop	Phil Vickery
Lock	Danny Grewcock
Lock	Martin Johnson (c)
Flanker	Neil Back
Flanker	Richard Hill
Number 8	Lawrence Dallaglio
Scrum-half	Matt Dawson
Fly-half	Jonny Wilkinson
Right Wing	Austin Healey
Centre	Phil de Glanville
Centre	Jerry Guscott
Left Wing	Dan Luger
Full-back	Matt Perry
Reserves	Martin Corry, Darren Garforth, Paul Grayson, Phil Greening, Tim Rodber

New Zealand

Prop	Craig Dowd
Hooker	Anton Oliver
Prop	Carl Hoeft
Lock	Robin Brooke
Lock	Norm Maxwell
Flanker	Josh Kronfeld
Flanker	Reuben Thorne
Number 8	Taine Randell (c)
Scrum-half	Justin Marshall
Fly-half	Andrew Mehrtens
Right Wing	Jonah Lomu
Centre	Christian Cullen
Centre	Alama Ieremia
Left Wing	Tana Umaga
Full-back	Jeff Wilson
Reserves	Tony Brown, Greg Feek, Daryl Gibson, Byron Kelleher, Royce Willis
Referee	Marshall P

Points Scorers

England

Name	Tries	Conv	Pen K	Drop G	Points
de Glanville PR	1	0	0	0	5
Wilkinson JP	0	1	3	0	11

New Zealand

Name	Tries	Conv	Pen K	Drop G	Points
Kelleher BT	1	0	0	0	5
Lomu JT	1	0	0	0	5
Mehrtens AP	0	3	3	0	15
Wilson JW	1	0	0	0	5

Pool B, Fourth Match
Italy v Tonga: 25-28
10 October 1999
Welford Road, Leicester

Players
Italy

Prop..	Andrea Castellani
Hooker..	Alessandro Moscardi
Prop..	Alejandro Moreno
Lock	Carlo Checchinato
Lock	Mark Giacheri
Flanker..	Massimo Giovanelli (c)
Flanker..	Stefano Saviozzi
Number 8..	Carlo Caione
Scrum-half..	Alessandro Troncon
Fly-half...	Diego Dominguez
Right Wing	Fabio Roselli
Centre...	Sandro Ceppolino
Centre	Cristian Stoica
Left Wing...	Paolo Vaccari
Full-back...	Matt Pini
Reserves..	Andrea Moretti, Nicola Mazzucato

Tonga

Prop..	Ta'u Fainga'anuku
Hooker..	Latiume Maka
Prop..	Ngalu Taufo'ou
Lock	Ben Hur Kivalu
Lock	Falamani Mafi
Flanker..	David Edwards
Flanker..	Jonathan Koloi
Number 8..	Kati Tu'ipulotu
Scrum-half..	Sililo Martens
Fly-half...	Brian Wooley
Right Wing..	Tauna'holo Taufahema
Centre...	Semi Taupeaafe
Centre	'Elisi Vunipola (c)
Left Wing...	Epi Taione
Full-back...	Sateki Tuipulotu
Reserves...............................	David Tiueti, Isi Fatani, Isi Tapueluelu, Matt Te Pou
Referee	McHugh D

Points Scorers
Italy

Name	Tries	Conv	Pen K	Drop G	Points
Dominguez D	0	1	6	0	20
Moscardi A	1	0	0	0	5

Tonga

Name	Tries	Conv	Pen K	Drop G	Points
Fatani I	1	0	0	0	5
Taufahema T	1	0	0	0	5
Tuipulotu S	1	2	2	1	18

Pool B, Fifth Match
New Zealand v Italy: 101–3
14 October 1999
McAlpine Stadium, Huddersfield

Players
New Zealand

Prop	Craig Dowd
Hooker	Mark Hammett
Prop	Greg Feek
Lock	Ian Jones
Lock	Royce Willis
Flanker	Andrew Blowers
Flanker	Dylan Mika
Number 8	Taine Randell (c)
Scrum-half	Byron Kelleher
Fly-half	Tony Brown
Right Wing	Jonah Lomu
Centre	Pita Alatini
Centre	Daryl Gibson
Left Wing	Glen Osborne
Full-back	Jeff Wilson
Reserves	Robin Brooke, Christian Cullen, Rhys Duggan, Kees Meeuws, Scott Robertson

Italy

Prop	Andrea Castellani
Hooker	Andrea Moretti
Prop	Alejandro Moreno
Lock	Carlo Checchinato
Lock	Mark Giacheri
Flanker	Massimo Giovanelli (c)
Flanker	Stefano Saviozzi
Number 8	Carlo Caione
Scrum-half	Alessandro Troncon
Fly-half	Diego Dominguez
Right Wing	Paolo Vaccari
Centre	Sandro Ceppolino
Centre	Cristian Stoica
Left Wing	Nicolas Zisti
Full-back	Matt Pini
Reserves	Orazio Arancio, Walter Cristofoletto, Francesco Mazzariol, Nicola Mazzucato, Alessandro Moscardi, Franco Properzi-Curti
Referee	Fleming J

Points Scorers
New Zealand

Name	Tries	Conv	Pen K	Drop G	Points
Brown TE	1	11	3	0	36
Cullen CM	1	0	0	0	5
Gibson DPE	1	0	0	0	5
Hammett MG	1	0	0	0	5
Lomu JT	2	0	0	0	10
Mika DG	1	0	0	0	5
Osborne GM	2	0	0	0	10
Randell TC	1	0	0	0	5
Robertson SM	1	0	0	0	5
Wilson JW	3	0	0	0	15

Italy

Name	Tries	Conv	Pen K	Drop G	Points
Dominguez D	0	0	1	0	3

Pool B, Sixth Match
England v Tonga: 101-10
15 October 1999
Twickenham, London

Players

England

Prop	Graham Rowntree
Hooker	Phil Greening
Prop	Phil Vickery
Lock	Garath Archer
Lock	Martin Johnson (c)
Flanker	Richard Hill
Flanker	Joe Worsley
Number 8	Lawrence Dallaglio
Scrum-half	Matt Dawson
Fly-half	Paul Grayson
Right Wing	Austin Healey
Centre	Will Greenwood
Centre	Jerry Guscott
Left Wing	Dan Luger
Full-back	Matt Perry
Reserves	Nick Beal, Mike Catt, Richard Cockerill, Danny Grewcock

Tonga

Prop	Ngalu Taufo'ou
Hooker	Fe'ao Vunipola
Prop	Tevita Taumoepeau
Lock	Isi Fatani
Lock	Ben Hur Kivalu
Flanker	David Edwards
Flanker	Jonathan Koloi
Number 8	Kati Tu'ipulotu
Scrum-half	Sililo Martens
Fly-half	'Elisi Vunipola (c)
Right Wing	David Tiueti
Centre	Salesi Finau
Centre	Fepiko Tatafu
Left Wing	Semi Taupeaafe
Full-back	Sateki Tuipulotu
Reserves	Ta'u Fainga'anuku, Latiume Maka, Falamani Mafi, Epi Taione, Isi Tapueluelu, Va'a Toloke, Sione Tuipulotu
Referee	Erickson W

Points Scorers

England

Name	Tries	Conv	Pen K	Drop G	Points
Dawson MJS	1	0	0	0	5
Grayson PJ	0	12	4	0	36
Greening PBT	2	0	0	0	10
Greenwood WJH	2	0	0	0	10
Guscott JC	2	0	0	0	10
Healey AS	2	0	0	0	10
Hill RA	1	0	0	0	5
Luger DD	2	0	0	0	10
Perry MB	1	0	0	0	5

Tonga

Name	Tries	Conv	Pen K	Drop G	Points
Tiueti TL	1	0	0	0	5
Tuipulotu S	0	1	1	0	5

Pool C, First Match
Fiji v Namibia: 67–18
1 October 1999
Stade de la Méditerranée, Béziers

Players

Fiji

Prop	Dan Rouse
Hooker	Greg Smith (c)
Prop	Joeli Veitayaki
Lock	Emori Katalau
Lock	Simon Raiwalui
Flanker	Alfi Mocelutu Vuivau
Flanker	Apisai Naevo
Number 8	Seta Tawake Naivaluwaqa
Scrum-half	Jacob Rauluni
Fly-half	Waisale Serevi
Right Wing	Fero Lasagavibau
Centre	Viliame Satala
Centre	Waisake Sotutu
Left Wing	Imanueli Tikomaimakogai
Full-back	Alfred Uluinayau
Reserves	Lawrence Little, Epeli Naituvau, Meli Nakauta, Koli Sewabu

Namibia

Prop	Mario Jacobs
Hooker	Hugo Horn
Prop	Joodt Opperman
Lock	Heino Senekal
Lock	Pieter Steyn
Flanker	Quinn Hough (c)
Flanker	Jaco Olivier
Number 8	Sean Furter
Scrum-half	Riaan Jantjies
Fly-half	Johan Zaayman
Right Wing	Dirk Farmer
Centre	Attie Samuelson
Centre	Schalk van der Merwe
Left Wing	Deon Mouton
Full-back	Lean van Dyk
Reserves	Andries Blaauw, Herman Lintvelt, Eben Smith, Johannes Theron, Glovin van Wyk, Sarel Janse van Rensburg, François van Rensburg
Referee	McHugh D

Points Scorers

Fiji

Name	Tries	Conv	Pen K	Drop G	Points
Serevi WT	0	8	2	0	22
Katalau ES	1	0	0	0	5
Lasagavibau FT	2	0	0	0	10
Mocelutu Vuibau A	1	0	0	0	5
Rauluni J	1	0	0	0	5
Satala V	1	0	0	0	5
Smith GJ	1	0	0	0	5
Tawakè Naivaluwaqa S	1	0	0	0	5
Tikomaimakogai I	1	0	0	0	5

Namibia

Name	Tries	Conv	Pen K	Drop G	Points
Jacobs M	1	0	0	0	5
Senekal H	1	0	0	0	5
van Dyk L	0	1	2	0	8

Pool C, Second Match
France v Canada: 33-20
2 October 1999
Stade de la Méditerranée, Béziers

Players

France

Prop	Christian Califano
Hooker	Raphael Ibanez (c)
Prop	Franck Tournaire
Lock	Abdelatif Benazzi
Lock	Fabien Pelous
Flanker	Marc Lievremont
Flanker	Olivier Magne
Number 8	Christophe Juillet
Scrum-half	Pierre Mignoni
Fly-half	Thomas Castaignede
Right Wing	Xavier Garbajosa
Centre	Richard Dourthe
Centre	Stephane Glas
Left Wing	Christophe Dominici
Full-back	Ugo Mola
Reserves	Olivier Brouzet, Christophe Lamaison, Lionel Mallier, Emile Ntamack, Cedric Soulette, Stephane Castaignede

Canada

Prop	Rod Snow
Hooker	Pat Dunkley
Prop	John Thiel
Lock	Mike James
Lock	John Tait
Flanker	Dan Baugh
Flanker	John Hutchinson
Number 8	Alan Charron
Scrum-half	Morgan Williams
Fly-half	Gareth Rees (c)
Right Wing	Courtney Smith
Centre	Scott Bryan
Centre	Dave Lougheed
Left Wing	Winston Stanley
Full-back	Scott Stewart
Reserves	Ryan Banks, Richard Bice, John Graf, Bobby Ross, Mike Schmid
Referee	Campsall B

Points Scorers

France

Name	Tries	Conv	Pen K	Drop G	Points
Castaignede T	1	0	0	0	5
Dourthe R	0	2	3	0	13
Glas S	1	0	0	0	5
Magne O	1	0	0	0	5
Ntamack E	1	0	0	0	5

Canada

Name	Tries	Conv	Pen K	Drop G	Points
Rees GL	0	1	1	0	5
Ross RP	0	1	1	0	5
Williams M	2	0	0	0	10

**Pool C, Third Match
France v Namibia: 47-13
8 October 1999
Stade Lescure, Bordeaux**

Players
France

Prop	Christian Califano
Hooker	Raphael Ibanez (c)
Prop	Franck Tournaire
Lock	Olivier Brouzet
Lock	Fabien Pelous
Flanker	Marc Lievremont
Flanker	Olivier Magne
Number 8	Thomas Lievremont
Scrum-half	Pierre Mignoni
Fly-half	Christophe Lamaison
Right Wing	Philippe Bernat-Salles
Centre	Richard Dourthe
Centre	Stephane Glas
Left Wing	Emile Ntamack
Full-back	Ugo Mola
Reserves	Abdelatif Benazzi, Arnaud Costes, Marc Dal Maso, Cedric Desbrosse, Xavier Garbajosa, Cedric Soulette, Stephane Castaignede

Namibia

Prop	Mario Jacobs
Hooker	Hugo Horn
Prop	Joodt Opperman
Lock	Heino Senekal
Lock	Pieter Steyn
Flanker	Quinn Hough (c)
Flanker	Thys van Rooyen
Number 8	Sean Furter
Scrum-half	Riaan Jantjies
Fly-half	Johan Zaayman
Right Wing	Attie Samuelson
Centre	Schalk van der Merwe
Centre	François van Rensburg
Left Wing	Lean van Dyk
Full-back	Glovin van Wyk
Reserves	Andries Blaauw, Herman Lintvelt, Cliff Loubscher, Eben Smith, Johannes Theron, Sarel Janse van Rensburg
Referee	White C

Points Scorers
France

Name	Tries	Conv	Pen K	Drop G	Points
Bernat-Salles P	1	0	0	0	5
Dourthe R	0	4	3	0	17
Mola U	3	0	0	0	15
Ntamack E	1	0	0	0	5
Mignoni P	1	0	0	0	5

Namibia

Name	Tries	Conv	Pen K	Drop G	Points
Samuelson A	1	0	0	0	5
van Dyk L	0	1	2	0	8

Pool C, Fourth Match
Fiji v Canada: 38-22
9 October 1999
Stade Lescure, Bordeaux

Players
Fiji

Prop	Dan Rouse
Hooker	Greg Smith (c)
Prop	Joeli Veitayaki
Lock	Emori Katalau
Lock	Simon Raiwalui
Flanker	Ilivasi Tamanivalu Tabua
Flanker	Seta Tawake Naivaluwaqa
Number 8	Alfi Mocelutu Vuivau
Scrum-half	Jacob Rauluni
Fly-half	Nicky Little
Right Wing	Fero Lasagavibau
Centre	Viliame Satala
Centre	Waisake Sotutu
Left Wing	Marika Vunibaka
Full-back	Alfred Uluinayau
Reserves	Waisale Serevi, Apisai Naevo, Mosese Rauluni, Koli Sewabu

Canada

Prop	Rod Snow
Hooker	Pat Dunkley
Prop	John Thiel
Lock	Mike James
Lock	John Tait
Flanker	Dan Baugh
Flanker	Alan Charron
Number 8	Mike Schmid
Scrum-half	Morgan Williams
Fly-half	Gareth Rees
Right Wing	Dave Lougheed
Centre	Scott Bryan
Centre	Kyle Nichols
Left Wing	Winston Stanley
Full-back	Scott Stewart
Reserves	Mark Cardinal, John Hutchinson, Duane Major
Referee	Morrison E

Points Scorers
Fiji

Name	Tries	Conv	Pen K	Drop G	Points
Lasagavibau FT	1	0	0	0	5
Little NT	0	3	3	1	18
Satala V	2	0	0	0	10
Vunibaka MD	1	0	0	0	5

Canada

Name	Tries	Conv	Pen K	Drop G	Points
James MB	1	0	0	0	5
Rees GL	0	1	4	1	17

Pool C, Fifth Match
Canada v Namibia: 72-11
14 October 1999
Stade Municipal, Toulouse

Players
Canada

Prop	Rod Snow
Hooker	Mark Cardinal
Prop	John Thiel
Lock	Mike James
Lock	John Tait
Flanker	Dan Baugh
Flanker	John Hutchinson
Number 8	Alan Charron
Scrum-half	Morgan Williams
Fly-half	Gareth Rees
Right Wing	Joe Pagano
Centre	Dave Lougheed
Centre	Kyle Nichols
Left Wing	Winston Stanley
Full-back	Scott Stewart
Reserves	Ryan Banks, Scott Bryan, Pat Dunkley, John Graf, Duane Major, Bobby Ross, Mike Schmid

Namibia

Prop	Joodt Opperman
Hooker	Hugo Horn
Prop	Eben Smith
Lock	Heino Senekal
Lock	Pieter Steyn
Flanker	Quinn Hough (c)
Flanker	Thys van Rooyen
Number 8	Sean Furter
Scrum-half	Riaan Jantjies
Fly-half	Johan Zaayman
Right Wing	Attie Samuelson
Centre	Schalk van der Merwe
Centre	François van Rensburg
Left Wing	Lean van Dyk
Full-back	Glovin van Wyk
Reserves	Andries Blaauw, Herman Lintvelt, Johannes Theron
Referee	Cole A

Points Scorers
Canada

Name	Tries	Conv	Pen K	Drop G	Points
Charron AJ	1	0	0	0	5
Nichols K	2	0	0	0	10
Rees GL	0	9	3	0	27
Ross RP	1	0	0	0	5
Snow RGA	2	0	0	0	10
Stanley WU	2	0	0	0	10
Williams M	1	0	0	0	5

Namibia

Name	Tries	Conv	Pen K	Drop G	Points
Hough Q	1	0	0	0	5
van Dyk L	0	0	2	0	6

Pool C, Sixth Match
France v Fiji: 28-19
16 October 1999
Stade Municipal, Toulouse

Players

France

Prop	Christian Califano
Hooker	Raphael Ibanez (c)
Prop	Franck Tournaire
Lock	Abdelatif Benazzi
Lock	Fabien Pelous
Flanker	Marc Lievremont
Flanker	Olivier Magne
Number 8	Christophe Juillet
Scrum-half	Stephane Castaignede
Fly-half	Christophe Lamaison
Right Wing	Philippe Bernat-Salles
Centre	Richard Dourthe
Centre	Emile Ntamack
Left Wing	Christophe Dominici
Full-back	Ugo Mola
Reserves	Olivier Brouzet, Arnaud Costes, Marc Dal Maso, Fabien Galthie, Xavier Garbajosa

Fiji

Prop	Dan Rouse
Hooker	Greg Smith (c)
Prop	Joeli Veitayaki
Lock	Emori Katalau
Lock	Simon Raiwalui
Flanker	Ilivasi Tamanivalu Tabua
Flanker	Seta Tawake Naivaluwaqa
Number 8	Alfi Mocelutu Vuivau
Scrum-half	Jacob Rauluni
Fly-half	Nicky Little
Right Wing	Manasa Bari
Centre	Viliame Satala
Centre	Waisake Sotutu
Left Wing	Fero Lasagavibau
Full-back	Alfred Uluinayau
Reserves	Meli Nakauta, Koli Sewabu
Referee	O'Brien P

Points Scorers

France

Name	Tries	Conv	Pen K	Drop G	Points
Dourthe R	0	2	2	0	10
Juillet C	1	0	0	0	5
Lamaison C	0	0	1	0	3
Dominici C	1	0	0	0	5
Penalty Try	1	0	0	0	5

Fiji

Name	Tries	Conv	Pen K	Drop G	Points
Little NT	0	1	4	0	14
Uluinayau AB	1	0	0	0	5

Pool D, First Match
Wales v Argentina: 23-18
1 October 1999
Millennium Stadium, Cardiff

Players

Wales

Prop	Peter Rogers
Hooker	Garin Jenkins
Prop	Dai Young
Lock	Craig Quinnell
Lock	Chris Wyatt
Flanker	Colin Charvis
Flanker	Brett Sinkinson
Number 8	Scott Quinnell
Scrum-half	Rob Howley (c)
Fly-half	Neil Jenkins
Right Wing	Dafydd James
Centre	Scott Gibbs
Centre	Mark Taylor
Left Wing	Gareth Thomas
Full-back	Shane Howarth
Reserve	Jason Jones-Hughes

Argentina

Prop	Roberto Grau
Hooker	Mario Ledesma Arocena
Prop	Mauricio Reggiardo
Lock	Alejandro Allub
Lock	Ignacio Fernandez Lobbe
Flanker	Lucas Ostiglia
Flanker	Santiago Phelan
Number 8	Gonzalo Longo Elia
Scrum-half	Agustin Pichot
Fly-half	Gonzalo Quesada
Right Wing	Diego Albanese
Centre	Lisandro Arbizu (c)
Centre	Eduardo Simone
Left Wing	Octavio Bartolucci
Full-back	Manuel Contepomi
Reserves	Gonzalo Camardon, Omar Hasan Jalil, Rolando Martin
Referee	O'Brien P

Points Scorers

Wales

Name	Tries	Conv	Pen K	Drop G	Points
Charvis CL	1	0	0	0	5
Jenkins NR	0	2	3	0	13
Taylor M	1	0	0	0	5

Argentina

Name	Tries	Conv	Pen K	Drop G	Points
Quesada G	0	0	6	0	18

Pool D, Second Match
Samoa v Japan: 43-9
3 October 1999
Racecourse Ground, Wrexham

Players
Samoa

Prop	Robbie Ale
Hooker	Trevor Leota
Prop	Brendan Reidy
Lock	Sene Ta'ala
Lock	Lama Tone
Flanker	Craig Glendinning
Flanker	Junior Paramore
Number 8	Pat Lam (c)
Scrum-half	Stephen So'oilao
Fly-half	Stephen Bachop
Right Wing	Brian Lima
Centre	Inga Tuigamala
Centre	To'o Vaega
Left Wing	Afato So'oalo
Full-back	Silao Leaega
Reserves	Earl Va'a, John Clarke, George Leaupepe, Mike Mika, Opeta Palepoi, Semo Sititi

Japan

Prop	Shin Hasegawa
Hooker	Masahiro Kunda
Prop	Kohei Oguchi
Lock	Robert Gordon
Lock	Naoya Okubo
Flanker	Greg Smith
Flanker	Yasunori Watanabe
Number 8	Jamie Joseph
Scrum-half	Graeme Bachop
Fly-half	Keiji Hirose
Right Wing	Terunori Masuho
Centre	Andrew McCormick (c)
Centre	Yukio Motoki
Left Wing	Daisuke Ohata
Full-back	Tsutomu Matsuda
Reserves	Takeomi Ito, Masaaki Sakata, Hiroyuki Tanuma, Patiliai Tuidraki, Akira Yoshida
Referee	Cole A

Points Scorers
Samoa

Name	Tries	Conv	Pen K	Drop G	Points
Leaega S	1	3	4	0	23
Lima BP	2	0	0	0	10
So'oalo A	2	0	0	0	10

Japan

Name	Tries	Conv	Pen K	Drop G	Points
Hirose K	0	0	3	0	9

Pool D, Third Match
Wales v Japan: 64-15
9 October 1999
Millennium Stadium, Cardiff

Players
Wales

Prop	Peter Rogers
Hooker	Garin Jenkins
Prop	Dai Young
Lock	Craig Quinnell
Lock	Mike Voyle
Flanker	Brett Sinkinson
Flanker	Martyn Williams
Number 8	Geraint Lewis
Scrum-half	Rob Howley (c)
Fly-half	Neil Jenkins
Right Wing	Jason Jones-Hughes
Centre	Scott Gibbs
Centre	Mark Taylor
Left Wing	Allan Bateman
Full-back	Shane Howarth
Reserves	David Llewellyn, Ben Evans, Jonathan Humphreys, Stephen Jones, Andrew Lewis, Gareth Thomas, Chris Wyatt

Japan

Prop	Shin Hasegawa
Hooker	Masahiro Kunda
Prop	Naoto Nakamura
Lock	Robert Gordon
Lock	Hiroyuki Tanuma
Flanker	Naoya Okubo
Flanker	Greg Smith
Number 8	Jamie Joseph
Scrum-half	Graeme Bachop
Fly-half	Keiji Hirose
Right Wing	Daisuke Ohata
Centre	Andrew McCormick (c)
Centre	Yukio Motoki
Left Wing	Patiliai Tuidraki
Full-back	Tsuyoshi Hirao
Reserves	Takeomi Ito, Wataru Murata, Toshikazu Nakamichi, Yoshihiko Sakuraba, Masaaki Sakata
Referee	Dume J

Points Scorers
Wales

Name	Tries	Conv	Pen K	Drop G	Points
Llewellyn DS	1	0	0	0	5
Penalty Try	1	0	0	0	5
Bateman AG	1	0	0	0	5
Gibbs IS	1	0	0	0	5
Howley R	1	0	0	0	5
Howarth SP	1	0	0	0	5
Jenkins NR	0	8	1	0	19
Taylor M	2	0	0	0	10
Thomas G	1	0	0	0	5

Japan

Name	Tries	Conv	Pen K	Drop G	Points
Hirose K	0	1	1	0	5
Ohata D	1	0	0	0	5
Tuidraki P	1	0	0	0	5

Pool D, Fourth Match
Argentina v Samoa: 32-16
10 October 1999
Stradey Park, Llanelli

Players

Argentina

Prop	Omar Hasan Jalil
Hooker	Mario Ledesma Arocena
Prop	Mauricio Reggiardo
Lock	Alejandro Allub
Lock	Ignacio Fernandez Lobbe
Flanker	Rolando Martin
Flanker	Santiago Phelan
Number 8	Gonzalo Longo Elia
Scrum-half	Agustin Pichot
Fly-half	Gonzalo Quesada
Right Wing	Diego Albanese
Centre	Lisandro Arbizu (c)
Centre	Eduardo Simone
Left Wing	Octavio Bartolucci
Full-back	Manuel Contepomi
Reserves	Gonzalo Camardon, Miguel Ruiz, Martin Scelzo

Samoa

Prop	Robbie Ale
Hooker	Trevor Leota
Prop	Brendan Reidy
Lock	Opeta Palepoi
Lock	Lama Tone
Flanker	Junior Paramore
Flanker	Sene Ta'ala
Number 8	Pat Lam (c)
Scrum-half	Stephen So'oilao
Fly-half	Stephen Bachop
Right Wing	Brian Lima
Centre	George Leaupepe
Centre	Inga Tuigamala
Left Wing	Afato So'oalo
Full-back	Silao Leaega
Reserves	Isaac Fea'unati, Onehunga Matauiau Esau, Mike Mika, Kalolo Toleafoa, Tanner Vili

Referee	Erickson W

Points Scorers

Argentina

Name	Tries	Conv	Pen K	Drop G	Points
Allub A	1	0	0	0	5
Quesada G	0	0	8	1	27

Samoa

Name	Tries	Conv	Pen K	Drop G	Points
Leaega S	0	1	3	0	11
Paramore PJ	1	0	0	0	5

Pool D, Fifth Match
Wales v Samoa: 31–38
14 October 1999
Millennium Stadium, Cardiff

Players
Wales

Prop	Peter Rogers
Hooker	Garin Jenkins
Prop	Dai Young
Lock	Gareth Llewellyn
Lock	Chris Wyatt
Flanker	Brett Sinkinson
Flanker	Martyn Williams
Number 8	Scott Quinnell
Scrum-half	Rob Howley (c)
Fly-half	Neil Jenkins
Right Wing	Dafydd James
Centre	Scott Gibbs
Centre	Mark Taylor
Left Wing	Gareth Thomas
Full-back	Shane Howarth
Reserves	Ben Evans, Andrew Lewis

Samoa

Prop	Robbie Ale
Hooker	Trevor Leota
Prop	Brendan Reidy
Lock	Lio Falaniko
Lock	Lama Tone
Flanker	Craig Glendinning
Flanker	Junior Paramore
Number 8	Pat Lam (c)
Scrum-half	Stephen So'oilao
Fly-half	Stephen Bachop
Right Wing	Brian Lima
Centre	George Leaupepe
Centre	To'o Vaega
Left Wing	Inga Tuigamala
Full-back	Silao Leaega
Reserves	Terry Fanolua, Earl Va'a, Onehunga Matauiau Esau, Mike Mika, Semo Sititi, Sene Ta'ala

Referee	Morrison E

Points Scorers
Wales

Name	Tries	Conv	Pen K	Drop G	Points
Penalty Try	2	0	0	0	10
Jenkins NR	0	2	4	0	16
Thomas G	1	0	0	0	5

Samoa

Name	Tries	Conv	Pen K	Drop G	Points
Bachop SJ	2	0	0	0	10
Falaniko FL	1	0	0	0	5
Lam PR	1	0	0	0	5
Leaega S	1	5	1	0	18

Pool D, Sixth Match
Argentina v Japan: 33-12
16 October 1999
Millennium Stadium, Cardiff

Players

Argentina

Prop	Omar Hasan Jalil
Hooker	Mario Ledesma Arocena
Prop	Mauricio Reggiardo
Lock	Alejandro Allub
Lock	Pedro Sporleder
Flanker	Rolando Martin
Flanker	Santiago Phelan
Number 8	Ignacio Fernandez Lobbe
Scrum-half	Agustin Pichot
Fly-half	Gonzalo Quesada
Right Wing	Diego Albanese
Centre	Lisandro Arbizu (c)
Centre	Eduardo Simone
Left Wing	Gonzalo Camardon
Full-back	Ignacio Corleto
Reserves	Felipe Contepomi, Lucas Ostiglia, Miguel Ruiz

Japan

Prop	Toshikazu Nakamichi
Hooker	Masahiro Kunda
Prop	Kohei Oguchi
Lock	Robert Gordon
Lock	Hiroyuki Tanuma
Flanker	Naoya Okubo
Flanker	Greg Smith
Number 8	Jamie Joseph
Scrum-half	Graeme Bachop
Fly-half	Keiji Hirose
Right Wing	Daisuke Ohata
Centre	Andrew McCormick (c)
Centre	Yukio Motoki
Left Wing	Patiliai Tuidraki
Full-back	Tsutomu Matsuda
Reserves	Shin Hasegawa, Takeomi Ito, Naoto Nakamura, Masaaki Sakata
Referee	Dickinson S

Points Scorers

Argentina

Name	Tries	Conv	Pen K	Drop G	Points
Albanese DL	1	0	0	0	5
Contepomi F	0	1	0	0	2
Pichot A	1	0	0	0	5
Quesada G	0	0	7	0	21

Japan

Name	Tries	Conv	Pen K	Drop G	Points
Hirose K	0	0	4	0	12

Pool E, First Match
Ireland v USA: 53-8
2 October 1999
Lansdowne Road, Dublin

Players

Ireland

Prop	Peter Clohessy
Hooker	Keith Wood
Prop	Paul Wallace
Lock	Jeremy Davidson
Lock	Paddy Johns
Flanker	Trevor Brennan
Flanker	Andy Ward
Number 8	Dion O'Cuinneagain (c)
Scrum-half	Tom Tierney
Fly-half	David Humphreys
Right Wing	Matt Mostyn
Centre	Brian O'Driscoll
Centre	Kevin Maggs
Left Wing	Justin Bishop
Full-back	Conor O'Shea
Reserves	Jonathan Bell, Eric Elwood, Eric Miller, Ross Nesdale, Malcolm O'Kelly, Brian O'Meara, Justin Fitzpatrick

USA

Prop	Ray Lehner
Hooker	Tom Billups
Prop	George Sucher
Lock	Luke Gross
Lock	Alec Parker
Flanker	Dave Hodges
Flanker	Richard Tardits
Number 8	Dan Lyle (c)
Scrum-half	Kevin Dalzell
Fly-half	Mark Williams
Right Wing	Vaea Anitoni
Centre	Juan Grobler
Centre	Tomasi Takau
Left Wing	Brian Hightower
Full-back	Kurt Shuman
Reserves	Kirk Khasigian, Tasi Mo'unga, David Niu, Shaun Paga, Mark Scharrenberg
Referee	Dume J

Points Scorers

Ireland

Name	Tries	Conv	Pen K	Drop G	Points
Elwood EP	0	2	0	0	4
Humphreys DG	0	4	2	0	14
O'Driscoll B	1	0	0	0	5
Wood KGM	4	0	0	0	20
Bishop JP	1	0	0	0	5
Penalty Try	1	0	0	0	5

USA

Name	Tries	Conv	Pen K	Drop G	Points
Dalzell K	1	0	1	0	8

Pool E, Second Match
Australia v Romania: 57-9
3 October 1999
Ravenhill Park, Belfast

Players
Australia
Prop	Andrew Blades
Hooker	Phil Kearns
Prop	Richard Harry
Lock	John Eales (c)
Lock	David Giffin
Flanker	Owen Finegan
Flanker	David Wilson
Number 8	Toutai Kefu
Scrum-half	George Gregan
Fly-half	Rod Kafer
Right Wing	Jason Little
Centre	Dan Herbert
Centre	Tim Horan
Left Wing	Ben Tune
Full-back	Matthew Burke
Reserves	Mark Connors, Dan Crowley, Nathan Grey, Jeremy Paul, Joe Roff, Tiaan Strauss, Chris Whitaker

Romania
Prop	Laurentiu Rotaru
Hooker	Petru Balan
Prop	Constantin Stan
Lock	Tiberiu Brinza
Lock	Ovidiu Slusariuc
Flanker	Alin Petrache
Flanker	Erdinci Septar
Number 8	Catalin Draguceanu
Scrum-half	Petre Mitu
Fly-half	Roland Vusec
Right Wing	Cristian Sauan
Centre	Gabriel Brezoianu
Centre	Romeo Gontineac (c)
Left Wing	Gheorghe Solomie
Full-back	Mihai Vioreanu
Reserves	Daniel Chiriac, Florin Corodeanu, Nicolae Dragos Dima, Razvan Mavrodin
Referee	Honiss P

Points Scorers
Australia
Name	Tries	Conv	Pen K	Drop G	Points
Burke MC	1	5	0	0	15
Eales JA	0	1	0	0	2
Horan TJ	1	0	0	0	5
Kafer R	1	0	0	0	5
Kefu RST	3	0	0	0	15
Little JS	1	0	0	0	5
Roff JWC	2	0	0	0	10

Romania
Name	Tries	Conv	Pen K	Drop G	Points
Mitu P	0	0	3	0	9

Pool E, Third Match
USA v Romania: 25-27
9 October 1999
Lansdowne Road, Dublin

Players

USA

Prop	Ray Lehner
Hooker	Tom Billups
Prop	George Sucher
Lock	Luke Gross
Lock	Alec Parker
Flanker	Dan Lyle (c)
Flanker	Tasi Mo'unga
Number 8	Rob Lumkong
Scrum-half	Kevin Dalzell
Fly-half	David Niu
Right Wing	Vaea Anitoni
Centre	Juan Grobler
Centre	Mark Scharrenberg
Left Wing	Brian Hightower
Full-back	Kurt Shuman
Reserves	Joe Clayton, Dave Hodges, Kirk Khasigian, Shaun Paga, Tomasi Takau, Richard Tardits

Romania

Prop	Razvan Mavrodin
Hooker	Petru Balan
Prop	Constantin Stan
Lock	Tiberiu Brinza
Lock	Tudor Constantin
Flanker	Alin Petrache
Flanker	Erdinci Septar
Number 8	Catalin Draguceanu
Scrum-half	Petre Mitu
Fly-half	Roland Vusec
Right Wing	Cristian Sauan
Centre	Gabriel Brezoianu
Centre	Romeo Gontineac
Left Wing	Gheorghe Solomie
Full-back	Mihai Vioreanu
Reserves	Daniel Chiriac, Florin Corodeanu, Nicolae Dragos Dima
Referee	Fleming J

Points Scorers

USA

Name	Tries	Conv	Pen K	Drop G	Points
Dalzell K	0	2	2	0	10
Hightower B	1	0	0	0	5
Lyle DJ	1	0	0	0	5
Shuman KD	1	0	0	0	5

Romania

Name	Tries	Conv	Pen K	Drop G	Points
Constantin T	1	0	0	0	5
Mitu P	0	2	1	0	7
Petrache AA	1	0	0	0	5
Solomie GL	2	0	0	0	10

**Pool E, Fourth Match
Ireland v Australia: 3-23
10 October 1999
Lansdowne Road, Dublin**

Players

Ireland

Prop	Paul Wallace
Hooker	Keith Wood
Prop	Justin Fitzpatrick
Lock	Paddy Johns
Lock	Malcolm O'Kelly
Flanker	Trevor Brennan
Flanker	Andy Ward
Number 8	Dion O'Cuinneagain (c)
Scrum-half	Tom Tierney
Fly-half	David Humphreys
Right Wing	Matt Mostyn
Centre	Brian O'Driscoll
Centre	Kevin Maggs
Left Wing	Justin Bishop
Full-back	Conor O'Shea
Reserves	Jonathan Bell, Bob Casey, Peter Clohessy, Eric Elwood, Eric Miller

Australia

Prop	Andrew Blades
Hooker	Phil Kearns
Prop	Richard Harry
Lock	John Eales (c)
Lock	David Giffin
Flanker	Mark Connors
Flanker	David Wilson
Number 8	Toutai Kefu
Scrum-half	George Gregan
Fly-half	Steve Larkham
Right Wing	Joe Roff
Centre	Dan Herbert
Centre	Tim Horan
Left Wing	Ben Tune
Full-back	Matthew Burke
Reserves	Dan Crowley, Owen Finegan, Nathan Grey, Jason Little, Jeremy Paul, Tiaan Strauss
Referee	Thomas C

Points Scorers

Ireland

Name	Tries	Conv	Pen K	Drop G	Points
Humphreys DG	0	0	1	0	3

Australia

Name	Tries	Conv	Pen K	Drop G	Points
Burke MC	0	2	2	0	10
Eales JA	0	0	1	0	3
Horan TJ	1	0	0	0	5
Tune BN	1	0	0	0	5

Pool E, Fifth Match
Australia v USA: 55–19
14 October 1999
Thomond Park, Limerick

Players
Australia

Prop	Dan Crowley
Hooker	Michael Foley
Prop	Rod Moore
Lock	Tom Bowman
Lock	Mark Connors
Flanker	Owen Finegan
Flanker	Tiaan Strauss
Number 8	Jim Williams
Scrum-half	Chris Whitaker
Fly-half	Steve Larkham
Right Wing	Matthew Burke
Centre	Nathan Grey
Centre	Jason Little (c)
Left Wing	Scott Staniforth
Full-back	Chris Latham
Reserves	Matt Cockbain, David Giffin, Rod Kafer, Joe Roff

USA

Prop	Joe Clayton
Hooker	Tom Billups
Prop	George Sucher
Lock	Luke Gross
Lock	Alec Parker
Flanker	Dave Hodges
Flanker	Tasi Mo'unga
Number 8	Rob Lumkong
Scrum-half	Kevin Dalzell (c)
Fly-half	David Niu
Right Wing	Vaea Anitoni
Centre	Juan Grobler
Centre	Mark Scharrenberg
Left Wing	Brian Hightower
Full-back	Kurt Shuman
Reserves	Jesse Coulson, Kirk Khasigian, Marc L'Huillier, Shaun Paga, Eric Reed, Tini Saulala, Tomasi Takau
Referee	Watson A

Points Scorers
Australia

Name	Tries	Conv	Pen K	Drop G	Points
Burke MC	1	5	1	0	18
Foley MA	1	0	0	0	5
Larkham SJ	1	0	0	0	5
Latham CE	1	0	0	0	5
Roff JWC	0	1	0	0	2
Staniforth SNG	2	0	0	0	10
Strauss CP	1	0	0	0	5
Whitaker C	1	0	0	0	5

USA

Name	Tries	Conv	Pen K	Drop G	Points
Dalzell K	0	1	3	1	14
Grobler J	1	0	0	0	5

Pool E, Sixth Match
Ireland v Romania: 44-14
15 October 1999
Lansdowne Road, Dublin

Players
Ireland

Prop	Paul Wallace
Hooker	Ross Nesdale
Prop	Justin Fitzpatrick
Lock	Paddy Johns
Lock	Malcolm O'Kelly
Flanker	Kieron Dawson
Flanker	Andy Ward
Number 8	Dion O'Cuinneagain (c)
Scrum-half	Tom Tierney
Fly-half	Eric Elwood
Right Wing	Matt Mostyn
Centre	Jonathan Bell
Centre	Mike Mullins
Left Wing	Jimmy Topping
Full-back	Conor O'Shea
Reserves	Jeremy Davidson, Gordon D'Arcy, Angus McKeen, Brian O'Meara, Brian O'Driscoll, Keith Wood, Alan Quinlan

Romania

Prop	Razvan Mavrodin
Hooker	Petru Balan
Prop	Constantin Stan
Lock	Tiberiu Brinza
Lock	Tudor Constantin (c)
Flanker	Alin Petrache
Flanker	Erdinci Septar
Number 8	Catalin Draguceanu
Scrum-half	Petre Mitu
Fly-half	Roland Vusec
Right Wing	Cristian Sauan
Centre	Gabriel Brezoianu
Centre	Romeo Gontineac
Left Wing	Gheorghe Solomie
Full-back	Mihai Vioreanu
Reserves	Marius Iacob, Daniel Chiriac, Florin Corodeanu, Nicolae Dragos Dima, Radu Fugigi, Laurentiu Rotaru, Ionut Tofan
Referee	Campsall B

Points Scorers
Ireland

Name	Tries	Conv	Pen K	Drop G	Points
Elwood EP	0	5	2	0	16
O'Cuinneagain D	1	0	0	0	5
O'Shea CMP	2	0	0	0	10
O'Driscoll B	0	0	0	1	3
Tierney T	1	0	0	0	5
Ward AJ	1	0	0	0	5

Romania

Name	Tries	Conv	Pen K	Drop G	Points
Mitu P	0	0	3	0	9
Sauan DC	1	0	0	0	5

First Quarter-Final Play-Off
Scotland v Samoa: 35-20
20 October 1999
Murrayfield, Edinburgh

Players

Scotland

Prop	George Graham
Hooker	Gordon Bulloch
Prop	Tom Smith
Lock	Scott Murray
Lock	Doddie Weir
Flanker	Budge Pountney
Flanker	Martin Leslie
Number 8	Gordon Simpson
Scrum-half	Gary Armstrong (c)
Fly-half	Gregor Townsend
Right Wing	Kenny Logan
Centre	Jamie Mayer
Centre	James McLaren
Left Wing	Cammie Murray
Full-back	Glenn Metcalfe
Reserves	Paul Burnell, Stuart Grimes, Duncan Hodge, Cameron Mather, Robbie Russell

Samoa

Prop	Polo Asi
Hooker	Trevor Leota
Prop	Brendan Reidy
Lock	Lio Falaniko
Lock	Lama Tone
Flanker	Craig Glendinning
Flanker	Semo Sititi
Number 8	Pat Lam (c)
Scrum-half	Stephen So'oialo
Fly-half	Stephen Bachop
Right Wing	Brian Lima
Centre	Terry Fanolua
Centre	To'o Vaega
Left Wing	Inga Tuigamala
Full-back	Silao Leaega
Reserves	Earl Va'a, Robbie Ale, Onehunga Matauiau Esau, Sene Ta'ala, Filipo Toala

Referee	Hawke C

Points Scorers

Scotland

Name	Tries	Conv	Pen K	Drop G	Points
Penalty Try	1	0	0	0	5
Leslie MD	1	0	0	0	5
Logan KMcK	0	1	5	0	17
Murray CA	1	0	0	0	5
Townsend GPJ	0	0	0	1	3

Samoa

Name	Tries	Conv	Pen K	Drop G	Points
Leaega S	0	2	2	0	10
Lima BP	1	0	0	0	5
Sititi S	1	0	0	0	5

Second Quarter-Final Play-Off
England v Fiji: 45-24
20 October 1999
Twickenham, London

Players
England

Prop	Darren Garforth
Hooker	Phil Greening
Prop	Jason Leonard
Lock	Garath Archer
Lock	Martin Johnson (c)
Flanker	Neil Back
Flanker	Joe Worsley
Number 8	Lawrence Dallaglio
Scrum-half	Austin Healey
Fly-half	Jonny Wilkinson
Right Wing	Nick Beal
Centre	Mike Catt
Centre	Will Greenwood
Left Wing	Dan Luger
Full-back	Matt Perry
Reserves	Richard Cockerill, Matt Dawson, Phil de Glanville, Paul Grayson, Richard Hill, Tim Rodber, Graham Rowntree

Fiji

Prop	Dan Rouse
Hooker	Greg Smith (c)
Prop	Joeli Veitayaki
Lock	Emori Katalau
Lock	Simon Raiwalui
Flanker	Koli Sewabu
Flanker	Seta Tawake Naivaluwaqa
Number 8	Ifereimi Tawake
Scrum-half	Mosese Rauluni
Fly-half	Waisale Serevi
Right Wing	Imanueli Tikomaimakogai
Centre	Meli Nakauta
Centre	Viliame Satala
Left Wing	Marika Vunibaka
Full-back	Alfred Uluinayau
Reserves	Nicky Little, Inoke Male, Epeli Naituvau, Jacob Rauluni, Isaia Rasila, Waisake Sotutu
Referee	Bevan D

Points Scorers
England

Name	Tries	Conv	Pen K	Drop G	Points
Back NA	1	0	0	0	5
Beal ND	1	0	0	0	5
Dawson MJS	0	1	0	0	2
Greening PBT	1	0	0	0	5
Luger DD	1	0	0	0	5
Wilkinson JP	0	1	7	0	23

Fiji

Name	Tries	Conv	Pen K	Drop G	Points
Serevi WT	0	0	1	0	3
Little NT	0	3	0	0	6
Nakauta M	1	0	0	0	5
Satala V	1	0	0	0	5
Tikomaimakogai I	1	0	0	0	5

Third Quarter-Final Play-Off
Argentina v Ireland: 28-24
20 October 1999
Stade Felix Bollaert, Lens

Players

Argentina

Prop	Omar Hasan Jalil
Hooker	Mario Ledesma Arocena
Prop	Mauricio Reggiardo
Lock	Alejandro Allub
Lock	Ignacio Fernandez Lobbe
Flanker	Rolando Martin
Flanker	Santiago Phelan
Number 8	Gonzalo Longo Elia
Scrum-half	Agustin Pichot
Fly-half	Gonzalo Quesada
Right Wing	Diego Albanese
Centre	Lisandro Arbizu (c)
Centre	Eduardo Simone
Left Wing	Gonzalo Camardon
Full-back	Ignacio Corleto
Reserves	Felipe Contepomi, Martin Scelzo

Ireland

Prop	Paul Wallace
Hooker	Keith Wood
Prop	Reg Corrigan
Lock	Jeremy Davidson
Lock	Malcolm O'Kelly
Flanker	Kieron Dawson
Flanker	Andy Ward
Number 8	Dion O'Cuinneagain (c)
Scrum-half	Tom Tierney
Fly-half	David Humphreys
Right Wing	Matt Mostyn
Centre	Brian O'Driscoll
Centre	Kevin Maggs
Left Wing	Justin Bishop
Full-back	Conor O'Shea
Reserves	Bob Casey, Eric Miller, Justin Fitzpatrick
Referee	Dickinson S

Points Scorers

Argentina

Name	Tries	Conv	Pen K	Drop G	Points
Albanese DL	1	0	0	0	5
Quesada G	0	1	7	0	23

Ireland

Name	Tries	Conv	Pen K	Drop G	Points
Humphreys DG	0	0	7	1	24

First Quarter-Final
Wales v Australia: 9-24
23 October 1999
Millennium Stadium, Cardiff

Players
Wales

Prop	Peter Rogers
Hooker	Garin Jenkins
Prop	Dai Young
Lock	Craig Quinnell
Lock	Chris Wyatt
Flanker	Colin Charvis
Flanker	Brett Sinkinson
Number 8	Scott Quinnell
Scrum-half	Rob Howley (c)
Fly-half	Neil Jenkins
Right Wing	Dafydd James
Centre	Scott Gibbs
Centre	Mark Taylor
Left Wing	Gareth Thomas
Full-back	Shane Howarth
Reserves	Allan Bateman, Ben Evans, Andrew Lewis, Mike Voyle

Australia

Prop	Andrew Blades
Hooker	Michael Foley
Prop	Richard Harry
Lock	John Eales (c)
Lock	David Giffin
Flanker	Matt Cockbain
Flanker	David Wilson
Number 8	Tiaan Strauss
Scrum-half	George Gregan
Fly-half	Steve Larkham
Right Wing	Joe Roff
Centre	Dan Herbert
Centre	Tim Horan
Left Wing	Ben Tune
Full-back	Matthew Burke
Reserves	Mark Connors, Owen Finegan, Jason Little, Jeremy Paul
Referee	Hawke C

Points Scorers
Wales

Name	Tries	Conv	Pen K	Drop G	Points
Jenkins NR	0	0	3	0	9

Australia

Name	Tries	Conv	Pen K	Drop G	Points
Burke MC	0	3	1	0	9
Gregan GM	2	0	0	0	10
Tune BN	1	0	0	0	5

Second Quarter-Final
England v South Africa: 21-44
24 October 1999
Stade de France, Paris

Players
England

Prop	Jason Leonard
Hooker	Phil Greening
Prop	Phil Vickery
Lock	Danny Grewcock
Lock	Martin Johnson (c)
Flanker	Neil Back
Flanker	Richard Hill
Number 8	Lawrence Dallaglio
Scrum-half	Matt Dawson
Fly-half	Paul Grayson
Right Wing	Nick Beal
Centre	Phil de Glanville
Centre	Will Greenwood
Left Wing	Dan Luger
Full-back	Matt Perry
Reserves	Mike Catt, Martin Corry, Austin Healey, Jonny Wilkinson

South Africa

Prop	Os Du Randt
Hooker	Naka Drotske
Prop	Cobus Visagie
Lock	Mark Andrews
Lock	Krynauw Otto
Flanker	Johan Erasmus
Flanker	Andre Venter
Number 8	Bobby Skinstad
Scrum-half	Joost van der Westhuizen (c)
Fly-half	Jannie de Beer
Right Wing	Deon Kayser
Centre	Robbie Fleck
Centre	Pieter Muller
Left Wing	Pieter Rossouw
Full-back	Percy Montgomery
Reserves	Ollie le Roux, Stefan Terblanche, Albert van den Bergh, Andre Vos

Referee	Fleming J

Points Scorers
England

Name	Tries	Conv	Pen K	Drop G	Points
Grayson PJ	0	0	6	0	18
Wilkinson JP	0	0	1	0	3

South Africa

Name	Tries	Conv	Pen K	Drop G	Points
de Beer JH	0	2	5	5	34
Rossouw PWG	1	0	0	0	5
van der Westhuizen J	1	0	0	0	5

Third Quarter-Final
Scotland v New Zealand: 18-30
24 October 1999
Murrayfield, Edinburgh

Players
Scotland

Prop	Paul Burnell
Hooker	Gordon Bulloch
Prop	Tom Smith
Lock	Scott Murray
Lock	Doddie Weir
Flanker	Budge Pountney
Flanker	Martin Leslie
Number 8	Gordon Simpson
Scrum-half	Gary Armstrong (c)
Fly-half	Gregor Townsend
Right Wing	Kenny Logan
Centre	Jamie Mayer
Centre	Alan Tait
Left Wing	Cammie Murray
Full-back	Glenn Metcalfe
Reserves	George Graham, Stuart Grimes, Robbie Russell

New Zealand

Prop	Craig Dowd
Hooker	Anton Oliver
Prop	Carl Hoeft
Lock	Robin Brooke
Lock	Norm Maxwell
Flanker	Josh Kronfeld
Flanker	Reuben Thorne
Number 8	Taine Randell (c)
Scrum-half	Justin Marshall
Fly-half	Andrew Mehrtens
Right Wing	Jonah Lomu
Centre	Christian Cullen
Centre	Alama Ieremia
Left Wing	Tana Umaga
Full-back	Jeff Wilson
Reserves	Tony Brown, Daryl Gibson, Mark Hammett, Ian Jones, Kees Meeuws
Referee	Morrison E

Points Scorers
Scotland

Name	Tries	Conv	Pen K	Drop G	Points
Pountney AC	1	0	0	0	5
Logan KMcK	0	1	1	0	5
Murray CA	1	0	0	0	5
Townsend GPJ	0	0	0	1	3

New Zealand

Name	Tries	Conv	Pen K	Drop G	Points
Lomu JT	1	0	0	0	5
Mehrtens AP	0	2	2	0	10
Umaga TJF	2	0	0	0	10
Wilson JW	1	0	0	0	5

Fourth Quarter-Final
Argentina v France: 26-47
24 October 1999
Lansdowne Road, Dublin

Players

Argentina

Prop	Roberto Grau
Hooker	Mario Ledesma Arocena
Prop	Mauricio Reggiardo
Lock	Alejandro Allub
Lock	Ignacio Fernandez Lobbe
Flanker	Rolando Martin
Flanker	Santiago Phelan
Number 8	Gonzalo Longo Elia
Scrum-half	Agustin Pichot
Fly-half	Gonzalo Quesada
Right Wing	Diego Albanese
Centre	Lisandro Arbizu (c)
Centre	Eduardo Simone
Left Wing	Gonzalo Camardon
Full-back	Ignacio Corleto
Reserves	Agustin Canalda, Manuel Contepomi, Felipe Contepomi, Nicolas Fernandez Miranda, Lucas Ostiglia, Miguel Ruiz, Martin Scelzo

France

Prop	Cedric Soulette
Hooker	Raphael Ibanez (c)
Prop	Franck Tournaire
Lock	Abdelatif Benazzi
Lock	Olivier Brouzet
Flanker	Marc Lievremont
Flanker	Olivier Magne
Number 8	Christophe Juillet
Scrum-half	Fabien Galthie
Fly-half	Christophe Lamaison
Right Wing	Philippe Bernat-Salles
Centre	Richard Dourthe
Centre	Emile Ntamack
Left Wing	Christophe Dominici
Full-back	Xavier Garbajosa
Reserves	David Auradou, Arnaud Costes, Marc Dal Maso, Pieter de Villiers, Stephane Glas, Ugo Mola, Stephane Castaignede
Referee	Bevan D

Points Scorers

Argentina

Name	Tries	Conv	Pen K	Drop G	Points
Arbizu L	1	0	0	0	5
Contepomi F	0	0	1	0	3
Pichot A	1	0	0	0	5
Quesada G	0	2	3	0	13

France

Name	Tries	Conv	Pen K	Drop G	Points
Bernat-Salles P	2	0	0	0	10
Garbajosa X	2	0	0	0	10
Lamaison C	0	5	4	0	22
Ntamack E	1	0	0	0	5

First Semi-Final
Australia v South Africa: 27-21
30 October 1999
Twickenham, London

Players

Australia

Prop	Andrew Blades
Hooker	Michael Foley
Prop	Richard Harry
Lock	John Eales (c)
Lock	David Giffin
Flanker	Matt Cockbain
Flanker	David Wilson
Number 8	Toutai Kefu
Scrum-half	George Gregan
Fly-half	Steve Larkham
Right Wing	Joe Roff
Centre	Dan Herbert
Centre	Tim Horan
Left Wing	Ben Tune
Full-back	Matthew Burke
Reserves	Mark Connors, Owen Finegan, Nathan Grey, Jason Little

South Africa

Prop	Os Du Randt
Hooker	Naka Drotske
Prop	Cobus Visagie
Lock	Mark Andrews
Lock	Krynauw Otto
Flanker	Johan Erasmus
Flanker	Andre Venter
Number 8	Bobby Skinstad
Scrum-half	Joost van der Westhuizen (c)
Fly-half	Jannie de Beer
Right Wing	Deon Kayser
Centre	Robbie Fleck
Centre	Pieter Muller
Left Wing	Pieter Rossouw
Full-back	Percy Montgomery
Reserves	Henry Honiball, Ollie le Roux, Stefan Terblanche, Albert van den Bergh, Andre Vos

Referee	Bevan D

Points Scorers

Australia

Name	Tries	Conv	Pen K	Drop G	Points
Burke MC	0	0	8	0	24
Larkham SJ	0	0	0	1	3

South Africa

Name	Tries	Conv	Pen K	Drop G	Points
de Beer JH	0	0	6	1	21

Second Semi-Final
France v New Zealand: 43-31
31 October 1999
Twickenham, London

Players
France

Prop	Cedric Soulette
Hooker	Raphael Ibanez (c)
Prop	Franck Tournaire
Lock	Abdelatif Benazzi
Lock	Fabien Pelous
Flanker	Marc Lievremont
Flanker	Olivier Magne
Number 8	Christophe Juillet
Scrum-half	Fabien Galthie
Fly-half	Christophe Lamaison
Right Wing	Philippe Bernat-Salles
Centre	Richard Dourthe
Centre	Emile Ntamack
Left Wing	Christophe Dominici
Full-back	Xavier Garbajosa
Reserves	Olivier Brouzet, Arnaud Costes, Pieter de Villiers, Stephane Glas, Ugo Mola, Stephane Castaignede

New Zealand

Prop	Craig Dowd
Hooker	Anton Oliver
Prop	Carl Hoeft
Lock	Robin Brooke
Lock	Norm Maxwell
Flanker	Josh Kronfeld
Flanker	Reuben Thorne
Number 8	Taine Randell (c)
Scrum-half	Byron Kelleher
Fly-half	Andrew Mehrtens
Right Wing	Jonah Lomu
Centre	Christian Cullen
Centre	Alama Ieremia
Left Wing	Tana Umaga
Full-back	Jeff Wilson
Reserves	Daryl Gibson, Justin Marshall, Kees Meeuws, Royce Willis
Referee	Fleming J

Points Scorers
France

Name	Tries	Conv	Pen K	Drop G	Points
Bernat-Salles P	1	0	0	0	5
Dourthe R	1	0	0	0	5
Lamaison C	1	4	3	2	28
Dominici C	1	0	0	0	5

New Zealand

Name	Tries	Conv	Pen K	Drop G	Points
Lomu JT	2	0	0	0	10
Mehrtens AP	0	2	4	0	16
Wilson JW	1	0	0	0	5

Third Place Play-Off
New Zealand v South Africa: 18-22
4 November 1999
Millennium Stadium, Cardiff

Players
New Zealand

Prop	Craig Dowd
Hooker	Mark Hammett
Prop	Kees Meeuws
Lock	Norm Maxwell
Lock	Royce Willis
Flanker	Josh Kronfeld
Flanker	Reuben Thorne
Number 8	Taine Randell (c)
Scrum-half	Justin Marshall
Fly-half	Andrew Mehrtens
Right Wing	Jonah Lomu
Centre	Christian Cullen
Centre	Alama Ieremia
Left Wing	Tana Umaga
Full-back	Jeff Wilson
Reserves	Pita Alatini, Carl Hoeft, Dylan Mika, Anton Oliver

South Africa

Prop	Os Du Randt
Hooker	Naka Drotske
Prop	Cobus Visagie
Lock	Mark Andrews
Lock	Krynauw Otto
Flanker	Johan Erasmus
Flanker	Andre Venter
Number 8	Andre Vos
Scrum-half	Joost van der Westhuizen (c)
Fly-half	Henry Honiball
Right Wing	Breyton Paulse
Centre	Robbie Fleck
Centre	Pieter Muller
Left Wing	Stefan Terblanche
Full-back	Percy Montgomery
Reserves	Ruben Kruger, Ollie le Roux, Chris Rossouw, Werner Swanepoel, Albert van den Bergh

Referee	Marshall P

Points Scorers
New Zealand

Name	Tries	Conv	Pen K	Drop G	Points
Mehrtens AP	0	0	6	0	18

South Africa

Name	Tries	Conv	Pen K	Drop G	Points
Honiball HW	0	1	3	0	11
Montgomery PC	0	0	0	2	6
Paulse BJ	1	0	0	0	5

Final
Australia v France: 35-12
6 November 1999
Millennium Stadium, Cardiff

Players

Australia

Prop	Andrew Blades
Hooker	Michael Foley
Prop	Richard Harry
Lock	John Eales (c)
Lock	David Giffin
Flanker	Matt Cockbain
Flanker	David Wilson
Number 8	Toutai Kefu
Scrum-half	George Gregan
Fly-half	Steve Larkham
Right Wing	Joe Roff
Centre	Dan Herbert
Centre	Tim Horan
Left Wing	Ben Tune
Full-back	Matthew Burke
Reserves	Mark Connors, Dan Crowley, Owen Finegan, Nathan Grey, Jason Little, Jeremy Paul, Chris Whitaker

France

Prop	Cedric Soulette
Hooker	Raphael Ibanez (c)
Prop	Franck Tournaire
Lock	Abdelatif Benazzi
Lock	Fabien Pelous
Flanker	Marc Lievremont
Flanker	Olivier Magne
Number 8	Christophe Juillet
Scrum-half	Fabien Galthie
Fly-half	Christophe Lamaison
Right Wing	Philippe Bernat-Salles
Centre	Richard Dourthe
Centre	Emile Ntamack
Left Wing	Christophe Dominici
Full-back	Xavier Garbajosa
Reserves	Olivier Brouzet, Arnaud Costes, Marc Dal Maso, Pieter de Villiers, Stephane Glas, Ugo Mola, Stephane Castaignede
Referee	Watson A

Points Scorers

Australia

Name	Tries	Conv	Pen K	Drop G	Points
Burke MC	0	2	7	0	25
Finegan ODA	1	0	0	0	5
Tune BN	1	0	0	0	5

France

Name	Tries	Conv	Pen K	Drop G	Points
Lamaison C	0	0	4	0	12

2003

Pool A, First Match
Australia v Argentina: 24-8
10 October 2003
Telstra Stadium, Sydney

Players

Australia

Prop	Alastair Baxter
Hooker	Brendan Cannon
Prop	Bill Young
Lock	David Giffin
Lock	Nathan Sharpe
Flanker	George Smith
Flanker	Phil Waugh
Number 8	David Lyons
Scrum-half	George Gregan (c)
Fly-half	Steve Larkham
Right Wing	Joe Roff
Centre	Matthew Burke
Centre	Elton Flatley
Left Wing	Wendell Sailor
Full-back	Mat Rogers
Reserves	Matt Cockbain, Matt Giteau, Jeremy Paul, Chris Whitaker, Ben Darwin, Daniel Vickerman, Lote Tuqiri

Argentina

Prop	Roberto Grau
Hooker	Mario Ledesma Arocena
Prop	Omar Hasan Jalil
Lock	Patricio Albacete
Lock	Ignacio Fernandez
Flanker	Rolando Martin
Flanker	Santiago Phelan
Number 8	Gonzalo Longo Elia
Scrum-half	Agustin Pichot (c)
Fly-half	Felipe Contepomi
Right Wing	Diego Albanese
Centre	Manuel Contepomi
Centre	Jose Orengo
Left Wing	Jose Nunez Piossek
Full-back	Ignacio Corleto
Reserves	Martin Durand, Juan Martin Hernandez, Mauricio Reggiardo
Unused	Rimas Alvarez Kairelis, Nicolas Fernandez Miranda, Federico Mendez, Gonzalo Quesada
Referee	Honiss P

Points Scorers

Australia

Name	Tries	Conv	Pen K	Drop G	Points
Sailor WJ	1	0	0	0	5
Flatley EJ	0	1	4	0	14
Roff JWC	1	0	0	0	5

Argentina

Name	Tries	Conv	Pen K	Drop G	Points
Corleto I	1	0	0	0	5
Contepomi F	0	0	1	0	3

Pool A, Second Match
Ireland v Romania: 45-17
11 October 2003
Central Coast Stadium, Gosford (NSW)

Players

Ireland

Prop	Reggie Corrigan
Hooker	Keith Wood (c)
Prop	Marcus Horan
Lock	Malcolm O'Kelly
Lock	Paul O'Connell
Flanker	Victor Costello
Flanker	Keith Gleeson
Number 8	Anthony Foley
Scrum-half	Peter Stringer
Fly-half	David Humphreys
Right Wing	Denis Hickie
Centre	Brian O'Driscoll
Centre	Kevin Maggs
Left Wing	Shane Horgan
Full-back	Girvan Dempsey
Reserves	Shane Byrne, Guy Easterby, John Hayes, John Kelly, Donncha O'Callaghan, Ronan O'Gara, Alan Quinlan

Romania

Prop	Petru Balan
Hooker	Razvan Mavrodin
Prop	Marcel Socaciu
Lock	Sorin Socol
Lock	Augustin Petrechei
Flanker	George Chiriac
Flanker	Ovidiu Tonita
Number 8	Cristian Petre
Scrum-half	Lucian Sirbu
Fly-half	Ionut Tofan
Right Wing	Gabriel Brezoianu
Centre	Romeo Gontineac (c)
Centre	Valentin Maftei
Left Wing	Cristian Sauan
Full-back	Dan Dumbrava
Reserves	Iulian Andrei, Marius Nicolae, Cezar Popescu, Ioan Teodorescu, Petrisor Toderasc, Marian Tudori, Mihai Vioreanu
Referee	Kaplan J

Points Scorers

Ireland

Name	Tries	Conv	Pen K	Drop G	Points
Horgan SP	1	0	0	0	5
Hickie DA	2	0	0	0	10
Humphreys DG	0	3	4	0	18
Wood KGM	1	0	0	0	5
Costello VCP	1	0	0	0	5
O'Gara RJR	0	1	0	0	2

Romania

Name	Tries	Conv	Pen K	Drop G	Points
Maftei VD	1	0	0	0	5
Tofan IR	0	1	1	0	5
Andrei I	0	1	0	0	2
Penalty Try	1	0	0	0	5

Pool A, Third Match
Argentina v Namibia: 67-14
14 October 2003
Central Coast Stadium, Gosford (NSW)

Players

Argentina

Prop	Mauricio Reggiardo
Hooker	Federico Mendez
Prop	Martin Scelzo
Lock	Rimas Alvarez Kairelis
Lock	Pedro Sporleder
Flanker	Martin Durand
Flanker	Lucas Ostiglia
Number 8	Pablo Bouza
Scrum-half	Nicolas Fernandez Miranda (c)
Fly-half	Gonzalo Quesada
Right Wing	Diego Albanese
Centre	Juan Fernandez Miranda
Centre	Martin Gaitan
Left Wing	Hernan Senillosa
Full-back	Juan Martin Hernandez
Reserves	F Contepomi, I Fernandez Lobbe, M Ledesma Arocena, R Roncero
Unused	Patricio Albacete, Ignacio Corleto, Agustin Pichot

Namibia

Prop	Neil Du Toit
Hooker	JM Meyer
Prop	Kees Lensing
Lock	Eben Isaacs
Lock	Heino Senekal
Flanker	Herman Lintvelt
Flanker	Schalk Van Der Merwe
Number 8	Sean Furter (c)
Scrum-half	Hakkies Husselman
Fly-half	Emile Wessels
Right Wing	Melrick Afrika
Centre	Du Preez Grobler
Centre	Corne Powell
Left Wing	Deon Mouton
Full-back	Jurie Booysen
Reserves	A Blaauw, R Pedro, N Swanepoel, V Dreyer, W Duvenhage, J Van Lill
Unused	Cor Van Tonder
Referee	Williams N

Points Scorers

Argentina

Name	Tries	Conv	Pen K	Drop G	Points
Gaitan M	3	0	0	0	15
Fernandez Miranda J	1	0	0	0	5
Quesada G	0	7	1	0	17
Fernandez Miranda N	1	0	0	0	5
Mendez FE	1	0	0	0	5
Bouza P	2	0	0	0	10
Penalty try	2	0	0	0	10

Namibia

Name	Tries	Conv	Pen K	Drop G	Points
Grobler Du P	1	0	0	0	5
Wessels E	0	2	0	0	4
Husselman D	1	0	0	0	5

Pool A, Fourth Match
Australia v Romania: 90-8
18 October 2003
Suncorp Stadium, Brisbane

Players

Australia

Prop	Alastair Baxter
Hooker	Brendan Cannon
Prop	Bill Young
Lock	Nathan Sharpe
Lock	Daniel Vickerman
Flanker	George Smith
Flanker	Phil Waugh
Number 8	David Lyons
Scrum-half	George Gregan (c)
Fly-half	Steve Larkham
Right Wing	Joe Roff
Centre	Matthew Burke
Centre	Elton Flatley
Left Wing	Wendell Sailor
Full-back	Mat Rogers
Reserves	Matt Cockbain, Matt Giteau, Stirling Mortlock, Jeremy Paul, Ben Darwin, Justin Harrison, Lote Tuqiri

Romania

Prop	Silviu Florea
Hooker	Razvan Mavrodin
Prop	Petrisor Toderasc
Lock	Sorin Socol
Lock	Cristian Petre
Flanker	Marius Nicolae
Flanker	Ovidiu Tonita
Number 8	George Chiriac
Scrum-half	Lucian Sirbu
Fly-half	Ionut Tofan
Right Wing	Gabriel Brezoianu
Centre	Romeo Gontineac (c)
Centre	Valentin Maftei
Left Wing	Cristian Sauan
Full-back	Dan Dumbrava
Reserves	Bogdan Tudor, Cristian Podea, Cezar Popescu, Marcel Socaciu, Ioan Teodorescu, Marian Tudori, Mihai Vioreanu

Referee	Deluca P

Points Scorers

Australia

Name	Tries	Conv	Pen K	Drop G	Points
Rogers MS	3	0	0	0	15
Burke MC	2	0	0	0	10
Flatley EJ	1	11	1	0	30
Roff JWC	1	0	0	0	5
Larkham SJ	2	0	0	0	10
Smith GB	1	0	0	0	5
Giteau M	1	0	0	0	5
Mortlock SA	1	0	0	0	5
Tuqiri L	1	0	0	0	5

Romania

Name	Tries	Conv	Pen K	Drop G	Points
Tofan IR	0	0	1	0	3
Toderasc P	1	0	0	0	5

Pool A, Fifth Match
Ireland v Namibia: 64-7
19 October 2003
Football Stadium, Sydney

Players

Ireland

Prop..John Hayes
Hooker...Keith Wood (c)
Prop...Marcus Horan
Lock...Malcolm O'Kelly
Lock...Paul O'Connell
Flanker...Simon Easterby
Flanker...Alan Quinlan
Number 8...Eric Miller
Scrum-half ....Peter Stringer
Fly-half ....Ronan O'Gara
Right Wing ....Denis Hickie
Centre ....Brian O'Driscoll
Centre ....Kevin Maggs
Left Wing ....Shane Horgan
Full-back ....Girvan Dempsey
Reserves.........................Shane Byrne, Guy Easterby, Simon Best, John Kelly
Unused ....Victor Costello, David Humphreys, Donncha O'Callaghan

Namibia

Prop ....Neil Du Toit
Hooker ....JM Meyer
Prop..Kees Lensing
Lock ....Heino Senekal
Lock...Archie Graham
Flanker..Schalk Van Der Merwe
Flanker ....Wolfie Duvenhage
Number 8 ....Sean Furter (c)
Scrum-half ....Hakkies Husselman
Fly-half ....Emile Wessels
Right Wing ....Deon Mouton
Centre...Du Preez Grobler
Centre...Corne Powell
Left Wing ....Vincent Dreyer
Full-back..Ronaldo Pedro
Reserves...............................Melrick Afrika, Andries Blaauw, Herman Lintvelt,
Niel Swanepoel, Mot Schreuder, Cor Van Tonder, Jurgens Van Lill

Referee..Cole A

Points Scorers

Ireland

Name	Tries	Conv	Pen K	Drop G	Points
Dempsey GT	1	0	0	0	5
Horgan SP	1	0	0	0	5
Hickie DA	1	0	0	0	5
O'Gara RJR	0	7	0	0	14
Horan M	1	0	0	0	5
Miller ERP	2	0	0	0	10
Quinlan A	2	0	0	0	10
Easterby G	1	0	0	0	5
Kelly JP	1	0	0	0	5

Namibia

Name	Tries	Conv	Pen K	Drop G	Points
Powell CJ	1	0	0	0	5
Wessels E	0	1	0	0	2

Pool A, Sixth Match
Argentina v Romania: 50-3
22 October 2003
Football Stadium, Sydney

Players
Argentina
Prop	Rodrigo Roncero
Hooker	Mario Ledesma Arocena
Prop	Martin Scelzo
Lock	Patricio Albacete
Lock	Pedro Sporleder
Flanker	Martin Durand
Flanker	Santiago Phelan (c)
Number 8	Pablo Bouza
Scrum-half	Nicolas Fernandez Miranda
Fly-half	Juan Fernandez Miranda
Right Wing	Jose Nunez Piossek
Centre	Manuel Contepomi
Centre	Martin Gaitan
Left Wing	Hernan Senillosa
Full-back	Juan Martin Hernandez
Reserves	Omar Hasan Jalil, Rolando Martin, Agustin Pichot, Gonzalo Quesada
Unused	Rimas Alvarez Kairelis, Federico Mendez, Jose Orengo

Romania
Prop	Silviu Florea
Hooker	Razvan Mavrodin
Prop	Petrisor Toderasc
Lock	Sorin Socol
Lock	Cristian Petre
Flanker	Ovidiu Tonita
Flanker	Marian Tudori
Number 8	George Chiriac
Scrum-half	Lucian Sirbu
Fly-half	Ionut Tofan
Right Wing	Ioan Teodorescu
Centre	Romeo Gontineac (c)
Centre	Valentin Maftei
Left Wing	Mihai Vioreanu
Full-back	Gabriel Brezoianu
Reserves	Vasile Ghioc, Iulian Andrei, Ion Paulica, Augustin Petrechei, Cezar Popescu, Cristian Sauan, Florin Tatu
Referee	White C

Points Scorers
Argentina
Name	Tries	Conv	Pen K	Drop G	Points
Hernandez JM	2	0	0	0	10
Gaitan M	1	0	0	0	5
Contepomi M	1	0	0	0	5
Fernandez Miranda J	0	4	1	0	11
Fernandez Miranda N	1	0	0	0	5
Bouza P	2	0	0	0	10
Quesada G	0	2	0	0	4

Romania
Name	Tries	Conv	Pen K	Drop G	Points
Tofan IR	0	0	1	0	3

Pool A, Seventh Match
Australia v Namibia: 142-0
25 October 2003
Adelaide Oval, Adelaide

Players

Australia

Prop	Ben Darwin
Hooker	Jeremy Paul
Prop	Matt Dunning
Lock	Justin Harrison
Lock	Nathan Sharpe
Flanker	David Croft
Flanker	George Smith
Number 8	David Lyons
Scrum-half	Chris Whitaker (c)
Fly-half	Matt Giteau
Right Wing	Mat Rogers
Centre	Nathan Grey
Centre	Stirling Mortlock
Left Wing	Lote Tuqiri
Full-back	Chris Latham
Reserves	M Burke, M Cockbain, D Giffin, J Roe, M Turinui
Unused	Brendan Cannon, Bill Young

Namibia

Prop	Neil Du Toit
Hooker	Cor Van Tonder
Prop	Kees Lensing
Lock	Eben Isaacs
Lock	Heino Senekal
Flanker	Herman Lintvelt
Flanker	Shaun Van Rooi
Number 8	Jurgens Van Lill
Scrum-half	Hakkies Husselman (c)
Fly-half	Mot Schreuder
Right Wing	Jurie Booysen
Centre	Du Preez Grobler
Centre	Emile Wessels
Left Wing	Deon Mouton
Full-back	Ronaldo Pedro
Reserves	Melrick Afrika, Andries Blaauw, Sean Furter, Phillipus Isaacs, Niel Swanepoel, Schalk Van Der Merwe, Deon Grunschloss
Referee	Jutge J

Points Scorers

Australia

Name	Tries	Conv	Pen K	Drop G	Points
Latham CE	5	0	0	0	25
Tuqiri L	3	0	0	0	15
Mortlock SA	1	0	0	0	5
Grey NP	1	0	0	0	5
Rogers MS	2	16	0	0	42
Giteau M	3	0	0	0	15
Paul JA	1	0	0	0	5
Lyons D	1	0	0	0	5
Roe JA	1	0	0	0	5
Turinui M	2	0	0	0	10
Burke MC	1	0	0	0	5
Penalty try	1	0	0	0	5

Pool A, Eighth Match
Argentina v Ireland: 15-16
26 October 2003
Adelaide Oval, Adelaide

Players

Argentina

Prop	Roberto Grau
Hooker	Federico Mendez
Prop	Mauricio Reggiardo
Lock	Rimas Alvarez Kairelis
Lock	Ignacio Fernandez Lobbe
Flanker	Rolando Martin
Flanker	Lucas Ostiglia
Number 8	Gonzalo Longo Elia
Scrum-half	Agustin Pichot (c)
Fly-half	Gonzalo Quesada
Right Wing	Diego Albanese
Centre	Felipe Contepomi
Centre	Jose Orengo
Left Wing	Jose Nunez Piossek
Full-back	Ignacio Corleto
Reserves	Martin Scelzo
Unused	Patricio Albacete, Nicolas Fernandez Miranda, Martin Gaitan, Juan Martin Hernandez, Mario Ledesma Arocena, Santiago Phelan

Ireland

Prop	John Hayes
Hooker	Keith Wood (c)
Prop	Reggie Corrigan
Lock	Malcolm O'Kelly
Lock	Paul O'Connell
Flanker	Simon Easterby
Flanker	Alan Quinlan
Number 8	Victor Costello
Scrum-half	Peter Stringer
Fly-half	David Humphreys
Right Wing	Denis Hickie
Centre	Brian O'Driscoll
Centre	Kevin Maggs
Left Wing	Shane Horgan
Full-back	Girvan Dempsey
Reserves	Eric Miller, Marcus Horan, Ronan O'Gara
Unused	Shane Byrne, Guy Easterby, John Kelly, Donncha O'Callaghan
Referee	Watson A

Points Scorers

Argentina

Name	Tries	Conv	Pen K	Drop G	Points
Corleto I	0	0	0	1	3
Quesada G	0	0	3	1	12

Ireland

Name	Tries	Conv	Pen K	Drop G	Points
Humphreys DG	0	1	1	0	5
Quinlan A	1	0	0	0	5
O'Gara RJR	0	0	2	0	6

Pool A, Ninth Match
Romania v Namibia: 37-7
30 October 2003
York Park, Launceston (Tasmania)

Players

Romania

Prop	Petru Balan
Hooker	Razvan Mavrodin
Prop	Marcel Socaciu
Lock	Cristian Petre
Lock	Augustin Petrechei
Flanker	George Chiriac
Flanker	Ovidiu Tonita
Number 8	Sorin Socol
Scrum-half	Lucian Sirbu
Fly-half	Ionut Tofan
Right Wing	Gabriel Brezoianu
Centre	Romeo Gontineac (c)
Centre	Valentin Maftei
Left Wing	Ioan Teodorescu
Full-back	Dan Dumbrava
Reserves	Silviu Florea, Iulian Andrei, Cezar Popescu, Cristian Sauan, Petrisor Toderasc, Marian Tudori, Mihai Vioreanu

Namibia

Prop	Neil Du Toit
Hooker	JM Meyer
Prop	Kees Lensing
Lock	Eben Isaacs
Lock	Heino Senekal
Flanker	Schalk Van Der Merwe
Flanker	Wolfie Duvenhage
Number 8	Sean Furter (c)
Scrum-half	Niel Swanepoel
Fly-half	Mot Schreuder
Right Wing	Deon Mouton
Centre	Du Preez Grobler
Centre	Emile Wessels
Left Wing	Vincent Dreyer
Full-back	Ronaldo Pedro
Reserves	Andries Blaauw, Deon Grunschloss, Corne Powell, Rudie Janse Van Vuuren, Cor Van Tonder, Jurgens Van Lill
Unused	Herman Lintvelt
Referee	Marshall P

Points Scorers

Romania

Name	Tries	Conv	Pen K	Drop G	Points
Teodorescu I	1	0	0	0	5
Tofan IR	0	3	2	0	12
Sirbu LM	1	0	0	0	5
Petrechei A	1	0	0	0	5
Chiriac G	1	0	0	0	5
Sauan DC	1	0	0	0	5

Namibia

Name	Tries	Conv	Pen K	Drop G	Points
Wessels E	0	1	0	0	2
Isaacs E	1	0	0	0	5

Pool A, Tenth Match
Australia v Ireland: 17-16
1 November 2003
Colonial Stadium, Melbourne

Players

Australia

Prop	Ben Darwin
Hooker	Brendan Cannon
Prop	Bill Young
Lock	David Giffin
Lock	Nathan Sharpe
Flanker	George Smith
Flanker	Phil Waugh
Number 8	David Lyons
Scrum-half	George Gregan (c)
Fly-half	Steve Larkham
Right Wing	Joe Roff
Centre	Matthew Burke
Centre	Elton Flatley
Left Wing	Wendell Sailor
Full-back	Mat Rogers
Reserves	Matt Cockbain, Matt Giteau, Jeremy Paul, Alastair Baxter, Daniel Vickerman, Lote Tuqiri
Unused	Chris Whitaker

Ireland

Prop	John Hayes
Hooker	Keith Wood (c)
Prop	Reggie Corrigan
Lock	Malcolm O'Kelly
Lock	Paul O'Connell
Flanker	Simon Easterby
Flanker	Keith Gleeson
Number 8	Anthony Foley
Scrum-half	Peter Stringer
Fly-half	Ronan O'Gara
Right Wing	Denis Hickie
Centre	Brian O'Driscoll
Centre	Kevin Maggs
Left Wing	Shane Horgan
Full-back	Girvan Dempsey
Reserves	David Humphreys, Eric Miller, Marcus Horan, John Kelly, Donncha O'Callaghan
Unused	Shane Byrne, Guy Easterby
Referee	O'Brien P

Points Scorers

Australia

Name	Tries	Conv	Pen K	Drop G	Points
Flatley EJ	0	0	3	0	9
Gregan GM	0	0	0	1	3
Smith GB	1	0	0	0	5

Ireland

Name	Tries	Conv	Pen K	Drop G	Points
O'Driscoll BG	1	0	0	1	8
O'Gara RJR	0	1	2	0	8

Pool B, First Match
France v Fiji: 61-18
11 October 2003
Lang Park, Brisbane

Players

France

Prop	Jean-Jacques Crenca
Hooker	Raphael Ibanez
Prop	Jean-Baptiste Poux
Lock	Fabien Pelous
Lock	Jerome Thion
Flanker	Serge Betsen Tchoua
Flanker	Olivier Magne
Number 8	Imanol Harinordoquy
Scrum-half	Fabien Galthie
Fly-half	Frederic Michalak
Right Wing	Aurelien Rougerie
Centre	Yannick Jauzion
Centre	Tony Marsh
Left Wing	Christophe Dominici
Full-back	Nicolas Brusque
Reserves	O Brouzet, G Merceron, P Elhorga, C Labit, D Traille
Unused	Yannick Bru, Olivier Milloud

Fiji

Prop	Richard Nyholt
Hooker	Greg Smith
Prop	Joeli Veitayaki
Lock	Apenisa Naevo
Lock	Ifereimi Rawaqa
Flanker	Sisa Koyamaibole
Flanker	Kitione Salawa
Number 8	Alifereti Doviverata (c)
Scrum-half	Mosese Rauluni
Fly-half	Nicky Little
Right Wing	Rupeni Caucaunibuca
Centre	Seru Rabeni
Centre	Aisea Tuilevu
Left Wing	Vilimoni Delasau
Full-back	Norman Ligairi
Reserves	Waisale Serevi, Kele Leawere, Sami Rabaka Nasagavesi, Naka Seru, Koli Sewabu, Marika Vunibaka
Unused	Bill Gadolo
Referee	Rolland A

Points Scorers

France

Name	Tries	Conv	Pen K	Drop G	Points
Jauzion Y	3	0	0	0	15
Dominici C	2	0	0	0	10
Michalak F	0	4	6	0	26
Ibanez R	1	0	0	0	5
Harinordoquy I	1	0	0	0	5

Fiji

Name	Tries	Conv	Pen K	Drop G	Points
Caucaunibuca R	1	0	0	0	5
Little NT	0	1	2	0	8
Naevo A	1	0	0	0	5

Pool B, Second Match
Scotland v Japan: 32-11
12 October 2003
Dairy Farmers Stadium, Townsville

Players

Scotland

Prop	Bruce Douglas
Hooker	Robbie Russell
Prop	Tom Smith
Lock	Stuart Grimes
Lock	Scott Murray
Flanker	Simon Taylor
Flanker	Jason White
Number 8	Jon Petrie
Scrum-half	Bryan Redpath (c)
Fly-half	Gordon Ross
Right Wing	Kenny Logan
Centre	Andrew Craig
Centre	James McLaren
Left Wing	Chris Paterson
Full-back	Ben Hinshelwood
Reserves	Gavin Kerr, Ross Beattie, Martin Leslie, Gregor Townsend, Simon Danielli
Unused	Michael Blair, Gordon Bulloch

Japan

Prop	Shin Hasegawa
Hooker	Masao Amino
Prop	Masahiko Toyoyama
Lock	Hajime Kiso
Lock	Adam Parker
Flanker	Naoya Okubo
Flanker	Takuro Miuchi (c)
Number 8	Takeomi Ito
Scrum-half	Takashi Tsuji
Fly-half	Keiji Hirose
Right Wing	Daisuke Ohata
Centre	Yukio Motoki
Centre	Reuben Parkinson
Left Wing	Hirotoki Onozawa
Full-back	Tsutomu Matsuda
Reserves	Toru Kurihara, Masaaki Sakata, Yuji Sonoda, Yasunori Watanabe, Andy Miller
Unused	Hiroyuki Tanuma, Masahito Yamamoto

Referee	Dickinson S

Points Scorers

Scotland

Name	Tries	Conv	Pen K	Drop G	Points
Paterson CD	2	1	1	0	15
Grimes SB	1	0	0	0	5
Taylor SM	1	0	0	0	5
Townsend GPJ	0	1	0	0	2
Danielli SCJ	1	0	0	0	5

Japan

Name	Tries	Conv	Pen K	Drop G	Points
Onozawa H	1	0	0	0	5
Hirose K	0	0	2	0	6

Pool B, Third Match
Fiji v USA: 19-18
15 October 2003
Lang Park, Brisbane

Players

Fiji

Prop	Naka Seru
Hooker	Greg Smith
Prop	Joeli Veitayaki
Lock	Apenisa Naevo
Lock	Ifereimi Rawaqa
Flanker	Alfi Mocelutu Vuivau
Flanker	Koli Sewabu
Number 8	Alifereti Doviverata (c)
Scrum-half	Mosese Rauluni
Fly-half	Nicky Little
Right Wing	Vilimoni Delasau
Centre	Seru Rabeni
Centre	Aisea Tuilevu
Left Wing	Marika Vunibaka
Full-back	Alfie Uluinayau
Reserves	Vula Maimuri, Sisa Koyamaibole, Richard Nyholt
Unused	Waisale Serevi, Bill Gadolo, Norman Ligairi, Epeli Ruivadra

USA

Prop	Dan Dorsey
Hooker	Kirk Khasigian
Prop	Mike MacDonald
Lock	Luke Gross
Lock	Alec Parker
Flanker	Dave Hodges (c)
Flanker	Kort Schubert
Number 8	Dan Lyle
Scrum-half	Kevin Dalzell
Fly-half	Mike Hercus
Right Wing	David Fee
Centre	Kain Cross
Centre	Phillip Eloff
Left Wing	Riaan Van Zyl
Full-back	Paul Emerick
Reserves	John Buchholz, Salesi Sika
Unused	Gerhard Klerck, Jurie Gouws, Kimball Kjar, John Tarpoff, Matt Wyatt
Referee	Jutge J

Points Scorers

Fiji

Name	Tries	Conv	Pen K	Drop G	Points
Little NT	0	1	4	0	14
Naevo A	1	0	0	0	5

USA

Name	Tries	Conv	Pen K	Drop G	Points
Van Zyl R	1	0	0	0	5
Hercus M	0	1	2	0	8
Schubert KS	1	0	0	0	5

Pool B, Fourth Match
France v Japan: 51-29
18 October 2003
Dairy Farmers Stadium, Townsville

Players

France

Prop	Olivier Milloud
Hooker	Yannick Bru
Prop	Jean-Baptiste Poux
Lock	Olivier Brouzet
Lock	Fabien Pelous
Flanker	Serge Betsen Tchoua
Flanker	Olivier Magne
Number 8	Christian Labit
Scrum-half	Fabien Galthie (c)
Fly-half	Frederic Michalak
Right Wing	Aurelien Rougerie
Centre	Tony Marsh
Centre	Damien Traille
Left Wing	Christophe Dominici
Full-back	Clement Poitreneaud
Reserves	D Auradou, Jean-Jacques Crenca, R Ibanez, G Merceron, S Chabal
Unused	Pepito Elhorga, Yannick Jauzion

Japan

Prop	Shin Hasegawa
Hooker	Masaaki Sakata
Prop	Ryo Yamamura
Lock	Adam Parker
Lock	Hiroyuki Tanuma
Flanker	Naoya Okubo
Flanker	Takuro Miuchi (c)
Number 8	Takeomi Ito
Scrum-half	Yuji Sonoda
Fly-half	Andy Miller
Right Wing	Daisuke Ohata
Centre	Hideki Nanba
Centre	George Konia
Left Wing	Hirotoki Onozowa
Full-back	Toru Kurihara
Reserves	Ryota Asano, Koichi Kubo
Unused	M Amino, Y Motoki, T Tsuji, M Yamamoto, T Yoshida

Referee	Lewis A

Points Scorers

France

Name	Tries	Conv	Pen K	Drop G	Points
Rougerie A	2	0	0	0	10
Dominici C	1	0	0	0	5
Michalak F	1	5	3	0	24
Pelous F	1	0	0	0	5
Crenca J-J	1	0	0	0	5
Merceron G	0	1	0	0	2

Japan

Name	Tries	Conv	Pen K	Drop G	Points
Kurihara T	0	2	5	0	19
Ohata D	1	0	0	0	5
Konia GN	1	0	0	0	5

Pool B, Fifth Match
Scotland v USA: 39-15
20 October 2003
Lang Park, Brisbane

Players
Scotland

Prop	Gavin Kerr
Hooker	Gordon Bulloch (c)
Prop	Tom Smith
Lock	Nathan Hines
Lock	Stuart Grimes
Flanker	Jon Petrie
Flanker	Ross Beattie
Number 8	Simon Taylor
Scrum-half	Michael Blair
Fly-half	Gregor Townsend
Right Wing	Chris Paterson
Centre	Andrew Craig
Centre	Andrew Henderson
Left Wing	Simon Danielli
Full-back	Glenn Metcalfe
Reserves	Bruce Douglas, Ben Hinshelwood, Martin Leslie, Kenny Logan, Bryan Redpath, Jason White
Unused	Robbie Russell

USA

Prop	Dan Dorsey
Hooker	Kirk Khasigian
Prop	Mike MacDonald
Lock	Luke Gross
Lock	Alec Parker
Flanker	Dave Hodges (c)
Flanker	Kort Schubert
Number 8	Dan Lyle
Scrum-half	Kevin Dalzell
Fly-half	Mike Hercus
Right Wing	David Fee
Centre	Kain Cross
Centre	Phillip Eloff
Left Wing	Riaan Van Zyl
Full-back	Paul Emerick
Reserves	Jason Keyter, Richard Liddington, Olo Fifita, Jurie Gouws, Kimball Kjar, Link Wilfley
Unused	Matt Wyatt
Referee	Kaplan J

Points Scorers
Scotland

Name	Tries	Conv	Pen K	Drop G	Points
Danielli SCJ	2	0	0	0	10
Paterson CD	1	4	2	0	19
Townsend GPJ	1	0	0	0	5
Kerr G	1	0	0	0	5

USA

Name	Tries	Conv	Pen K	Drop G	Points
Hercus M	0	0	5	0	15

Pool B, Sixth Match
Fiji v Japan: 41–13
23 October 2003
Dairy Farmers Stadium, Townsville

Players

Fiji

Prop	Isaia Rasila
Hooker	Greg Smith
Prop	Naka Seru
Lock	Emori Katalau
Lock	Kele Leawere
Flanker	Alfi Mocelutu Vuivau
Flanker	Koli Sewabu
Number 8	Alifereti Doviverata (c)
Scrum-half	Sami Rabaka Nasagavesi
Fly-half	Waisale Serevi
Right Wing	Vilimoni Delasau
Centre	Seru Rabeni
Centre	Epeli Ruivadra
Left Wing	Aisea Tuilevu
Full-back	Norman Ligairi
Reserves	Vula Maimuri, Bill Gadolo, Sisa Koyamaibole, Nicky Little, Mosese Rauluni, Joeli Veitayaki, Marika Vunibaka

Japan

Prop	Masahiko Toyoyama
Hooker	Masaaki Sakata
Prop	Masahito Yamamoto
Lock	Hajime Kiso
Lock	Adam Parker
Flanker	Naoya Okubo
Flanker	Takuro Miuchi (c)
Number 8	Takeomi Ito
Scrum-half	Takashi Tsuji
Fly-half	Andy Miller
Right Wing	Daisuke Ohata
Centre	Yukio Motoki
Centre	Reuben Parkinson
Left Wing	Hirotoki Onozowa
Full-back	Tsutomu Matsuda
Reserves	Masao Amino, Ryota Asano, Shin Hasegawa, Toru Kurihara, Koichi Kubo, Yuji Sonoda, George Konia
Referee	Williams N

Points Scorers

Fiji

Name	Tries	Conv	Pen K	Drop G	Points
Ligairi N	2	0	0	0	10
Tuilevu A	2	0	0	0	10
Serevi WT	0	0	1	0	3
Little NT	0	2	3	0	13
Vunibaka MD	1	0	0	0	5

Japan

Name	Tries	Conv	Pen K	Drop G	Points
Miller AJ	1	1	1	1	13

Pool B, Seventh Match
France v Scotland: 51-9
25 October 2003
Telstra Stadium, Sydney

Players

France

Prop	Jean-Jacques Crenca
Hooker	Raphael Ibanez
Prop	Sylvain Marconnet
Lock	Fabien Pelous
Lock	Jerome Thion
Flanker	Serge Betsen Tchoua
Flanker	Olivier Magne
Number 8	Imanol Harinordoquy
Scrum-half	Fabien Galthie (c)
Fly-half	Frederic Michalak
Right Wing	Aurelien Rougerie
Centre	Yannick Jauzion
Centre	Tony Marsh
Left Wing	Christophe Dominici
Full-back	Nicolas Brusque
Reserves	Y Bru, O Brouzet, G Merceron, O Milloud, P Tabacco, D Traille
Unused	Pepito Elhorga

Scotland

Prop	Gavin Kerr
Hooker	Gordon Bulloch
Prop	Tom Smith
Lock	Stuart Grimes
Lock	Scott Murray
Flanker	Cameron Mather
Flanker	Jason White
Number 8	Simon Taylor
Scrum-half	Bryan Redpath (c)
Fly-half	Gregor Townsend
Right Wing	Kenny Logan
Centre	Andrew Craig
Centre	Andrew Henderson
Left Wing	Chris Paterson
Full-back	Glenn Metcalfe
Reserves	B Douglas, N Hines, J Petrie, J McLaren, R Russell
Unused	Michael Blair, Simon Danielli
Referee	McHugh D

Points Scorers

France

Name	Tries	Conv	Pen K	Drop G	Points
Brusque N	1	0	0	1	8
Michalak F	1	4	4	1	28
Galthie F	1	0	0	0	5
Betsen Tchoua S	1	0	0	0	5
Harinordoquy I	1	0	0	0	5

Scotland

Name	Tries	Conv	Pen K	Drop G	Points
Paterson CD	0	0	3	0	9

Pool B, Eighth Match
Japan v USA: 26-39
27 October 2003
Central Coast Stadium, Gosford

Players

Japan

Prop	Shin Hasegawa
Hooker	Masao Amino
Prop	Masahiko Toyoyama
Lock	Hajime Kiso
Lock	Adam Parker
Flanker	Naoya Okubo
Flanker	Takuro Miuchi (c)
Number 8	Takeomi Ito
Scrum-half	Yuji Sonoda
Fly-half	Andy Miller
Right Wing	Toru Kurihara
Centre	Yukio Motoki
Centre	George Konia
Left Wing	Daisuke Ohata
Full-back	Tsutomu Matsuda
Reserves	Hirotoki Onozowa, Yuya Saito, Takashi Tsuji, Masahito Yamamoto
Unused	Koichi Kubo, Hideki Nanba, Masaaki Sakata

USA

Prop	Dan Dorsey
Hooker	Kirk Khasigian
Prop	Mike MacDonald
Lock	Gerhard Klerck
Lock	Luke Gross
Flanker	Dave Hodges (c)
Flanker	Kort Schubert
Number 8	Dan Lyle
Scrum-half	Kevin Dalzell
Fly-half	Mike Hercus
Right Wing	David Fee
Centre	Phillip Eloff
Centre	Salesi Sika
Left Wing	Riaan Van Zyl
Full-back	Paul Emerick
Reserves	John Buchholz, Kimball Kjar, Jacob Waasdorp, Matt Wyatt
Unused	Jason Keyter, Olo Fifita, Jurie Gouws
Referee	Walsh S

Points Scorers

Japan

Name	Tries	Conv	Pen K	Drop G	Points
Ohata D	1	0	0	0	5
Kurihara T	1	2	4	0	21

USA

Name	Tries	Conv	Pen K	Drop G	Points
Eloff P	1	0	0	0	5
Van Zyl R	1	0	0	0	5
Hercus M	1	4	2	0	19
Khasigian KA	1	0	0	0	5
Schubert KS	1	0	0	0	5

Pool B, Ninth Match
France v USA: 41-14
31 October 2003
WIN Stadium, Wollongong

Players

France

Prop	Olivier Milloud
Hooker	Yannick Bru (c)
Prop	Jean-Baptiste Poux
Lock	David Auradou
Lock	Olivier Brouzet
Flanker	Sebastien Chabal
Flanker	Patrick Tabacco
Number 8	Christian Labit
Scrum-half	Dimitri Yachvili
Fly-half	Gerald Merceron
Right Wing	David Bory
Centre	Brian Liebenberg
Centre	Damien Traille
Left Wing	Pepito Elhorga
Full-back	Clement Poitreneaud
Reserves	Sylvain Marconnet
Unused	R Ibanez, O Magne, A Rougerie, Y Jauzion, F Michalak, J Thion

USA

Prop	Dan Dorsey
Hooker	Kirk Khasigian
Prop	Mike MacDonald
Lock	Luke Gross
Lock	Alec Parker
Flanker	Dave Hodges (c)
Flanker	Kort Schubert
Number 8	Dan Lyle
Scrum-half	Kevin Dalzell
Fly-half	Mike Hercus
Right Wing	David Fee
Centre	Phillip Eloff
Centre	Salesi Sika
Left Wing	Riaan Van Zyl
Full-back	John Buchholz
Reserves	J Keyter, M Sherman, J Gouws, M Timoteo, J Waasdorp, M Wyatt
Unused	Gerhard Klerck
Referee	Honiss P

Points Scorers

France

Name	Tries	Conv	Pen K	Drop G	Points
Liebenberg B	3	0	0	0	15
Merceron G	0	2	3	0	13
Yachvili D	0	0	0	1	3
Bru Y	1	0	0	0	5
Poux J-B	1	0	0	0	5

USA

Name	Tries	Conv	Pen K	Drop G	Points
Hercus M	1	2	0	0	9
Schubert KS	1	0	0	0	5

Pool B, Tenth Match
Scotland v Fiji: 22-20
1 November 2003
Football Stadium, Sydney

Players
Scotland

Prop	Bruce Douglas
Hooker	Gordon Bulloch
Prop	Tom Smith
Lock	Nathan Hines
Lock	Stuart Grimes
Flanker	Ross Beattie
Flanker	Cameron Mather
Number 8	Simon Taylor
Scrum-half	Bryan Redpath (c)
Fly-half	Chris Paterson
Right Wing	Kenny Logan
Centre	Andrew Henderson
Centre	Gregor Townsend
Left Wing	Simon Danielli
Full-back	Glenn Metcalfe
Reserves	Ben Hinshelwood, James McLaren, Robbie Russell, Jason White
Unused	Michael Blair, Gordon McIlwham, Jon Petrie

Fiji

Prop	Isaia Rasila
Hooker	Greg Smith
Prop	Joeli Veitayaki
Lock	Apenisa Naevo
Lock	Ifereimi Rawaqa
Flanker	Vula Maimuri
Flanker	Koli Sewabu
Number 8	Alifereti Doviverata (c)
Scrum-half	Mosese Rauluni
Fly-half	Nicky Little
Right Wing	Rupeni Caucaunibuca
Centre	Seru Rabeni
Centre	Epeli Ruivadra
Left Wing	Aisea Tuilevu
Full-back	Norman Ligairi
Reserves	Vilimoni Delasau, Sisa Koyamaibole, Isikeli Nacewa, Jacob Rauluni, Kitione Salawa, Naka Seru
Unused	Seta Tawake Naivaluwaqa

Referee	Spreadbury T

Points Scorers
Scotland

Name	Tries	Conv	Pen K	Drop G	Points
Paterson CD	0	1	5	0	17
Smith TJ	1	0	0	0	5

Fiji

Name	Tries	Conv	Pen K	Drop G	Points
Caucaunibuca R	2	0	0	0	10
Little NT	0	2	2	0	10

Pool C, First Match
South Africa v Uruguay: 72-6
11 October 2003
Subiaco Oval, Perth

Players

South Africa

Prop	Richard Bands
Hooker	Danie Coetzee
Prop	Lawrence Sephaka
Lock	Victor Matfield
Lock	Bakkies Botha
Flanker	Danie Rossouw
Flanker	Joe Van Niekerk
Number 8	Juan Smith
Scrum-half	Joost Van Der Westhuizen
Fly-half	Louis Koen
Right Wing	Ashwin Willemse
Centre	Jaque Fourie
Centre	De Wet Barry
Left Wing	Thinus Delport
Full-back	Werner Greeff
Reserves	Derick Hougaard, Neil De Kock, Faan Rautenbach, Hendro Scholtz, John Smit, Selborne Boome, Ricardo Loubscher

Uruguay

Prop	Pablo Lemoine
Hooker	Diego Lamelas
Prop	Rodrigo Sanchez
Lock	Juan Alzueta
Lock	Juan Carlos Bado
Flanker	Nicolas Brignoni
Flanker	Marcelo Gutierrez
Number 8	Rodrigo Capo Ortega
Scrum-half	Emiliano Caffera
Fly-half	Sebastian Aguirre
Right Wing	Alfonso Cardoso
Centre	Diego Aguirre
Centre	Martin Mendaro
Left Wing	Emiliano Ibarra
Full-back	Joaquin Pastore
Reserves	Bernardo Amarillo, Eduardo Berruti, Nicolas Grille, Juan Menchaca, Guillermo Storace, Juan Andres Perez, Hernan Ponte

Referee	O'Brien P

Points Scorers

South Africa

Name	Tries	Conv	Pen K	Drop G	Points
Greeff WW	1	0	0	0	5
Fourie J	1	0	0	0	5
Delport GM	1	0	0	0	5
Koen LJ	0	5	0	0	10
Van Der Westhuizen J	3	0	0	0	15
Bands RE	1	0	0	0	5
Botha JP	2	0	0	0	10
Van Niekerk JC	1	0	0	0	5
Rossouw D	1	0	0	0	5
Scholtz H	1	0	0	0	5
Hougaard DJ	0	1	0	0	2

Uruguay

Name	Tries	Conv	Pen K	Drop G	Points
Aguirre D	0	0	2	0	6

Pool C, Second Match
England v Georgia: 84-6
12 October 2003
Subiaco Oval, Perth

Players
England

Prop	Phil Vickery
Hooker	Steve Thompson
Prop	Trevor Woodman
Lock	Ben Kay
Lock	Martin Johnson (c)
Flanker	Neil Back
Flanker	Richard Hill
Number 8	Lawrence Dallaglio
Scrum-half	Matt Dawson
Fly-half	Jonny Wilkinson
Right Wing	Jason Robinson
Centre	Will Greenwood
Centre	Mike Tindall
Left Wing	Ben Cohen
Full-back	Josh Lewsey
Reserves	A Gomarsall, P Grayson, J Leonard, D Luger, M Regan, L Moody
Unused	Danny Grewcock

Georgia

Prop	Goderdzi Shvelidze
Hooker	Akvsenti Guiorgadze
Prop	Aleko Margvelashvili
Lock	Victor Didebulidze
Lock	Zurab Mtchedlishvili
Flanker	Guia Labadze
Flanker	Gregoire Yachvili
Number 8	George Chkhaidze
Scrum-half	Irakli Abusseridze
Fly-half	Paliko Jimsheladze
Right Wing	Makho Urjukashvili
Centre	Irakli Guiorgadze
Centre	Tedo Zibzibadze
Left Wing	Vassil Katsadze (c)
Full-back	Bessik Khamashuridze
Reserves	D Bolghashvili, D Dadunashvili, V Nadiradze, B Khekhelashvili, S Nikolaenko, M Kvirikashvili, I Machkhaneli
Referee	Deluca P

Points Scorers
England

Name	Tries	Conv	Pen K	Drop G	Points
Robinson JT	1	0	0	0	5
Greenwood WJH	2	0	0	0	10
Tindall MJ	1	0	0	0	5
Cohen BC	2	0	0	0	10
Wilkinson JP	0	5	2	0	16
Dawson MJS	1	0	0	0	5
Thompson S	1	0	0	0	5
Dallaglio LBN	1	0	0	0	5
Back NA	1	0	0	0	5
Regan MP	1	0	0	0	5
Grayson PJ	0	4	0	0	8
Luger DD	1	0	0	0	5

Georgia

Name	Tries	Conv	Pen K	Drop G	Points
Urjukashvili M	0	0	1	0	3
Jimsheladze P	0	0	1	0	3

Pool C, Third Match
Samoa v Uruguay: 60-13
15 October 2003
Subiaco Oval, Perth

Players

Samoa

Prop	Jeremy Tomuli
Hooker	Jonathan Meredith
Prop	Kas Lealamanu'a
Lock	Leo Lafaiali'i
Lock	Opeta Palepoi
Flanker	Maurie Fa'asavalu
Flanker	Peter Poulos
Number 8	Semo Sititi (c)
Scrum-half	Steven So'oialo
Fly-half	Earl Va'a
Right Wing	Lome Fa'atau
Centre	Terry Fanolua
Centre	Brian Lima
Left Wing	Sailosi Tagicakibau
Full-back	Tanner Vili
Reserves	Dominic Feaunati, Des Tuiali'i, Simon Lemalu, Mahonri Schwalger, Denning Tyrell, Kitiona Viliamu, Dale Rasmussen

Uruguay

Prop	Pablo Lemoine
Hooker	Diego Lamelas
Prop	Rodrigo Sanchez
Lock	Juan Alzueta
Lock	Juan Carlos Bado
Flanker	Nicolas Grille
Flanker	Marcelo Gutierrez
Number 8	Rodrigo Capo Ortega
Scrum-half	Juan Campomar
Fly-half	Bernardo Amarillo
Right Wing	Carlos Baldassari
Centre	Diego Aguirre (c)
Centre	Martin Mendaro
Left Wing	Joaquin Pastore
Full-back	Juan Menchaca
Reserves	Juan Alvarez, Nicolas Brignoni, Juan Machado, Jose Viana, Ignacio Conti, Joaquin De Freitas, Juan Andres Perez

Referee	McHugh D

Points Scorers

Samoa

Name	Tries	Conv	Pen K	Drop G	Points
Vili TA	1	2	0	0	9
Fa'atau LM	1	0	0	0	5
Lima BP	2	0	0	0	10
Tagicakibau S	1	0	0	0	5
Va'a EV	0	3	0	0	6
Palepoi O	1	0	0	0	5
Fa'asavalu M	2	0	0	0	10
Lemalu S	1	0	0	0	5
Feaunati D	1	0	0	0	5

Uruguay

Name	Tries	Conv	Pen K	Drop G	Points
Aguirre D	0	0	1	0	3
Lemoine PA	1	0	0	0	5
Capo Ortega R	1	0	0	0	5

Pool C, Fourth Match
England v South Africa: 25-6
18 October 2003
Subiaco Oval, Perth

Players

England

Prop	Phil Vickery
Hooker	Steve Thompson
Prop	Trevor Woodman
Lock	Ben Kay
Lock	Martin Johnson (c)
Flanker	Neil Back
Flanker	Lewis Moody
Number 8	Lawrence Dallaglio
Scrum-half	Kyran Bracken
Fly-half	Jonny Wilkinson
Right Wing	Jason Robinson
Centre	Will Greenwood
Centre	Mike Tindall
Left Wing	Ben Cohen
Full-back	Josh Lewsey
Reserves	Jason Leonard, Dan Luger, Joe Worsley
Unused	Martin Corry, Andy Gomarsall, Paul Grayson, Dorian West

South Africa

Prop	Richard Bands
Hooker	Danie Coetzee
Prop	Christo Bezuidenhout
Lock	Victor Matfield
Lock	Bakkies Botha
Flanker	Corne Krige (c)
Flanker	Joe Van Niekerk
Number 8	Juan Smith
Scrum-half	Joost Van Der Westhuizen
Fly-half	Louis Koen
Right Wing	Ashwin Willemse
Centre	De Wet Barry
Centre	Jorrie Muller
Left Wing	Thinus Delport
Full-back	Jaco Van Der Westhuyzen
Reserves	Derick Hougaard, Werner Greeff, John Smit, Lawrence Sephaka
Unused	Neil De Kock, Selborne Boome, Danie Rossouw

Referee	Marshall P

Points Scorers

England

Name	Tries	Conv	Pen K	Drop G	Points
Greenwood WJH	1	0	0	0	5
Wilkinson JP	0	1	4	2	20

South Africa

Name	Tries	Conv	Pen K	Drop G	Points
Koen LJ	0	0	2	0	6

Pool C, Fifth Match
Georgia v Samoa: 9-46
19 October 2003
Subiaco Oval, Perth

Players

Georgia

Prop	Sosso Nikolaenko
Hooker	Akvsenti Guiorgadze
Prop	Goderdzi Shvelidze
Lock	Vano Nadiradze
Lock	Zurab Mtchedlishvili
Flanker	Guia Labadze
Flanker	Gregoire Yachvili
Number 8	Ilia Zedguinidze (c)
Scrum-half	Irakli Abusseridze
Fly-half	Paliko Jimsheladze
Right Wing	Makho Urjukashvili
Centre	Irakli Guiorgadze
Centre	Tedo Zibzibadze
Left Wing	Vassil Katsadze
Full-back	Badri Khekhelashvili
Reserves	David Bolghashvili, Victor Didebulidze, Bessik Khamashuridze, Merab Kvirikashvili, Irakli Machkhaneli, Aleko Margvelashvili
Unused	David Dadunashvili

Samoa

Prop	Jeremy Tomuli
Hooker	Jonathan Meredith
Prop	Kas Lealamanu'a
Lock	Leo Lafaiali'i
Lock	Opeta Palepoi
Flanker	Maurie Fa'asavalu
Flanker	Peter Poulos
Number 8	Semo Sititi (c)
Scrum-half	Steven So'oialo
Fly-half	Earl Va'a
Right Wing	Ron Fanuatanu
Centre	Terry Fanolua
Centre	Brian Lima
Left Wing	Sailosi Tagicakibau
Full-back	Tanner Vili
Reserves	Dominic Feaunati, Simon Lemalu, Mahonri Schwalger, Denning Tyrell, Siaosi Vaili, Kitiona Viliamu, Dale Rasmussen
Referee	Rolland A

Points Scorers

Georgia

Name	Tries	Conv	Pen K	Drop G	Points
Jimsheladze P	0	0	2	1	9

Samoa

Name	Tries	Conv	Pen K	Drop G	Points
Lima BP	1	0	0	0	5
Tagicakibau S	1	0	0	0	5
Va'a EV	1	5	2	0	21
So'oialo S	1	0	0	0	5
Sititi S	1	0	0	0	5
Feaunati D	1	0	0	0	5

Pool C, Sixth Match
South Africa v Georgia: 46-19
24 October 2003
Football Stadium, Sydney

Players

South Africa

Prop	Faan Rautenbach
Hooker	John Smit (c)
Prop	Lawrence Sephaka
Lock	Bakkies Botha
Lock	Selborne Boome
Flanker	Hendro Scholtz
Flanker	Danie Rossouw
Number 8	Joe Van Niekerk
Scrum-half	Neil De Kock
Fly-half	Derick Hougaard
Right Wing	Breyton Paulse
Centre	Jaque Fourie
Centre	Werner Greeff
Left Wing	Stefan Terblanche
Full-back	Ricardo Loubscher
Reserves	Schalk Burger Jr, Jorrie Muller, Dale Santon
Unused	V Matfield, C Bezuidenhout, L Koen, J Van Der Westhuizen

Georgia

Prop	Avtandil Kopaliani
Hooker	David Dadunashvili
Prop	Aleko Margvelashvili
Lock	Victor Didebulidze
Lock	Sergo Gujaraidze
Flanker	David Bolghashvili
Flanker	George Tsiklauri
Number 8	George Chkhaidze
Scrum-half	Irakli Modebadze
Fly-half	Paliko Jimsheladze
Right Wing	Archil Kavtarahvili
Centre	Otar Eloshvili
Centre	Vassil Katsadze (c)
Left Wing	Gocha Khonelidze
Full-back	Irakli Machkhaneli
Reserves	Irakli Abusseridze, Akvsenti Guiorgadze, Bessik Khamashuridze, Sosso Nikolaenko, Merab Kvirikashvili, Ilia Zedguinidze
Unused	Gregoire Yachvili
Referee	Dickinson S

Points Scorers

South Africa

Name	Tries	Conv	Pen K	Drop G	Points
Fourie J	1	0	0	0	5
Hougaard DJ	1	4	1	0	16
Botha JP	1	0	0	0	5
Van Niekerk JC	1	0	0	0	5
Rossouw D	2	0	0	0	10
Burger Jr SWP	1	0	0	0	5

Georgia

Name	Tries	Conv	Pen K	Drop G	Points
Jimsheladze P	0	1	3	0	11
Dadunashvili D	1	0	0	0	5
Kvirikashvili M	0	0	1	0	3

Pool C, Seventh Match
England v Samoa: 35-22
26 October 2003
Colonial Stadium, Melbourne

Players
England

Prop	Jason Leonard
Hooker	Mark Regan
Prop	Julian White
Lock	Ben Kay
Lock	Martin Johnson (c)
Flanker	Neil Back
Flanker	Joe Worsley
Number 8	Lawrence Dallaglio
Scrum-half	Matt Dawson
Fly-half	Jonny Wilkinson
Right Wing	Iain Balshaw
Centre	Mike Tindall
Centre	Stuart Abbott
Left Wing	Ben Cohen
Full-back	Jason Robinson
Reserves	Mike Catt, Phil Vickery, Lewis Moody, Steve Thompson
Unused	Martin Corry, Andy Gomarsall, Dan Luger

Samoa

Prop	Jeremy Tomuli
Hooker	Jonathan Meredith
Prop	Kas Lealamanu'a
Lock	Leo Lafaiali'i
Lock	Opeta Palepoi
Flanker	Maurie Fa'asavalu
Flanker	Peter Poulos
Number 8	Semo Sititi
Scrum-half	Steven So'oialo
Fly-half	Earl Va'a
Right Wing	Lome Fa'atau
Centre	Terry Fanolua
Centre	Brian Lima
Left Wing	Sailosi Tagicakibau
Full-back	Tanner Vili
Reserves	Dominic Feaunati, Des Tuiali'i, Simon Lemalu, Mahonri Schwalger, Denning Tyrell, Kitiona Viliamu, Dale Rasmussen
Referee	Kaplan J

Points Scorers
England

Name	Tries	Conv	Pen K	Drop G	Points
Balshaw IR	1	0	0	0	5
Wilkinson JP	0	3	2	1	15
Back NA	1	0	0	0	5
Vickery PJ	1	0	0	0	5
Penalty try	1	0	0	0	5

Samoa

Name	Tries	Conv	Pen K	Drop G	Points
Va'a EV	0	1	5	0	17
Sititi S	1	0	0	0	5

Pool C, Eighth Match
Georgia v Uruguay: 12-24
28 October 2003
Football Stadium, Sydney

Players

Georgia

Prop	Avtandil Kopaliani
Hooker	David Dadunashvili
Prop	Goderdzi Shvelidze
Lock	Sergo Gujaraidze
Lock	Zurab Mtchedlishvili
Flanker	George Chkhaidze
Flanker	Gregoire Yachvili
Number 8	Ilia Zedguinidze (c)
Scrum-half	Irakli Modebadze
Fly-half	Paliko Jimsheladze
Right Wing	Makho Urjukashvili
Centre	Irakli Guiorgadze
Centre	Tedo Zibzibadze
Left Wing	Archil Kavtarahvili
Full-back	Irakli Machkhaneli
Reserves	Akvsenti Guiorgadze, Vassil Katsadze, Bessik Khamashuridze, Sosso Nikolaenko, Merab Kvirikashvili, George Tsiklauri
Unused	David Bolghashvili

Uruguay

Prop	Pablo Lemoine
Hooker	Diego Lamelas
Prop	Rodrigo Sanchez
Lock	Juan Alzueta
Lock	Juan Carlos Bado
Flanker	Nicolas Grille
Flanker	Hernan Ponte
Number 8	Rodrigo Capo Ortega
Scrum-half	Juan Campomar
Fly-half	Sebastian Aguirre
Right Wing	Carlos Baldassari
Centre	Diego Aguirre (c)
Centre	Martin Mendaro
Left Wing	Alfonso Cardoso
Full-back	Juan Menchaca
Reserves	Bernardo Amarillo, Eduardo Berruti, Nicolas Brignoni, Joaquin Pastore, Guillermo Storace, Marcelo Gutierrez, Juan Andres Perez
Referee	Deaker K

Points Scorers

Georgia

Name	Tries	Conv	Pen K	Drop G	Points
Urjukashvili M	0	0	1	0	3
Kvirikashvili M	0	0	3	0	9

Uruguay

Name	Tries	Conv	Pen K	Drop G	Points
Menchaca JR	0	1	1	0	5
Cardoso A	1	0	0	0	5
Aguirre D	0	2	0	0	4
Lamelas D	1	0	0	0	5
Brignoni N	1	0	0	0	5

Pool C, Ninth Match
South Africa v Samoa: 60-10
1 November 2003
Lang Park, Brisbane

Players

South Africa

Prop	Faan Rautenbach
Hooker	John Smit
Prop	Christo Bezuidenhout
Lock	Victor Matfield
Lock	Bakkies Botha
Flanker	Corne Krige (c)
Flanker	Joe Van Niekerk
Number 8	Juan Smith
Scrum-half	Joost Van Der Westhuizen
Fly-half	Derick Hougaard
Right Wing	Ashwin Willemse
Centre	De Wet Barry
Centre	Jorrie Muller
Left Wing	Thinus Delport
Full-back	Jaco Van Der Westhuyzen
Reserves	Jaque Fourie, Neil De Kock, Richard Bands, Schalk Burger Jr, Danie Coetzee, Louis Koen, Danie Rossouw

Samoa

Prop	Jeremy Tomuli
Hooker	Jonathan Meredith
Prop	Kas Lealamanu'a
Lock	Leo Lafaiali'i
Lock	Opeta Palepoi
Flanker	Maurie Fa'asavalu
Flanker	Peter Poulos
Number 8	Semo Sititi (c)
Scrum-half	Steven So'oialo
Fly-half	Earl Va'a
Right Wing	Lome Fa'atau
Centre	Romi Ropati
Centre	Brian Lima
Left Wing	Sailosi Tagicakibau
Full-back	Tanner Vili
Reserves	D Feaunati, D Tuiali'i, T Leupolu, D Tyrell, K Viliamu, D Rasmussen
Unused	Mahonri Schwalger
Referee	White C

Points Scorers

South Africa

Name	Tries	Conv	Pen K	Drop G	Points
Van Der Westhuyzen J	1	0	0	0	5
Willemse AK	1	0	0	0	5
Muller GP	1	0	0	0	5
Hougaard DJ	1	5	1	1	21
Smith JH	1	0	0	0	5
Van Niekerk JC	1	0	0	0	5
De Kock NA	1	0	0	0	5
Koen LJ	0	2	0	0	4
Fourie J	1	0	0	0	5

Samoa

Name	Tries	Conv	Pen K	Drop G	Points
Va'a EV	0	1	1	0	5
Palepoi O	1	0	0	0	5

Pool C, Tenth Match
England v Uruguay: 111-13
2 November 2003
Lang Park, Brisbane

Players
England

Prop	Jason Leonard
Hooker	Dorian West
Prop	Phil Vickery (c)
Lock	Martin Corry
Lock	Danny Grewcock
Flanker	Joe Worsley
Flanker	Lewis Moody
Number 8	Lawrence Dallaglio
Scrum-half	Andy Gomarsall
Fly-half	Paul Grayson
Right Wing	Dan Luger
Centre	Mike Catt
Centre	Stuart Abbott
Left Wing	Iain Balshaw
Full-back	Josh Lewsey
Reserves	K Bracken, W Greenwood, M Johnson, J Robinson, J White
Unused	Ben Kay, Steve Thompson

Uruguay

Prop	Eduardo Berruti
Hooker	Diego Lamelas
Prop	Pablo Lemoine
Lock	Juan Alvarez
Lock	Juan Carlos Bado
Flanker	Nicolas Brignoni
Flanker	Nicolas Grille
Number 8	Rodrigo Capo Ortega
Scrum-half	Juan Campomar
Fly-half	Sebastian Aguirre
Right Wing	Joaquin Pastore
Centre	Diego Aguirre (c)
Centre	Joaquin De Freitas
Left Wing	Jose Viana
Full-back	Juan Menchaca
Reserves	Juan Alzueta, Rodrigo Sanchez, Guillermo Storace, Emiliano Caffera, Marcelo Gutierrez, Juan Andres Perez, Diego Reyes
Referee	Williams N

Points Scorers
England

Name	Tries	Conv	Pen K	Drop G	Points
Lewsey OJ	5	0	0	0	25
Balshaw IR	2	0	0	0	10
Abbott SR	1	0	0	0	5
Catt MJ	2	2	0	0	14
Luger DD	1	0	0	0	5
Grayson PJ	0	11	0	0	22
Gomarsall ACT	2	0	0	0	10
Moody LW	1	0	0	0	5
Greenwood WJH	1	0	0	0	5
Robinson JT	2	0	0	0	10

Uruguay

Name	Tries	Conv	Pen K	Drop G	Points
Menchaca JR	0	1	2	0	8
Lemoine PA	1	0	0	0	5

Pool D, First Match
New Zealand v Italy: 70-7
11 October 2003
Colonial Stadium, Melbourne

Players

New Zealand

Prop	David Hewett
Hooker	Keven Mealamu
Prop	Greg Somerville
Lock	Chris Jack
Lock	Brad Thorn
Flanker	Richie McCaw
Flanker	Reuben Thorne (c)
Number 8	Jerry Collins
Scrum-half	Justin Marshall
Fly-half	Carlos Spencer
Right Wing	Doug Howlett
Centre	Daniel Carter
Centre	Tana Umaga
Left Wing	Joe Rokocoko
Full-back	Mils Muliaina
Reserves	Marty Holah, Leon MacDonald, Rodney So'oialo, Mark Hammett, Kees Meeuws, Ma'a Nonu
Unused	Steve Devine

Italy

Prop	Ramiro Martinez-Frugoni
Hooker	Carlo Festuccia
Prop	Salvatore Perugini
Lock	Cristian Bezzi
Lock	Carlo Checchinato (c)
Flanker	Scott Palmer
Flanker	Mauro Bergamasco
Number 8	Matthew Phillips
Scrum-half	Matteo Mazzantini
Fly-half	Francesco Mazzariol
Right Wing	Mirco Bergamasco
Centre	Matteo Barbini
Centre	Andrea Masi
Left Wing	Nicola Mazzucato
Full-back	Gert Peens
Reserves	Andrea Benatti, Gonzalo Canale, Leandro Castrogiovanni, Fabio Ongaro, Sergio Parisse, Alessandro Troncon
Unused	Rima Wakarua-Noema
Referee	Cole A

Points Scorers

New Zealand

Name	Tries	Conv	Pen K	Drop G	Points
Howlett DC	2	0	0	0	10
Carter DW	1	6	0	0	17
Rokocoko J	2	0	0	0	10
Spencer CJ	2	0	1	0	13
Marshall JW	1	0	0	0	5
Thorn BC	1	0	0	0	5
Thorne RD	1	0	0	0	5
MacDonald LR	1	0	0	0	5

Italy

Name	Tries	Conv	Pen K	Drop G	Points
Peens G	0	1	0	0	2
Phillips M	1	0	0	0	5

Pool D, Second Match
Wales v Canada: 41-10
12 October 2003
Colonial Stadium, Melbourne

Players

Wales

Prop	Gethin Jenkins
Hooker	Robin McBryde
Prop	Duncan Jones
Lock	Brent Cockbain
Lock	Gareth Llewellyn
Flanker	Dafydd Jones
Flanker	Martyn Williams
Number 8	Colin Charvis (c)
Scrum-half	Gareth Cooper
Fly-half	Ceri Sweeney
Right Wing	Mark Jones
Centre	Iestyn Harris
Centre	Sonny Parker
Left Wing	Gareth Thomas
Full-back	Kevin Morgan
Reserves	Huw Bennett, Adam Jones, Dwayne Peel, Robert Sidoli, Mark Taylor
Unused	Rhys Williams, Jonathan Thomas

Canada

Prop	Rod Snow
Hooker	Mark Lawson
Prop	John Thiel
Lock	Mike James
Lock	Colin Yukes
Flanker	Alan Charron (c)
Flanker	Adam Van Staveren
Number 8	Josh Jackson
Scrum-half	Morgan Williams
Fly-half	Bobby Ross
Right Wing	Dave Lougheed
Centre	Marco Di Girolomo
Centre	Nik Witkowski
Left Wing	Winston Stanley
Full-back	James Pritchard
Reserves	Garth Cooke, Jamie Cudmore, Kevin Tkachuk, Ryan Smith
Unused	Aaron Abrams, Ryan Banks, Ed Fairhurst
Referee	White C

Points Scorers

Wales

Name	Tries	Conv	Pen K	Drop G	Points
Jones MA	1	0	0	0	5
Parker S	1	0	0	0	5
Harris IR	0	5	2	0	16
Thomas G	1	0	0	0	5
Cooper GJ	1	0	0	0	5
Charvis CL	1	0	0	0	5

Canada

Name	Tries	Conv	Pen K	Drop G	Points
Pritchard J	0	1	0	0	2
Ross RP	0	0	0	1	3
Tkachuk K	1	0	0	0	5

Pool D, Third Match
Italy v Tonga: 36-12
15 October 2003
Bruce Stadium, Canberra

Players

Italy

Prop	Leandro Castrogiovanni
Hooker	Fabio Ongaro
Prop	Andrea Lo Cicero
Lock	Marco Bortolami
Lock	Santiago Dellape
Flanker	Andrea De Rossi
Flanker	Aaron Persico
Number 8	Sergio Parisse
Scrum-half	Alessandro Troncon (c)
Fly-half	Rima Wakarua-Noema
Right Wing	Denis Dallan
Centre	Manuel Dallan
Centre	Cristian Stoica
Left Wing	Nicola Mazzucato
Full-back	Gonzalo Canale
Reserves	Carlo Festuccia, Mirco Bergamasco, Carlo Checchinato, Andrea Masi, Salvatore Perugini
Unused	Matteo Mazzantini, Francesco Mazzariol

Tonga

Prop	Tonga Lea'aetoa
Hooker	Ephraim Taukafa
Prop	Heamani Lavaka
Lock	Milton Ngauamo
Lock	Viliami Vaki
Flanker	'Inoke Afeaki (c)
Flanker	'Ipolito Fenukitau
Number 8	Ben Hur Kivalu
Scrum-half	Sililo Martens
Fly-half	Sateki Tuipulotu
Right Wing	Sione Fonua
Centre	Gus Leger
Centre	John Payne
Left Wing	Tevita Tu'ifua
Full-back	Pierre Hola
Reserves	Johnny Ngauamo, Stanley Afeaki, Usaia Latu, Viliami Ma'asi, Kisi Pulu, Sila Va'enuku
Unused	Tony Alatini
Referee	Walsh S

Points Scorers

Italy

Name	Tries	Conv	Pen K	Drop G	Points
Dallan M	1	0	0	0	5
Dallan D	2	0	0	0	10
Wakarua-Noema R	0	3	5	0	21

Tonga

Name	Tries	Conv	Pen K	Drop G	Points
Payne J	1	0	0	0	5
Tu'ifua T	1	0	0	0	5
Tuipulotu S	0	1	0	0	2

Pool D, Fourth Match
New Zealand v Canada: 68-6
17 October 2003
Colonial Stadium, Melbourne

Players

New Zealand

Prop	Carl Hoeft
Hooker	Mark Hammett
Prop	Kees Meeuws
Lock	Chris Jack
Lock	Brad Thorn
Flanker	Marty Holah
Flanker	Reuben Thorne (c)
Number 8	Rodney So'oialo
Scrum-half	Steve Devine
Fly-half	Carlos Spencer
Right Wing	Mils Muliaina
Centre	Daniel Carter
Centre	Ma'a Nonu
Left Wing	Caleb Ralph
Full-back	Leon MacDonald
Reserves	Cory Flynn, Doug Howlett, Richie McCaw, Daniel Braid
Unused	David Hewett, Greg Somerville, Byron Kelleher

Canada

Prop	Garth Cooke
Hooker	Aaron Abrams
Prop	Kevin Tkachuk
Lock	Jamie Cudmore
Lock	Ed Knaggs
Flanker	Ryan Banks (c)
Flanker	Jim Douglas
Number 8	Jeff Reid
Scrum-half	Ed Fairhurst
Fly-half	Jared Barker
Right Wing	Sean Fauth
Centre	John Cannon
Centre	Marco Di Girolomo
Left Wing	Matt King
Full-back	Quentin Fyffe
Reserves	Rod Snow, Adam Van Staveren, Nik Witkowski, Colin Yukes, Ryan Smith
Unused	Mark Lawson, Morgan Williams
Referee	Spreadbury T

Points Scorers

New Zealand

Name	Tries	Conv	Pen K	Drop G	Points
Muliaina M	4	0	0	0	20
Nonu M	1	0	0	0	5
Carter DW	0	9	0	0	18
Ralph CS	2	0	0	0	10
Meeuws KJ	1	0	0	0	5
So'oialo R	2	0	0	0	10

Canada

Name	Tries	Conv	Pen K	Drop G	Points
Barker J	0	0	2	0	6

Pool D, Fifth Match
Wales v Tonga: 27–20
19 October 2003
Bruce Stadium, Canberra

Players
Wales

Prop	Gethin Jenkins
Hooker	Mefin Davies
Prop	Iestyn Thomas
Lock	Robert Sidoli
Lock	Gareth Llewellyn
Flanker	Dafydd Jones
Flanker	Colin Charvis (c)
Number 8	Alix Popham
Scrum-half	Gareth Cooper
Fly-half	Stephen Jones
Right Wing	Mark Jones
Centre	Iestyn Harris
Centre	Mark Taylor
Left Wing	Tom Shanklin
Full-back	Rhys Williams
Reserves	Huw Bennett, Adam Jones, Dwayne Peel, Martyn Williams, Chris Wyatt
Unused	Shane Williams, Garan Evans

Tonga

Prop	Heamani Lavaka
Hooker	Viliami Ma'asi
Prop	Kisi Pulu
Lock	Usaia Latu
Lock	Viliami Vaki
Flanker	Stanley Afeaki
Flanker	'Ipolito Fenukitau
Number 8	Ben Hur Kivalu (c)
Scrum-half	Sililo Martens
Fly-half	Pierre Hola
Right Wing	Sione Fonua
Centre	Sukanaivalu Hufanga
Centre	John Payne
Left Wing	Tevita Tu'ifua
Full-back	Sila Va'enuku
Reserves	Tonga Lea'aetoa, Milton Ngauamo, Nisifolo Naufahu, Ephraim Taukafa
Unused	Gus Leger, David Palu, Sateki Tuipulotu

Referee	Honiss P

Points Scorers
Wales

Name	Tries	Conv	Pen K	Drop G	Points
Jones S	0	1	4	0	14
Cooper GJ	1	0	0	0	5
Williams ME	1	0	0	1	8

Tonga

Name	Tries	Conv	Pen K	Drop G	Points
Hola P	1	1	1	0	10
Lavaka H	1	0	0	0	5
Kivalu DBH	1	0	0	0	5

Pool D, Sixth Match
Italy v Canada: 19-14
21 October 2003
Bruce Stadium, Canberra

Players

Italy

Prop	Leandro Castrogiovanni
Hooker	Fabio Ongaro
Prop	Andrea Lo Cicero
Lock	Marco Bortolami
Lock	Santiago Dellape
Flanker	Andrea De Rossi
Flanker	Aaron Persico
Number 8	Sergio Parisse
Scrum-half	Alessandro Troncon (c)
Fly-half	Rima Wakarua-Noema
Right Wing	Denis Dallan
Centre	Manuel Dallan
Centre	Cristian Stoica
Left Wing	Mirco Bergamasco
Full-back	Gonzalo Canale
Reserves	Carlo Festuccia, Matteo Mazzantini, Scott Palmer, Carlo Checchinato, Francesco Mazzariol, Andrea Masi
Unused	Salvatore Perugini

Canada

Prop	Rod Snow
Hooker	Mark Lawson
Prop	John Thiel
Lock	Alan Charron (c)
Lock	Colin Yukes
Flanker	Jamie Cudmore
Flanker	Jim Douglas
Number 8	Ryan Banks
Scrum-half	Morgan Williams
Fly-half	Jared Barker
Right Wing	Dave Lougheed
Centre	John Cannon
Centre	Marco Di Girolomo
Left Wing	Winston Stanley
Full-back	Quentin Fyffe
Reserves	Josh Jackson, Kevin Tkachuk
Unused	Aaron Abrams, Sean Fauth, Jeff Reid, Bobby Ross, Matt King
Referee	O'Brien P

Points Scorers

Italy

Name	Tries	Conv	Pen K	Drop G	Points
Wakarua-Noema R	0	1	4	0	14
Parisse SM	1	0	0	0	5

Canada

Name	Tries	Conv	Pen K	Drop G	Points
Fyffe Q	1	0	0	0	5
Barker J	0	0	3	0	9

Pool D, Seventh Match
New Zealand v Tonga: 91-7
24 October 2003
Lang Park, Brisbane

Players

New Zealand

Prop	Greg Somerville
Hooker	Cory Flynn
Prop	Kees Meeuws
Lock	Brad Thorn
Lock	Ali Williams
Flanker	Daniel Braid
Flanker	Reuben Thorne (c)
Number 8	Rodney So'oialo
Scrum-half	Justin Marshall
Fly-half	Carlos Spencer
Right Wing	Doug Howlett
Centre	Daniel Carter
Centre	Leon MacDonald
Left Wing	Caleb Ralph
Full-back	Mils Muliaina
Reserves	Ben Atiga, David Hewett, Marty Holah, Richie McCaw, Ma'a Nonu
Unused	Keven Mealamu, Jerry Collins

Tonga

Prop	Heamani Lavaka
Hooker	Viliami Ma'asi
Prop	Kisi Pulu
Lock	Usaia Latu
Lock	Viliami Vaki
Flanker	Stanley Afeaki
Flanker	'Ipolito Fenukitau
Number 8	Ben Hur Kivalu (c)
Scrum-half	Sililo Martens
Fly-half	Pierre Hola
Right Wing	Sione Fonua
Centre	Sukanaivalu Hufanga
Centre	John Payne
Left Wing	Tevita Tu'ifua
Full-back	Sila Va'enuku
Reserves	Tonga Lea'aetoa, Milton Ngauamo, Edward Langi, Gus Leger, Ephraim Taukafa, Sateki Tuipulotu
Unused	David Palu
Referee	Deluca P

Points Scorers

New Zealand

Name	Tries	Conv	Pen K	Drop G	Points
Muliaina M	2	0	0	0	10
Howlett DC	2	0	0	0	10
MacDonald LR	1	12	0	0	29
Carter DW	1	0	0	0	5
Ralph CS	2	0	0	0	10
Spencer CJ	1	1	0	0	7
Meeuws KJ	1	0	0	0	5
Flynn CR	1	0	0	0	5
Braid DJ	1	0	0	0	5
Penalty try	1	0	0	0	5

Tonga

Name	Tries	Conv	Pen K	Drop G	Points
Hola P	1	0	0	0	5
Tuipulotu S	0	1	0	0	2

Pool D, Eighth Match
Italy v Wales: 15-27
25 October 2003
Bruce Stadium, Canberra

Players

Italy

Prop	Leandro Castrogiovanni
Hooker	Fabio Ongaro
Prop	Andrea Lo Cicero
Lock	Carlo Checchinato
Lock	Santiago Dellape
Flanker	Andrea De Rossi
Flanker	Aaron Persico
Number 8	Sergio Parisse
Scrum-half	Alessandro Troncon (c)
Fly-half	Rima Wakarua-Noema
Right Wing	Denis Dallan
Centre	Andrea Masi
Centre	Cristian Stoica
Left Wing	Nicola Mazzucato
Full-back	Gonzalo Canale
Reserves	Cristian Bezzi, Carlo Festuccia, Matthew Phillips, Scott Palmer, Mauro Bergamasco, Francesco Mazzariol, Salvatore Perugini

Wales

Prop	Duncan Jones
Hooker	Robin McBryde
Prop	Adam Jones
Lock	Brent Cockbain
Lock	Gareth Llewellyn
Flanker	Dafydd Jones
Flanker	Martyn Williams
Number 8	Colin Charvis (c)
Scrum-half	Dwayne Peel
Fly-half	Ceri Sweeney
Right Wing	Mark Jones
Centre	Iestyn Harris
Centre	Sonny Parker
Left Wing	Gareth Thomas
Full-back	Kevin Morgan
Reserves	Gareth Cooper, Gethin Jenkins, Robert Sidoli, Rhys Williams, Jonathan Thomas, Stephen Jones
Unused	Mefin Davies
Referee	Cole A

Points Scorers

Italy

Name	Tries	Conv	Pen K	Drop G	Points
Wakarua-Noema R	0	0	5	0	15

Wales

Name	Tries	Conv	Pen K	Drop G	Points
Jones MA	1	0	0	0	5
Parker S	1	0	0	0	5
Harris IR	0	3	2	0	12
Jones DR	1	0	0	0	5

Pool D, Ninth Match
Canada v Tonga: 24-7
29 October 2003
WIN Stadium, Wollongong

Players

Canada

Prop	Garth Cooke
Hooker	Mark Lawson
Prop	Rod Snow
Lock	Alan Charron (c)
Lock	Mike James
Flanker	Jamie Cudmore
Flanker	Adam Van Staveren
Number 8	Josh Jackson
Scrum-half	Morgan Williams
Fly-half	Bobby Ross
Right Wing	Sean Fauth
Centre	Marco Di Girolomo
Centre	Nik Witkowski
Left Wing	Winston Stanley
Full-back	Quentin Fyffe
Reserves	Aaron Abrams, Ed Fairhurst, Jeff Reid, Kevin Tkachuk, Colin Yukes, James Pritchard, Ryan Smith

Tonga

Prop	Tonga Lea'aetoa
Hooker	Ephraim Taukafa
Prop	Heamani Lavaka
Lock	Milton Ngauamo
Lock	'Inoke Afeaki (c)
Flanker	Nisifolo Naufahu
Flanker	Sione Tu'amoheloa
Number 8	Ben Hur Kivalu
Scrum-half	Sililo Martens
Fly-half	Pierre Hola
Right Wing	Pila Fifita
Centre	Johnny Ngauamo
Centre	John Payne
Left Wing	Sione Fonua
Full-back	Gus Leger
Reserves	'Ipolito Fenukitau, Sukanaivalu Hufanga, Usaia Latu, Viliami Ma'asi, David Palu, Kafalosi Tonga, Viliami Vaki

Referee	Rolland A

Points Scorers

Canada

Name	Tries	Conv	Pen K	Drop G	Points
Fauth S	1	0	0	0	5
Ross RP	0	0	4	0	12
Abrams A	1	0	0	0	5
Pritchard J	0	1	0	0	2

Tonga

Name	Tries	Conv	Pen K	Drop G	Points
Hola P	0	1	0	0	2
Afeaki IU	1	0	0	0	5

Pool D, Tenth Match
New Zealand v Wales: 53-37
2 November 2003
Telstra Stadium, Sydney

Players
New Zealand

Prop	David Hewett
Hooker	Keven Mealamu
Prop	Greg Somerville
Lock	Brad Thorn
Lock	Ali Williams
Flanker	Richie McCaw
Flanker	Reuben Thorne (c)
Number 8	Jerry Collins
Scrum-half	Justin Marshall
Fly-half	Carlos Spencer
Right Wing	Doug Howlett
Centre	Leon MacDonald
Centre	Aaron Mauger
Left Wing	Joe Rokocoko
Full-back	Mils Muliaina
Reserves	Marty Holah, Rodney So'oialo, Mark Hammett, Kees Meeuws
Unused	Daniel Carter, Byron Kelleher, Ma'a Nonu

Wales

Prop	Adam Jones
Hooker	Robin McBryde
Prop	Iestyn Thomas
Lock	Brent Cockbain
Lock	Robert Sidoli
Flanker	Jonathan Thomas
Flanker	Colin Charvis (c)
Number 8	Alix Popham
Scrum-half	Gareth Cooper
Fly-half	Stephen Jones
Right Wing	Tom Shanklin
Centre	Sonny Parker
Centre	Mark Taylor
Left Wing	Shane Williams
Full-back	Garan Evans
Reserves	Mefin Davies, Gethin Jenkins, Dafydd Jones, Dwayne Peel, Ceri Sweeney, Gareth Thomas, Chris Wyatt

Referee	Watson A

Points Scorers
New Zealand

Name	Tries	Conv	Pen K	Drop G	Points
Howlett DC	2	0	0	0	10
MacDonald LR	1	5	1	0	18
Mauger AJD	1	0	0	0	5
Rokocoko J	2	0	0	0	10
Spencer CJ	1	0	0	0	5
Williams AJ	1	0	0	0	5

Wales

Name	Tries	Conv	Pen K	Drop G	Points
Williams SM	1	0	0	0	5
Taylor M	1	0	0	0	5
Parker S	1	0	0	0	5
Jones S	0	4	3	0	17
Charvis CL	1	0	0	0	5

First Quarter-Final
New Zealand v South Africa: 29-9
8 November 2003
Colonial Stadium, Melbourne

Players

New Zealand

Prop	David Hewett
Hooker	Keven Mealamu
Prop	Greg Somerville
Lock	Chris Jack
Lock	Ali Williams
Flanker	Richie McCaw
Flanker	Reuben Thorne (c)
Number 8	Jerry Collins
Scrum-half	Justin Marshall
Fly-half	Carlos Spencer
Right Wing	Doug Howlett
Centre	Leon MacDonald
Centre	Aaron Mauger
Left Wing	Joe Rokocoko
Full-back	Mils Muliaina
Reserves	Daniel Carter, Steve Devine, Marty Holah, Brad Thorn, Mark Hammett, Kees Meeuws, Caleb Ralph

South Africa

Prop	Faan Rautenbach
Hooker	John Smit
Prop	Christo Bezuidenhout
Lock	Victor Matfield
Lock	Bakkies Botha
Flanker	Corne Krige (c)
Flanker	Danie Rossouw
Number 8	Juan Smith
Scrum-half	Joost Van Der Westhuizen
Fly-half	Derick Hougaard
Right Wing	Ashwin Willemse
Centre	De Wet Barry
Centre	Jorrie Muller
Left Wing	Thinus Delport
Full-back	Jaco Van Der Westhuyzen
Reserves	Jaque Fourie, Neil De Kock, Richard Bands, Selborne Boome, Schalk Burger Jr, Danie Coetzee, Louis Koen
Referee	Spreadbury T

Points Scorers

New Zealand

Name	Tries	Conv	Pen K	Drop G	Points
MacDonald LR	1	1	3	0	16
Mauger AJD	0	0	0	1	3
Rokocoko J	1	0	0	0	5
Mealamu KF	1	0	0	0	5

South Africa

Name	Tries	Conv	Pen K	Drop G	Points
Hougaard DJ	0	0	3	0	9

Second Quarter-Final
Australia v Scotland: 33-16
8 November 2003
Lang Park, Brisbane

Players

Australia

Prop	Ben Darwin
Hooker	Brendan Cannon
Prop	Bill Young
Lock	Justin Harrison
Lock	Nathan Sharpe
Flanker	George Smith
Flanker	Phil Waugh
Number 8	David Lyons
Scrum-half	George Gregan (c)
Fly-half	Steve Larkham
Right Wing	Wendell Sailor
Centre	Elton Flatley
Centre	Stirling Mortlock
Left Wing	Lote Tuqiri
Full-back	Mat Rogers
Reserves	Matt Cockbain, Matt Giteau, Jeremy Paul, Joe Roff, Chris Whitaker, Alastair Baxter, Daniel Vickerman

Scotland

Prop	Bruce Douglas
Hooker	Gordon Bulloch
Prop	Tom Smith
Lock	Nathan Hines
Lock	Stuart Grimes
Flanker	Cameron Mather
Flanker	Jason White
Number 8	Simon Taylor
Scrum-half	Bryan Redpath (c)
Fly-half	Chris Paterson
Right Wing	Kenny Logan
Centre	Andrew Henderson
Centre	Gregor Townsend
Left Wing	Simon Danielli
Full-back	Glenn Metcalfe
Reserves	Gordon McIlwham, Jon Petrie, Ben Hinshelwood, James McLaren, Scott Murray, Robbie Russell
Unused	Michael Blair
Referee	Walsh S

Points Scorers

Australia

Name	Tries	Conv	Pen K	Drop G	Points
Mortlock SA	1	0	0	0	5
Flatley EJ	0	3	4	0	18
Gregan GM	1	0	0	0	5
Lyons D	1	0	0	0	5

Scotland

Name	Tries	Conv	Pen K	Drop G	Points
Paterson CD	0	1	2	1	11
Russell RR	1	0	0	0	5

Third Quarter-Final
France v Ireland: 43-21
9 November 2003
Colonial Stadium, Melbourne

Players

France

Prop	Jean-Jacques Crenca
Hooker	Raphael Ibanez
Prop	Sylvain Marconnet
Lock	Fabien Pelous
Lock	Jerome Thion
Flanker	Serge Betsen Tchoua
Flanker	Olivier Magne
Number 8	Imanol Harinordoquy
Scrum-half	Fabien Galthie (c)
Fly-half	Frederic Michalak
Right Wing	Aurelien Rougerie
Centre	Yannick Jauzion
Centre	Tony Marsh
Left Wing	Christophe Dominici
Full-back	Nicolas Brusque
Reserves	Yannick Bru, Olivier Brouzet, Pepito Elhorga, Brian Liebenberg, Olivier Milloud, Patrick Tabacco
Unused	Gerald Merceron

Ireland

Prop	John Hayes
Hooker	Keith Wood (c)
Prop	Reggie Corrigan
Lock	Malcolm O'Kelly
Lock	Paul O'Connell
Flanker	Simon Easterby
Flanker	Keith Gleeson
Number 8	Victor Costello
Scrum-half	Peter Stringer
Fly-half	Ronan O'Gara
Right Wing	Shane Horgan
Centre	Brian O'Driscoll
Centre	Kevin Maggs
Left Wing	John Kelly
Full-back	Girvan Dempsey
Reserves	Guy Easterby, David Humphreys, Eric Miller, Marcus Horan
Unused	Shane Byrne, Anthony Horgan, Donncha O'Callaghan
Referee	Kaplan J

Points Scorers

France

Name	Tries	Conv	Pen K	Drop G	Points
Dominici C	1	0	0	0	5
Michalak F	0	4	5	0	23
Crenca J-J	1	0	0	0	5
Harinordoquy I	1	0	0	0	5
Magne O	1	0	0	0	5

Ireland

Name	Tries	Conv	Pen K	Drop G	Points
O'Driscoll BG	2	0	0	0	10
Maggs KM	1	0	0	0	5
Humphreys DG	0	3	0	0	6

Fourth Quarter-Final
England v Wales: 28-17
9 November 2003
Lang Park, Brisbane

Players

England

Prop	Jason Leonard
Hooker	Steve Thompson
Prop	Phil Vickery
Lock	Ben Kay
Lock	Martin Johnson (c)
Flanker	Neil Back
Flanker	Lewis Moody
Number 8	Lawrence Dallaglio
Scrum-half	Matt Dawson
Fly-half	Jonny Wilkinson
Right Wing	Dan Luger
Centre	Will Greenwood
Centre	Mike Tindall
Left Wing	Ben Cohen
Full-back	Jason Robinson
Reserves	Kyran Bracken, Mike Catt, Trevor Woodman, Stuart Abbott
Unused	Simon Shaw, Dorian West, Joe Worsley

Wales

Prop	Adam Jones
Hooker	Robin McBryde
Prop	Iestyn Thomas
Lock	Brent Cockbain
Lock	Robert Sidoli
Flanker	Dafydd Jones
Flanker	Colin Charvis (c)
Number 8	Jonathan Thomas
Scrum-half	Gareth Cooper
Fly-half	Stephen Jones
Right Wing	Mark Jones
Centre	Iestyn Harris
Centre	Mark Taylor
Left Wing	Shane Williams
Full-back	Gareth Thomas
Reserves	Mefin Davies, Gethin Jenkins, Dwayne Peel, Ceri Sweeney, Gareth Llewellyn, Martyn Williams
Unused	Kevin Morgan
Referee	Rolland A

Points Scorers

England

Name	Tries	Conv	Pen K	Drop G	Points
Greenwood WJH	1	0	0	0	5
Wilkinson JP	0	1	6	1	23

Wales

Name	Tries	Conv	Pen K	Drop G	Points
Harris IR	0	1	0	0	2
Jones S	1	0	0	0	5
Charvis CL	1	0	0	0	5
Williams ME	1	0	0	0	5

First Semi-Final
Australia v New Zealand: 22-10
15 November 2003
Telstra Stadium, Sydney

Players

Australia

Prop	Ben Darwin
Hooker	Brendan Cannon
Prop	Bill Young
Lock	Justin Harrison
Lock	Nathan Sharpe
Flanker	George Smith
Flanker	Phil Waugh
Number 8	David Lyons
Scrum-half	George Gregan (c)
Fly-half	Steve Larkham
Right Wing	Wendell Sailor
Centre	Elton Flatley
Centre	Stirling Mortlock
Left Wing	Lote Tuqiri
Full-back	Mat Rogers
Reserves	Matt Cockbain, David Giffin, Nathan Grey, Jeremy Paul, Joe Roff, Alastair Baxter
Unused	Chris Whitaker

New Zealand

Prop	David Hewett
Hooker	Keven Mealamu
Prop	Greg Somerville
Lock	Chris Jack
Lock	Ali Williams
Flanker	Richie McCaw
Flanker	Reuben Thorne (c)
Number 8	Jerry Collins
Scrum-half	Justin Marshall
Fly-half	Carlos Spencer
Right Wing	Doug Howlett
Centre	Leon MacDonald
Centre	Aaron Mauger
Left Wing	Joe Rokocoko
Full-back	Mils Muliaina
Reserves	Marty Holah, Brad Thorn, Byron Kelleher, Kees Meeuws
Unused	Daniel Carter, Mark Hammett, Caleb Ralph
Referee	White C

Points Scorers

Australia

Name	Tries	Conv	Pen K	Drop G	Points
Mortlock SA	1	0	0	0	5
Flatley EJ	0	1	5	0	17

New Zealand

Name	Tries	Conv	Pen K	Drop G	Points
MacDonald LR	0	1	1	0	5
Thorne RD	1	0	0	0	5

Second Semi-Final
England v France: 24-7
16 November 2003
Telstra Stadium, Sydney

Players

England

Prop	Phil Vickery
Hooker	Steve Thompson
Prop	Trevor Woodman
Lock	Ben Kay
Lock	Martin Johnson (c)
Flanker	Neil Back
Flanker	Richard Hill
Number 8	Lawrence Dallaglio
Scrum-half	Matt Dawson
Fly-half	Jonny Wilkinson
Right Wing	Jason Robinson
Centre	Mike Catt
Centre	Will Greenwood
Left Wing	Ben Cohen
Full-back	Josh Lewsey
Reserves	Kyran Bracken, Jason Leonard, Mike Tindall, Dorian West, Lewis Moody
Unused	Martin Corry, Iain Balshaw

France

Prop	Jean-Jacques Crenca
Hooker	Raphael Ibanez
Prop	Sylvain Marconnet
Lock	Fabien Pelous
Lock	Jerome Thion
Flanker	Serge Betsen Tchoua
Flanker	Olivier Magne
Number 8	Imanol Harinordoquy
Scrum-half	Fabien Galthie (c)
Fly-half	Frederic Michalak
Right Wing	Aurelien Rougerie
Centre	Yannick Jauzion
Centre	Tony Marsh
Left Wing	Christophe Dominici
Full-back	Nicolas Brusque
Reserves	Gerald Merceron, Christian Labit, Olivier Milloud, Clement Poitreneaud
Unused	David Auradou, Yannick Bru, Damien Traille
Referee	O'Brien P

Points Scorers

England

Name	Tries	Conv	Pen K	Drop G	Points
Wilkinson JP	0	0	5	3	24

France

Name	Tries	Conv	Pen K	Drop G	Points
Michalak F	0	1	0	0	2
Betsen Tchoua S	1	0	0	0	5

Third-Place Play-Off
France v New Zealand: 13-40
20 November 2003
Telstra Stadium, Sydney

Players

France

Prop	Sylvain Marconnet
Hooker	Yannick Bru (c)
Prop	Jean-Baptiste Poux
Lock	David Auradou
Lock	Thibault Privat
Flanker	Sebastien Chabal
Flanker	Patrick Tabacco
Number 8	Christian Labit
Scrum-half	Dimitri Yachvili
Fly-half	Gerald Merceron
Right Wing	David Bory
Centre	Tony Marsh
Centre	Damien Traille
Left Wing	Pepito Elhorga
Full-back	Clement Poitreneaud
Reserves	Nicolas Brusque, Jean-Jacques Crenca, Raphael Ibanez, Olivier Magne, Fabien Pelous, Brian Liebenberg, Frederic Michalak

New Zealand

Prop	David Hewett
Hooker	Keven Mealamu
Prop	Greg Somerville
Lock	Chris Jack
Lock	Ali Williams
Flanker	Richie McCaw
Flanker	Reuben Thorne (c)
Number 8	Jerry Collins
Scrum-half	Steve Devine
Fly-half	Carlos Spencer
Right Wing	Doug Howlett
Centre	Leon MacDonald
Centre	Aaron Mauger
Left Wing	Joe Rokocoko
Full-back	Mils Muliaina
Reserves	D Carter, M Holah, B Thorn, M Hammett, C Hoeft, C Ralph
Unused	Byron Kelleher
Referee	White C

Points Scorers

France

Name	Tries	Conv	Pen K	Drop G	Points
Elhorga P	1	0	0	0	5
Yachvili D	0	1	1	1	8

New Zealand

Name	Tries	Conv	Pen K	Drop G	Points
Muliaina M	1	0	0	0	5
Howlett DC	1	0	0	0	5
MacDonald LR	0	1	0	0	2
Rokocoko JT	1	0	0	0	5
Jack CR	1	0	0	0	5
Thorn BC	1	0	0	0	5
Holah MR	1	0	0	0	5
Carter DW	0	4	0	0	8

Final
Australia v England: 17-20
22 November 2003
Telstra Stadium, Sydney

Players

Australia

Prop	Alastair Baxter
Hooker	Brendan Cannon
Prop	Bill Young
Lock	Justin Harrison
Lock	Nathan Sharpe
Flanker	George Smith
Flanker	Phil Waugh
Number 8	David Lyons
Scrum-half	George Gregan (c)
Fly-half	Steve Larkham
Right Wing	Wendell Sailor
Centre	Elton Flatley
Centre	Stirling Mortlock
Left Wing	Lote Tuqiri
Full-back	Mat Rogers
Reserves	Matt Cockbain, Matt Giteau, Jeremy Paul, Joe Roff, Matt Dunning
Unused	David Giffin, Chris Whitaker

England

Prop	Phil Vickery
Hooker	Steve Thompson
Prop	Trevor Woodman
Lock	Ben Kay
Lock	Martin Johnson (c)
Flanker	Neil Back
Flanker	Richard Hill
Number 8	Lawrence Dallaglio
Scrum-half	Matt Dawson
Fly-half	Jonny Wilkinson
Right Wing	Jason Robinson
Centre	Will Greenwood
Centre	Mike Tindall
Left Wing	Ben Cohen
Full-back	Josh Lewsey
Reserves	Mike Catt, Jason Leonard, Iain Balshaw, Lewis Moody
Unused	Kyran Bracken, Martin Corry, Dorian West

Referee	Watson A

Points Scorers

Australia

Name	Tries	Conv	Pen K	Drop G	Points
Flatley EJ	0	0	4	0	12
Tuqiri L	1	0	0	0	5

England

Name	Tries	Conv	Pen K	Drop G	Points
Robinson JT	1	0	0	0	5
Wilkinson JP	0	0	4	1	15

Index